D1190482

Legal Aspects
of
International Lending
and
Economic Development
Financing

Legal Aspects
of
International Lending
and
Economic Development
Financing

by

Georges R. Delaume

Docteur en Droit (Paris)
M.C.L. (George Washington University)

Published for the
PARKER SCHOOL OF FOREIGN
AND COMPARATIVE LAW
COLUMBIA UNIVERSITY IN THE CITY OF NEW YORK

1967
Oceana Publications, Inc.
Dobbs Ferry, New York

Acknowledgements

The author is particularly indebted to Professor Willis L. M. Reese for deciding to include this book in the Parker School Series and for his most valuable observations and suggestions, especially in connection with chapters 3 and 4. He wishes also to acknowledge his debt to his colleagues in the IBRD Legal Department and in the legal departments of the various international and domestic financial institutions whose practice could not have been accurately described without the benefit of their personal experience.

The author is grateful to Mr. A. Broches, Member of the President's Council and General Counsel of the IBRD for his authoritative advice on several chapters and for his encouragement throughout many years of literary gestation. The author also acknowledges the invaluable assistance of Mrs. Rose S. Porras, Librarian of the Joint Law Library of the IBRD and the IMF, in finding comparative material, and of Mrs. Clara Ledan for the typing of a work which, at times, bore some likeness to Penelope's tapestry.

Table of Contents

Abbreviations

Books Referred to by the Author's Name

BORCHARD: State Insolvency and Foreign Bondholders, vol. I (1951)

BROCHES: International Legal Aspects of the Operations of the World Bank, 98 Recueil des Cours 301 (1959)

DUNN: American Foreign Investments (1926)

McDANIELS: International Financing and Investment (1964), published for the World Community Association, edited by John F. McDaniels

MADDEN and NADLER: Foreign Securities (1929)

MANN: The Legal Aspect of Money (2d. ed. 1953)

MOREAU-NERET: Les Valeurs Mobilières (1939)

NUSSBAUM: Money in the Law, National and International (revised ed. 1950)

PALMER'S: Palmer's, Company Precedents, vol. 3 (16th ed. 1952)

SALMON: Le Rôle des Organisations Internationales en Matière de Prêts et d'Emprunts (1958)

SURREY: A Lawyer's Guide to International Business Transactions (1963), published by the Joint Committee of Continuing Legal Education, edited by Walter Sterling, Surrey and Crawford Shaw

VAN HECKE: Problèmes Juridiques des Emprunts Internationaux (2d ed. 1964)

WORLD BANK (THE): Policies and Operations of the World Bank, IFC and IDA (as amended 1963)

WYNNE: State Insolvency and Foreign Bondholders, vol. II (1951)

Lending Agencies and International Organizations

AID: Agency for International Development (successor to the DLF)

BIS: Bank for International Settlements

CAISSE CENTRALE: Caisse Centrale de Coopération Economique (formerly Caisse Centrale de la France d'Outre-Mer)

CDC: Commonwealth Development Corporation (formerly Colonial Development Corporation)
CDFC: Commonwealth Development Finance Company
DLF: Development Loan Fund (predecessor of the AID)
ECSC: European Coal and Steel Community
EDF: European Development Fund for Overseas Countries and Territories
EEC: European Economic Community
EIB. European Investment Bank
EURATOM: European Atomic Energy Community
EUROFIMA: European Company for the Financing of Railway Equipment
EXPORT-IMPORT BANK: Export-Import Bank of Washington
FAO: Food and Agriculture Organization
IADB: Inter-American Development Bank
IBRD: International Bank for Reconstruction and Development
ICJ: International Court of Justice
IFC: International Finance Corporation
ILO: International Labour Organization
IMF: International Monetary Fund
KREDITANSTALT: Kreditanstalt für Wiederaufbau
PCIJ: Permanent Court of International Justice
UNESCO: United Nations Educational, Scientific and Cultural Organization
UN SPECIAL FUND: United Nations Special Fund (Now: United Nations Development Programme/Special Fund)
WHO: World Health Organization

Other Abbreviations

ACT OF PLEDGE: Act of Pledge dated November 28, 1954 between the High Authority of the ECSC and the BIS (238 UNTS 340)
AM. J. COMP. L.: American Journal of Comparative Law
AM. J. INT'L L.: American Journal of International Law
B.I.J.I.: Bulletin de l'Institut Juridique International
B.Y.B.I.L.: British Year Book of International Law
CASS.: Cour de Cassation; when used without reference to any specific country, the French Supreme Court
C.E.: Conseil d'Etat, when used without reference to any specific country, the French Administrative Court

CLUNET: Journal du Droit International
D. (P.), (H.): Dalloz (Périodique), (Hebdomadaire)
GAZ. PAL.: Gazette du Palais
INT'L & COMP. L. Q.: International and Compative Law
      Quarterly
INT'L L. REP.: International Law Reports
J.C.P.: Juris-Classeur Périodique, also called la Semaine Juridique
J.O.: Journal Officiel
J.T.: Journal des Tribunaux (Switzerland)
JOURNAL DES TRIBUNAUX: Journal des Tribunaux
      (Belgium)
L.N. REPORT: Report of the Committee for the Study of Inter-
      national Loan Contracts, League of Nations, Official Docu-
      ment C.145.M.93. 1939.II.A
LNTS: League of Nations Treaty Series
PASICRISIE: Pasicrisie Belge
RECUEIL DES COURS: Recueil des Cours, Hague Academy
REV.: Revue de Droit International Privé, since 1934: Revue
      Critique de Droit International Privé
RGZ: Entscheidungen des Reichsgerichts in Zivilsachen
R.O.: Recueil Officiel des Arrêts du Tribunal Fédéral Suisse
S.: Recueil Sirey
SEC.: Securities and Exchange Commission
SEC REPORT: Securities and Exchange Commission, Report
      on the Study and Investigation of the Work, Activities,
      Personnel and Functions of Protective and Reorganization
      Committees, Part VI, Trustees under Indentures (1936)
T.F.: Swiss Federal Tribunal
T.G.I.: Tribunal de Grande Instance (see also Trib. Civ.)
TIAS: Treaties and other International Acts Series
TRIB. CIV.: Tribunal Civil
TRIB. COMM.: Tribunal de Commerce
UNTS: United Nations Treaty Series
NOTE: When statutes are found in private or official editions of
      domestic Codes, no reference is given to official gazettes or
      similar publications containing the relevant statutes, and it
      is assumed that the reader will simply refer to the current
      edition of the pertinent Code.

Preface

Since the second World War there have been dramatic changes
in the nature of international finance. Because of a variety of factors
new patterns of finance have developed, patterns which are changing
rapidly and which are difficult to assess.

There are many factors which have led to these changing patterns,
but it is possible to isolate and examine several which are of most
significance to an understanding of the changes in the legal system
which have developed as financing patterns themselves have changed.
In the first place, as colonial empires have dwindled or changed in
form, traditional mechanisms for financing investments in the less
developed areas of the world have likewise changed. In the past the
colonies looked primarily to their parent country and its investors for
finance and the relationship between them influenced the nature of
the legal framework in which financing took place. Now, however,
the newly independent countries have wider and more flexible sources
of finance, both private and governmental, open to them. While the
traditional methods of finance still prevail to some extent, entirely
new sources of finance have developed and the old patterns of finance,
and the legal relationships as well, have changed substantially. At the
same time, the interests of the more developed countries have also
changed. They have come realize that it is in their interest, without
regard to considerations of direct financial return, to help the less
developed world build more advanced economies. This has resulted
in their organizing and supporting new national and international
institutions designed to achieve that end.

Probably the most striking of all these economic developments has
been the formation, growth and increasing importance of international institutions designed to promote economic development. There
are the global development institutions, particularly the International Bank for Reconstruction and Development, known as the
World Bank (IBRD) and its affiliated organizations, the International
Development Association (IDA) and the International Finance

xvii

Corporation (IFC); the regional development institutions, such as the Inter-American Development Bank (IADB), the European Investment Bank (EIB), the African Development Bank, and the Asian Development Bank; the supra-national organizations, such as the European Atomic Energy Community (Euratom) and the European Coal and Steel Community (ECSC), the technical assistance institutions such as the United Nations Development Programme (UNDP) and the European Development Fund for the Overseas Countries and Territories (FED). Then there are the institutions which seek to regulate international currency movements and trade, such as the International Monetary Fund (IMF) and the General Agreement on Tariffs and Trade (G.A.T.T.). The lexicon of international organizations is reminiscent of the lexicon of the New Deal agencies created in the United States during the Roosevelt era; as those agencies have had a great effect on the economy of the United States, so the international organizations have had a great effect on the international economy.

Much has been written from the point of view of the economist or the specialist in governmental affairs about the changing scope and nature of international investment and trade and the emergence of these new institutions, but for the lawyer the picture is different.

From the point of view of the lawyer an analysis of these factors is exceptionally complicated, involving, as it does, not only an examination of legal practice and problems on three different levels—the municipal, the international and the comparative—but also of the effect which each has on the other. While a considerable body of legal literature has been produced during the past 20 years on various aspects of these problems, with few exceptions no attempt has been made to review and analyze current practice on a comprehensive basis, that is on a basis which compares one municipal system with another, which shows the effect of differing treatment by countries of public international law standards and which compares the various legal devices used by the international institutions and shows their effect on the legal practices of others.

This book is the first comprehensively to review and analyze contemporary legal theory and practice in the important field of international financial transactions. It is a particular virtue of this book that the author has managed to assemble, with painstaking care, specific examples of various types of provisions included in agreements used by many different types of lenders operating under different legal systems. These examples and an analysis of the theoretical considerations which underly them should prove to be of great value to the practicing lawyer who, up to now, must have found it most difficult to evaluate contemporary practice.

A good example of the inter-play between various legal systems and the requirements of different institutions can be found in the review of the contractual arrangements made by international institutions, particular attention being given to the practice of the World Bank family of institutions which has served, in varying degrees, as the model for the practice of others. The lenders in these cases do not simply turn over the proceeds of a loan to the borrower, relying only on a promise to pay. Instead they seek to get assurances that the loan will be used for certain agreed purposes and only in an agreed manner. These assurances can be far-reaching and may involve changes in existing legal arrangements or in the law of the borrowing country, as for example where power rates may have to be raised as a condition of a loan for electric power expansion. Or the agreement may provide for the furnishing by the borrower of certain security which in turn may require the incorporation of provisions specially designed to be enforceable only locally. Thus municipal law may become directly relevant to an agreement which, in all other respects, constitutes an international agreement. Or to take another example, the agreement may provide for compulsory international arbitration, which in turn may involve constitutional questions for the borrowing country. While many of these provisions can be found in ordinary domestic practice, they raise problems in the context of an international agreement for which law and practice provide little guidance.

In view of the growing tendency for joint operations among both international and domestic financing institutions, the practices of each institution may have a decided effect on the practices of others; and the review of these practices in this book is most useful.

A good example of the value of this kind of comparison is found in the analysis of so-called negative pledge clauses. A negative pledge is a provision whereby the borrower agrees in substance that if a lien shall be created on assets of the borrower to secure debt, the lien will equally and ratably secure the debt with respect to which the negative pledge is given. This is an important contractual provision and for years has been standard equipment in debt contracts, both private and governmental, entered into in common-law countries. It has also become common in the agreements entered into by most international institutions. Yet the problems which a negative pledge clause may raise in an international agreement have never before been described.

Particularly complex problems arise when attempts are made to carry over from one country to another devices to safeguard the interests of creditors, such as an attempt to apply the common-law trust concept in a civil law country, or to use a United States form of bond indenture in a country where its numerous complications, statutory and otherwise, would make it incomprehensible or illegal or both. Here too, the book contains a most useful analysis of theory and practice in an important branch of the law which has largely been neglected.

Problems in the field of conflicts in international contracts have plagued lawyers for years and recent developments have made these problems even more difficult to resolve. In the first place, international contracts have become far more complex. The attempt by many parties to "internationalize" agreements and to have disputes settled by international arbitration has tended to dim traditional distinctions between private and public international law. The advent of the International Monetary Fund has changed traditional conflict rules in the important area of exchange contracts. The fact that governments have become increasingly involved in owning and operating financial and commercial businesses has complicated the problem, already complicated enough, of sovereign immunity. And finally, a whole new class of persons—the international development or financing institutions—has developed and these institutions have had to be fitted into the legal order. These new factors are reviewed and analyzed in a particularly helpful section.

In order to provide a thorough study of the theories and practice of international lending, the author has carried out the heavy burden of marshalling a vast amount of primary and secondary materials and of analyzing a representative collection of loan contracts. The result is a work which should prove to be a manual for both the lawyer and the international banker.

LESTER NURICK, *Deputy General Counsel, International Bank for Reconstruction and Development Professorial Lecturer, George Washington University Law School*

Introduction

International loan agreements are concluded by a great variety of entities. These include corporations which may be privately or governmentally owned or controlled, autonomous or semi-autonomous agencies or other public bodies, governments of old and new nations, and, with increasing frequency in recent years, regional and international organizations.

Loans are made or contracted for vastly different reasons ranging from purely financial considerations to the pursuit of political goals or the achievement of such objectives as economic development, monetary cooperation, or peace operations in countries beset by internal or external strife.

The identity and motivation of the parties in making or contracting loans have a direct impact on the structure and content of international loan agreements, particularly since these agreements must be prepared and implemented within the context of different juridical systems and business practices. In a highly technical field such as this, in which legal tradition and commercial or diplomatic usages play an important part, differences in contractual trends are unavoidable.

There is, therefore, reason to expect that international loan agreements will exhibit substantial variations. Yet, although specific situations may require unique and imaginative treatment, and often offer draftsmen fascinating and challenging problems, it is possible to discern in the practice of the international financial community a common background of legal thinking.

One generally accepted premise is the assumption that all international loan transactions are legally binding on the parties. There is no room in the contemporary law of international lending for such outdated doctrines as that which, stressing the possible absence of effective remedies against sovereign states, contends that a state's public debt is not binding in law, but in honor only.

Another important consideration is that, both in the private and in the public sector of international lending, financiers and their legal advisers have a natural inclination to rely on contractual devices and legal techniques whose merits and effectiveness have been tested by years of commercial practice. There is thus in existence a body of rules, the domestic origin of which is frequently apparent, which constitutes a common heritage capable of supplying both the devices necessary to the solution of technical problems and the general principles of an international financial law far advanced in its development. In this last respect, the increasingly frequent association in recent years of private persons, governments and international organizations in financial ventures can only, by offering renewed opportunities for juxtaposing legal concepts and business practices, contribute to the acceleration of the process of legal interaction which is a characteristic feature of the modern financial world.

It is questionable, however, whether as a result of this association and of new developments, such as contractual innovations which particularly in the public sector of lending can be expected to make a significant contribution to the elaboration of new techniques, it will be possible to identify certain rules sufficiently uniform to lend themselves to codification. It is symptomatic that nothing has come of the attempt[1] made some twenty years ago to elaborate a code of uniform rules applicable to foreign bonds issued by states and public bodies. In a period of transition, such as the present one, it would appear entirely unrealistic to assume that the law of international financial relations can be frozen into immobility.

Furthermore, as a result of the unprecedented growth of economic development lending, new legal patterns and contractual trends have made their appearance. Though it is too early to forecast the solutions which will ultimately prevail, there is reason to believe that in the process of evolution a sharper distinction will be made between international financial loans, following more or less conventional patterns, and economic development loans. The latter, together with other types of economic agreements, might constitute the proper subject-matter of a new "law of international economic development."[2]

---

[1] See the Preliminary Draft Uniform Rules Applicable to International Loans, prepared by the International Institute for the Unification of Private Law, 20 Institute Papers: International Loans (Doc. 5a (1) (1947)). Professor Van Hecke correctly points out that the scope of this document, which is limited to bonds publicly issued by foreign governments or public bodies, is too narrow and that there is no reason to distinguish between public bonds and direct loans (see *Van Hecke*, p. 314). However, Professor Van Hecke's endorsement (subject to the above qualification) of the recommendations of the Institute appears to this writer somewhat over optimistic.

[2] Friedmann, *The Changing Structure of International Law* (1964), pp. 176, 373-4.

Current proposals for the creation of new arbitration and conciliation

A few additional remarks may be in order. Most often contractual stipulations referred to or quoted in this book have been taken from documents in the public domain, such as prospectuses and agreements published in treaty series or official gazettes. Though the author has been authorized to make reference to certain contractual covenants in documents which are otherwise confidential, it has not been possible in all cases to identify these documents with precision. Nor has it been possible in certain cases to publish information supplied by eminent lawyers and financiers who have been good enough to give the author the benefit of their own experience. As background material, however, this information has been most helpful in clarifying a number of issues which might otherwise have been omitted or treated differently. The author expresses his deepest thanks to his correspondents.

A description of contractual practice would be of limited usefulness if it were not accompanied by reference to the particular legal system or systems within which loan transactions take place and are implemented. An attempt has therefore been made to include the comparative law background necessary to a proper understanding of the function and effectiveness of stipulations currently found in international loan agreements. It is hoped, that this approach will make this book useful to both scholars and practitioners.

Most of the material included in this book is new. However, Chapters III, IV and VI include portions of articles originally published in *Law and Contemporary Problems* (Summer 1956), the *American Journal of Comparative Law* (1957 and 1960), the *American Journal of International Law* (1962), the *Arbitration Journal* (1955) and the *Columbia Journal of Transnational Law* (1964). The author is deeply grateful to the editors of these publications for their permission to use this material.

A final word. Though extensive reference has been made throughout this book to the practice of the World Bank, with which the author has been associated for many years, the views expressed are his entirely and do not necessarily represent those of the World Bank.

G. R. Delaume

1966

---

facilities for the settlement of investment disputes, or a system of multilateral investment insurance can only intensify the process of evolution referred to in the text above. Though reference to these proposals is made in various chapters, a full treatment of the problems which they raise would require a separate study.

Part One

THE GENERAL LEGAL FRAMEWORK
OF INTERNATIONAL LOANS

Chapter I

The Conclusion of International Loan Transactions

The procedures surrounding the conclusion of international loan transactions necessarily vary from case to case. Certain transactions, such as public offerings of foreign securities or agreements cast in the mold of treaties or other conventional compacts between international persons, are subject to strict substantive requirements and formalistic rituals. Other transactions are very informal. Examples are financial arrangements between loan partners of long standing, affiliated corporations or other institutions, credit or banking establishments, including central banks, or between such establishments and international organizations, and sometimes between governments. Arrangements such as these may consist of no more than an exchange of correspondence, possibly supplemented by the delivery of notes or similar instruments issued by the borrower to represent his indebtedness to the lender.[1]

These variations are not all attributable to legal considerations. The climate of mutual trust and confidence in which the parties operate, the nature or purpose of the transaction or the degree of solemnity that the parties intend to bestow upon it, are additional factors which may greatly affect the character and complexity of the procedures followed in making or contracting loans and may significantly vary the number of conditions (including those of a legal nature) that must be satisfied before the loan proceeds are made available to the borrower.[2]

---

[1] See e.g., the arrangements between the IBRD and the Deutsche Bundesbank, the Central Bank of Germany, for the purchase by the German bank of notes issued by the IBRD in *The World Bank,* p. 86.

Comp., the following agreements between the United Kingdom and (i) Austria (88 UNTS 93) ; (ii) Chile (385 UNTS 15) ; (iii) Jordan (312 UNTS 373, 379; 385 UNTS 81); or (iv) Yugoslavia (88 UNTS 329; 102 UNTS 29; 343 UNTS 153); or between the United States and Pakistan (227 UNTS 77) .

[2] See e.g., in connection with the public offering of securities: Stevenson, "Legal Aspects of the Public Offering of Foreign Securities in the United States Market," 28 Geo. Wash. L. Rev. 194 (1959); Cohen and Throop, "Invest-

SECTION I. THE VALIDITY OF
INTERNATIONAL LOANS

A. AUTHORIZING PROCEDURES

1. *Corporate Loans*

There are striking differences between corporation laws involving the borrowing powers of corporations and the procedures required to authorize corporate borrowings. Thus, statutes in certain countries, such as Italy, Japan or Mexico, restrict the power of corporations to issue bonds by limiting the amount of bonded debt to a sum not exceeding the paid-in capital of the borrower;[3] and in France, though no such limitation exists, the law provides nevertheless that a corporation cannot issue bonds before its capital stock (which under French law must be fully subscribed *ab initio*) has been fully paid in.[4] Further-

---

ment of Private Capital in Foreign Securities," in *Surrey,* p. 519; Althaus, "The Stock Exchanges of Europe and the Free Transfer of Securities," in *Finance and Investment in the Common Market,* Two-Day Conference February 7-8, 1962, sponsored by the Federal Trust for Education and Research (London 1962), p. 14; Conard, "Organizing for Business," in *American Enterprises in the European Common Market, A Legal Profile,* vol. II (1960), at pp. 141-147.

See also, in connection with the conclusion of economic development agreements: *The World Bank,* pp. 45, 98 and 108; Delaume, "International Machinery for Financing Economic Development," 28 Geo. Wash. L. Rev. 533 (1960), at pp. 547 et seq.; Swacker, "Procedural Guide for Processing a Loan with International Lending Institutions," 17 The Business Lawyer 369 (1962) ; Nurick, "International Bank for Reconstruction and Development and the International Development Association," in *Surrey,* 427, at pp. 430 and 442; Richards, "International Finance Corporation," Id. op. 443, at pp. 445 and 450; Arnold, "The Inter-American Development Bank," Id. op. 471, at pp. 477-481; Dupont, "Les Institutions Internationales Bancaires de Financement du Développement," in *Les Banques de Développement dans le Monde* (1963) 67, at pp. 178-182.

Comp., in respect of loans made by governmental lending agencies, Middleton, "The Export-Import Bank," in *Surrey,* 391, at pp. 395-396; Grant, "Agency for International Development," Id. op. 403, at pp. 408-412, 415-417.

[3] Italy, Civil Code, article 2410; Japan, Commercial Code, article 297; Mexico, Law of Negotiable Instruments of August 26, 1932, article 212; Spain, Corporation Law of July 1, 1951, article 111; Venezuela, Commercial Code, article 305. Some of these statutes make exception to the general rule when the bonds are specifically secured on assets of the borrower, or are government guaranteed, or represent the value or the price of property which the issuer has contracted to build or to purchase. See e.g., Italy, Civil Code, article 2410, Mexico, Law of Negotiable Instruments, article 212; Spain, Corporation Law, article 114.

[4] Law of March 4, 1943 (article 2). In addition, French law requires that the issuing corporation must have established its first balance sheet before it can issue bonds, unless the bonds to be issued are guaranteed or secured under certain conditions. See Decree-Law of October 30, 1935, article 2.

more, in some countries the right to issue bonds, at least by way of a public issue, is denied to certain corporate entities, such as the French "société à responsabilité limitée",[5] or the Latin American corporations other than "sociedades anonimas" or similar corporations.[6]

There are also many differences with respect to the type of corporate action necessary to authorize borrowings. Aside from matters regarding quorum or majority, the most important question involves the division of powers between the board of directors and the shareholders in general meeting. In most countries, the respective rights of directors and shareholders are set forth in the corporate charter or articles of association and, even though certain basic standards have been developed in each country, any attempt at generalization must be made with caution. A preliminary comparison of the solutions generally obtaining would seem to indicate that the powers of directors, at least in respect of loans other than loans raised in the ordinary course of business, are usually greater in common law than in civil law systems.[7] In practice, however, these differences often tend

---

[5] Law of March 4, 1925 (article 4).

[6] See e.g., Argentina, Law No. 8875 of February 12, 1912 (article 1); Chile, Law No. 4657 of September 25, 1929 (articles 1 and 2); Mexico, General Law on Negotiable Instruments of August 27, 1932 (article 208).

[7] These variations are apparent from the following statements (as translated) in prospectuses issued in Switzerland by an English company:
   "Pursuant to a resolution adopted by its board of directors . . . the British Aluminium Company Limited, contracts in Switzerland a loan . . ." (The British Aluminium Company, London, 4¼% Loan of 1961),
or by an American corporation:
   "Pursuant to the resolution adopted by its board of directors, IBM, World Trade Corporation contracts in Switzerland a loan . . ." (IBM, World Trade Corporation 4¼% Loan of 1961),
which contrasts with other statements such as those concerning an Italian company:
   "On the proposal of the board of directors, the extraordinary general meeting [of shareholders] of MONTECATINI. . . . has decided to contract a loan . . ." (Montecatini, Societa Generale per l'Industria Mineraria e Chimica, Anonima, 4½% External Loan of 1955),
or a French company:
   "The board of directors has decided, in accordance with the authorization given by the general meeting [of shareholders], to contract an external loan . . ." (Saint Gobain, Société Anonyme des Manufactures des Glaces et Produits Chimiques de Saint Gobain, Chauny et Cirey, 4½% External Loan of 1958),
or a Spanish company:
   "Pursuant to the authorization given by the general meeting of shareholders on May 16, 1961, in accordance with the statutes [of the Company], the board of directors . . . has decided to contract in Switzerland a loan . . ." (Compania Sevillana de Electricidad, Sevilla, 5% Loan of 1963).

to disappear. On the one hand, charter provisions in civil law countries not infrequently increase the normal powers of directors to such an extent as to make them comparable to those ordinarily granted to directors in common law countries.[8] On the other hand contemporary legislation in both civil and common law systems subjects an increasing number of corporate financial commitments to the control of the shareholders.[9]

Modern statutes in point fall into two categories. Some are permissive and provide that the consent of the shareholders must be obtained only in the absence of a contrary provision in the articles of association.[10] Other statutes are mandatory and make the validity of certain borrowing operations depend upon the prior approval of the shareholders. Such is the case in Italy and Mexico in regard to corporate bond issues.[11] The Italian law is particularly severe since it not only makes the shareholders' consent a requisite to the validity of the operation, but provides also that the resolution authorizing the issuance of bonds, which must be recorded in a special register, can be recorded only after judicial determination that all legal requirements have been satisfied.[12]

Another form of limitation, which is not confined to any particular kind of borrowing, imposes a ceiling on the amount of loans the directors can raise on their own authority. Thus, under the Indian

---

[8] Comp. with the statements quoted in the foregoing note, the following statements in other Swiss prospectuses concerning a French company:
"Pursuant to the resolution of its board of directors [the company] . . . contracts an external loan . . ." (Société Concessionnaire Française pour la Construction et l'Exploitation du Tunnel Routier sous le Mont-Blanc, 4½% External Loan of 1961),
or a German company:
"In accordance with the authority vested in it under § 9 letter (d) of the articles of association, the board of directors of Tauernkraftwerke, Aktiengesellschaft, Salzburg, has decided to contract a loan . . ." (Tauernkraftwerke, Aktiengesellschaft, Salzburg, 5% Loan of 1958).
See also note 14 infra.

[9] See e.g., New York, Stock Corporation Law, Section 16; Indian Companies Act of 1956, Section 293. See also notes 10 to 13 infra.

[10] See e.g., France, Commercial Code, article 18; Japan, Commercial Code, article 296.

[11] Italy, Civil Code, articles 2365 and 2411; Mexico, General Law on Commercial Companies of August 4, 1934, article 182.

[12] see e.g., Autostrade Concessioni e Costruzioni Autostrade, S.A., US $15 million 5½% Guaranteed Bonds 1972/78, issued in England in 1963:
"The issue of the Bonds was authorized by a Resolution passed at an Extraordinary General Meeting of the Company on 17th June, 1963 and sanctioned by the Tribunal of Rome on 25th June, 1963."
(Prospectus p. 1).

Companies Act,[13] the board of directors may not, without the consent of the shareholders in general meeting, borrow money if "the moneys to be borrowed, together with the moneys already borrowed by the company (apart from temporary loans obtained from the company's bankers in the ordinary course of business) [would] exceed the aggregate of the paid-up capital of the company and its free reserves . . . ." This last limitation, which is found also in the charters of corporations in countries other than India, raises a practical difficulty when the corporation attempts to obtain foreign currency loans. In that case, the question whether the loan must be approved by the shareholders can be answered only by determining the ratio between debt and equity on the basis of some conversion rate between the local currency in which the capital stock and the foreign currency in which the loan are respectively expressed. In most cases, this determination is made on an *ad hoc* basis, at or about the time of the proposed loan. Sometimes, however, and especially in the case of corporations which are expected to engage in important and possibly frequent international financial operations, the conversion formula is found in the charter of the corporation involved.[14]

---

[13] Section 293.

[14] See e.g., the following provision (as translated) found with increasing frequency in the "statuts" of modern French corporations:

"Subject to complying with legal requirements, the company may contract any loans in France and abroad, in French or foreign currencies . . . by issuing bonds or notes or by any other means.

The Board of Directors, without the intervention of the General Assembly [of shareholders], approves such loans and is authorized to fix the amount, terms and conditions of issue and of repayment, pro vided, however, that the aggregate nominal amount of loans so approved by the Board of Directors alone, together with the nominal amount of outstanding loans already contracted, shall never exceed the nominal amount of the capital stock.

For the purpose of the above provision [and] in respect to foreign currency loans previously issued and outstanding, or loans the issuance of which is under consideration, the nominal amount of said loans shall be deemed to be the equivalent in French francs of such foreign currency determined on the basis of the last spot rate of exchange for such currency on the Paris Stock Exchange before the date on which the Board of Directors shall approve the issuance of the new loan. In the case of a loan denominated in several foreign currencies, the highest nominal amount in French francs, as determined on the basis of the above method of computation, shall be determinative. Any issuance of bonds, notes or loans of any kind in excess of the nominal amount of the capital stock, must be authorized by the General Assembly [of shareholders] in extraordinary meeting . . . the form of the borrowing and the conditions of issue and repayment being determined, however, by the board of directors."

2. *Governmental Loans*

In most countries, governmental borrowing requires legislative sanction.[15] Only in relatively few instances does the executive branch of the government have constitutional authority to contract foreign loans without the consent of the Legislature.[16] Constitutional requirements and customs, however, vary considerably from country to country. In certain cases, either as a matter of law or practice, each loan transaction must be submitted to the legislature for approval or ratification, and the enabling legislation, therefore, takes the form of a specific authorization.[17] In other cases, the enabling legislation

---

[15] See e.g., the Constitutions of: Argentina (Article 67 (3)) ; Chile (Article 44) ; Denmark (Article 43); Ecuador (Article 53 (6))); Ghana (Article 36) ; Japan (Article 85); Lebanon (Article 88) ; Mexico (Article 73 (VIII)) ; Panama (Article 118) ; and Peru (Article 15). See also, *Broches,* pp. 383-408; Stevenson, op. cit. note 2 supra, pp. 196-197.

[16] See e.g., the Constitution of India, Article 292.

[17] The form of the authorization varies. Sometimes, the procedures regarding the approval of governmental financial undertakings are followed. In the case of loan agreements with other international persons, however, the transaction may be approved in accordance with constitutional procedures concerning the approval of international agreements or treaties. See *Broches,* pp. 404-408.

The following provisions in intergovernmental loan agreements are typical:
> "The Government of the United Kingdom and the Government of the French Republic will, subject to the previous approval of their legislature, jointly and severally guarantee . . ." (Agreement of January 27, 1939 concerning financial assistance to Czechoslovakia, Hudson, VIII, *International Legislation.* p. 260) ;

Financial Agreement dated April 9, 1946 between Canada and France (43 UNTS 43), Article 10 (agreement subject to ratification by the French Constituent Assembly) ; and Financial Agreement dated March 6, 1946, between Canada and the United Kingdom (20 UNTS 13) , Article 9 (agreement subject to "such legislative approval" as may be necessary) .

See also, in connection with IBRD loans, the following provisions in: (i) the Luxembourg Law of October 17, 1947 (Memorial of October 18, 1947):
> "The Loan Agreement concluded at Washington on August 28, 1947 between the Government of the Grand Duché de Luxembourg and the International Bank for Reconstruction and Development is approved" (as translated).

and (ii) the Commonwealth of Australia, Loan (International Bank for Reconstruction and Development) Act, 1957:
> "The Treasurer may, on behalf of the Commonwealth, borrow from the International Bank for Reconstruction and Development, in accordance with the provisions of the Loan Agreement, moneys in various currencies not exceeding in the whole an amount equivalent to fifty million dollars in the currency of the United States of America."

Similar provisions are found in other legislative enactments concerning

confers upon the government the right to contract loans within certain stated limits,[18] or for specific purposes, such as the financing of imports or economic development projects or programs.[19]

such IBRD loans as those in Ecuador, Law of October 18, 1957 (Registro Oficial, October 21, 1957); El Salvador, Legislative Decree No. 3149 (Diario Oficial, October 14, 1960); Iran, Law of May 23, 1960 (Official Gazette June 22, 1960); Kenya, Ordinance No. 13 of 1960 (Kenya Gazette, Suppl. Ordinances 1960, May 17, 1960); Mauritania, Law of July 13, 1960 (Journal Officiel, August 3, 1960); Nigeria, The Railway Loan (International Bank for Reconstruction and Development) Ordinance 1958 (Official Gazette, April 17, 1958).

For examples of provisions found in prospectuses regarding public bond issues, see e.g.:

Kingdom of Denmark 4½% Loan of 1959 (Swiss issue):
"Pursuant to Law No. 148 of May 13, 1959, the Government of the Kingdom of Denmark issues in Switzerland a Loan. . ." (as translated).

Republic of Finland 6% Loan of 1964 (German issue):
"Pursuant to Resolutions adopted by Parliament on December 12, 1963 and January 25, 1964, and the Resolutions adopted by the Council of State of June 11, 1964 and July 3, 1964, the Republic of Finland. . . issues. . . a 6% Bearer Bonds Loan . . ." (as translated).

Republic of Austria US $18 million 6% Bonds 1979/84 (English issue):
"The issue of the Bonds is authorized by Federal Law No. 1 of 1964 of the Republic of Austria."

Crédit Foncier de France 5½% Guaranteed External Loan Bonds due 1979 (U.S. issue):
"Pursuant to the authorization in article 2 of the [French] Republic Law No. 59-958 dated July 1, 1959 (The "Guarantee Law"), the Republic will unconditionally guarantee the payment of principal and interest on the Bonds."

[18] See e.g., in Chile, Law No. 14,171 of October 24, 1960 (Diario Oficial December 6, 1960), Articles 7 and 8:
"The President of the Republic is authorized to: (a) Contract directly with governments, governmental organizations or banking or financial institutions, either foreign or national, short or long term loans. . .

Loans. . .may be contracted in national or foreign currency. Their aggregate amount. . .shall not exceed the sum of US $500 million or its equivalent in current [Chilean] currency at the rate of exchange in force at the time of the operation." (as translated).

Comp., in Belgium, the prospectus of the Société Nationale des Chemins de Fer Belges, External Loan 4% of 1948, issued (jointly with the Kingdom of Belgium) in Switzerland, clause 5:
"Pursuant to art. 4 of the Arrêté-loi of November 30, 1946 authorizing the Société Nationale des Chemins de Fer Belges to issue loans up to a maximum amount of Belgian francs 3 billion within or without Belgium, the Belgian State undertakes, as joint co-debtor, to pay interest on, and to repay the principal of, this loan, in "effective" Swiss francs. . ."

[19] See e.g., in Austria, Federal Law No. 239 of October 30, 1958, (Bundesgesetzblatt No. 68 of November 10, 1958):
"*ARTICLE I — General Provisions*
1. The Federal Republic is empowered to raise loans, obtain advances

This last procedure, which imports an appreciable degree of flexibility into borrowing operations, not infrequently raises various problems of implementation. Thus, if the legislative authorization is broadly formulated, it may be necessary for the appropriate official, such as the Minister of Finance to obtain a Presidential or Royal Decree specifically authorizing the proposed transaction before he proceeds to negotiate with foreign lenders the terms and conditions of a loan.[20]

Another practical question is the following. Frequently, general authorizations impose a ceiling upon the amount of loans that can be raised by the government. Sometimes, particularly when it is not known at the time of the authorization from which foreign source borrowed funds are likely to be forthcoming or when the authorization applies to both domestic and external borrowings, the ceiling of the authorization is expressed in domestic currency. When this is the case, and the government seeks to raise foreign currency loans, a problem of conversion arises. In order to make certain that the proposed loan, together with possibly existing loans contracted under the relevant authorization, does not exceed the unused balance of the authorization, it becomes necessary to establish a formula for determining the equivalent in the borrower's currency of foreign currency loans and to fix the rate or rates of exchange at which the

---

and negotiate credits on behalf of the Republic of Austria to a maximum value, at any given time, of 250 million U.S. dollars or its equivalent in foreign currency, and to assume guarantees, to the said maximum value in respect of loans, advances or credits furnished to Austrian concerns, and to accept liability for loss, or liability as guarantor or obligor.

2. The proceeds of agreements concluded in accordance with (1) above are to be employed for the purpose of covering, to a partial extent, the import and investment requirements of Austria.

3. The Federal Republic must inform the main committee of the National Assembly regarding any loans, advances or credits raised, or any guarantees or liabilities assumed, by virtue of this Federal Law, and produce the agreements that have been concluded." (as translated).

See also, in France, Decree of December 26, 1961 (Journal Officiel of December 27, 1961, p. 11,959) regarding the guarantee of economic development loans by the French Government. Comp., the constitutions of Mexico (Article 73) and Peru (Article 15).

[20] See e.g., Chile, Law No. 14,171, cited in part in note 18 supra providing in substance (Article 8) that the conditions of amortization of bonds issued in pursuance thereof should be determined by Supreme Decrees of the President of the Republic at the time of each issue. See also, the Royal "Arrêtés" of September 9, 1957 authorizing the Minister of Finance of Belgium to borrow $40 million by means of a public offering of $30 million Belgian bonds and of a $10 million loan from the IBRD (Moniteur of September 9-10, 1957).

necessary determination should be made on the relevant date or dates when this determination is required. This can be done by adopting the rate of exchange prevailing at the time the authorization is given,[21] or the rate in force at the time of each borrowing operation,[22] or some other rate as may be appropriate under the circumstances.

These are considerations which may prove cumbersome but are not particularly insurmountable. Other constitutional requirements or limitations, however, sometimes create extremely difficult problems. For example a provision customarily found in the loan agreements and bonds of foreign governments is that the borrower shall not create any lien or priority on its assets or revenues as security for future loans unless the loan or the bonds shall be equally and ratably secured thereby. These "negative pledge" clauses, while they do not prevent the borrower from contracting new debts, give to the lenders

---

[21] See e.g., the Resolution of the Norweigan Storting of November 16, 1960:

> "The Storting agrees that the King or the Ministry to which he delegates his authority, be authorized to obtain new State loans in foreign currencies for an amount not exceeding the equivalent of 500 million kroner, calculated at the present rate of exchange." (as translated) .

[22] See e.g., Chile Law No. 14,171 cited in note 18 supra. See also, the Kenya Ordinance No. 13 of 1960 (cited note 17 supra), reading in part as follows:

> "3. (1) The Governor is hereby authorised, in the name of the Government, to borrow from the Bank, the sum of two million pounds sterling or the equivalent in pounds sterling and other currencies, or the equivalent in other currencies.
>
> (2) The borrowing shall be deemed—
>> (a) to be made on the date that any agreement providing therefore is signed, notwithstanding any other date on which the Loan or any part thereof may be made available or may be drawn; and
>> (b) to be in such amount of pounds sterling as is the equivalent, at the rate of exchange in force at the date of such signature, to the amount of loan as expressed in the currency in which the loan is denominated in or for the purpose of such agreement."

Comp., Peru Law No. 13505 of 1961 (article 1) authorizing the government to raise domestic and foreign loans "up to six billion gold soles or its equivalent in foreign currency, calculated at the average rate of exchange prevailing in the country on the day on which the relevant agreement is signed." (as translated) .

In cases such as these, lenders normally insist upon receiving, by way of corroboration of their own analysis of the situation, a certificate from an appropriate official of the borrower giving a detailed statement of existing borrowings and certifying that the amount of the proposed loan falls within the outstanding balance of the authorization.

the assurance that new creditors shall not be placed in a more favorable position since, to the extent that the rights of such creditors would be secured, the existing lenders would be entitled to claim their shares of the security.[23]

Such a clause, so long as it is limited to the creation by the obligor of liens on its own assets, raises no particular difficulty. Sometimes, however, attempts are made to widen the scope of the clause in order to prevent the borrower not only from using its own resources to secure other creditors, but also from using its authority to mobilize for the same purpose other resources, including those of its political subdivisions, central bank or other public entities.[24] It is in this case that delicate constitutional issues may arise. In certain countries, constitutional limitations may make it difficult, if not impossible, for

___

[23] See Chapter V text and notes 95 to 100.

[24] See e.g., the following provision in the Union of South Africa External Loan Bonds 5-5½% of December 1, 1958, issued in the United States of America:

"This Bond. . .ranks *pari passu*, without any preference one above the other by reason of priority of date of issue or otherwise, with all other loan indebtedness of the Union and all loan indebtedness guaranteed by the Union, except for the preference accorded by the terms of the South Africa Act to the Cape of Good Hope Perpetual Stock. . .outstanding in the aggregate amount of £383,350. It is the intention of the Union that no other external debt, direct or contingent, shall enjoy any prioriy over the Bonds by way of a mortgage or lien on public assets. To that end the Union specifically undertakes that, except as the bearer or registered owner of this Bond at the time shall otherwise agree, if any mortgage or lien shall be created on any assets of the Union or any Province or other political subdivision of the Union or any agency or any of them (including local governing authorities) or the South African Reserve Bank as security for any external debt, direct or contingent, such mortgage or lien shall *ipso facto* equally and ratably secure the payment of the principal of and interest on this Bond and all other External Loan Bonds of December 1, 1958, then outstanding, and that in the creation of any such mortgage or lien express provision to that effect shall be made; provided, however, that the foregoing provisions shall not apply to (i) any mortgage or lien created on any property at the time of purchase thereof solely as security for the payment of the purchase price of such property, (ii) any mortgage or lien on commercial goods to secure debt maturing not more than one year after its date and to be paid out of the proceeds of sale of such commercial goods, (iii) any mortgage or lien, created as security for bonds or notes of the Union or any such Province or other political subdivision or agency, on revenues of any new project for which such bonds or notes are issued, or (iv) any mortgage or lien created by the South African Reserve Bank on any of its assets in the ordinary course of its banking business to secure any indebtedness maturing not more than one year after its date."

the central government to undertake negative pledge clause commitments on behalf of its political subdivisions or more or less autonomous public entities.[25] In such instances, some compromise must be found to give satisfaction to the lenders while also taking into account the constitutional difficulty.

Although each case must be decided on its own merits and any generalization should be made only with extreme caution, it seems nevertheless possible to distinguish two major areas of difficulty. The first area covers those situations where it appears probable that the government involved does not have the authority to make the negative pledge clause effective with respect to its political subdivisions or autonomous entities. In that case, all that may be possible is to provide that if a situation occurs which would normally call for the implementation of the negative pledge clause and the borrower is unable within the limits of its constitutional powers to implement the clause effectively, the borrower shall give to the lenders an equivalent lien on assets within its reach satisfactory to the lenders.[26]

This situation, however, is relatively exceptional. In the majority of cases the obligor government will have sufficient power to enforce, however indirectly, the negative pledge clause by reason of its control over foreign exchange or because of specific legislation regarding external borrowing by public entities. In these cases, all that may be necessary is to acknowledge the existence of the constitutional problem and to rely for the implementation of the clause upon the use by the government of its general power to control foreign public borrowing or to administer the foreign exchange resources of the country as a whole.[27]

---

[25] See e.g., the Constitutions of: (i) Argentina (Article 107); (ii) Ecuador (Article 128 and Ley de Regimen Municipal, Articles 8, 10(3) and (7); (iii) Japan (Articles 92 and 94); and (iv) Uruguay (Sections XI and XIV).

[26] See e.g., the Guarantee Agreement dated October 9, 1958 between the Republic of Ecuador and the IBRD (section 3.01, 337 UNTS 299); the Loan Agreement dated December 30, 1959 between Republica Oriental del Uruguay and the IBRD (Section 5.03, 384 UNTS 275); the Loan Agreement dated June 1, 1961 between the Argentine Republic and the IBRD (Section 5.03, 445 UNTS 85).

Comp. the Argentine Republic 6½% External Loan 1961/1973 of US $25 million, issued in Switzerland, General Bond, Article XII.

[27] See e.g., the Guarantee Agreement dated March 17, 1960 between Japan and the IBRD (Section 3.03, 362 UNTS 43 and Annexed Letter, p. 52); the Guarantee Agreement dated September 25, 1959 between Republic of Austria and the IBRD (Section 3.01, 355 UNTS 223); the Loan Agreement dated December 3, 1956 between the Commonwealth of Australia and the IBRD (Section 5.03, 288 UNTS 99). For an interesting situation involving the "Community" (as it then existed) between France and African Republics,

3. *Loans Raised by Political Subdivisions and Other Domestic Public Entities*

External borrowing by political subdivisions and other public entities ordinarily requires the sanction of the central government, in addition to the approval of the competent organ of the borrower, such as a city council or a state or provincial legislature, or a managing board.[28]

---

see the Guarantee Agreement dated March 17, 1960 between France and the IBRD (Section 3.01, 452 UNTS 147, and letter of even date therewith from France to the IBRD, at pp. 156-161).

[28] See e.g., among recent examples, the prospectus of the City of Oslo 5% Dutch Guilders Loan of 1961:

"The present loan is issued pursuant to the Municipal Corporations Act of 1954, as subsequently amended, and in accordance with the resolution of the Municipal Council of March 24, 1960 and that of the College of Aldermen of October 12, 1961, approved by Royal Decree of October 20, 1961 and Decision of the Minister for Commerce and Shipping of October 20, 1961." (as translated).

or that of the City of Copenhagen 5¾% DM Bonds of 1964:

"The City Council of the City of Copenhagen resolved at its meeting of June 11, 1964, to issue a 5¾% Deutsche Mark Loan of 1964 in the Federal Republic of Germany in the total amount of DM 75,000,000. The issue was approved by the Danish Minister of the Interior on June 12, 1964." (as translated).

or that of the Mortgage Bank of the State of Vorarlberg in Bregenz (Austria) 4½% (Swiss Francs) Bonds of 1959:

"In accordance with its articles of incorporation and after approval by the Austrian Ministry of Finance as well as with the consent of the National Bank, the Mortgage Bank of the State of Vorarlberg offers for sale a loan of 4½% bonds series 5. . ." (as translated).

or that of the City of Milan 5½% External Loan Bonds due 1978 (issued in the United States in 1963):

"Borrowings and guarantees must be authorized by the City Council and approved by the Provincial Administrative Board and in certain cases by the Central Commission for Local Finance, an agency of the national government. If municipal borrowings are evidenced by negotiable instruments, the issue must also be authorized by the Minister of the Treasury in agreement with the Minister of Interior and upon the advice of the Central Commission for Local Finance and the Provincial Administrative Board."

Governmental action in this case should be carefully distinguished from that which may be necessary under exchange control regulations. The latter regulations, whose impact upon international borrowing is discussed elsewhere, are essentially intended to meet transitory situations, even though they may be maintained for many years. Specific statutes providing for governmental control of public borrowing, on the contrary, are of a permanent nature. Although the same authority, e.g. the Minister of Finance, may be responsible for taking either action and the loan documents do not always indicate with precision in which capacity such authority intervenes, the distinction nevertheless remains important.

Governmental control of foreign public borrowing may be limited to specific transactions, such as the issuance of bonds,[29] or apply indiscriminately to any kind of borrowing operations.[30] Most

Comp., the prospectus of the Kraftlaget Opplandskraft (Opplandskrapt Electricity Supply Company), Oslo 5¼% Loan of 1962 issue in the Netherlands:

"The issue of the present loan was approved on June 6, 1962 by the Board of Directors of Kraftlaget Opplandskraft and on June 27, 1962 by the Norwegian Minister of Trade and Shipping; this approval was confirmed by Royal Decree on August 3, 1962."

[29] See e.g., Article 267 of the French Code de l'Administration Communale, Annexed to Decree No. 57-657 of May 22, 1957 (Dalloz, Code Administratif (1961), p. 74) stating in substance that cities may be authorized by governmental decree to issue foreign bonds up to 30 years' maturity and that individual decree shall fix the maximum amount of the issue, the rate of interest and the conditions of repayment. See also the City of Milan prospectus cited in the preceding note.

[30] See Section 51 of the Norwegian Municipalities Act of 1954, as amended, summarized in the prospectus of the City of Oslo $10 million 5½% Sinking Fund External Loan Bonds of 1962, p. 12.

Comp., the Colombian law No. 6a of March 6, 1928, which (as translated by *Madden and Nadler*, p. 207-209, original Spanish text in Legislacion Administrativa Colombiana, Constitucion Nacional y Codigo Political Municipal (3d ed. 1946), p. 159) reads as follows:

'Article I. The Departments through their Governors may contract domestic or foreign loans for works of recognized public interest. The Departmental Assemblies, upon authorizing the contraction of a loan, shall indicate the projects that meet this requirement. The respective loan contracts, when they refer to a foreign loan, require for validity the approval of the President of the Republic after the latter has heard the opinion of the Cabinet.

Article 2. When the Governor of a Department, in conformity with the provisions of the preceding Article, proposes to negotiate a foreign loan, he shall notify the Government through the Minister of Finance, giving the general terms of the proposed negotiation in order that the Government may be acquainted with its general character.

Article 3. The Government shall not approve a contract for a Departmental foreign loan unless there is a definite understanding as to the work or works to be carried out, supported by studies demonstrating the utility of the project and the advantages to accrue therefrom to the respective Department, together with a copy of the legislation authorizing the operation and indicating the application of the funds.

Article 4. The Municipal Councils may, with the authorization of the National Government, contract foreign or domestic loans to be employed exclusively in improvements of distinct public benefit. To this end the Government may authorize the Municipality to hypothecate its properties and pledge the municipal revenues for the purpose of insuring the payment of interest and principal on obligations so contracted.

Article 5. The application (by a municipality) for such authorization shall be accompanied by a statement of the work or works to be carried out, together with economic studies demonstrating their desir-

frequently, the basis for governmental intervention is set forth in ordinary statutory enactments, although in certain countries it is found in the national constitution. Thus, pursuant to the March 1, 1962 Constitution of Pakistan:

"A Province may not without the consent of the Federal Government borrow outside Pakistan. . ."[31]

Another example is that of Australia, which offers many original features. In order to improve the credit of the Commonwealth, which had been somewhat impaired by the past borrowings of the States and the Commonwealth, and also in order to regulate future public borrowings, the Commonwealth and the States concluded in 1927 a so-called "Financial Agreement," which was given statutory authority under an amendment of the Commonwealth Constitution and the enactment of implementing legislation by the Commonwealth and State Parliaments.[32] Pursuant to the Agreement, the Commonwealth took over the public debts of the States as of July 1, 1929 and undertook under certain conditions to make interest payments to the

---

ability and utility, and a copy of the resolution authorizing the execution of the work.

Article 6. The Councils (municipal) shall not undertake any loan negotiations without having obtained the authorization referred to in the previous articles.

Article 7. Foreign loan contracts that are entered into by Municipal Councils in accordance with this law require the approval of the Government, based upon the favorable opinion of the Cabinet.

Article 8. The Government shall not approve foreign loans of the Departments or Municipalities in cases where, according to its judgment, the administration of public affairs will be embarrassed by the payment of interest and sinking fund charges. In no case shall the Government give its consent when the sums necessary for the service of the public debt of the respective entity, including the loan under consideration, represent more than 20 per cent of the ordinary annual income, exclusive, in the case of the Departments, of that part of their revenues which, by law, reverts to the Municipalities. In the case of loans guaranteed by public enterprises, the income of which is not included in the ordinary budget, the charge imposed by the debt service may equal the amount of the net revenues of the enterprise.

Article 9. The Departments and Municipalities may, with the authorization and approval of the Government, contract loans for the purpose of converting debts already in existence."

[31] Article 140 (2).

[32] The full text of the Agreement (as amended) is reproduced in Nicholas, *The Australian Constitution* (2d ed. 1952), pp. 414-429. See also, Article 105 A of the Commonwealth Constitution, Ibid. pp. 409-410; and the Prospectus of the Commonwealth of Australia Twenty Year 5½% Bonds due July 1, 1982, issued in the United States. p. 37.

States' creditors;[33] sinking funds were established in respect of existing public debts of the States;[34] and the Commonwealth and the States undertook to submit their borrowing programs for each financial year to the Australian Loan Council, composed of a representative of the Commonwealth (entitled to two votes and a casting vote) and of representatives of the six States (each entitled to one vote).[35]

Under this arrangement, if the Loan Council decides that the total amount of the loan program for the year cannot be borrowed at reasonable rates and conditions, it determines by a majority vote what amount shall be borrowed. By a unanimous decision, the Council may allocate such amount between the Commonwealth and the States; in the absence of such unanimity, the amount to be borrowed is to be distributed in accordance with an allocation formula set forth in the Agreement.[36] Borrowings, either by the Commonwealth or by the States, are arranged by the Commonwealth. The securities issued are Commonwealth securities, unless the Loan Council, by a unanimous decision, authorizes a State to contract a foreign loan in its name and issue its own securities. In that case, the Agreement provides that the Commonwealth must guarantee performance by the borrower of its obligations to the bondholders.[37]

Although the Agreement contains no provision regarding borrowing by local bodies or governmental agencies, the Commonwealth and the States informally agreed, by a "gentlemen's agreement" concluded in 1936, that the total borrowing program of these bodies or agencies and the terms of large loans contracted by them be submitted, together with those of the State concerned, to the Loan Council for approval.[38]

4. *Borrowings by International Organizations*

Unlike governmental borrowings which are frequently the object of subsequent approval or ratification, borrowings by international

---

[33] Agreement, Clauses 10 and 11.

[34] Agreement, Clause 12.

[35] Agreement, Clause 3 (8) and (14) (b).

[36] Agreement, Clause 3 (9) and (10). The Commonwealth is entitled to one-fifth of the total amount approved by the Council; the share of each State is proportionate to the State's borrowing during the past five years.

[37] Agreement, Clause 4 (1) and (2).

[38] Nicholas, op. cit. note 32 supra, p. 182. Notwithstanding the above, it should be noted that the 1927 Agreement authorizes the Commonwealth and the States to contract loans, without the Loan Council's approval, for "temporary purposes," or, in the case of the Commonwealth, for "defense purposes" (Agreement, Clause 3 (8)).

organizations are normally authorized before the loan is actually concluded, although it may already have been negotiated. This consistent practice is followed regardleess of whether the borrowing takes the form of an issuance of bonds, notes or other securities,[39] or that of a direct loan contract,[40] and it is unaffected by the identity of the other contracting party or parties. Thus prior authorization remains the rule regardless of whether the loan-partner is another international organization,[41] a government,[42] a governmental agency,[43] a political

---

[39] See e.g., the following statements in prospectuses concerning: (a) *the IBRD* (i) $4\frac{1}{2}\%$ Netherlands Guilder Bonds of 1955: "These bonds are issued pursuant to Resolution No. 331 dated July 28, 1955, of the Executive Directors of the International Bank for Reconstruction and Development" (as translated); (ii) 5% DM Bonds of 1959: "Pursuant to the authorization granted to it by Resolution No. 474 of March 26, 1959 of the Executive Directors, and with the consent of the Federal Republic of Germany, as required under Article IV, Section 1, paragraph (b) of the Articles of Agreement of the International Bank for Reconstruction and Development (BGBI, II, No. 13 of August 1, 1952), the International Bank for Reconstruction and Development (hereinafter called the "World Bank") has decided to issue 5% Deutsche Mark Bonds of 1959. . ." (as translated); or (iii) 5% Belgian Franc Bonds of 1959: "Pursuant to the authorization granted to it by Resolution No. 478 of April 20, 1959, of its Board (Executive Directors), the International Bank for Reconstruction and Development has decided to issue a Loan. . ." (as translated); (b) *the High Authority of the ECSC* Swiss Franc $4\frac{1}{4}\%$ Loan of 1956: "Pursuant to Article 49 of the Treaty of April 18, 1951, between the States member of the European Coal and Steel Community, the High Authority has decided to contract in Switzerland a Loan. . ." (as translated); (c) *the EIB* $4\frac{1}{2}\%$ Netherlands Guilder Bonds of 1961: "In accordance with a Resolution of its Board of Directors of May 8, 1961, the European Investment Bank. . . has decided to issue a $4\frac{1}{2}\%$ Loan. . ."; or (d) the *IADB* $5\frac{1}{2}\%$ DM Bonds of 1964: "Pursuant to Resolution No. DE-64/64 of July 6, 1964 of its Executive Directors, and with the consent of the Federal Republic of Germany, the Inter-American Development Bank has decided to issue $5\frac{1}{2}\%$ Deutsche Mark Bonds of 1964. . ." (as translated).

Comp., the Resolution 1739 (XVI) dated December 20, 1961, of the General Assembly authorizing the Secretary-General to issue United Nations bonds in accordance with the terms and conditions set forth in the Annex to the Resolution. In this connection, see Salmon, "L'Emprunt de 200 Millions de Dollars de l'Organisation des Nations Unies," Annuaire Français de Droit International 556 (1962).

[40] See notes 41 to 44 infra.

[41] See the 1950 loan from the United Nations to the FAO to finance part of the costs of the transfer of the FAO's headquarters from Washington, D.C. to Rome, consisting of a request from the FAO and a Resolution of the General Assembly. See Resolution 457 (V), November 16, 1950. See also Jenks, *The Proper Law of International Organizations* (1962), p. 186.

[42] See e.g., the Loan Agreement dated March 23, 1948 between the

subdivision of a foreign government,[44] or a private entity.[45]

Subject to this general observation, authorizing procedures vary considerably. Depending upon the circumstances, and particularly the degree of financial autonomy enjoyed by the relevant organization, borrowings may require the approval of the plenary organ of the borrower or be authorized by the executive body responsible for the general conduct of the borrower's operations. The first alternative is a characteristic feature of borrowings made by such organizations as the United Nations,[46] UNESCO, [47] or the ILO,[48] which have no resources of their own and are financially dependent upon the contributions of their respective members. The second alternative is consistently adopted by those organizations which enjoy financial autonomy, such as the IBRD,[49] the EIB,[50] the IADB,[51] or the ECSC.[52]

United States of America and the United Nations (19 UNTS 43) for the construction of the headquarters building; authorized by Resolution 182 (II) of the General Assembly, dated November 20, 1947; the 1957 arrangements between the Swiss Government and the United Nations for financing the cost of modernization of the Palais des Nations, in Geneva, authorized by Resolution 1101 (XI) dated February 25, 1957; the IMF borrowing arrangements authorized by Resolution of the Fund Executive Directors of January 12, 1962 (Int. Fin. News Survey, Suppl. January 12, 1962).

[43] See e.g., the 1953 financial arrangements between the Caisse Centrale des Dépôts et Consignation and the UNESCO for the construction of the UNESCO headquarters building, authorized by Resolution 13 of the General Conference of the UNESCO, dated July 3, 1953. See also, *Salmon,* pp. 114 and 313.

[44] See the Loan Contract dated July 25, 1950 between the Canton of Geneva and the ILO for the extension of the ILO's headquarters building, authorized by Decision of the Governing Body dated June 10, 1950, ILO, Off. Bull., vol. 33 (1950), 255. See also the Loan Agreement dated March 30/April 15, 1957 between the Swiss Government and the ILO, ILO, Off. Bull.; vol. 40 (1957), 352.

[45] See note 39 supra.

[46] See notes 39 and 42 supra.

[47] See note 43 supra.

[48] See note 44 supra.

[49] See note 39 supra.

[50] See note 39 supra.

[51] See note 39 supra.

[52] See note 39 supra. In the case of EURATOM, the borrowing power of the organization is vested in the Council of Ministers, and the Commission has no power comparable to those of the High Authority of the ECSC. See Sertoli, "The Structure and Financial Activities of the European Communities," 26 Law and Contemporary Problems (Summer 1961) 515, at pp. 525-526. See also, Pescatore, *Les Relations Extérieures des Communautés Européennes,* 103 Rec. Cours (1961) 1, at pp. 116-117 and 121-123.

B. COMPLIANCE WITH THE LAWS OF THE LENDER'S COUNTRY

1. *Governmental Control of Foreign Loans*

Foreign loans may significantly affect the economy and the balance of payments of capital-exporting countries or, as in the case of loans to foreign governments, have political implications that deserve consideration.

Conscious of the problem, most European countries have imposed restrictions upon foreign borrowings and subject foreign loan transactions (particularly the issuance, sale or listing of foreign securities) to the prior approval of the local Treasury, the National Bank, or other controlling institutions or bodies.[53]

In contrast, the United States has an established tradition of free capital markets. Except for such powers as are vested in the Government by the Neutrality Acts or the Trading with the Enemy Act,[54] or such restrictions as are imposed by the Johnson Act (at present of no practical significance),[55] governmental control over foreign borrowings in the United States has been achieved primarily with the voluntary co-operation of the financial community.[56] This tradi-

---

[53] See, *A Description and Analysis of Certain European Capital Markets* (hereinafter *Description*), Paper No. 3, 88th Congress, 2d Session, Joint Committee Print (Washington 1964), pp. 34-36, 62-63, 107-108, 122, 181, 187-189, 212-214, 242-244, 250-251, 262-268; Larcier, "Le Placement Mobilier dans le Marché Commun," Revue de la Banque 1959, 62; Piguet, *La Banque dans le Cadre de la Réglementation Bancaire Suisse* (1953) pp. 358-361; Soutendijk, "Local Financing Facilities in the Netherlands," in *McDaniels*, 306, at pp. 309-311.
Though, in Germany, there is no restriction on international transactions, the Government is nevertheless, through the administration of securities taxes, in a position to exercise an important influence upon the capital market. See, *Description*, pp. 153-154. "Foreign Loan Issues in the Federal Republic of Germany", 16 Monthly Report of the Deutsche Bundesbank 3 (December 1964); Dragon, "Regulation of Capital Influx; Recent Developments in France, Germany and Switzerland," 14 Am. J. Comp. L. 38 (1965).

[54] See e.g., *Borchard*, p. 151; 7 Hackworth, *Digest of International Law*, pp. 657-661; 3 Hyde, *International Law* (2d ed. 1945), pp. 2302-5; "Laws and Regulations Affecting United States Trade," in *Surrey*, 43, at pp. 85 et seq.

[55] The Johnson Act of 1934 made it unlawful for any person in the United States to purchase or sell securities issued by, or make loans to, foreign governments, or their political subdivisions or agencies, in default in the payment of its obligations to the Government of the United States. Already subject to restrictive interpretation before the last World War, the Act was tacitly repealed by the enactment of the Bretton Woods Agreements Act and the Export-Import Bank Act. See, *Borchard*, pp. 175-176.

[56] See e.g., *Borchard*, pp. 224-229; *Madden and Nadler*, pp. 221-230.

tion is so well established that when in 1963 the Government sought to introduce measures appropriate to stem a rising outflow of capital, it refused to consider governmental control over foreign issues as a possible solution. It proposed instead to slow down foreign borrowings by imposing an "interest equalization" tax on American purchases of foreign securities, thus increasing the cost to foreigners of capital in the United States market.[57] However, since the administration of the tax is largely left to governmental discretion, it is questionable whether the regulatory power retained by the United States Government substantially differs from that which it could have acquired under a direct and selective method of control such as obtains in European countries.[58]

2. Securities Laws and Regulations

Regulatory requirements vary considerably from country to country. A comprehensive comparative analysis of the securities laws and regulations in leading financial markets and, most important of all, the manner in which such laws and regulations are implemented or administered, would require a separate study.[59]

In essence, there are three major types of regulatory systems:

[57] Interest Equalization Tax Act of September 2, 1964, 78 Stat. 809. As a result of many exemptions in favor of less developed countries and Canada, the tax applies chiefly to borrowings by Western European countries and Japan.

[58] See e.g., The New York Times, June 25, 1964, op. 30, col. 2; "Interest and Equalization Tax: A Deceptive Tourniquet," First National City Bank, New York, Monthly Economic Letter, April 1964, pp. 45-47.

[59] For comparative literature, see e.g., Loss, Securities Regulations (2d ed. 1961) vol. I, pp. 427-454; Althaus, "The Stock Exchanges of Europe and the Free Transfer of Securities," in Finance and Instrument in the Common Market, Two-day Conference, February 7-8, 1962, sponsored by the Federal Trust for Education and Research (London 1962), pp. 14-21; Larcier, "Le Placement Mobilier dans le Marché Commun," Revue de la Banque 1959, 62; Gower, "Some Contrasts between British and American Corporation Law," 69 Harv. L. Rev. 1369 (1956), at pp. 1381-2; Stevenson, "Legal Aspects of the Public Offering of Foreign Securities in the United States Market," 28 Geo. Wash. L. Rev. 194 (1959) ; Cohen and Throop, "Investment of Private Capital in Foreign Securities," in Surrey, p. 519; Conard, "Organizing for Business," in American Enterprises in the European Common Market, A Legal Profile, vol. II (1960), pp. 141-147. The Principal Stock Exchanges of the World (edited by David E. Spray (1964).

For older publications, see also Nussbaum, "American and Foreign Stock Exchange Legislation," 21 Va. L. Rev. 839 (1935); Kessler, "The American Security Act and its Foreign Counterparts: a Comparative Study," 44 Yale L. J. 1133 (1935); May, "Financial Regulations Abroad: The Contracts with American Technique," 41 J. Pol. Econ. 457 (1939) .

the American, the Continental and, intermediate between these two, the English system.

The American system is based on a philosophy of full and fair disclosure of information intended to enable investors to form a reasonable judgment as to the merits of offered securities. Thus, under the American Securities Act, and subject to certain exceptions, no public offering of securities can be made before filing a registration statement (together with a form of the prospectus to be furnished to investors) with a federal agency, the Securities and Exchange Commission (SEC) and no securities can be sold until the registration statement is "effective," (normally the 20th day after the date of filing).[60] This waiting (also popularly called "cooling") period, in addition to giving dealers and traders in securities the opportunity to study the merits of a proposed offering, enables the SEC to examine the information submitted by the registrant and request him to correct or supplement deficient or inaccurate statements in the prospectus. Although the SEC has no authority to approve or disapprove any security or to pass judgment on the merits of a security, this initial screening of information by the SEC is an important factor of reliability.[61]

The contrast between United States and Continental disclosure standards and practices is striking. In most Continental countries, publicity requirements, which are ordinarily found in companies laws rather than in specific securities acts, are much more limited in scope and in detail than their American counterpart.[62] Furthermore, the screening of securities offerings in Continental markets is not normally vested in separate agencies, such as the SEC, but is the responsibility of stock-exchange committees. These committees, which frequently include government-appointed members and operate in collaboration with financial, economic or public institutions, have authority to examine the quality of securities introduced to the public through listing and trading. If they administer with intelligent discretion their own technical rules (which are far more

---

[60] For the SEC's power to shorten this period by granting "acceleration" or to issue "stop orders" for non-compliance with statutory requirements, see Cohen, "Federal Legislation Affecting the Public Offering of Securities," 28 Geo. Wash. L. Rev. 119 (1959); Cohen and Throop, op. cit. preceding note, p. 551. As to the powers of commissioners under state "blue sky laws," see Id. op., pp. 596-597.

[61] Cohen, op. cit. preceding note, p. 155.

[62] See e.g., Conard, op. cit. note 59 supra, pp. 141-147; Althaus, op. cit. note 2 supra, p. 19.

elaborate than the rather scanty requirements found in Continental statutes) they are able to exert a profound influence upon the distribution of securities and the disclosure of information to potential investors.[63] In effect, stock-exchange committees are the cardinal agencies of securities regulation in Western Europe.[64]

The English system combines some of the features of the United States and the Continental regulatory machinery. Like the American Securities Act, the English Companies Act provides for the registration of prospectuses with an official, the Registrar of Companies, and prescribes in great detail the content of prospectuses.[65] The English Act however, differs from its American counterpart in several respects,[66] not the least significant of which concerns the powers of the Registrar of Companies. The Registrar operates as a mere filing authority, without power to investigate the accuracy of the information contained in prospectuses. In England, as on the Continent, the real regulatory bodies are stock-exchange committees. As a practical matter, no public offering can be made in England without making arrangements for the listing and quotation of the securities on one or more stock exchanges, which, in the case of foreign securities, nearly always include the London Stock Exchange. The Share and Loan Department of this Exchange has authority to scrutinize the accuracy of the information supplied by the applicant and its policies regarding disclosure of information and publicity are possibly stricter than those of Continental committees. In practice, therefore, the English system achieves indirectly, but most effectively, results substantially similar to those which can be obtained under the American securities laws.[67]

---

[63] Stock Exchange Committees have the power to determine the type of information to be supplied in each case and the extent to which such information should be disclosed to potential investors either in the prospectus or in public announcements in the specialized or general press.

[64] See, however, in respect to the powers of the Belgian "Commission Bancaire," De Voghel and Grégoire, Le Statut Légal des Banques (1949), pp. 146 et seq.; Conard, op. cit. note 59 supra, pp. 145-147; Description (see note 53 supra), p. 62.

[65] Companies Act, 1948, Fourth Schedule, reproduced in Palmer's, Company Law (20th ed. 1959), p. 1063.

[66] Thus, although the Companies Act provides for a waiting period, the short span of the period (three days only) gives it a significance far less important than that of the American "cooling" period. Another important difference is that, unlike the Securities Act, the Companies Act does not apply to foreign governmental borrowings.

[67] See e.g., Gower, op. cit. note 59, supra, at p. 1382.

SECTION II. SIGNATURE AND ENTRY
INTO FORCE

A. SIGNATURE

The particular nature of each loan transaction and the character of the parties thereto explain the many variations in signing procedures which can be found in contemporary loan instruments. Depending upon the circumstances, these instruments may be signed by the general manager or president of private or public corporate entities,[68] or international organizations;[69] ministers of state, finance, economy, public works, or similar officials;[70] or by such other persons as may be designated for the purpose.[71]

[68] See e.g., the following Loan Agreements between the IBRD and: (i) The Pakistan Industrial Credit and Investment Corporation Limited (September 25, 1959, 355 UNTS 169, General Manager); (ii) Cassa per il Mezzogiorno (September 16, 1959, 375 UNTS 159, President); (iii) The Japanese Development Bank (November 12, 1959, 354 UNTS 313, Director); or (iv) Autoridad Portuaria de Guayaquil (October 9, 1958, 337 UNTS 299, President).

[69] See e.g., (i) the Loan Contract dated July 25, 1950 between the Canton of Geneva and the ILO, signed on behalf of the ILO by its Director General (ILO, Off. Bull. vol. 33 (1950) 255); (ii) the Loan Agreement dated April 23, 1954 between the United States and the ECSC, signed on behalf of the ECSC by its President (229 UNTS 229); (iii) the Agreement dated March 23, 1948 between the United States and the United Nations, signed on behalf of the U.N. by the Secretary General (19 UNTS 43) or (iv) the Loan Agreement dated October 20, 1961 between Switzerland and the IBRD, signed on behalf of the IBRD by its President (415 UNTS 395). IBRD Loan and Guarantee Agreements are normally signed by the IBRD's President or in his absence a Vice President.

[70] See e.g.: (a) *Prime Minister:* Economic Agreement dated June 16, 1954, between the USA and Italy (236 UNTS 149); Exchange of Notes March 31, 1961, between the United Kingdom and Jordan (385 UNTS 81); Special Agreement on Financial Matters Dated October 19, 1939, between France, the United Kingdom and Turkey (CC LNTS 172); (b) *Secretary of State:* Exchange of Notes Dated February 3, 1959 between the United Kingdom and Yugoslavia (343 UNTS 153); Exchange of Notes Dated June 27, 1959, between the United States and Ecuador (317 UNTS 52); Exchange of Notes Dated September 17, 1952 between the United States and Pakistan (227 UNTS 77); Exchange of Notes Dated December 18-23, 1946, between the United Kingdom and Austria (88 UNTS 93); (c) *Minister of Finance:* Financial Agreement dated October 25, 1945, between Canada and Belgium (230 UNTS 127); Financial Agreement dated April 9, 1946, between Canada and France (43 UNTS 43); Exchange of Notes dated July 2, 1947, between New Zealand and France (16 UNTS 219); (d) *Minister of the Economy:* Guarantee Agreement dated September 16, 1959, between the Republic of Italy and the IBRD relating to the IBRD loan referred to note 68 supra (375 UNTS 159).

[71] The majority of agreements between the IBRD and member governments are signed by the ambassadors of such governments in Washington.

References in loan documents to the source of authority of the signatories vary greatly in detail and precision. Certain agreements are quite specific and expressly refer to all governmental, legislative or corporate action taken to authorize signature.[72] Other agreements merely contain the perfunctory statement that the documents have been signed by the duly authorized representatives of the parties, without identifying the source of their authority.[73] Even in this last

See also, the following agreements signed by diplomatic or consular representatives: (i) Financial Agreement dated October 25, 1945, between Canada and Belgium (see preceding note); Financial Agreement dated April 9, 1946, between Canada and France (id, loc.); Exchange of Notes dated June 27, 1959, between the United States and Ecuador (id. loc.); Exchange of Notes dated September 17, 1952, between the United States and Pakistan (id. loc); Exchange of Notes dated February 3, 1959, between the United Kingdom and Yugoslavia (id. loc.); Exchange of Notes dated December 18-23, 1946, between the United Kingdom and Austria (id. loc.); Special Agreement dated October 19, 1939, between France, the United Kingdom and Turkey (id. loc.); Financial Agreement dated December 6, 1945, between the United States and the United Kingdom (126 UNTS 13).

Comp., Loan Agreement dated July 24, 1957, between the IBRD and Corporación de Fomento de la Producción (New York Representative of the Corporación) and Compania Carbonifera e Industrial de Lota (General Manager of the Company) (282 UNTS 139); Project Agreement dated September 16, 1959 (relating to the IBRD loan to the Cassa per il Mezzogiorno referred to note 68 supra), between the IBRD and (i) SENN (President); (ii) Finelettrica (Director General); (iii) SME (New York Representative Banca di Napoli); and (iv) SIP (New York Representative of Banca Commerciale Italiana).

[72] See e.g., Financial Agreement dated February 5, 1964, between Canada and the Netherlands (43 UNTS 3); Financial Agreement dated October 25, 1945, between Canada and Belgium (referred to note 70 supra); Loan Agreement dated July 15, 1950, between the Canton of Geneva and the ILO (referred to in note 69 supra).

Comp., the following provision in a Loan Contract between the Republic of Cuba and American bankers, January 26, 1923, executed in Havana (*Dunn*, 290, at p. 291):

"... Deponent, as President of the Republic of Cuba, and in the exercise of the authority given to him by the law of October 9, 1922, enacted by the Congress, and sanctioned by the National Executive, hereinabove set forth, executes his deed of bond issue in the following manner ..."

See also the Trust Contract dated May 31, 1922, between the Republic of Bolivia and The Equitable Trust Company of New York (*Dunn*, 256, at p. 257, Article First, Sections 1 and 2).

[73] See e.g., Agreement dated March 25, 1953, between the United Kingdom and Lybia (172 UNTS 281); Agreement dated April 6, 1954, between the United States and Yugoslavia (237 UNTS 78); Agreement dated July 2, 1947, between New Zealand and France (see note 70 supra); Financial Agreement between Canada and the United Kingdom, March 6, 1946 (20 UNTS 13); Agreement dated October 21, 1960, between the United Kingdom and Chile (385 UNTS 15).

Comp., the following loan agreements between the USSR and: (i) China,

case, however, it is customary for each party to supply the other with sufficient evidence of the authority of its representatives. This may take the form of enabling legislation, executive orders or regulations, corporate resolutions, full powers or other appropriate delegation of authority.[74]

Delegations of authority take different forms. Some entities, such as commercial or banking establishments or international organizations, find it convenient to designate from time to time a number of persons generally authorized to sign all or specific kinds of agreements in the name of the entity concerned.[75] In other cases, delegations of authority are given on an *ad hoc* basis. Examples are full powers given to ambassadors or other representatives, public or private, designated by foreign borrowers.[76]

In selecting the appropriate representative or representatives many factors, not all of a legal nature, may be relevant. One is the particular degree of solemnity surrounding the transaction. Although there is no uniform rule, in practice only the most solemn agreements are signed by the highest officials of the contracting parties, while other agreements, which are the object of less attention and publicity, are executed by officials of lower rank.[77]

---

dated February 14, 1950 (226 UNTS 25); (ii) Finland, dated February 6, 1954 (221 UNTS 143); (iii) Yugoslavia, dated February 2, 1956 (259 UNTS 111); (iv) Iraq, dated March 16, 1959 (346 UNTS 107); and (v) Cuba, dated February 13, 1960 (329 UNTS 3).

[74] See e.g., the following formula in a loan contract between American bankers and a foreign government:

"The Government hereby authorizes the person who from time to time shall be recognized by the Secretary of State of the United States as the fully accredited Ambassador or Chargé d'Affaires of the Government to the United States Government, or [name of the representative] so long as he shall be Financial Counselor of the Embassy of [the Government] in the United States, or any other person thereunto specifically authorized by the Government, to act for and in the name of the Government or in the name of its Minister of Finance, or both, as to any and all matters relating to the Agreement or the Notes, or to the performance hereof or thereof, and the Government agrees that it will be fully bound by any act of such Ambassador or Chargé d'Affaires or [name of the representative] or other person so authorized."

See also, in respect of the IBRD practice, *Broches*, pp. 386-387.

[75] For a concrete example, see e.g. Annex B to the Act of Pledge.

[76] See note 74 supra. See also, Loan Agreement dated September 7, 1949, between the United Kingdom and Belgium (106 UNTS 61); Agreement dated May 21, 1959, between the United Kingdom and Greece (344 UNTS 3); Exchange of Notes dated January 22, 1948, between New Zealand and Czechoslovakia (16 UNTS 229); Agreement dated July 4, 1948, between the United States and Turkey (24 UNTS 67).

[77] Thus, it is not without significance that the President of the High Au-

Another pertinent factor may be one of pure convenience. Thus, if there are established channels of communication between the parties, the loan documents will naturally be processed through those channels. Examples are loans made to the United Nations by member or non-member governments through their respective permanent representatives or observers to that organization,[78] or loan or financial agreements executed by diplomatic agents, officers of banking institutions or corporations affiliated with the borrower; or other representatives stationed or doing business at the place of signing.[79]

Except when the existence of such channels makes it particularly convenient for the parties to proceed with the signing in the country of the borrower,[80] and in other exceptional situations,[81] the execution of the loan documents normally takes place in the lender's country or in the country in which the lender's headquarters are located. This rule applies regardless of whether the loan is made or contracted by private entities,[82] governmental agencies,[83] governments,[84] or international organizations.[85]

---

thority of the ECSC came in person to the United States to participate in the negotiations for the 1954 American loan which provided the ECSC with its first lending resources. Other agreements concerning subsequent borrowings by the ECSC have been executed on its behalf by officers of that organization.

[78] See e.g., the 1957 arrangements between the Swiss Government and the United Nations referred to in note 42 supra; the 1948 Agreement between the United States and the United Nations, id loc. See also the Loan Agreement dated September 7, 1949 between the United Kingdom and Belgium (106 UNTS 61) signed in Paris at the offices of the Belgian mission to the OEEC.

[79] See notes 71 and 76 supra.

[80] See e.g., Exchange of Notes dated May 4, 1960, between the United Kingdom and Jordan (385 UNTS 81); Exchange of Notes dated December 18-23 1946, between the United Kingdom and Austria (88 UNTS 93); Exchange of Notes dated June 16, 1954, between the United States and Italy (236 UNTS 149); and Exchange of Notes dated January 30, 1958, between Japan and Indonesia (325 UNTS 13). See also the 1923 loan made to Cuba by American bankers referred to in note 72 supra.

[81] Occasionally the agreement is executed in a third country. See e.g., the 1949 Loan Agreement between the United Kingdom and Belgium referred to in note 78 supra; and the Agreement dated January 22, 1948, between New Zealand and Czechoslovakia (16 UNTS 229), signed in London.

[82] See e.g., the Agreement dated December 5, 1921, between Bolivia and American bankers (Dunn, p. 252). This writer is not at liberty to refer specifically to contemporary private loan contracts but can vouch that this general rule prevails in all leading financial markets.

[83] See e.g., the Agreement dated February 25, 1957, between the United Kingdom and the Export-Import Bank of Washington (cmnd. 104); the Agreement dated December 4, 1945, between the French Government and the Export-Import Bank of Washington (Journal Official December 27, 1945, p. 8606).

[84] See e.g., the agreements between (a) Canada and (i) the United King-

Loan documents are normally signed or exchanged on the same day. There are however, a few exceptions to this general rule. Informal arrangements between banking or other financial institutions operating in different countries, for example, are common. These arrangements frequently consist merely of a letter of understanding dispatched by one party to the other, which is acknowledged either by separate letter or by returning a duly confirmed copy of the original. Whether, in the absence of an express stipulation, these arrangements are to be regarded as concluded in the country of the lender or of the borroweer or in some other country with which the transaction may be connected is a question, which, in the event of a dispute between the parties, must be determined in accordance with the conflict of law rules of the forum.[86] Exceptions involving governmental loans to international organizations are also worth mentioning. Thus, the 1961 agreement providing for a loan of 100 million Swiss Frs. from the Swiss Government to the IBRD was signed by a Federal Councillor at Berne on October 11, 1961, and by the President of the IBRD at Washington, D.C. nine days later.[87] The 1957 loan from the Swiss Government to the United Nations for the modernization of the Palais des Nations, in Geneva, was concluded pursuant to an offer made in a letter dated January 29, 1957 from the Permanent Observer of Switzerland to the United Nations, which was acknowledged a month later in a resolution of the General Assembly and was duly approved by the Swiss Parliament on September 16, 1957.[88]

Questions of timing and location are of particular importance

---

dom, dated March 6, 1946 (note 73 supra), (ii) Belgium, dated October 25, 1945 (note 70 supra), (iii) France, dated April 9, 1946 (id. loc.); (b) the United Kingdom and (i) Yugoslavia, dated May 10, 1951 (102 UNTS 29); (ii) Chile, dated October 21, 1960 (385 UNTS 15); (c) the United States and (i) Ecuador, dated June 27, 1959 (note 70 supra); (ii) Pakistan, dated September 17, 1952 (id. loc.); (d) India and Burma, dated March 12, 1957 (312 UNTS 139); and (e) New Zealand and France, dated July 2, 1947 (note 70 supra).

[85] See e.g., the 1954 Loan Agreement between the United States and the ECSC (note 69 supra); the Loan Agreement dated September 17, 1956, between the Swiss Government and the IBRD (340 UNTS 311). As a rule, IBRD loan, and related guarantee agreements are signed at the IBRD's headquarters in Washington, D.C.

[86] Examples are the various arrangements between the IBRD and the Deutsche Bundesbank. See *The World Bank,* pp. 88-89.

[87] Article 10 (415 UNTS 395).

[88] UN Doc. A/C.5/659/Add. 1, February 1, 1957; Resolution 1101 (XI) of February 27, 1957 (UN Yearbook 1956, p. 404); and Arrêté Fédéral dated September 16, 1957 (Feuille Fédérale Suisse 1957, II, 677).

in the case of joint financing operations. When joint financing is provided from a number of sources all parties, including the borrower, have a direct interest in seeking assurances that every participant is committed to contribute its share of the over-all financial scheme. This can be done either by having all the parties join in a common announcement that the financing of the over-all transaction is assured or, if the progress of negotiations permits it, by having all loan documents executed at the same time in a joint closing session. The selection of the particular place at which the announcement or the closing should be made is largely a matter of taste and circumstances. Depending upon the facts of the case, this may be the place where one or several lenders have their main offices[89] or, as in the case of joint operations involving public bond issues or private placements in the private capital market, the particular market in which funds are raised.[90] On rare occasions the closing formalities take place in the borrower's own country. This, for example, was the solution adopted in connection with the conclusion of the various agreements settling the long-standing dispute between India and Pakistan over the economic uses of the waters of the Indus river, and the financing of a plan for the development of the peaceful uses of these waters. These agreements, including loan agreements to Pakistan from the IBRD and the DLF and an international financial agreement creating an Indus Basin Development Fund equal to almost $900 million, were all executed in Karachi on September 19, 1960.[91]

---

[89] In 1962, when the IBRD, the AID, The Export-Import Bank of Washington and the United Kingdom, through its Export Credits Guarantee Department, agreed to provide funds to the Volta River Authority, an agency of the Government of Ghana, the final closing of the entire transaction took place at the IBRD's headquarters. See also text and note 107 infra.

[90] Thus, several IBRD loan agreements, concomitant with public offerings of the borrower in New York, have been signed in that city. See e.g., the following agreements with: (i) Norway, dated April 19, 1955 (211 UNTS 159); (ii) South Africa, dated November 28, 1955 (230 UNTS 101) and October 1, 1957 (280 UNTS 285); (iii) Belgium, dated September 10, 1957 (286 UNTS 291); (iv) Denmark, dated February 4, 1959 (328 UNTS 143); and (v) The Japanese Development Bank (guaranteed by Japan), dated February 17, 1959 (337 UNTS 205).

[91] 444 UNTS 259. It is noteworthy that the Water Treaty and the Indus Basin Development Fund Agreement between the participating Governments and the IBRD came into force on January 12, 1961, i.e. the date of the exchange of the instruments of ratification of the Treaty, which is also the date on which the DLF Loan Agreement, in force since the date of signature, became operative. The IBRD Loan Agreement was declared effective on January 17, 1961. Note also that, pursuant to an express provision of the fund

As a practical matter, once such a joint venture has been publicly announced, it would be very difficult morally for a participant to refuse to perform its part of the bargain. Nevertheless, that possibility cannot be excluded altogether. It is therefore understandable that the parties to such ventures insist on making performance of their respective promises mutually interdependent, either by co-ordinating disbursements.[92] arranging for the concomitant entry into force and effect of all related arrangements,[93] or by providing both for such coming into force and co-ordination.[94]

B. ENTRY INTO FORCE

No reputable lender will enter into a foreign loan contract, or agree to underwrite or purchase foreign securities, without being assured that all requirements essential to the validity of the borrower's obligations have been met. This, of course, is the paramount question which must be answered to the lender's complete satisfaction before the loan proceeds are made available to the borrower.[95]

Agreement, its effect was retrospectively set as from April 1, 1960 (Section 13.01).

Of course, the problem may be considerably simplified if the overall transaction is contained in a single document or, if contained in several instruments, all instruments are executed by the same parties. An example of the first situation is the Agreement dated June 28, 1950 between the Governments of the United Kingdom, Australia, India, Pakistan and Ceylon, and the Government of Burma (87 UNTS 153), providing for a £6 million loan to Burma, which came into force upon signature. The second situation is illustrated by the Financial Agreement dated October 19, 1939 (CC LNTS 168) between France, Great Britain and Turkey. This agreement, which was intended to provide Turkey with financial and economic assistance and facilitate Turkey's acquisition of war material, was signed on the same day as the Treaty of Mutual Assistance between the three Governments and came into force simultaneously with the Treaty, upon the deposit of the instruments of ratification at Ankara.

[92] See e.g., the Loan Agreement dated April 1, 1959 between the IBRD and the Cassa per il Mezzogiorno (359 UNTS 191, Schedule 3 (d)), concluded as part of a combined operation including a loan from the EIB to, and a public offering of securities by, the borrower.

[93] See e.g., the IBRD agreements referred to in note 90 supra.

[94] See e.g., the Loan Agreement dated February 8, 1962, between the IBRD and the Volta River Authority (449 UNTS 207, Sections 2.02, 7.01 and 7.02).

[95] Although information supplied by the borrower can greatly assist the lender in making the proper determination, it is clear that representations made, or evidence furnished, by the borrower do not preclude the lender from proceeding with its own investigation of the matter, frequently with the assistance of foreign counsel. See e.g., *Broches,* pp. 392-396; Richards, op. cit. note 2 supra, p. 456; Stevenson, op. cit. note 2 supra, p. 197; Cohen and Throop, op. cit. note 2 supra, p. 523.

Although in most cases the lender performs its part of the bargain at the outset and attention naturally focuses on the borrower's repayment and other obligations, it should be emphasized that matters of legal validity are no less the borrower's concern than they are the lender's. This is particularly true if, as in the case of many contemporary lines of credit, economic development loans or similar arrangements, the lender's commitments, like the borrower's own obligations, are stretched over a period of time. Provisions commonly found in international loan agreements show clearly that the parties to such agreements are quite conscious of the importance of the problem. Examples are provisions such as those regarding notices of approval or ratification or appropriation of funds by the lender or its competent organs,[96] as well as the practice of certain institutional lenders to supply borrowers with sufficient evidence of authority.[97]

What constitutes satisfactory evidence and the methods used in obtaining it vary from case to case. The complexity of the transaction, the personality of the parties, the continuity of relations between them or their familiarity with each other's legal systems, all are factors which considerably affect the character and the extent of the necessary investigation. In certain cases, this investigation may (or must as in the case of public offerings of foreign securities), be completed before

---

[96] See e.g., the following agreements between: (a) Canada and (i) the United Kingdom, dated March 6, 1946 (note 73 supra), (ii) France, dated April 9, 1946 (note 70 supra); (b) the United Kingdom and Belgium, dated September 7, 1949 (note 76 supra); (c) New Zealand and France, dated July 2, 1947 (note 70 supra); (d) India and Burma, dated March 12, 1957 (note 84 supra); (e) the USSR and Yugoslavia, dated February 2, 1956 (259 UNTS 111). See also, note 99 infra.

Comp., the Loan Contract dated June 24, 1922, between the Republic of El Salvador and Minor C. Keith (*Dunn*, p. 222). This contract, which expressly refers to the authority of the Republic's representative (given by way of full powers, id. op., p. 223), also provides that

"This contract shall not become operative for any purpose until the same shall have been authorized, ratified and sanctioned in accordance with the Constitution and the Laws of the Republic and until all other legal conditions and necessary pre-requisites shall have been duly performed and complied with and official notification thereof shall have been transmitted to the Fiscal Agent through the Department of State of the United States of America, and all liens on the Custom House have been duly cancelled by the creditors to the satisfaction of Keith and the Fiscal Agent." (Article XXIII (e), id. op., p. 247).

See also, the Agreement between the Republic of Nicaragua and American bankers, October 8, 1913, *Dunn,* p. 372 (Article 19th, p. 379).

[97] Thus, it is the consistent practice of the IBRD to deliver to borrowers and guarantors a copy, duly certified by the Secretary of the IBRD, of the resolution of its board of directors authorizing the loan.

the date of the loan.[98] Frequently, however, the loan cannot be fully operative from the date of signing and some time must elapse between that date and the date on which the borrower becomes entitled to draw the proceeds of the loan. This may be either because the loan is subject to specific conditions, including ratification, or simply because of the complexity of the corporate, constitutional or other issues involved.[99]

---

[98] See e.g., Agreement dated January 22, 1948, between New Zealand and Czechoslovakia (Article VI, not 76 supra); Agreement dated July 10, 1954, between the United Kingdom and Germany (Article X, 199 UNTS 135); Agreement dated July 9, 1954, between the United Kingdom and the Netherlands (Article X, 199 UNTS 157); Exchange of Notes dated June 16, 1954, between the United States and Italy (note 80 supra); Agricultural Commodities Agreement dated March 13, 1959, between the United States and Ceylon (Article VI, 342 UNTS 51).

See also, Loan Contract dated July 25, 1950, between the Canton of Geneva and the ILO (note 69 supra); the agreements referred to in note 106 and 107 infra; the Social Progress Trust Fund Agreement dated June 19, 1961, between the United States and the IADB (Article VII, TIAS 4763).

[99] Although the following examples in the text above focus primarily on action to be taken by borrowers in fulfilment of the various requirements set forth in the loan documents or otherwise requested by lenders, it should be noted that the entry into force of international loan contracts may be delayed by the lender's own procedures. Typical examples are those concerning governmental loans to international organizations. It will be recalled that it is the general practice of these organizations to seek prior approval of their borrowing operations by their respective organs (see text and notes 39 to 45 supra). Under the circumstances, the question whether loan agreements between these organizations and governmental parties becomes effective upon signature or at a later date, depends essentially upon the parties' intention or the complexity of the legislative or other requirements which must be satisfied by the governmental contracting party.

If all governmental action is taken before the execution of the loan agreement, the entry into force of the agreement may coincide with the date of signature. See e.g., the 1954 Loan Agreement between the United States and the ECSC (note 69 supra), and the 1961 Loan Agreement between the Swiss Government and the IBRD (note 69 supra).

If, however, ratification, parliamentary appropriation or some other governmental action is needed after signature, the entry into force of the agreement must be postponed until such time as the necessary action is taken. Thus, the 1948 loan from the United States Government to the United Nations for the construction of the headquarters building (note 69 supra), though signed on March 23, 1948, on behalf of the UN by the Secretary General (duly authorized by the General Assembly) and on behalf of the United States by its Representative to the United Nations, came into force about five months after signature, when the United States notified the Secretary General that all governmental action necessary to perfect the validity of the agreement had been taken by the President and the American Congress. (See UN Yearbook 1947-48, pp. 224-226). Another example is the 1956 Loan Agreement between the Swiss Government and the IBRD (340 UNTS

Several solutions are possible. If the lender has good reason to believe that the satisfaction of unfulfilled requirements is only a matter of time, it may be willing to make available to the borrower part of the loan proceeds by anticipation, reserving the right, however, to claim immediate repayment of the monies advanced if the necessary requirements are not satisfied within a specified time.[100]

Sometimes specific conditions attach only to certain provisions of the loan contract, which are separable from the remainder of the contract. In such a case, the parties may agree to let the remainder of the contract take effect and postpone the effectiveness of the provisions in question until such time as the relevent conditions have been duly satisfied. This situation is nicely illustrated by the financial agreement of March 6, 1946 between Canada and the United Kingdom. This agreement, which required legislative approval, came into force on May 30, 1946, with the exception of certain provisions whose effectiveness was postponed until after approval by the United States Congress of the Anglo-American financial agreement signed in Washington on December 6, 1945. This last approval having been given on July 15, 1946, the latter provisions of the Anglo-Canadian agreement came into effect on the following day.[101]

---

311) which entered into force upon ratification by the Swiss Parliament, some three months after signature.

[100] See e.g., the Agreement dated December 5, 1921, between Bolivia and American bankers (*Dunn*, p. 252). In anticipation of the loan, the bankers had deposited with one of them the sum of $1 million. The Agreement (Article I) provided that:

"From this sum the Minister of Finance may immediately withdraw a sum not to exceed One Hundred Thousand Dollars; against the remainder, he may draw as soon as the Congress of the Republic has authorized the Executive to contract the present loan on the terms of this contract; with the condition, however, that such authorization be conferred not later than 17 December of this year; the legality of such authorization shall be confirmed by the lawyers of the Bankers. If the Republic, through mediation of its Congress, should not authorize the present loan before 17 December, 1921, the sums loaned to the Republic before that date shall be immediately repaid, but in that case, the other dispositions of this contract shall continue in effect." (p. 253).

Comp., the Agreement dated February 13, 1960, between the USSR and Cuba (329 UNTS 3), which was said to be "provisionally effective" as of the date of signature, though its entry into force was subject to ratification Article 12). See also, the Agreement dated February 14, 1950, between the USSR and China (226 UNTS 25) which "entered into force from the date of signature," subject to ratification.

[101] 20 UNTS 13. The Anglo-American Agreement is found in 126 UNTS 13. See also, ibid. p. 34, the letter from the Acting Secretary of State to the British Ambassador.

Another solution, is to declare the entire loan effective at a given time, but to make disbursement under the loan contingent upon the fulfilment of certain conditions. In this case, although the agreement comes into force on a certain date, which is usually the date of signature, its operative effect, insofar as drawings against the loan are concerned, is delayed until all specified conditions are satisfied. This solution, which sometimes obtains in the agreements between private lenders and foreign borrowers,[102] is consistently favored by certain lending institutions, which include the Export-Import Bank of Washington, other American lending agencies, and international lending organizations like the IADB.[103]

An entirely different procedure is adopted by other institutional lenders, and in particular by the IBRD and other organizations or agencies which have followed its example. The IBRD Loan Regulations provide in substance that before a loan agreement can be

---

[102] The conditions stipulated by private lenders which occur with the greatest frequency relate to the submission of documents evidencing corporate or governmental action, governmental consents, including exchange licenses and transfer assurances, the registration of mortgages or other forms of security, and opinions of counsel regarding the validity of the foregoing actions. Another stipulation sometimes found in loan agreements with foreign governments, governmental agencies or municipalities, concerns the furnishing of opinions establishing the validity of waivers of sovereign immunity contained in the agreement.

[103] Thus, it is a standard provision in agreements between the Export-Import Bank and foreign governments that:

"Prior to and as a condition precedent to the first disbursement under the credit, Eximbank shall be furnished with:

    (a) Evidence of authority of the person who has executed this Agreement and the promissory note and otherwise acts as the representative of [the borrower] in connection with the credit; and

    (b) An opinion of legal counsel satisfactory to Eximbank, demonstrating to the satisfaction of Eximbank that [the borrower] has taken all action necessary under its constitutional laws to authorize the contracting of the credit and that the promissory note given to evidence the credit constitutes the valid and binding obligations of [the borrower] in accordance with its terms."

For other examples, see e.g., the agreements between the Export-Import Bank and: (i) France, dated December 4, 1945, Article 11 (Journal Officiel December 27, 1945, p. 8606) ; or (ii) the United Kingdom, dated February 25, 1957, Article XIV (Cmnd. 104). Comp., the Agreement dated April 23, 1954, between the United States Government and the ECSC, Article XIII (as amended by a supplemental agreement dated December 16, 1954, 229 UNTS 229, and 238 UNTS 340); the agreements between the United States and (i) Ecuador, dated June 27, 1958, Section 4 (317 UNTS 52) ; and (ii) Burma, dated March 21, 1957, Article VII, (1) (8 UNTS 1862) .

Similar provisions are also found in agreements between lending agencies and borrowers other than foreign governments.

declared effective, the IBRD must have received satisfactory evidence, including opinions of counsel, that the execution and delivery of the agreement on behalf of the borrower have been duly authorized or ratified by the requisite corporate or governmental action, and that all events specified in the agreement as conditions to its effectiveness have occurred. It is only after the IBRD has had an opportunity to review the evidence submitted, and upon notification to the borrower of the its acceptance of such evidence, that the agreement becomes effective.[104]

The IBRD's loan agreements normally become effective at some time after the date of signature, since conditions of effectiveness, other than those regarding evidence of due authorization or ratification, are frequent,[105] and some time is required before these conditions can be fulfilled. In fact, in the whole history of the IBRD's lending operations, only two of its several hundred loans have come into force upon signature. These are a 1949 agreement with the Kingdom of Belgium for the financing of industrial projects in that country,[106] and a 1962 agreement with Volta River Authority to finance part of the cost of a hydro-electric project in Ghana.[107] These two agreements however, differ in other respects. In the Belgian case, all conditions of effectiveness, including all necessary authorizations and the submission of legal opinions, had been satisfied before signature. In the Volta case, the project involved was a joint international venture, financed in part by the IBRD, by sources in the United Kingdom and the United States and by contributions from the Government of Ghana, and each party, even though entering into separate agreements, had a common interest in making all agreements effective at the same time.

---

[104] *Broches,* pp. 392-396.

[105] Id. op., id. loc.

[106] Loan Agreement dated March 1, 1949 (154 UNTS 133).

[107] Loan Agreement (together with a Guarantee Agreement between the Republic of Ghana and the IBRD dated February 8, 1962 (449 UNTS 207)

Chapter II

The Administration of International Loans

Both international and domestic lenders have a direct interest in seeking to maintain a close relationship with the borrower throughout the life of each loan. It is not surprising, therefore, that attempts have been made, by means of contractual stipulations or statutory enactments, to import into the international sector many of the devices which, in the domestic sector, are the essential parts of a sound loan administration machinery.

While such attempts are understandable, it cannot be said that they have all met with equal success. The use of the trust device in international loans made in the nineteen twenties and the early thirties is a perfect illustration. Sometimes with the enthusiastic support, sometimes with the passive assistance of Continental lawyers and financiers, the trust device was employed in all kinds of loans, ranging from private loans to such governmental loans as the Young Loan and loans made under the auspices of the League of Nations.[1] As might have been expected, this sudden transplantation of the trust into a soil as yet unprepared to receive it did not live up to the expectations of its sponsors. When difficulties occurred, puzzled Continental courts felt obliged to rely on public policy or to transform the trust into concepts such as agency, which differed from common law institution, but were more acceptable to the Continental mind.[2]

This example, though it may be the most spectacular, does not stand alone. Indiscriminate extension of domestic legal devices to international situations is fraught with danger. First of all, regula-

---

[1] See e.g., Zahn, "The Trustee in German-American Industrial Loans", 12 Boston L. Rev. 187 and 428 (1932); *Borchard*, p. 45; Weiser, *Trust on the Continent of Europe* (1936); Kuczynski, *American Loans to Germany* (1927).

[2] See text and notes 62, 95 to 96 infra.

tions or contractual stipulations which are acceptable as a matter of course to domestic borrowers may appear unduly complicated or inconvenient to foreign borrowers, and thus constitute a source of constant friction detrimental to the harmonious continuity of the lender-borrower relationship. Secondly, domestic devices when transposed into an international context, are bound to lose some, if not a great deal, of their effectiveness, for geographical, legal or other reasons. International lenders and their legal advisers must realize that, short of subjecting the borrower to the strictest supervision, they must rely, much more extensively than would a domestic lender operating within the bounds of his own commercial and legal systems, upon the good faith of the borrower and his willingness to abide by his contractual commitments.

Furthermore, it is apparent that the preoccupations of domestic and international lenders in administering their respective loans are not necessarily the same, Domestically, the primary purpose of financial or other controls over the borrower's affairs is to preserve the lenders' interests and facilitate the timely exercise of their remedies. Internationally, this objective, which clearly cannot be ignored, is supplemented by other considerations. Not the least important of these is the increasing realization that many borrowers, especially in underdeveloped countries, need guidance and assistance in the planning and development of their economy or in carrying out their business. By keeping close contact with borrowers, international lenders may satisfy themselves that their original appraisal of the merits of the loan and the risks involved is not put in jeopardy by the subsequent behavior of the borrower, and also be in a position to help the borrower in meeting specific structural, technical or economic problems.[3] Appreciation of such factors is essential to a correct understanding of modern international loan administration machinery; otherwise one might be misled by the apparent similarity between the devices used in the international and the domestic field of lending.

---

[3] Historically this new orientation of international loan administration can be traced back to the creation of the League of Nations. See e.g., *Borchard*, pp. 277 et seq.; Andréades, *Les Contrôles Financiers Internationaux*, 5 Recueil des Cours. 1 (1942); John Fisher Williams, *L'Entr'Aide Financière Internationale*, 5 Recueil des Cours 113 (1924), and *La Convention Financière pour l'Assistance aux Etats Victimes d'Agression*, 34 Recueil des Cours 81 (1930); Strupp, *L'Intervention en Matière Financière*, 8 Recueil des Cours 5 (1925): Cosoiu, *Le Rôle de la Société des Nations en Matière d'Emprunts d'Etat* (1934), pp. 181 et seq.; *Salmon*, pp. 205-206.

SECTION I. THE OBJECT OF INTERNATIONAL
LOAN ADMINISTRATION

A. APPLICATION OF PROCEEDS

One of the most elementary assurances to be sought by lenders is that the loan proceeds reach their intended destination and are not diverted to purposes other than those for which the loan was made,[4] Of necessity, however, the scope of the lenders' control over the use of the loan monies varies extensively from case to case.

Sometimes, as when the proceeds of the loan are intended to be used in the general operations of the borrower, all that may be feasible or necessary is to state in the loan documents, in more or less comprehensive terms, the general purpose of the loan,[5] and to provide additional covenants to protect the lenders against a possible deterioration of the borrower's financial position.

At other times, especially when the loan is made to finance expenditures on a specific project, it is possible to include specific provisions in the loan documents regarding the use of the proceeds. In this respect, two major situations must be distinguished: (a) when the loan proceeds are made available to the borrower in a lump sum, at or about the time of the loan,[6] and (b) when the disbursements are spread over a period of time which generally corresponds to the time

---

[4] In exceptional cases, such as those involving inter-governmental relations, the lender may, for reasons of political discretion, foresake this requirement, See e.g., the Agreement dated February 6, 1954, between the U.S.S.R. and Finland concerning a Soviet loan to the latter country (221 UNTS 143), Article I. "The U.S.S.R. shall grant to Finland, for use in its discretion, a ten-year loan . . ."

[5] See e.g., the following statements in documents relating to loans raised by private borrowers: "The net proceeds [of the loan] will be used to finance the cost of the expansion of [the Borrower] . . . and for general corporate purposes of [the Borrower]"; "the proceeds of the loan shall be used to finance partially the expansion programme of the [Borrower in its home and foreign countries]";—and by foreign governments: "The proceeds of the loan will increase the foreign exchange reserves of [the Borrower]", "the proceeds of the loan will ease the financial relations between the two countries";—and by such international organizations as the IBRD: "The net proceeds to the Bank of the sale of the Bonds will be used in the general operations of the Bank", or the High Authority of the ECSC: "The proceeds from this Loan shall be used to make loans to enterprises or institutions which, under the Treaty [creating the ECSC] may borrow from [the High Authority]. . . ." (as translated from French).

[6] This is the situation in public offerings of foreign securities and sometimes in loans made directly to foreign borrowers by banking or credit institutions.

estimated for the successful completion of the project involved. Clearly, the lenders' controlling power is greater in the second than in the first situation. In the first situation the lenders initially have the means to obtain satisfactory assurances, e.g. in the forms of appropriate evidence showing that orders for the delivery of goods or contracts with contractors, consultants or other persons whose services are required for the carrying out of the project, have been placed or concluded. However, once the proceeds of the loan have been disbursed, they must rely essentially on the good faith of the borrower. In the second situation the lenders' continuing power to scrutinize evidence furnished in support of the borrowers withdrawal applications provides an effective means to follow up the application of the loan proceeds and to suspend or terminate disbursements if the borrower fails to comply with his obligations.[7]

---

[7] This situation exists in most economic development loans made by governmental lending agencies and international lending organizations. The following provisions in the IBRD Loan Regulations are reproduced for the convenience of the reader:

"Section 4.01. *Withdrawal from the Loan Account.* The Borrower shall be entitled to withdraw from the Loan Account (i) such amounts as shall have been paid for the reasonable cost of goods to be financed under the Loan Agreement; and (ii), if the Bank shall so agree, such amounts as shall be required to meet payments to be made for the reasonable cost of such goods. Except as shall be otherwise agreed between the Bank and the Borrower, no withdrawals shall be made on account of (a) expenditures prior to [the Effective Date] or (b) expenditures in the currency of the Borrower or for goods produced in (including services supplied from) the territories of the Borrower or (c) expenditures in the territories of any country which is not a member of the Bank (other than Switzerland) or for goods produced in (including services supplied from) such territories.

Section 4.02. *Special Commitments by the Bank.* Upon the Borrower's request and upon such terms and conditions as shall be agreed upon between the Bank and the Borrower, the Bank may enter into special commitments in writing to pay amounts to the Borrower or others in respect of the cost of goods notwithstanding any subsequent suspension or cancellation.

Section 403. *Applications for Withdrawal or for Special Commitment.* When the Borrower shall desire to withdraw any amount from the Loan Account or to request the Bank to enter into a special commitment pursuant to Section 4.02, the Borrower shall deliver to the Bank a written application in such form, and containing such statements and agreements, as the Bank shall reasonably request. Applications for withdrawal, with the necessary documentation as hereinafter in this Article provided, shall, except as the Bank and the Borrower shall otherwise agree, be made promptly in relation to expenditures for the Project.

Section 4.04. *Supporting Evidence.* The Borrower shall furnish to the Bank such documents and other evidence in support of the application

Another device is to attach economic conditions to the loan. For example, the borrower may be required to use all or part of the loan proceeds to pay for services supplied, or goods produced, by the lenders or by enterprises with which they are more or less intimately associated or in which they have a particular interest. Commonly called a "tied" loan, this type of agreement is not foreign to contractual arrangements between private lenders and borrowers,[8] and is a char-

---

as the Bank shall reasonably request, whether before or after the Bank shall have permitted any withdrawal requested in the application.
Section 4.05 *Sufficiency of Applications and Documents.* Each application and the accompanying documents and other evidence must be sufficient in form and substance to satisfy the Bank that the Borrower is entitled to withdraw from the Loan Account the amount applied for and that the amount to be withdrawn from the Loan Account is to be used only for the purposes specified in the Loan Agreement.
Section 4.06. *Payment by the Bank.* Payment by the Bank of amounts which the Borrower is entitled to withdraw from the Loan Account shall be made to or on the order of the Borrower."

Similar provisions are sometimes found in intergovernmental loan agreements. See e.g., the Exchange of Notes dated January 24, 1947, between Australia and The Netherlands (10 UNTS 77, Article 8):
"The Netherlands Indies Government will give full information to the Commonwealth Bank of Australia regarding payments made, or to be made, under the Credit, whenever such information is requested by the Commonwealth Government or the Commonwealth Bank of Australia."

Comp., The Exchange of Notes dated June 27, 1958, between the United States and Ecuador (317 UNTS 51, Article 3).

See also, in connection with loans issued under the auspices of the League of Nations, *Salmon,* pp. 204-205.

[8] See e.g., the arrangement between Metro-Goldwyn-Mayer Company and the German Universum Film Company, incidental to a loan made by the former to the latter company, providing for the distribution of motion pictures, referred to by Zahn, op. cit., supra note 1, p. 216, and by Kuczinski, op. cit. id. loc., p. 361.

Comp., the Kingdom of Norway (Shipping) 4½% Sterling Registered Stock 1961/66:
"The whole of the net proceeds of the Issue will be expended in the United Kingdom in respect to vessels constructed or to be constructed in United Kingdom yards."

See also, in Switzerland, the following statements in prospectuses regarding: (i) the Aktieselskapet Union (Union Co.) Oslo, 4½% Loan of 1956:
"The corporation has undertaken, in connection with this loan, to place orders in Switzerland up to an amount of 3 million Swiss francs [i.e., 1/5 of the aggregate amount of the Loan], provided that tenders submitted by Swiss enterprises can withstand comparison with those submitted by competitive enterprises" (as translated).

and (ii) the Mortgage Bank of the State of Vorarlberg 4½% Loan of 1959:
"The proceeds of this issue serve to make loans to various Vorarlberg enterprises, most of which are important and steady customers for products of the Swiss economy." (as translated).

acteristic feature of most contemporary governmental financing operations, either in the form of economic cooperation, mutual assistance
or export-financing facilities.[9] Although frequently warranted by purely domestic political and economic considerations, these arrangements
have the major inconvenience of limiting financial cooperation to
strictly bilateral relations and of interfering with the normal development of international trade. These considerations explain why such
cooperative institutions as international lending organizations, whose
purpose it is to promote the growth of international trade and economic cooperation, are forbidden by their respective charters from
imposing any condition that the proceeds of loans made by them be
spent in the territories of any particular country. In furtherance of
their corporate purpose, these organizations have adopted policies
which, though they are sufficiently flexible to take into account the
particular circumstances of each operation, generally encourage borrowers to obtain supplies and services on a competitive international
basis.[10]

B. Managerial and Policy Issues

The quality and experience of the borrower's management and
the soundness of its operational policies are factors of primary importance in assessing the merits of any loan transaction. Clearly, however, the scope and intensity of the lenders' investigation and the
particular assurances required by the lenders vary considerably from
case to case. These variations are reflected in the relevant provisions
of loan documents.

In the case of loans to borrowers with experienced and skillful
management, reference to the managerial issue, if included in the
loan documents at all, may consist of no more than a description of
the most characteristic features of the borrower's corporate, constitu-

---

[9] See e.g., Arnold, *Aid For Developing Countries* (1962); Luchaire, "L'Aide
Internationale aux Pays Sous-Développés", Penant 1964, 21, 295, 423—1965,
1, 177; Grant, "Agency for International Development", in *Surrey*, 403, at
pp. 404 and 411; Middleton, "The Export-Import Bank", id. op., 391, at
p. 392; Billerbeck, *Reform of Development Aid* (1962), at p. 43; Billerbeck,
Soviet Bloc Foreign Aid to Underdeveloped Countries (1960), p. 36; Boguslavski, "Legal Aspects of the Soviet Technical Aid Programme for Economically Under-Developed Countries", 8 Review of Contemporary Law 41 (1961),
at p. 46.

[10] IBRD, Articles of Agreement, Article III, Section 5 (a); IDA, Articles
of Agreement, Article V, Section 1 (f); IFC, Articles of Agreement, Article
III, Section 3 (iii); IADB, Articles of Agreement, Article III, Section 9 (a);
EIB, Statutes, Article 20 (4).

tional or administrative set up;[11] and inquiry into the borrower's policies may be limited to requesting more or less periodic information concerning the borrower's financial condition or the progress of the particular project involved.[12]

Frequently, however, additional assurances must be obtained and provision made for organizational or managerial changes,[13] the employment of outside experts or consultants,[14] or the undertaking by the borrower of specific commitments regarding the conduct of its affairs. Depending upon the circumstances, these commitments may take the form of positive assurances by the borrower that it will adopt

---

[11] Description of foreign legal institutions may create interesting problems for draftsmen. See e.g., Stevenson, "Legal Aspects of the Public Offering of Foreign Securities in the United States Market", 28 Geo. Wash. L. Rev. 194 (1959), at pp. 206-207, 211-212.

[12] This kind of control may take various forms ranging from the borrower's submission of balance sheets, annual audits, external debt or balance of payments statements to direct end-use supervision in the field by representatives of the lenders.

[13] See, e.g., the following agreements between the IBRD and: The Government of Ceylon June 6, 1961 (414 UNTS 349, Section 5.09); the Empire of Ethiopia September 10, 1950 (157 UNTS 233, Sections 4.05 and 6.01 (a)); the Republic of Peru December 10, 1960 (417 UNTS 275, Section 5.02 (b)); the Port Authority of Thailand October 12, 1956 (261 UNTS 117, Section 7.01); and the State of Israel September 9, 1960 (406 UNTS 3, Section 5.09). See also *The World Bank*, pp. 36-37.

[14] These may be financial experts, such as the commissioner general and financial advisers to central banks appointed in connection with most loans issued under the auspices of the League of Nations (See e.g., Cosoiu, op. cit. note 3 supra, p. 200; *Borchard,* p. 296; Sir John Fisher Williams, *Chapters on Current International Law and The League of Nations* (1929), p. 378) or technical experts or consultants as in the case of economic development loans. Most loans of this type contain provisions to the effect that the borrower shall employ engineering, agricultural or other consultants to assist it in the carrying on of the project financed under the loan. See e.g., the following agreements between the IBRD and: Servicios Electricos del Gran Buenos Aires, S. A., January 19, 1962 (446 UNTS 305, Section 5.02); the Government of Ceylon, June 6, 1961 (414 UNTS 349, Section 5.01 (b)); Empresa de Energia Electrica de Bogota, May 23, 1962 (447 UNTS 39, Section 5.01 (a)); the Republic of Chile, June 28, 1961 (426 UNTS 33, Section 5.01 (a)); the Volta River Authority, February 8, 1962 (449 UNTS 207, Section 5.01 (b)); Iran, February 20, 1960 (384 UNTS 313, Section 5.01 (b)); Dead Sea Works Limited, July 11, 1961 (429 UNTS 3, Section 5.01 (b)); and the Republic of the Sudan, June 14, 1961 (415 UNTS 25, Section 5.01 (b)).

See also, the reference made by Zahn, op. cit. note 1 supra, p. 216, to a provision in an American indenture concerning a loan to a German cable company, according to which the lenders had the right to appoint the chief engineer for the construction of an Atlantic cable, while the borrower had only the right to appoint the second engineer.

certain policies considered necessary to the success of its business or the improvement of its economy. Alternatively, the covenants may be formulated in a negative fashion, prohibiting the borrower from taking certain measures possibly detrimental to its own as well as to the lenders' interests, without prior consultation with, or agreement by, the lenders.

On the positive side, the basic consideration is to make sure that the borrower has at all times sufficient funds to enable it to meet working expenses and financial liabilities. This consideration underlies various covenants, such as those which require the borrower (a) to make additional calls upon its shareholders, by means of advances or subscriptions to additional shares of capital stock, to the extent that may be required by its operations;[15] (b) to request promptly all budgetary appropriations required for the financing of its operational expenses;[16] or (c) to maintain its revenues at levels sufficient to yield enough income to service the loan and possibly to build up reserves and surplus necessary for the future expansion of the borrower's operations.[17] Similar considerations explain also the more or

---

[15] See e.g., the following provisions in agreements between the IBRD and: Société Pétrolière de Gérance, December 10, 1959 (380 UNTS 319, Section 4.04); Société Anonyme des Mines de Fer de Mauritanie, March 17, 1960 (452 UNTS 67, Section 5.05); Central Elétrica de Furnas, S.A., October 3, 1958 (337 UNTS 177, Section 5.09); and Lima Light and Power Company, June 29, 1960 (400 UNTS 99, Section 5.17).

[16] This covenant is often used in connection with loans made to governmental or other public agencies. In many countries, however, the rule that budgetary appropriations must be voted annually is an obstacle to such long-term undertakings. Lenders may have to be satisfied with moral, rather than legally binding, commitments of the borrower or the relevant authorities, to request adequate annual appropriations in accordance with the local budgetary procedure, unless some provision of the local law authorizes long-term budgetary appropriations. As to "supply of funds" covenants in guaranteed loans see Chapter V, text and notes 26 and 27.

[17] See e.g., the following provision in a Loan Agreement between the IBRD and National Power Corporation, dated October 13, 1961 (415 UNTS 69, Section 5.08):
"The Borrower shall from time to time take all steps necessary or desirable to obtain such adjustment in rates as will provide revenues sufficient: (a) to cover operating expenses, including adequate maintenance and depreciation, taxes and interest; (b) to meet repayments on long-term indebtedness but only to the extent that such repayments shall exceed provision for depreciation; and (c) to leave a surplus for financing a reasonable portion of future expansion of its power facilities."
Similar provisions are found, in addition to many other power loans, in IBRD agreements with port authorities (see e.g., Loan Agreement dated May 22, 1956 with Autoridad Portuaria de Corinto, 253 UNTS 233, Section

less elaborate provisions whereby the borrower agrees to maintain a sound ratio between debt and equity so that the aggregate amount of its funded indebtedness does not exceed its financial capacity.[18]

These provisions, although bearing a great resemblance to those currently obtaining in domestic practice, are nevertheless frequently more complex than their domestic counterparts because they must account for many issues normally not present in domestic transactions. Thus, a debt-equity ratio covenant of the type already mentioned may become meaningless in an international loan if it is not complemented by an additional provision determining the rate or rates of exchange between the currency or currencies in which debts may be incurred and the currency in which the equity capital of the borrower is expressed.[19] Indeed, failure to provide for such determination would

5.08; Loan Agreement dated October 12, 1956, with Port Authority of Thailand, 261 UNTS 117, Section 5.07) and railway companies (see e.g., Loan Agreement dated March 13, 1963, with the Peruvian Corporation Limited (478 UNTS 245, Section 5.13).

[18] See e.g., the IBRD loan agreements with: Companía de Cemento Portland del Norte, S.A., dated April 19, 1955 (221 UNTS 153, Section 5.08); Litani River Authority, dated August 25, 1955 (230 UNTS 233, Section 5.04); Dead Sea Works Limited, dated July 11, 1961 (429 UNTS 3, Section 5.18); the Karachi Electric Supply Commission, dated June 20, 1955 (230 UNTS 41, Sections 5.13 and 5.14).

Comp., the Canadian prospectus regarding the Pétrofina, S.A. 5½%-7½% Debentures of 1957, p. 5, according to which the related Trust Agreement would contain inter alia a covenant by the Company:

"that so long as any of the Debentures are outstanding it will not . . . (ii) create or issue any funded obligations (other than the Debentures) unless the principal amount of all funded obligations to be outstanding after such proposed creation or issue shall, as at a date not more than 90 days preceding the date of the proposed creation or issue, be less than 65% of the net worth (as defined) of the company . . ."

In this connection, it is noteworthy that several legislative attempts have been made in various countries to establish certain objective ratios between debt, and especially bonded debt, and equity. See Chapter I, text and notes 3 and 4.

[19] International loan documents, after stating the ratio of debt to equity, normally contain an additional provision to the effect that the equivalent in local currency of debts contracted in foreign currencies shall be determined on the basis of a certain rate of exchange, which may be the official or some other mutually agreed rate of exchange, between these currencies at the date on which the borrower proposes to incur the debt in question.

See e.g., the following provision in the Indenture dated March 1, 1962, between Société du Pipe-Line Sud-Européen and Morgan Guaranty Trust Company of New York, relating to the Société's 5½% Sinking Fund Debentures Due 1982:

". . . the New Franc equivalent of the principal amount of any Funded Debt of the Company payable in a currency other than the New Franc

make it extremely difficult, if not impossible, to make the calculation necessary to implement such covenants. Again, a rate covenant in an international loan, even though it may be perfectly adequate to provide the borrower with sufficient revenues to meet its obligations under the loan, may have little practical significance if it is not supported by specific undertakings from the appropriate authorities to sell or grant to the borrower the foreign exchange necessary to service the loan.[20]

Similar considerations obtain in the case of negative covenants. International loan instruments, like their domestic counterparts, bristle with negative covenants prohibiting the borrower from incurring additional indebtedness;[21] creating liens on its assets in favor of

> shall be determined by converting the principal amount of such Funded Debt into New Francs at the official rate of exchange, if any, established by the French Finance Ministry (or such other monetary authority as shall have jurisdiction thereof) and in effect on the date of issue of such Funded Debt, and, if there shall be no such official rate of exchange, then at the average rate of exchange generally applicable to cable transfers in the principal exchange market in the country of such currency other than the New Franc on such date or on the last previous date at which such rate of exchange was available; . . ." (Section 5.03 (c). See also Section 5.10).

See also the following IBRD loan agreements with: KLM, Royal Dutch Airlines, dated March 20, 1952 (159 UNTS 207, Section 70.5); Corporación de Fomento de la Producción and Compania Manufacturera de Papeles y Cartones, dated September 10, 1953 (188 UNTS 25, Section 6.04); The Tata Iron and Steel Company, Limited, dated November 20, 1957 (301 UNTS 47, Section 5.06); Volta River Authority, dated February 8, 1962 (449 UNTS 207, Section 5.12); National Power Corporation (referred to in note 17 supra, Section 5.09).

[20] See Chapter VII, Section 2.

[21] See e.g., the following IBRD agreements with: National Power Corporation (referred to note in 17 supra, Section 5.09); Volta River Authority (referred to in note 19 supra, Section 5.12); Instituto Costarricense de Electricidad, dated February 3, 1961 (414 UNTS 313, Section 5.08); Société Pétrolière de Gérance (referred to note in 15 supra, Section 4.08); Société Anonyme des Mines de fer de Mauritanie (referred to in note 15 supra, Section 5.09).

Comp. the IBRD agreements with: Grand-Duchy of Luxembourg dated August 28, 1947 (153 UNTS 3, Article VII, Section 2); Republic of Haiti dated May 7, 1956 (252 UNTS 279, Section 5.02 (b)).

See also, Article 22 of the Convention of June 3, 1955, between France and Tunisia (Clunet 1956, 220):

> "In order that France, so long as it shall be a creditor of the Tunisian Government or shall guarantee its loans, may follow the evolution of the Tunisian public debt, any loan contracted by the Tunisian Government shall be decided by mutual agreement between the two governments. The same shall apply to any loan directly or indirectly guaranteed by the Tunisian Government, the amount of which shall bring the aggre-

other creditors, at least without causing the lenders to share equally
in any such security;[22] paying dividends or making cash distributions
to its shareholders;[23] reducing its source of income below a level satisfactory to the lenders;[24] undertaking new ventures which might conflict with the completion of the particular project involved or have an
adverse effect upon the borrower's operations or financial condition;[25]
or amending its statutes, articles of association[26] or arrangements with
third parties, including advisors, consumers or purchasers of the borrower's goods and services, which are deemed essential to the successful operation of the borrower or the maintenance of its financial position.[27]

---

gate amount of commitments undertaken by said government, within one
calendar year, above two billion francs, subject to any modification of
this ceiling by mutual agreement of the parties."
and in this connection, Silvera, "L'Evolution des Rapports Financiers et
Economiques Franco-Tunisiens", Rev. Jur. et Pol. d'Outre-Mer 1960, 89, at
pp. 100-102.

[22] See Chapter V, text and notes 95 to 101.

[23] See e.g., the following IBRD agreements with: The Tata Iron and
Steel Company, Limited (referred to in note 19 supra, Section 5.08) ; Karnaphuli Paper Mills Limited dated August 4, 1955 (236 UNTS 195, Section
5.03) ; Dead Sea Works Limited (referred to in note 18 supra, Section 5.19);
Société Anonyme des Mines de Fer de Mauritanie (referred to note in 15
supra, Section 5.08) .

[24] See e.g., the Arbitral Award dated June 23, 1926, Dawes Plan Interpretation (Commissioner of Controlled Revenues) Case, Annual Digest 1925-
1926, 208, regarding the binding character of the Dawes Plan after the borrower had attempted, without the consent of the Commissioner, to reduce the
rate of the duties and other revenues charged as security for the Dawes Loan.
    See also, the Loan Agreement dated April 23, 1954, between the United
States and the ECSC (229 UNTS 229, Article VII, para. (b)) stipulating
that the ECSC will maintain and collect levies sufficient to provide the sums
necessary to meet its loan commitments; and the Act of Pledge, Article VI,
Section 6.04 to the same effect.

[25] See e.g., the following IBRD agreements with: Société Pétrolière de
Gérance (referred to in note 15 supra, Section 4.14); Société des Mines de
Fer de Mauritanie (referred to in note 15 supra, Section 5.15) ; Dead Sea
Works Limited (referred to in note 18 supra, Section 5.21) ; Lima Light and
Power Company (referred to in note 15 supra, Section 5.12. Comp., the IBRD
agreements with: Iran, dated February 20, 1960 (384 UNTS 213, Section
5.11), and the Republic of Haiti, dated May 7, 1956 (252 UNTS 279, Sec-
tion 5.08) .

[26] See e.g., the following IBRD agreements with: Société Pétrolière de
Gérance (referred to in note 15 supra, Section 4.07) ; Dead Sea Works Limited
(referred to in note 18 supra, Section 5.14); The Tata Iron and Steel Company (referred to in note 19 supra, Section 5.14) .

[27] See e.g., the following IBRD agreements with: the Volta River Authority (referred to in note 19 supra, Section 5.10, power contract) ; Dead Sea
Works Limited (referred to in note 18 supra, Section 5.17, concession);

In this respect also international loans raise problems which have no equivalent in domestic practice. In addition to currency problems which may be as vitally important to the implementation of negative covenants as they are to the administration of positive undertakings,[28] other issues may complicate considerably the operation of stipulations whose enforcement in the domestic field would raise little or no difficulty. These include difficult constitutional issues[29] or problems of legal co-ordination, such as those related to the power of a majority of bondholders to waive the provisions of loan covenants in appropriate circumstances.[30]

C. Right to Carry on Business—Maintenance of the Borrower's Juridical Existence

Knowledge that the loan proceeds have been, or will be, used in the intended way; that the borrower's management is exceptionally qualified and experienced; and that its policies are particularly sound may afford lenders little satisfaction if during the life of the loan the borrower ceases to carry on operations.

Since international loans are normally made for protracted periods of time, it is essential that the lenders be assured that the borrower will not abruptly cease to exist as a juridical entity and that its right to carry on business will not be suspended or terminated before the loan is repaid. Covenants to that effect are commonly included in loan documents, especially those involving loans to private borrowers or to public borrowers, other than foreign governments or international organizations, whose existence and operations are subject to fluctuations unlikely to affect such governments or organizations.

Loans made to private entities frequently provide that the borrower, usually a foreign corporation, shall maintain its corporate existence and take, or cause to be taken, all such action as may from time to time be necessary to maintain, preserve or renew such corpo-

---

Lima Light and Power Company (referred to in note 15 supra, Section 5.10, power contract) ; Société Anonyme des Mines de Fer de Mauritanie (referred to in note 15 supra, Section 5.03 (a) , concession, establishment convention, commercial arrangements, etc.); Sui Gas Transmission Company Limited dated June 2, 1954 (324 UNTS 59, Section 5.09, gas purchase agreement, lease and managing agency agreement) .

[28] For example, a debt limitation convenant may be expressed in a currency other than the revenues or assets of the borrower. See note 21 supra.

[29] See Chapter I, text and notes 25 to 27.

[30] See text and note 75 to 88 infra.

rate existence in accordance with the applicable laws.[31] A natural complement to this type of provision is the frequent stipulation, which has received legislative sanction in a number of countries,[32] that the borrower shall not, without the lenders' prior approval and subject to various conditions, merge or consolidate with another corporation.[33]

Sometimes, as in the case of loans to private companies operating under a governmental license or concession or to autonomous public

---

[31] See e.g., the Copenhagen Telephone Company, Incorporated, 5⅜% Sinking Fund Dollar Debentures due April 15, 1978, issued in 1963, prospectus p. 17:

"The company will agree to take all steps necessary to maintain its corporate existence and to obtain, preserve and renew all licenses, concessions and franchises necessary or useful in the conduct of its business."

Comp., the following provision in a trust deed between an English company and a continental borrower:

"[The borrower] will at all times do or cause to be done all things necessary to be done to preserve and keep in full force and effect its corporate rights and concessions and to obtain such further concessions as it may require for the purpose of its business and will comply with all the laws of . . . or any other place to the laws of which it may be subject . . ."

See also, the following provisions in IBRD agreements with: Dead Sea Works Limited (referred to in note 18 supra, Section 5.06 (b) ; Sui Gas Transmission Company Limited (referred to in note 27 supra, Section 5.11 (b); Lima Light and Power Company (referred to in note 15 supra, Section 5.09 (a) ; Société Pétrolière de Gérance (referred to in note 15 supra, Section 4.15).

[32] See e.g., Argentina, Law No. 8875 on Debentures, February 12, 1912, art. 9; Brazil, Decree-Law No. 781 on the Protection of Bondholders, October 12, 1938, art. 3 (2) (g),—Decree-Law No. 2627, Corporation Law, September 26, 1940, arts, 151 and 154; France, Decree-Law on the Protection of Bondholders, October 30, 1935, art. 20; Germany, Corporation Law, January 30, 1937, art. 241; Italy, Civil Code, art. 2503; Japan, Commercial Code, art. 100; Spain, General Corporation Law, July 7, 1951, art. 145; Switzerland, Code of Obligations, art. 748; Venezuela, Commercial Code, art. 318.

In addition to the consent of creditors of the corporation, some statutes provide for judicial sanction of the proposed merger or consolidation. See e.g., India, Companies Act, 1956, Section 101; United Kingdom, Companies Act, 1948, Section 67.

On other occasions, all that the statute provides is that the merger or consolidation shall not impair in any way the rights of the creditors of the corporation or corporations involved. See e.g., New York Business Corporation Law, § 906.

[33] For example, the indenture may prohibit any merger, consolidation, or sale of the borrower's property and assets, except between the borrower and its subsidiaris; or subject any such transaction to specific conditions such as that the corporation resulting from the merger or consolidation will remain of the same nationality as that of the borrower, agree to be bound to the lenders by the terms of the indenture, assume the due and punctual payment of the principal of, and interest on, the loan, proceed with the neces-

agencies engaged in public works, transportation or industrial production, attempts are made to obtain additional assurances from the grantor of the license or concession or from the governmental or other authorities having jurisdiction over the borrower that they will not interfere with its affairs (and particularly with the performance of its loan obligations) or otherwise put an end to its operations;[34] or that, if the borrower is dissolved, its rights and obligations will be transferred to a successor organization or the relevant authorities.[35]

---

sary publications and modifications in the appropriate registers, including the mortgage register if the loan is so secured, etc.

[34] See e.g., the following IBRD agreements with: British Guiana, dated June 23, 1961, (415 UNTS 357); Islamic Republic of Mauritania, dated March 17, 1960 (452 UNTS 211, relating to the loan to Société Anonyme des Mines de Fer de Mauritanie, note 15 supra, Guarantee Agreement, Section 3.07); Dominion of Pakistan (referred to in connection with the loan to Sui Gas Transmission Company Limited, note 27 supra, Guarantee Agreement, Section 3.06); the Republic of Peru (referred to in connection with the loan to Lima Light and Power Company, note 15 supra, Guarantee Agreement, Section 3.06).

[35] See e.g., the prospectus concerning the Southern Italy Development Fund (Cassa per il Mezzogiorno) Guaranteed External Loan Bonds, issued in the United States in 1959, p. 5:

"The Cassa's activities were originally limited to the ten-year period 1950 to 1960, but by subsequent legislation were extended to June 30, 1965. The statutes relating to the Cassa provide that, upon termination of the Cassa or upon its dissolution, all of its rights and obligations shall be transferred to the Republic and also that if the duration of external loans entered into by the Cassa should exceed the period of its activities, another agency or organization will, prior to termination of the activities of the Cassa, be appointed to assume liability for such loans. The legislation also provides that the Republic's guarantees of payment of principal and interest on such loans will be valid subsequent to termination of the Cassa's activities. The Republic's guarantees on the Bonds will provide that such guarantees will continue regardless of any change in the Cassa's legal status or termination of its activities."

See also, the prospectus relating to the Société Internationale de la Moselle (GmbH), Trèves, 4½% Loan of 1961, issued in Switzerland with the Guarantee of the Republic of France, clause 5:

"Furthermore, the Republic of France, acting by the Minister for Finance and Economic Affairs, covenants to substitute herself for the Company as principal debtor in the event that the Company, as a result of its transformation or dissolution, could no longer act in that capacity" (as translated).

Comp., the following provision in a loan agreement dated April 12, 1954 between the IBRD and the Republic of Peru (190 UNTS 231, Section 5.09):

"If SCIPA's (a governmental agency of the borrower) legal or administrative status should be changed or its existence be ended during the term of the Loan, the Borrower shall maintain or establish a successor organization which shall fulfill SCIPA's functions under this Agreement. Such successor organization shall be under the direction of a qualified

As a rule, none of the above covenants are found in agreements relating to loans made to foreign governments or international organizations. There are several reasons for this. One reason is that such covenants, which would appear to question the continued existence of the borrower, would be, for obvious psychological reasons, unobtainable. A second, and technically more pertinent, reason is that in the majority of cases such covenants would not be justified by the risks involved in the loan transaction. This is true in the case of loans contracted by international organizations, especially those involved in international lending activities, whose charters usually contain elaborate provisions to safeguard the rights of their respective creditors in the event of dissolution, liquidation, or suspension of the organization's operations.[36] This is also true of loans made to foreign governments since, short of dismemberment or other change of sovereignty, changes in the internal structure of a debtor government would not, under the views which generally prevail in this respect,[37] affect the continuity of its existence and the binding character of its external financial obligations.

It is only, therefore, in exceptional cases, as when it is expected or feared at the time of the transaction that the borrower's constitutional or institutional set up might undergo considerable changes during the life of the loan, that provision may be made in loan docu-

---

and experienced director mutually satisfactory to the Borrower and the Bank, and it shall have such staff, legal and administrative status, organization, financial resources, fiscal and accounting procedures and powers as in the opinion of the Borrower and the Bank are required to enable such successor organization to carry out its responsibilities efficiently."

[36] See e.g., the Articles of Agreement of the IBRD (Article VI, Section 5); IDA (Article VII, Section 5); IFC (Article V, Section 5); IADB (Article X, Sections 3 and 4) and the Statutes of the EIB (Article 27). These provisions should be read in conjunction with other provisions in the respective charters of these organizations concerning their immunities and particularly those exempting their assets from restrictions (See e.g., the Articles of Agreement of the IBRD (Article VII, Section 6); IDA (Article VIII, Section 6); IFC (Article VI, Section 6); IADB (Article XI, Section 6) and the Statutes of the EIB (Article 25)). This last consideration is particularly important. It will be recalled that a substantial part of these assets is usually set aside in the the form of uncalled capital, reserves or guarantee funds to meet the financial obligations of these organizations. Freedom of these assets from restriction is, therefore, a particularly appropriate means of helping lending organizations recruit loan capital since it gives to creditors the assurance that, if necessary, the debtor organization will have freely available the funds required to meet their obligations. See also, Bowett, *The Law of International Institutions* (1963), p. 307; Chiu, "Succession in International Organizations", 14 Int'l & Comp. L.Q 83 (1965).

[37] See Chapter VIII, text and notes 4 to 10.

ments to anticipate the possible consequences of such changes. Examples are stipulations found in the 1954 Loan Agreement between the United States and the ECSC, the Act of Pledge between the ECSC and the BIS,[38] and in agreements with dependent territories concluded at the dawn of political independence.[39]

D. THE PROBLEM OF FOREIGN SUBSIDIARIES

For various purposes, including tax considerations or qualification to do business in foreign countries, many corporations operating on an international scale own and operate foreign subsidiaries. When a loan is made to a parent corporation or to its subsidiary, it may be advisable or necessary to take steps to insure that covenants agreed to by the borrower will not be defeated by subsequent arrangements between it and the related corporation. Sometimes, as when a loan to a subsidiary is guaranteed jointly and severally by the parent or holding corporation, there is no real difficulty since any concerted action between the borrower and the guarantor which would violate the terms of the loan would also put the guarantee into effect. On other occasions, however, especially when the loan is made to the parent corporation, the possibility exists that the borrower may use the subsidiary to obtain indirectly results that it could not achieve directly without openly violating its loan commitments. In such circumstances, it is a matter of elementary prudence to widen the scope of contractual undertakings by making them applicable to both the borrower and its subsidiaries. This can be done either by making express reference to each subsidiary, as well as to the parent corporation, on each occasion where such reference is deemed necessary[40]; or by stipulating in general terms that the borrower's obligations shall be deemed applicable to all of its subsidiaries, with the borrower undertaking specifically to cause its subsidiary or subsidiaries to carry out such obligations.[41]

---

[38] Loan Agreement (referred to note in 24 supra), Article X, first paragraph, letter (c) ; and Act of Pledge, Article VII, Section 7.01 (c), both referring to possible modifications of the ECSC Treaty "adversely affecting the capacity of the High Authority to perform its obligations".

[39] See Chapter VIII, text and note 33.

[40] See e.g., the following IBRD agreements with: Brazilian Traction, Light and Power Company Limited, dated January 27, 1949 (153 UNTS 264, Article VI, Sections 1 and 2) ; Mexican Light and Power Company, dated January 14, 1958 (293 UNTS 167, Sections 5.01, 5.03, 5.06, 5.09 to 5.12 and 5.15); Dead Sea Works Limited (referred to in note 18 supra, Section 5.03 (c)).

[41] See e.g., the following IBRD agreements with: Société Pétrolière de Gérance (referred to in note 15 supra, Section 4.16) ; Société Anonyme des

SECTION II. LOAN ADMINISTRATION MACHINERY

A. DIRECT LOANS

A continuing relationship between lenders and borrowers is essential to the successful implementation of the various supervisory devices currently set up in loan documents. In the case of loans from a single lender to a particular borrower, loan supervision usually presents no fundamental difficulty and can be carried out effectively through continuous contacts and exchange of information between the parties. This information include progress, audit or other reports concerning the borrower's operations and financial condition or, in the case of loans to governments, reports concerning the borrower's economy and the position of its international balance of payments.[42]

Additional, though not insurmountable, complexities may occur if the number of parties is increased, as in the case of loans made to co-borrowers,[43] guaranteed loans,[44] or joint lending operations under-

Mines de Fer de Mauritanie (referred to in note 15 supra, Section 5:17 (b)) ; The Tata Iron and Steel Company Limited (referred to in note 19 supra, Section 5.03 (c)).

[42] See e.g., *The World Bank,* pp. 42-43; Townsend, "The Export-Import Bank of Washington: Organization and Operation", U. of Ill., *Law Forum, Legal Problems of International Trade* 237 (1959 Spring Number), pp. 234-244. Comp., Boskey, *Problems and Practices of Development Banks* (1959), pp. 96-99.

[43] See e.g., the IBRD agreements with: Osterreichische Elektrizitätswirtschafts-Aktiengesellschaft (Verbundgesellschaft) and Osterreichische Donaukraftwerke Aktiengesellschaft, dated September 21, 1956 (259 UNTS 43); Companhia de Electricidade do Alto Rio Grande and Centrais Elétricas de Minas Gerais, S.A., dated July 17, 1953 (190 UNTS 149) ; Corporación Autónoma Regional del Cauca and Central Hydroelectrica del Rio Anchicaya Limitada, dated May 10, 1960 (379 UNTS 217) ; and The Tata Hydro-Electric Power Supply Company, Limited, the Andhra Power Supply Company, Limited and The Tata Power Company, Limited, dated November 19, 1954 (309 UNTS 159).
An interesting situation was presented to the IBRD when it agreed in 1953 to make a loan to the "Territory of Northern Rhodesia" (as it was then called) for the financing of a railway project. As much of the project was to be carried out in the territories of Southern Rhodesia, then a British "Colony," and the execution and the financing of the project were dependent on the joint efforts of the Rhodesias, it was agreed that, in addition to the Loan Agreement between the IBRD and Northern Rhodesia, both Rhodesias would enter into a Subsidiary Agreement with the IBRD concerning the carrying out of the project. See the Agreements dated March 11, 1953 (172 UNTS 115). A somewhat similar situation occurred in the case of the IBRD loan to Compagnie Minière de l'Ogooné in connection with the financing of a mining project extending over the territories of both the Republics of Congo (Brazzaville) and Gabon. See Loan Agreement dated June 30, 1959 and related Guarantee Agreement with (i) Republic of France (452 UNTS

taken by a number of lenders, including international organizations,[45] governments,[46] public lending agencies[47] or private banking or credit institutions.[48] The joint aspects of the operation are normally reflected in stipulations in the loan documents (and also usually in confidential

67); (ii) Republic of Congo (Brazzaville) (Ibid., 123) ; and (iii) Republic of Gabon (Ibid., p. 135) .

[44] See Chapter V, notes 26 to 34.

[45] See e.g., the joint financing by the IBRD and the EIB of projects in Southern Italy. Only the IBRD loan agreement has been published, see Loan Agreement dated April 21, 1959, with the Cassa per il Mezzogiorno (359 UNTS 191) ; in July 1964, the IDA and the IADB joined in the financing of power projects in Bolivia (The IDA Credit Agreements dated July 24, 1964 have been registered with the United Nations Secretariat under Nos. 7762 and 7763) .

The IBRD and its affiliate the IDA have joined forces in several combined operations, See e.g., the IBRD Loan Agreements and the IDA Credit Agreements with: the Republic of Costa Rica, dated October 13, 1961 (430 UNTS 27, 431 UNTS 3) ; the Republic of Colombia, dated August 28, 1961 (416 UNTS 3 and 23); and the Republic of Chile, dated June 28, 1961 (426 UNTS 33 and 89) . See also note 47 infra.

[46] See e.g., the Agreement dated June 28, 1950, between the United Kingdom, Australia, India, Pakistan, Ceylon and Burma concerning a loan to Burma (87 UNTS 153) . See also the Indus Basin Development Fund Agreement dated September 19, 1960 (444 UNTS 259) (supplemented in 1964 503 UNTS 388) , between Australia, Canada, the Federal Republic of Germany, New Zealand, Pakistan, the United Kingdom, the United States, and the IBRD regarding the creation of a Fund to finance the construction of irrigation and other works in Pakistan.

[47] See e.g., the arrangements regarding the financing of the Volta River project consisting of an IBRD loan and long-term loans from the United States (through the AID) , the Export-Import Bank of Washington, the United Kingdom (through its Export Credits Guarantee Department) and an equity contribution from the Government of Ghana (See in this connection the IBRD Loan Agreement with the Volta River Authority, dated February 8, 1962, 449 UNTS 207); the arrangements regarding the financing of a land settlement and development project in Kenya, consisting of an IBRD loan (Loan Agreement dated November 29, 1961, 426 UNTS 49), loans and grants from the United Kingdom and a loan from the Colonial Development Corporation; the arrangements concerning the Roseires Irrigation project in the Sudan, consisting of an IBRD Loan Agreement, an IDA Credit Agreement, dated June 14, 1961 (415 UNTS 25 and 49) and a loan from the Kreditanstalt für Wiederaufbau; and arrangements concerning the financing of a gas liquefaction plant in Algeria consisting of an IBRD loan, and a loan from Caisse d'Equipement pour le Développement de l'Algérie, to Compagnie Algérienne du Méthane Liquide (See the IBRD Loan Agreement dated May 14, 1964 and the related Algeria Guarantee Agreement and Shareholders Guarantee Agreement, registered with the United Nations Secretariat under No. 7552) .

[48] See e.g., the IBRD Loan Agreement with Air-India International Corporation, dated March 5, 1957 (272 UNTS 201) forming part of a joint financing operation including loans made pursuant to a Credit Agreement dated January 31, 1957 between the Borrower and several American banking institutions.

arrangements between the lenders) regarding such matters as disbursements;[49] questions of common interest, including consultation between the lenders or the designation of common representatives to act on their behalf;[50] or remedial provisions such as those concerning the suspension, termination or accelaration of the various loans involved.[51]

B. BOND ISSUES

Modern statutory developments in both common-law[52] and civil-law[53] countries have substantially increased the duties of indenture trustees and strengthened the powers of bondholders' communities. There is as yet no sure solution, however, to the problem of establish-

---

[49] See e.g., the IBRD agreements regarding loans to: the Cassa per il Mezzogiorno (Section 2.02, note 45 supra); the Volta River Authority (Section 2.02, note 47 supra) ; the Republic of Costa Rica (Section 2.02, note 45 supra) ; the Republic of Colombia (Section 2.02, note 45 supra) ; Kenya (Section 2.02, note 47 supra) .

[50] See e.g., the Indus Basin Development Fund Agreement (note 46 supra) pursuant to which the IBRD is designated as Administrator of the Fund; the Administration Agreement dated June 14, 1961 between the Republic of the Sudan, Kreditanstalt für Wiederaufbau, the IDA and the IBRD in connection with the joint operation referred to note 47 supra; the IBRD Loan Agreement with Compagnie Algérienne du Méthane Liquide (note 47 supra, Section 5.14) .

[51] See e.g., the IBRD agreements regarding loans to: the Cassa per il Mezzogiorno (Schedule 3 (i) and (k), note 45 supra); the Volta River Authority (Schedule 3 (a) " (j) " and " (q) ", note 47 supra) ; the Republic of Colombia (Section 6.02, note 45 supra); the Republic of the Sudan (Section 6.02, note 47 supra) ; and Compagnie Algérienne du Méthane Liquide (Schedule 3 (e) " (j)", note 47 supra) .
See also, in connection with repayments in advance of maturity, the following provisions in IBRD agreements regarding loans to: the Republic of the Sudan (Section 5.08, note 47 supra) ; Kenya (Section 5.11, note 47 supra) ; the Volta River Authority (Section 5.11, note 47 supra) . Comp., the Agreement of June 28, 1950 (Article 3, note 46 supra) .

[52] See e.g., in the United States, the Trust Indenture Act of 1939, 53 Stat. 1149 (1939), 15 U.S.C. § 77 aaa (1940) ; in the United Kingdom, the Trustee Act 1925, 15 Geo. 5, c.19, and the Companies Act 1948, 11 & 12 Geo. 6, c.38, Section 88.

[53] Prior to the 'thirties, with the exception of some countries financially tied to the common-law world (see e.g., Argentina, Law No. 8875 of February 12, 1912, on Debentures, hereinafter referred to as L.D.; Annual Report of the Special Committee on Private International Law and Conflict of Laws for 1924-25 to the Association of the Bar of the City of New York, pp. 422 et seq., now outdated in many respects but historically interesting) , the representation of bondholders had been systematically organized in only a few civil-law countries, such as Austria (Law on the common "Curator" of bondholders of April 24, 1874, hereinafter L.C.B.) , Germany (Law concern-

ing Bondholders' Common Interests dated December 4, 1899, hereinafter *L.B.*) or Belgium (Commercial Code, Title IX, as amended in 1913, hereinafter *Comm. Code*).

Since then, however, an increasing number of countries have become conscious of the problem and have taken steps to find it a satisfactory answer.

(a) On occasion, the solution has been found by duplicating more or less the essential features of the trust indenture machinery. See e.g., Chile Law No. 4657 of September 25, 1929, concerning the Issuance of Bonds (hereinafter *L.I.B.*); Mexico, Law of August 26, 1932, on Negotiable Instruments (hereinafter *L.N.I.*); Spain, Joint Stock Company Law of July 7, 1951 (hereinafter *J.C.L.*); Switzerland, Code of Obligations (as amended on April 1, 1949), articles 1157 et seq. (hereinafter *C.O.*).

Even though vested with duties similar to those of a trustee, none of these bondholders' representatives ("Representate" in Chile, "Representante Comun" in Mexico, "Comisario" in Spain, "Représentant" in Switzerland) is a real trustee. Because the duties of such representatives are somewhat more extensive than those of an ordinary agent, and also because their appointment, in the original documents, precedes the constitution of the bondholders' community, writers in civil-law countries have had some difficulty in finding the proper qualification, although that of agent is still commonly favored. See e.g., generally, De Arrillaga, *Emision de Obligacionesy Proteccion de los Obligacionistas* (1952) pp. 256-266; and specifically, in Chile, Avila, 2 *Manual de Derecho Mercantil* (1950), pp. 192 et seq.; in Mexico, Tena, 2 *Derecho Mercantil Mexicano* (2d ed 1945), p. 330; Rodriguez, 2 *Tratado de Sociedades Mercantiles* (3d ed 1965, p. 336); Ahumada, *Titulos y Operaciones de Credito* (1955), p. 177; in Spain, Garrigues and Uria, 2 *Comentario a la Ley de Sociedades Anonimas* (2d ed 1953), pp. 483-4; in Switzerland, Reymond, "Le Trust et le Droit Suisse," Zeitschrift für Schweizerisches Recht 1954, 119a; Gubler, "Besteht in der Schweiz ein Bedürfnis nach Einführung des Instituts der Angelsächsischen Treuhand (Trust)?", Ibid, 215.

Writers also generally agree that the Germanic concept of "Treuhaender" is not a real trustee. See e.g., Zahn, op. cit. note 1 supra, at pp. 438 et seq.; Guisan, "La Fiducie en Droit Suisse", *Travaux de la Semaine Internationale de Droit*, Paris, 1937, Part V, p. 93, p. 101; Meyer, "Trusts and Swiss Law", 1 Int'l & Comp. L.Q., 378 (1952). But see Huber, "Trust and 'Treuhand' in Swiss Law", Ibid., 64 (1952).

(b) On other occasions, where the prevailing legal climate was not favorable to the reception of the trust, adequate substitutes were thought to satisfy the needs of the financial community and to increase the common representation of bondholders. See e.g., Brazil, Decree-Law No. 781 of October 12, 1938, concerning Bondholders' Associations (hereinafter *D.L.B.A.*); France, Decree-Law of October 30, 1935, concerning the Protection of Bondholders (hereinafter *D.L.P.B.*); Italy, *Civil Code*, articles 2415 et seq.

(c) It should be noted that civil-law statutes sometimes give to common representatives greater powers than those normally vested in trustees. Thus, in Argentina (*L.D.*, article 18), Chile (*L.I.B.* article 65), Germany (*L.B.*, article 15), Italy (*Civil Code*, article 2418), Mexico (*L.N.I.*, article 217 (XI)), Spain (*J.C.L.*, article 119) or Switzerland (*C.O.*, article 1160, para. (2)), the common representative is given power to attend shareholders' meetings or meetings of the board of directors. In Argentina (*L.D.*, article 18), Chile (*L.I.B.*, article 65) and Spain (*J.C.L.*, article 119), the common representative may request the suspension or revocation of directors of the obligor.

ing between borrowers and bondholders an effective channel of communication capable of assuring a continuing representation of the bondholders' interests and of providing the borrower with a representative of the bondholders who has authority to discuss, and, most important of all, in sufficient time financial or other matters of common interest.

This conclusion, which is true enough in the field of domestic lending, is even more pertinent in the international field. In the first place, a number of international transactions, especially those involving governments or international organizations, fall outside the scope of the relevant statutes.[54] Furthermore, it is now apparent that legislative enactments have not resolved all conflict of laws problems. Though modern legislative trends, by bringing into sharper focus the fundamentals of collective loan administration, have to a considerable extent filled the former gap between common-law and civil-law institutions, basic conceptual differences between the two legal systems remain as overwhelming as ever. Thus, it is not without significance that in all cases found, with one exception,[55] courts in civil-law countries have proved unable to understand or unwilling to acknowledge the common-law distinction between legal and equitable title. Instead, when giving effect to foreign indentures, these courts have felt compelled to "re-characterize" the trust in terms of civil-law concepts.[56] Equally significant is the caution exhibited recently by drafters of international indentures in avoiding any reference to a trust in provisions otherwise similar to those found in common-law countries.[57]

There is another important consideration. Whatever may be the contribution made by contemporary statutory developments to the promotion of mutual understanding between common-law and civil-law countries, these developments have created substantial disparities between the laws of countries belonging to the same legal system. Paradoxical as this may appear, it is now more difficult, in a country like

---

[54] Such is the case, for example, of the American Trust Indenture Act, the English Companies Act or the French *D.L.P.B.*

As to the status of international organizations, see e.g., *The World Bank*, pp. 83 to 91; Note "The Status of International Organizations under the Law of the United States," 71 Harv. L. Rev. 1300 (1958) at p. 1319; Stevenson, "Legal Aspects of the Public Offering of Foreign Securities in the United States Market", 28 Geo Wash. L. Rev. 194 (1959), at p. 201; II Loss, *Securities Regulation* (2d ed. 1961), pp. 560-562, 748.

[55] See text and note 98 infra.

[56] See text and notes 96 to 99 infra.

[57] See the Act of Pledge.

France, to enforce resolutions passed by bondholders' communities operating under foreign civil-law statutes more liberal than the French,[58] than it is to enforce in France trust indenture provisions regulating, for example, the respective right of action of the trustee and individual bondholders.[59] Though the extraterritorial effect given to the French statute may be primarily responsible for situations of this kind, it is also possible that substantial differences between such statutes as the American Trust Indenture Act and the English Companies Act may create interesting problems.[60]

All that can be stated at present is that the whole matter is in a state of flux. In some respects, new developments are definitely encouraging. In other respects, there are still many limitations upon the successful co-ordination of legal systems and the implementation of workable arrangements mutually advantageous to borrowers and foreign bondholders.

1. *The Impact of Statutory Enactments on International Loan Relations*

(a) *The status of trustees and bondholders' representatives.* In the absence of statutory provisions to the contrary, common-law countries impose no particular conditions of eligibility or qualification upon the trustee.[61] This situation and the potential abuses inherent in it, rather than wilful hostility towards the concept of trust, explain such adverse decisions as an early judgment of the Supreme Court of Austria denying effect in that country to the appointment of English trustees whose affiliation with the obligor appeared irreconcilable with the standard of independence required by Austrian law from representatives of bondholders.[62]

---

[58] See text and note 90 infra.

[59] See text and note 95 infra.

[60] See e.g., Gower, *The Principles of Modern Company Law* (1954) pp. 408-409; Loss, op. cit. note 54 supra, at p. 754.

[61] See e.g. the *Cohen Committee Report,* Cmd. 6659/45, para. 63.

[62] Supreme Court, May 4, 1904, Sammlung von Zivilrechtlichen Entscheidungen, vol. 41, New Series, vol. 7, p. 283. This decision has been subject to dramatic criticism by Weiser, op. cit. note 1 supra p. 45, who reproaches to the Austrian court to have found that the appointment of an English trustee constituted "a danger" to the effective protection of the Austrian bondholders. In view of the intimate relationship between the obligor and the trustee, such a finding is not as surprising as the learned author wished to state. Indeed, there is much in common between the analysis of the facts of the case by the Austrian court and the views expressed by the authors of the S.E.C. Report on the Practices and Activities of Trustees. *S.E.C. Report,* pp. 71 et seq.

To the extent, however, that such statutes as the Trust Indenture Act impose upon trustees conditions of eligibility and qualification which are substantially similar to those set forth in civil-law statutes regarding the appointment of bondholders representatives, it is to be expected that the recognition of foreign trustees in civil-law countries will be greatly facilitated. A comparison of the American and French statutes may illustrate this remark.

Under the Trust Indenture Act, at least one of the trustees must be at all times a corporation organized and doing business in the United States, with a combined capital and surplus of at least $150,-000, authorized to exercise trust powers and subject to the supervision of a governmental authority.[63] Under French law, the bondholders' representative must be either a French citizen domiciled in France or a French association or corporation having its central place of business in that country, and must be professionally eligible to act as common representative.[64] In addition, both the American and the French statutes disqualify persons affiliated with the obligor or having an active and interested participation in the conduct of its business.[65] In view of these similarities between the two laws, it is highly improbable that French ethics would, like those of Austria in the above mentioned case, create an obstacle to the recognition of American trustees in France.

---

[63] Section 310 (a).

[64] *D.L.P.B.*, art. 25. The French statute is formulated negatively in the sense that it provides that to act as common representative a person must not have been deprived of the right to exercise such profession as that of banker, manager or director of a corporation.

As to other civil law countries, see e.g., Argentina, *L.D.*, art. 15; Chile, *L.I.B.*, art. 61; Italy, *Civil Code*, art. 2417. In Peru, the common representative must be the Central Mortgage Bank (*Banco Central Hypotecario*), Civil Code, art. 1807. This provision applies, however, only to bearer bonds which are secured by a mortgage on real property to the exclusion of registered bonds (*Civil Code*, art. 1814). In Mexico, the *L.N.I.* art. 350 provides that only institutions expressly authorized by the Banking Law may act as trustee. In regard to common representatives of bondholders, the law provides only that the representative must not be a bondholder, *L.N.I.*, art. 216. When the law sets forth no requirements of eligibility or qualification, as in Spain, it is, however, generally agreed that persons whose interests are liable to conflict with those of the bondholders cannot be appointed to act as common representatives. (See 2 Garrigues and Uria, op. cit. note 53 supra, p. 485).

[65] Section 310 (b) of the Act; Article 25 of the *D.L.P.B.* It is noteworthy, however, that the French requirements for disqualification are not as extensive as those set forth by the Trust Indenture Act. The only persons disqualified under the French *D.L.P.B.* are agents or officers of the obligor or of other corporations acting as guarantors of the loan, and accountants and their employees connected with the affairs of same corporations.

On the other hand, these statutes, despite their similarity, may be the source of new difficulties. Suppose that, as in a recent case,[66] a corporation issues, both in France and in the United States, bonds equally and ratably secured by a mortgage, an assignment of accounts receivable or similar security. In such a case, it may be necessary, in order to comply with the respective requirements of the American and the French law, to organize two separate machineries for the representation of bondholders and the protection of their rights. It may also be necessary to provide for the appointment of a co-ordinating agency capable of acting as an intermediary between the American trustee and the French representative as well as between them and the obligor.

Other problems may arise, particularly in connection with the enforcement of exculpatory clauses in trust indentures or agency agreements. The domestic practice of limiting the liability of trustees by means of exculpatory clauses,[67] is not foreign to international indentures. Sometimes with the blessing of such bodies as the League of Nations Committee for the Study of International Loans,[68] provisions have been included in international indentures to exonerate trustees from all liability other than for wilful default or gross negligence.[69]

---

[66] The example cited in the text concerns the borrowings made in 1961 and 1962 in France, the Netherlands and the United States by the Société du Pipe-Line Sud-Européen (see the American prospectus dated March 13, 1962). All these issues are equally and ratably secured by amounts receivable by the borrower from its shareholders assigned to the French common representative, the Dutch "trustee," Morgan Guaranty Trust Company of New York as trustee for the holders of bonds issued in the United States, and Lazard Frères & Cie, acting as "tiers détenteur" for the pro rata benefit of all the bondholders.

[67] The remark made by an American writer (Palmer, "The Liability of the Trustee under the Corporate Indenture", 42 Harv. L. Rev. 198 (1928), at p. 240) that "the ordinary indenture is impregnated with negatives" applies to indentures used in connection with foreign loans as well as to those concerning domestic operations.

[68] "Loan contracts by which trustees are appointed generally stipulate that the latter will be 'freed from any responsibility whatsoever, except in the case of breach of trust knowingly and wifully committed'. This provision should be maintained, for it is unlikely that anybody would accept such a task if liability were involved outside of cases of manifest breach of trust."
L.N. Report, para. 58, p. 18. See also Annex II to the L.N. Report, para. 2, p. 34.

[69] See e.g., in regard to government loans, Article 22 of the General Bond of the Austrian Government Guaranteed Loan 1923-1943:
"No Trustee of these present shall be liable or responsible for anything whatsoever except a breach of trust knowingly and intentionally committed by him."

Since this type of stipulation, when used in agency agreements, is generally deemed valid, though not necessarily viewed with favor, in civil-law countries,[70] there has been little opportunity in those countries to test the enforceability of common-law exculpatory clauses. In the one case in point, involving the liability of the BIS as trustee for the Young Loan, the issue was avoided and the court based its decision on entirely different considerations.[71] It would seem likely,

---

Comp., Article 17 of the General Bond of the German External Loan 1924 (Dawes Loan); Article XXVII of the General Bond of the Austrian Government International Loan of 1930.

In regard to private loans, see e.g., the relevant provisions of American-German industrial loans of the 'twenties referred to by Zahn, op. cit. note 1 supra, at pp. 444 et seq.

The parties to the Act of Pledge carefully avoided any reference to the concept of trust in regard to the nature of the obligations of the BIS as "Pledgee or Depositary" of Notes delivered to it by the High Authority to secure the latter's undertakings to its own creditors. However the relevant provisions of the Act of Pledge are worth mentioning. Art. X, Section 10.03 (d) reads as follows:

"The Depositary shall not be responsible for the performance of any duties under this Indenture except such duties as are specifically set forth in this Indenture, and no implied covenants or obligations shall be read into this Indenture against the Depositary, but the duties and obligations of the Depositary shall be determined solely by the express provisions of this Indenture."

and paragraph (f) of the same Section also reads:

"The Depositary shall not be responsible or accountable to anyone, either by reason of its execution of this Indenture or any indenture supplemental hereto or any certificate of authentication on any Note or for any other reason whatsoever, with respect to the validity of this Indenture or of any indenture supplemental hereto or of the Notes, or for the validity or value of any Pledged Property, or for any act done or omitted by it in good faith, or for anything whatever in connection with this Indenture or any indenture supplemental hereto or any Note, except for its own wilful misconduct or failure to exercise reasonable care in the performance of its duties hereunder."

In regard to the liability of the BIS for acts done by sub-depositaries or agents, see para. (b) of Section 10.03.

[70] See e.g., Planiol, Ripert et Savatier, *Traité Pratique de Droit Civil Français*, vol. XI (2d ed. 1954), pp. 909 and 914. Comp., the following provision in an indenture dated September 6, 1954, between Compagnie Financière Belge des Pétroles, Pétrofina," S.A. and N. V. Nederlandsch-Administratie-en Trustkantoor, attached as an exhibit to the prospectus concerning the Pétrofina 4% Fifteen Year Bonds of 1954:

"The trustee carries no further responsibility with respect to the administration assumed by him than for wilful misconduct or gross negligence. He is not responsible for any act or omission on the part of persons or institutions chosen by him in good faith," (Article XX, as translated).

[71] T.F. May 26, 1936, Aktiebolaget Obligationinteressenter v. the BIS, R.O.62, II, 140. See also, League of Nations, Doc. I.L. 18 Geneva February

however, that if the issue were squarely raised, exculpatory clauses in foreign indentures would be upheld in civil-law countries, provided that such clauses did not attempt to relieve the trustee of liability for bad faith or wilful failure to act.

A different result might be reached in such countries, as the United Kingdom which now limit strictly the scope of exculpatory clauses.[72] In the absence of any known decision in point, it is possible that an American court would refuse to enforce an exculpatory clause prohibited by the Trust Indenture Act but permitted by the law governing the indenture, on the ground that the Act represents American public policy. Similar reasoning inspired the solution of maritime cases following the enactment of the Harter Act.[73]

(b) *Bondholders' communities.* The powers of bondholders' communities vary considerably from country to country.[74] On the one hand, all systems of law hold that no resolution taken at bondholders' meeting can affect the essential rights of the bondholders or introduce discriminations among bondholders of the same class. Any such modi-

---

11, 1937, containing all the judgments of the Swiss Courts in this case. See also text and notes 105-106 infra.

[72] Trust Indenture Act, Section 315 (a) and (d) ; Companies Act, Section 88.

[73] See e.g., Knauth, "Renvoi and Other Conflicts Problems in Transportation Law", 49 Col. L. Rev. 1 (1949), p. 12; Paulson and Sowern, "Public Policy in the Conflict of Laws", 56 Col. L. Rev. 969 (1956), at p. 992; Note, "Conflict of Laws: "Party Autonomy in Contracts"", 57 Col. L. Rev. 553 (1957) at p. 562; Note, "Ocean Bills of Lading and Some Problems of Conflicts of Laws", 58 Col. L. Rev. 212 (1958).

[74] As a rule, meetings are called at the discretion of the debtor corporation, the trustee or other common representative of the bondholders. However, indentures and statutes usually provide that the trustee or common representative, or the obligor, may be compelled to call a meeting upon the request of a certain percentage of bondholders. This percentage is subject to considerable variations. Thus in the United States, England and Canada, the percentage generally varies from 10% to 25%, although the majority of English and Canadian indentures usually adopt a lower percentage (generally 10%) than the American indentures (frequently 20%). The same remark holds true in civil-law countries. Thus whereas in Brazil (*D.L.B.A.*, Art. 4), France (*D.L.P.B.*, art. 12), Germany (*L.B.*, art. 3), Spain (*J.C.L.*, art. 126), and Switzerland (*C.O.*, art. 1165) a percentage of 5% of the bondholders is sufficient, the percentage rises to 10% in Mexico (*L.N.I.*, art. 218) and 20% in Belgium (*Comm. Code*, Title IX, art. 91), Chile (*L.I.B.*, art. 47) and Luxembourg (*C.C.L.*, art. 86).

The difference between American indentures and English or Canadian indentures (the former providing much less frequently than the latter for bondholders' meetings) noted by the S.E.C. (*S.E.C. Report,* pp. 135 et seq.) does not seem to obtain in international loans. American, like English or Canadian indentures relating to international financial transactions, rarely fail to provide for bondholders meetings.

fication requires the assent of each bondholder. Beyond this general principle, however, the power of a majority to pass resolutions binding upon the minority, and to sanction modifications of the rights of bondholders as a class, differs considerably throughout the world.

In the first place, whereas in most common-law countries and in a number of civil-law countries, possible modifications are exhaustively listed in the indenture or the relevant statute,[75] some civil-law countries authorize such modifications in the most general terms.[76]

In the second place, the range of authorized modifications is generally more restricted in the United States than in other countries. Thus, English or Canadian indentures and civil-law statutes generally empower specified majorities of bondholders to sanction such modifications of the bondholders' rights as: (a) the reconstruction of the debtor corporation or its amalgamation with another corporation;[77] (b) the creation of a prior lien;[78] (c) the release or cancellation of

[75] For examples of American, English and Canadian trust indentures, see *S.E.C. Report,* pp. 135 et seq. As to civil-law countries, see e.g., Belgium, *Comm. Code,* Title IX, art. 93; Luxembourg, *C.C.L.,* art. 88; Switzerland, *C.O.,* art. 1170.

The French system is rather defective and quite illustrative of the dangers inherent to the enumerative system. Thus, the *D.L.P.B.* lists certain matters which can be passed upon by extraordinary resolution (art. 20) and other matters (art. 21) which can be settled only with the agreement of the individual bondholder. Since neither list exhausts the possible areas of dispute, it rested with the courts to decide whether matters not specifically mentioned could be acted upon by the association of bondholders or only by each individual holder of bonds. At first, the courts tentatively favored the former alternative, but finally adopted the latter and more restrictive solution. It is now well established that bondholders' associations enjoy no other prerogatives than those expressly conferred upon them by the decree-law. See text and note 90 infra.

[76] Thus in Brazil (*D.L.B.A.,* art. 3 (2)), Chile (*L.I.B.,* art. 48) Germany (*L.B.,* art. 1), Italy (*Civil Code,* art. 2415), Mexico (*L.N.I.,* art. 220 (III)), and Spain (*J.C.L.,* art 127), the law states generally that modifications are permissible and makes express reference to a few major modifications only to illustrate the general rule. No further reference to any of these statutes shall be made hereafter, except to mention the illustrations expressly contained therein.

[77] As to this modification and all the others subsequently listed in the text above, see generally for England and Canada, 3 *Palmer's,* pp. 134 et seq., 360 et seq.; De Forest-Billyou, "Corporate Mortgage Bonds and Majority Clauses", 57 Yale J.J. 595 (1948). See also, *S.E.C. Report,* pp. 138 et seq.

As to civil-law countries, see e.g.: Argentina, *L.D.,* art. 9; Brazil, *D.L.B.A.,* art. 3 (2) (g); France, *D.L.P.B.,* art. 20 (1) (a) and (b); Luxembourg, *C.C.L.,* art. 88 (7). See also note 32 supra.

[78] See e.g., Argentina *L.D.,* art. 12; Belgium, *Comm. Code,* Title IX, art. 93 (1); Chile, *L.I.B.,* art. 27; France, *D.L.P.B.,* art. 20 (1) (c); Luxembourg, *C.C.L.,* art. 88 (1); Switzerland, *C.O.,* art. 1170 (7).

pledged security;[79] (d) the modification of sinking fund provisions;[80] (e) the extension of the maturity of the bonds;[81] (f) the postponement of the payment of interest;[82] and (g) the reduction of the rate of interest.[83] In addition, some systems authorize such major modifications as the cancellation of arrears of interest,[84] the reduction of the principal amount of the bonds,[85] or their conversion into shares of stock of the debtor corporation.[86]

In contrast, the American practice appears rather restrictive. Especially since the enactment of the Trust Indenture Act, possible modifications of indenture provisions of a majority of bondholders have

[79] See e.g., Belgium, *Comm. Code,* Title IX, art. 93 (1); Chile, *L.I.B.,* art. 29; France, *D.L.P.B.,* art. 20 (2) ; Luxembourg, *C.C.L.,* art. 88 (1) ; Switzerland, *C.O.,* art. 1170 (7) .

[80] See e.g., Belgium, *Comm. Code,* Title IX, art. 93 (3) ; Brazil, *D.L.B.A.,* art. 3 (2) (a) (c) and (e); France, *D.L.P.B.,* art. 20 (2); Mexico, *L.N.I.,* art. 200 (III) ; Switzerland, *C.O.,* art. 1170 (4) .

[81] See e.g., Belgium, *Comm. Code,* Title IX, art. 93 (3) ; Brazil, *D.L.B.A.,* Art. 3 (2) (b); Luxembourg, *C.C.L.,* art. 88 (3) ; Mexico, *L.N.I.,* art. 220 (III); Switzerland, *C.O.,* art. 1170 (5) . In France, there is some difference of opinion as to whether a majority can pass a resolution extending the maturity of the bonds or whether the consent of each individual holder of bonds is required. See Hureau, *Les Pouvoirs des Assemblées d'Obligataires* (1948), p. 227. In Germany, an extension of maturity may be approved only when it is the only means of preventing the debtor's bankruptcy (*L.B.,* art. 11) .

[82] See e.g., Belgium, *Comm. Code,* Title IX, art. 93 (2) ; Brazil, *D.L.B.A.,* art. 3 (2) (a) ; France, *D.L.P.B.,* art. 20 (2); Luxembourg, *C.C.L.,* art. 88 (2) ; Switzerland, *C.O.,* art. 1170 (1) .

[83] See e.g., Belgium, *Comm. Code,* Title IX, art. 93 (2); Brazil, *D.L.B.A.,* art. 3 (2) (f); Luxembourg, *C.C.L.,* art. 88 (2) ; Switzerland, *C.O.,* art. 1170 (3) . In France, the prevailing view seems to be that the consent of each individual holder of security is necessary. See e.g., Hureau, op. cit., note 81 supra, p. 264; I Hamel and Lagarde, *Traité de Droit Commercial* (1954) p. 841. In Germany, the interest rate can only be reduced if necessary to prevent the debtor's bankruptcy (*L.B.,* art. 11) .

[84] Such a cancellation is authorized in Switzerland (*C.O.,* art. 1170 (2)) for a limited period of time. In France, the status of the law is not altogether clear (see Hureau, op. cit. note 81 supra, p. 264). Spanish law requires the consent of each individual security holder (see 2 Garrigues and Uria, op. cit. note 53 supra, p. 528).

[85] Such a reduction is permitted in Brazil (*D.L.B.A.,* art. 3 (2) (f). It is prohibited in France (see Hureau, op. cit. note 81 supra, p. 267) ; Spain (see 2 Garrigues and Uria, op. cit. note 81 supra, p. 528) ; and in Germany (*L.B.,* article 12, para. 3).

[86] Such a conversion is possible in Belgium (*Comm. Code,* Title IX, art. 93 (4)), Luxembourg (*C.C.L.,* art. 88 (4)), Switzerland (*C.O.,* art. 1170 (9) . It is prohibited in France (*D.L.P.B.,* art. 21) , Spain (2 Garrigues and Uria, op. cit. note 84 supra, p. 528) . In Brazil (I Valverde, *Sociedades por Agoes* (1941) , p. 523) and Chile (*L.I.B.,* art. 39) , the answer depends upon the conditions of issue and the terms of the indenture.

become rather limited in scope and in number.[87] In addition, American indentures not infrequently stipulate that such modifications of the right of bondholders as a reduction of the interest rate or the creation of a prior lien, require the consent of the holders of all outstanding bonds.[88]

-----

[87] Pursuant to the Act, the indenture may permit the holders of not less than a majority in principal amount of outstanding bonds to direct the trustee in conducting proceedings or in exercising any trust or power conferred upon it by the indenture; and to consent, on behalf of the holders of all outstanding bonds, to the waiver of any past default and its consequences (Section 316 (a) (1)). The indenture may also provide that the holders of not less than 75% of outstanding bonds may consent on behalf of all the holders to the postponement of any interest payment for a period not exceeding three years (Section 316 (a) (2) and (b)). Subject to these limitations, however, the general rule is that the indenture must provide that the right of any security holder to receive payment of principal and interest on or after the respective due dates or to institute suit for the enforcement of any such payment, shall not be impaired or affected without the consent of such holder (Section 316 (b)).

[88] A typical provision is the following:
    "With the consent of the holders . . . of more than 50 per cent majority in aggregate principal amount of the Bonds at the time outstanding, the Company and the Trustees may from time to time and at any time enter into an indenture or indentures supplemental hereto (which shall conform to the provisions of the Trust Indenture Act of 1939 as then in effect) for the purpose of adding any provisions to or changing in any manner or eliminating any of the provisions of this Indenture or any supplemental indenture or of modifying in any manner the rights and obligations of the Company, the Trustees and of the holders of the Bonds and coupons; *provided,* that no such supplemental indenture shall, without the consent of the holders of all outstanding Bonds, (i) extend the fixed maturity of any Bonds or reduce the principal amount thereof, or reduce the rate or extend the time of payment of interest or additional interest payable thereon or, except as otherwise provided in the Indenture, permit the creation of any lien ranking prior to or on parity with the lien of the Indenture with respect to any property covered thereby, or (ii) reduce the aforesaid percentage of Bonds, the holders of which are required to consent to any such supplemental indenture."
The attitude of the New York Stock Exchange and the fact that majority clauses may affect the negotiability of bonds, have been cited, among other factors, as possible explanations for the prevailing American practice. See De Forest Billyou, op. cit. note 77 supra, p. 597. As the author correctly remarks:
    "The difference in attitude is carried so far that Canadian securities, while normally subject to such a clause, if intended to be sold or listed in the United States are devoid of majority clauses."
It is noteworthy that the American practice has to a certain extent influenced transactions involving international organizations. For example, the Act of Pledge (Article VIII, Section 8.02) provides that the consent of each individual holder of notes issued by the High Authority is required for the postponement or reduction of interest payments, even though these modi-

(c) *The individual bondholder.* These variations between legal systems may have an adverse effect upon the implementation of working arrangements concluded with the borrower and approved by the majority of bondholders. Although it would be desirable that a resolution validly adopted under the applicable law should be binding upon all bondholders, wherever they reside,[89] it cannot be said that this solution will always prevail. Thus statutes like the French decree-law of October 30, 1935 regarding the protection of bondholders and the powers of bondholders' communities has made it easier for individual bondholders or minority groups to challenge successfully the validity of schemes approved by the majority under foreign laws more liberal than the French law.[90]

Interesting problems may arise in other respects also, particularly in connection with the exercise by bondholders of their individual

---

fications could be approved by a majority of note holders under the law of Luxembourg, where the Act was entered into and where the High Authority has its seat, or under the law of Switzerland where the Pledgee is incorporated.

[89] See e.g., Canada Southern R.R. Co. v. Gebhard, 109 U.S. 527, 3 S. Ct. 363, 27 L. Ed. 1020 (1883). See also, Chalmers v. Nederlandsch-Amerikaansche Stoomvaart Maatschappij, Holland Amerika Lijn, 36 N.Y.S. 2d 717 (1942); Nadelmann, "Composition-Reorganization and Arrangements in the Conflict of Laws", 61 Harv. L. Rev. 804 (1948).

[90] Thus, the French Supreme Court refused to enforce, on the ground of public policy, a Portuguese judicial order confirming a plan approved by 91% of the holders of bonds of a Portuguese railway company which waived a gold clause and authorized the obligor to issue preferential bonds (Cass. March 22, 1944, Chemins de Fer Portugais v. Ash, S. 1945.I. 77, Rev. 1940-46, 107). In another case, the Court quashed a bondholder's resolution waiving the benefit of a gold clause in bonds issued in France by a Syrian company on the ground that the waiver was *ultra vires* (Cass. March 10, 1954, Société Tramways et Electricité de Damas v. Caumartin, D. 1954, 489; S.1954.I.153). A similar solution was reached in another case involving an arrangement between a Brazilian company and French bondholders, which waived the benefit of a gold clause and provided for the settlement of controversies by arbitration (Cass. June 18, 1958, Association Nationale des Porteurs Français de Valeurs Mobilières v. Auribault, Revue de l'Arbitrage 1958, 91; J.C.P. 1958, IV, 114).

Because the *D.L.P.B.* has been construed to produce these undesirable results, suggestions for liberalizing the French law are certainly welcome. See e.g., Hamel, "La Protection des Porteurs d'Obligations Étrangères", Travaux du Comité Français de Droit International Privé 1935-36, pp. 121 et seq., "Un Difficile Problème de Protection de l'Epargne: Comment Défendre les Porteours d'Obligations Etrangères?" D.H.1936, No. 9, p. 17 et seq.; Hureau, op. cit. note 81 supra, pp. 352-354.

A recent decree-law of May 20, 1955 now authorizes the community of bondholders to refer disputes with foreign issuers to arbitration, a resolution previously prohibited. See Delaume, "Arbitration of Loan Disputes under French Law", 10 The Arbitration Journal (N.S.) 196 (1955). See also, Chapter IV, text and notes 88-90.

right of action. Thus, whereas in recent years an effort to preserve the bondholder's individual right of action is noticeable in common law systems,[91] strict limitations upon the exercise of remedies by individual bondholders are characteristic of civil-law systems. Subject to minor variations, the cases in which the exercise of individual remedies remains possible are limited to actions affecting one or several bondholders only, such as an action for fraud or misrepresentation directed particularly at the plaintiff, or an action intended to remedy the failure of the community or of its representative to act.[92] As a rule, individual bondholders cannot institute any action or proceeding concerning matters of common interest to all bondholders, such as those relating to (1) the construction and enforcement of the loan contract, (2) the creation or the foreclosure of a mortgage security, or (3) the appointment of a receiver.[93] A good illustration, though an

---

[91] In England, debenture holders retain their individual right to sue at law upon the debenture. In regard to the enforcement of the security, if any, the action may be brought either by the trustee or more commonly, by a debenture holder against both the corporation and the trustee. See Palmer, *Company Law* (19th ed. 1949), pp. 312 et seq.; 6 Halsbury's *Laws of England,* pp. 500 et seq., 507 et seq. In the United States, there is, at least since the enactment of the Trust Indenture Act (Section 316 (b)), a clear trend to give strict construction to "no-action" clauses. For cases prior to the Trust Indenture Act, see e.g., Central Hanover Bank and Trust Co. v. Siemens and Halske A.G., 15 F. Supp. 927 (D.C.N.Y. 1936) and Anglo-Continentale Trust Maatschappij v. Allgemeine Elektrizitaets-Gesellschaft, 171 Misc. 714, 13 N.Y.S. 2d 397 (1939), enforcing "no action" clauses in bonds issued by German corporations in New York. But see, Deutsch v. Gutehoffnungshuette Aktienverein fuer Bergbau und Huettenbetrieb, 168 Misc. 872, 6 N.Y.S. 2d 319 (1938) holding that a "no-action" clause in a mortgage indenture securing bonds issued in the United States by a German corporation related only to the enforcement of the mortgage, so that the right of action of bondholders on the bonds themselves remained unimpaired. See also, generally, Posner, "The Trustee and the Trust Indenture: a Further Study", 46 Yale L.J., 737 (1937), 774 et seq.; Domke, "La No-Action Clause dans les Emprunts Internationaux", Revue Internationale des Sociétés, II (1936), No. 2.

[92] See e.g., France, Hureau, op. cit. note 81 supra, pp. 163 et seq.; Brazil, I Valverde, op. cit. note 86 supra, pp. 519 et seq.; Mexico, 2 Rodriguez, op. cit. note 53 supra, pp. 274-275 et seq.

[93] Most frequently, the law contains a general statement that all rights of action affecting the common interests of the bondholders shall vest in the community of bondholders and shall be exercised by the common representative, upon the direction of the community. See e.g., France, *D.L.P.B.,* art. 30; Brazil, *D.L.B.A.,* art. 2; Chile, *L.I.B.,* art. 67; Mexico, *L.N.I.,* art. 217 (VIII); Switzerland, *C.O.,* arts. 1159 and 1164. An exception to the general rule is found in Germany: German law does not consider that the appointment of a common representative automatically deprives bondholders of their individual right of action. However, the community of bondholders

old one, is found in a case decided by the Mixed Court of Appeals of Alexandria involving the respective rights of action of the Commissioners of the Egyptian Debt Commission and of individual holders of Egyptian bonds. In 1896, certain members of the Egyptian Debt Commission had approved a resolution to take out of the reserve fund various sums to finance an expedition in the Sudan. Actions to have the resolution quashed as *ultra vires* were brought by dissenting members of the Commission and individual holders of bonds. The action of the Commissioners succeeded; that brought by individual holders was dismissed on the group that, under the relevant loan documents, the bondholders had relinquished to the Commissioners all rights of action relating to their common interests.[94]

Even more pertinent example is *Kerr v. Société Pyrénées Minerals,* a leading French case.[95] Pyrénées Minerals, an English company, had issued bonds secured by a mortgage on French mines. The English trust deed and the French deed of mortgage each provided that the bondholders renounced their individual right of action in favor of the trustee. In an action by a bondholder to foreclose the mortgage, the court denied the plaintiff's right to sue individually.

---

may pass a resolution that the right to bring action against the debtor corporation shall be vested exclusively in the common representative (*L.B.*, art. 14, para. 3). See Zahn, op. cit. note 1 supra, p. 431. In some countries, the individual right of action of bondholders, although not expressly eliminated, is subjected to such conditions as to make its exercise highly improbable. Thus, both in Italy (*Civil Code,* art. 2419) and in Spain (*J.C.L.*, art. 123) the exercise of individual remedies is permissible only if such exercise does not conflict with the terms of a resolution validly passed by the community of bondholders. In addition, in Spain, the exercise of individual remedies must not conflict with any of the powers vested in the community. Since the community has power to pass any resolution and take any steps necessary to the safeguard of the common interests of bondholders, the chances that an individual bondholder may exercise his personal right of action are very dim indeed. See e.g., 2 Garrigues and Uria, op. cit. note 53 supra, p. 530. In Argentina, there is some difference of opinion as to the extent to which the individual right of action of bondholders is paralyzed by the powers vested in the community of bondholders and the common representative. See e.g., I Fernandez, *Codigo de Comercio de la Republica Argentina Comentado* (1946), p. 572.

[94] M.C.A. Alexandria December 2, 1896, Le Gouvernement Egyptien et Money, Morana, de Richthofen et Zaluski v. Herbault et Consorts, Louis, Yonine, Bouteron et Autres, S. 1898.4.1. In the same connection it is noteworthy that the League of Nations Committee for the Study of International Loan Contracts recommended strict limitations upon the bondholders' individual right of action. See *L.N. Report,* Annex II, p. 32.

[95] Cass. February 19, 1908, Clunet 1912, 243, affirming Court of Appeals of Toulouse July 18, 1905, Clunet 1906, 451.

Comparing the situation existing under the trust deed to that which
would obtain in France as between bondholders and their representative, the court held that the no-action clause in the deed was not contrary to public policy and should be enforced in France. A similar
solution prevailed in at least one decision of the Supreme Court of
Colombia.[96]

2. *An Outstanding Problem of Characterization*

From a practical standpoint, decisions such as those in the *Kerr*
and other cases are excellent. To the extent at least that the trust
"permits certain arrangements which are not repugnant to the property law existing in [civil-law countries],"[97] there is no reason why
the trust, though as an institution it is foreign to the civil law, should
be denied effect in civil-law countries. Judicial attempts to achieve
results consistent with the parties' intention are, therefore, encouraging. Yet it is only fair to remark that, with the exception of pre-
Castro Cuba where the trust had acquired "letters of naturalization,"[98]

---

[96] June 23, 1939, Palau v. Departamento de Antioquia, 48 Gaceta Judicial
808-817 (with a French summary in Clunet 1940-45, 589) dismissed a bondholder's action for the deposit of service monies because, in the Court's
opinion, the trustee had the right to maintain such an action. It is noteworthy that in this case the indenture provided only that the trustee was to
act as "representante general de los tenedores de bonos" (general representative of the bondholders) and that no express provision was made to bar
the claims of individual bondholders. The court found, nevertheless, that the
parties' intention was to vest all rights of action in the trustee and held that
this intention could not be defeated by the unilateral action of one of the
bondholders.

In the case of P.P.G.G. v. Siemens & Halske and Siemens Schuckertwerke
(Trib. Civ. Seine July 23, 1936, English translation by Plesh, *The Gold
Clause* (1936), p. 76, French text (minus the part of the judgment concerning the no-action clause considered as "sans intérêt" in S.1938.2.25), it was
held that holders of gold dollar bonds of a German corporation were not
bound by a no-action clause in the bonds, where they had subscribed to the
bonds on the basis of a prospectus which did not contain any such clause.
In view of the exceptional circumstances of this case and the fact that the
judgment is merely that of a lower court, it is difficult to agree with Professor Nussbaum that "it may be said that the non-action clause . . . apparently can no longer count on enforcement by continental courts". See
Nussbaum, "Sociological and Comparative Aspects of the Trust", 38 Col. L.
Rev. 408, 428 (1938).

[97] Toulouse July 18, 1905, Clunet 1906, 451, at p. 455.

[98] Supreme Court of Cuba February 12, 1938, The National City Bank of
New York v. The Potomac Insurance Company, La Jurisprudencia al Dia
1938, Sentencia No. 6, p. 99, at p. 104. The Court authorized an American
trustee to bring action in its own name and in its capacity as trustee to recover insurance indemnities after the destruction of properties mortgaged in
Cuba as security for the loan.

these attempts have succeeded only at the expense of legal orthodoxy, usually on the basis of a more or less arbitrary assimilation of the trustee's functions to those of an agent.[99]

This assimilation, regardless of its legal weakness, is not at times without inconvenience. Since an agent has no title of his own, the trustee, if the loan is secured by a mortgage or similar lien on assets located in a civil-law country, may be forced to produce some evidence of authority before it can record the security. This may take the form, for example, of a resolution passed at a bondholders' meeting. Since no such meeting can take place before the bonds are subscribed, this requirement may mean in practice that, unless some other alternative is found under the *lex situs*,[100] recordation may be delayed for some time. Furthermore, the artificial transmutation of the trustee into an agent may substantially complicate the administration of the loan security. It is a settled general rule in civil-law countries that releases or substitution of security require the approval of a specified majority of bondholders.[101] The consequence of this rule, if it is strictly enforced at the situs, may be to render inoperative the usual indenture provision authorizing the trustee to consent, under certain conditions, to releases or substitution of security. Before such a release or substitution can be made effective, the trustee may be forced to prove that the proposed transaction has been sanctioned by the bondholders.[102]

---

[99] See e.g., the Court of Appeals of Toulouse judgment on the Kerr Case, note 97 supra:

"Whereas it follows from article 4 [of the Trust deed] that the trustee who is considered in certain respects *fictitious owner,* should be considered *more exactly as agent,* since in those cases specified in art. 4 the bondholders have the right to compel the trustee to foreclose the mortgage . . ." (as translated, emphasis added, Clunet 1906, at p. 453).

See also, McMahon, "Parties Litigant in Louisiana", 10 Tulane L. Rev. 489 (1936) who, commenting on Buck v. Larcade (183 La. 570, 164 So. 593 (1935)) writes:

"It would appear that in the absence of special statutory authority the 'trustee' is without capacity to enforce judicially the rights of the 'trustee' in the courts of Louisiana. Such actions must be maintained either by the beneficiaries in their individual capacity or by the 'trustee' in the capacity of mandatary of the beneficiaries." (Ibid., at p. 513).

[100] See Chapter V, text and notes 78 and 79.

[101] See note 79 supra. The only area of disagreement in this connection is whether the resolution authorizing such a release or substitution must be passed at an extraordinary or an ordinary meeting. In the latter case, the conditions of quorum and majority would be easier to satisfy.

[102] See e.g., Hureau, op. cit. note 81 supra, pp. 214-218. Comp. in Belgium, III Resteau, *Traité des Sociétés Anonymes* (2d ed. 1933), pp. 407-416; I Van Ryn, *Principes de Droit Commercial* (1954), p. 450.

Another area in which delicate problems have arisen relates to the functions of trustees in connection with debt service payments. Indentures frequently provide that principal and interest payments shall be made by the trustee as they come due with service monies remitted by the borrower to the trustee, generally a few days in advance of the payment date. If the wording of such a provision is not specific enough, the question may arise whether the trustee is to hold the service monies "in trust" for distribution to the bondholders, in which case the borrower loses control over the funds remitted to the trustee; or whether the trustee is to receive and hold the service monies as a depository for the obligor, acting only on the obligor's instructions. The question essentially is one of intent and must be decided in the light of the circumstances of each case. The solution of the problem which, even for courts in common-law countries may be far from easy,[103] is made considerably more difficult when the question is brought before a civil-law court. To the Continental mind, the notion that, in the absence of a specific pledge or similar arrangement, the borrower may lose control over the service monies before the same are effectively paid to the bondholders is somewhat disconcerting.[104] The case of *Aktiebolaget Obligationinteressenter v. The Bank for International Settlements* is a well-known example.[105]

---

[103] See e.g., Ehag Eisenbahnwerke Holding, A.G. v. Banca Nationala A Romanei, 117 N.E. 2d 346, 306 N.Y. 242 (1954); Erb v. Banco di Napoli, 243 N.Y. 45, 152 N.E. 460 (1926); Nacional Financiera S.A. v. Speyer, 26 N.Y.S. 2d 865, 261 App. Div. 599 (1941); Carr v. Yokohama Specie Bank, 69 N.Y.S. 2d 262, 272 App. Div. 64 (1947), affirmed 297 N.Y. 674, 76 N.E. 2d 330. See also, Lamont v. Travelers Ins. Co. 24 N.E. 2d 81, 281 N.Y. 362 (1939); McClelland and Fisher, *Law of Corporate Mortgage Bond Issues* (1937), pp. 516 et seq.

[104] See e.g., the following statement in a French judgment dismissing, on the ground of sovereign immunity, an action for payment on bonds issued in France by Morocco:

"Whereas [the service monies deposited by Morocco with French banks] cannot be considered a pledge or deposit granted by the foreign state to its creditors, who have not been granted, either personally or through their agents, effective possession of the assumed pledge . . .; and whereas, on the contrary, Morocco *retains the ownership of this deposit* which cannot be disposed of . . . and is immune from attachment [and must be considered] as a liquid fund solely for the service of the loan by the Banque de Paris et des Pays-Bas . . .; and whereas the immunity [of Morocco] benefits the bankers . . . who are *agents* of the foreign government . . ." (as translated, emphasis added).

Aix, December 30, 1929, Gouvernement du Maroc v. Laurans, S.1930.2.153, 156, affirmed Cass. November 5, 1934, S.1935.1.31. See also 2 *Moreau-Néret*, pp. 63 et seq.

[105] T.F. May 26, 1936, R.O.62, II, 140. All the decisions, including those of the lower courts in this case are reproduced in League of Nations, Doc. I.L. 18 (Geneva February 11, 1937).

The General Bond of the Young Loan of 1930 provided that the German Government: (i) was "indebted" to the BIS for the entire amount of the loan; and (ii) agreed "to pay to the Bondholder the principal and interest secured by the Bonds of the Loan as and when the same shall become due and payable . . ." (Article VII). This double-barrelled provision resulted in inextricable difficulties when it became necessary to determine the exact nature of the BIS duties after the German Reich, in violation of the *pari passu* and gold clauses in the Bond, had instructed the BIS to pay only the nominal amount of their share in the service monies to holders of bonds in countries which, like Sweden, had gone off the gold standard. The issue was raised in an action brought against the BIS by a Swedish bondholder for the payment of the gold differential. The question was whether, in construing the ambiguous provision in the General Bond, emphasis should be placed on the first or the second covenant. In the first instance, the acknowledgement by the obligor that it was "indebted" to the BIS for the aggregate amount of the loan would have required the BIS, as trustee in full control of the service monies, to distribute the same among all the bondholders in accordance with the terms of the General Bond, any instructions from the obligor to the contrary notwithstanding. In the second instance, where the emphasis was on the obligor's promise to pay monies to individual bondholders, the so-called "indebtedness" of the obligor to the BIS could be construed as a mere undertaking by the obligor to remit to the BIS, as an intermediary between it and its real creditors, the sums necessary to satisfy the latter's claims against the obligor. In this case, of course, the obligor would not lose control over the service monies and the BIS, as its agent, could not ignore its payment instructions. The Swiss courts rejected the first alternative as improper under the Swiss law (the *lex loci solutionis*) which was held to be the proper law of the loan. Although it is clear that the courts favored the second alternative, they were faced with a technical difficulty which made it impossible for them to qualify the BIS as the ordinary agent of the obligor, namely the absence in the loan documents of any provision for revocation by the BIS, an essential feature of the law of agency. Determined not to impose on the BIS the duties of a trustee, the Swiss courts finally held that:

> "The legal relationship should rather be construed as a mandate like, a three-sided contract sui generis, for the purport of which the conditions of the loan contract are exclusively decisive."[106]

---

[106] League of Nations. Doc. I.L. 18, p. 12.

This decision, whose merits are somewhat questionable from the view of both comparative law[107] and conflict of laws,[108] is a clear reminder of "the hopelessness of the attempt to press a highly unusual transaction into forms not made for it".[109] There may be reasons to believe, especially as a result of contemporary legislative developments, that some of the past misapprehensions caused by the fatal word "trustee" can be cured by a revision of current practice, in both common-law and civil-law countries. Nevertheless, in a field in which the needs of the financial community are fundamentally identical the world-over, it would be quite unrealistic to assume that basic historical differences between the two systems of law can be removed in the foreseeable future.

---

[107] See e.g., *Borchard*, pp. 52-53; Weiser, op. cit. note 1 supra, at p. 87.

[108] At the time the BIS case was decided, the Swiss courts generally held that, in the absence of a conflict-of-laws provision in a contract, the *lex loci solutionis* governed. Since then, the Swiss courts have adopted the "center of gravity" theory and now hold that the applicable law is that of the country with which the contract is most closely connected. See e.g., Secrétan, "Evolution Récente de la Jurisprudence Suisse Relative aux Conflits de Lois en Matière de Contrats," 7 Revue Hellénique de Droit International 137 (1954); Schnitzer, "Le Droit International Privé Suisse," Ibid., 143, 157; Flattet, case annotation, Rev. 1954, 799. It does not seem that this change of Swiss case law would affect the solution reached in the BIS case, since the contacts between the loan and the Swiss Territory were sufficient to justify, at least from the Swiss point of view, the applicability of Swiss law.

The interesting question, however, is whether the General Bond should have been governed by Swiss law at all or by international law. See Mann, "The Law Governing State Contracts," 21 B.Y.B.I.L. 11 (1944), at p. 21. See also, Chapter III, text and note 106.

[109] Mann, op. cit. preceding note, at p. 18.

Chapter III

The Quest for a System of Law

In approaching the problem of determining the law applicable to contracts with international elements, it is customary to stress the state of confusion of the existing law[1] and not at all uncommon to add that the parties, by their neglect of the relevant rules of private and public international law, are largely responsible for this chaotic situation.[2]

In the case of international loans, neither statement is wholly accurate. It is true that controversies sometimes arise because a careful investigation of the issues involved was not made at the time of the loan negotiations. Nevertheless, the many stipulations of applicable law currently found in loan contracts certainly are not indicative of a lack of interest in the fundamental problem.

Also, in many respects, the rules of determination are neither complex nor unsettled. In this connection, it is imperative to distinguish between the three types of transactions which might give rise to uncertainty, namely: (i) loans between private individuals or private or public legal entities subject to a domestic law, hereinafter referred to, for want of a better generic expression, as "private persons"; (ii) loans between international persons; and (iii) loans between private and international persons.

The first category creates no special difficulty: The law or laws applicable to the transaction, or certain aspects of it, must be determined in accordance with normal conflict-of-laws principles. In the

[1] For references to such statements, see Ehrenzweig, *"A Treatise on the Conflict of Laws"* (1962), p. 453, note 1. See also, *L. N. Report,* pp. 21-24.

[2] See e.g., Mann, "The Law Governing State Contracts" (hereinafter "State Contracts") 21 B.Y.B.I.L. 11 (1944), at pp. 12-13; *Van Hecke,* p. 68; Schmitthoff, "The International Government Loan", 19 J. Comp. Leg. and Int'l L. (3d Series) 179 (1937), at p. 180.

case of "adhesion" contracts like current loan transactions contracted by foreign borrowers directly from, or through the intermediary of, bankers or institutional lenders, these rules are fairly well settled. Although certain issues may give rise to uncertainty these are relatively limited in number.

The determination of the law applicable to loans in the second category is also usually free of difficulty. These loans are normally governed by international law. They may be subject to domestic law in certain respects, such as authority to contract. However, the application of domestic law is not to be presumed and is most likely to result from express stipulations in the loan contract which leave no doubt as to the intention of the parties.

The real difficulty arises in connection with the third type of loans. Until recently the general consensus was that these loans could be subject only to some domestic law. If there was somewhat less agreement as to what this law should be, it could nevertheless be stated that:

> ". . . . any contract which is not a contract between states in their capacity as subjects of international law is based on the municipal law of some country."[3]

In recent years, however, new developments have taken place. The increasingly frequent association of international persons (which now include, in addition to states, a profusion of international organizations) with private persons in economic, commercial or financial transactions of a highly technical character, has thrown a new light on the problem.[4]

---

[3] Serbian and Brazilian Loans Cases, P.C.I.J., Series A, Nos. 20 and 21, at p. 42 and p. 121. See also the Arbitral Award dated July 5, 1901, in the Guano Loans Case, Descamps and Renault, *Recueil International des Traités du XXème Siècle* (year 1901), p. 188. As security for external loans, Peru had given to lenders a "Guano Guarantee" authorizing them to exploit guano deposits and to retain the profits derived from the exploitation. Under Peruvian law, the "guarantee" amounted at best to a personal obligation of Peru and did not create any valid and effective security. To overcome the consequences of this conclusion, one plaintiff argued that the guarantee was not subject to the law of Peru but rather to international law and constituted "un droit réel identique à l'hypothèque et consacré par le droit des gens" (Ibid., p. 370; see also pp. 252-3). It was held that since only transactions between states can be subject to international law, the guano guarantee was governed by Peruvian law and the claim was consequently denied (Ibid., p. 370).

[4] See e.g., among current literature, the following publications dealing particularly with the determination of the law applicable to international loans: *Broches; Salmon;* Jenks, *The Proper Law of International Organizations* (1962), pp. 178-188; Bowett, *The Law of International Institutions* (1963), pp. 296-300; Sommers, Broches and Delaume, "Conflict Avoidance

Today, the idea that contracts between persons subject to a different legal order can be governed by international law has made much progress. Contemporary attempts to insulate such contracts from the consequences of municipal law, call for a reconsideration of the respective spheres of application of the two systems of law into which the rules of international intercourse are traditionally divided.[5] This is not the same, of course, as saying that the distinction between private and public international law, blurred as it may be by the necessities of modern international economic relations, is now obsolete and that intermediate legal systems are likely to emerge or be desirable.[6] What is proposed is that contracting parties, when at least

in International Loans and Monetary Agreements", 21 Law & Contemporary Problems 463 (Summer 1956); Delaume, "The Proper Law of Loans Concluded by International Persons: a Restatement and a Forecast", 56 Am. J. Int'l L. 63 (1962); Nurick, "Choice of Law Clauses and International Contracts", 1960 Proceedings Am. Soc. Int'l L. 56; Scott, "The Enforceability of Loan Agreements between the World Bank and its Member Countries", 13 Am. U. L. Rev. 185 (1964); Zimmer, "Legal Experience of the European Coal and Steel Community in International Loan Operations", in McDaniels, p. 266; Olmstead, "Economic Development Agreements, Part I, Public Economic Development Loan Agreements; Choice of Law and Remedy", 48 Calif. L. Rev. 424 (1960), and "Part II, Agreements between State and Aliens; Choice of Law and Remedy", 49 Calif. L. Rev. 504 (1961).

[5] See e.g., Sereni, *International Economic Institutions and the Municipal Law of States*, 96 Recueil des Cours 133 (1959); Hyde, *Economic Development Agreements*, 105 Recueil des Cours 271 (1962); Friedmann, *The Changing Structure of International Law* (1964); Jessup, *Transnational Law* (1956); Mann, "State Contracts", "The Proper Law of Contracts Concluded by International Persons" (hereinafter "The Proper Law"), 35 B.Y.B.I.L. 34 (1959); McNair, "The General Principles of Law Recognized by Civilized Nations" (hereinafter "The General Principles"), 33 B.Y.B.I.L. 1 (1957); Schwarzenberger, "The Protection of British Property Abroad", 5 Current Legal Problems 294 (1952); Verdross, "Protection of Private Property under Quasi-International Agreements", 6 Nederlands Tijdschrift voor Int'l Recht 355 (1959); Bourquin, "Arbitration and Economic Development Agreements", 15 The Business Lawyer 860 (1960). Broches, "Choice of Law Provisions in Contracts with Governments", *International Contracts: Choice of Law and Language* (Parker School 1962), p. 64.

[6] According to Professor Verdross' theory, "quasi-international agreements" between international and private persons, constitute "a new legal order, created by the concurring wills of the parties, i.e. the agreed *lex contractus*" which would regulate "the relation between the parties exhaustively" (op. cit. preceding note, p. 358). The idea that a contract can be the "law" of the parties is not new; it is characteristic of the well-known hypertrophy of the doctrine of autonomy proper to the French notion of "international payments" sometimes referred to by Professor Verdross' followers (not always correctly, see e.g., Ray, "Law Governing Contracts between States and Foreign Nationals", *Proceedings of the 1960 Institute on Private Investment Abroad* (1960) 5, at p. 30.) Under the circumstances, it is not surprising that Professor Verdross' proposal has encountered the same criticism as that which

one of them is an international person, should be permitted to select international law as the law of their contract; and in the absence of any express statement of intention, the court should be free to apply, from either system of law, the rules most suitable for a reasonable solution to the issue or issues in controversy.[7]

So far, these proposals have had limited success with lenders. Except for certain international organizations, such as the IBRD, whose operations take place in the context of an unusual setup, private as well as international lenders have shown no disposition to depart from established patterns of transacting business and have made no real effort to "de-nationalize" or "internationalize" the loan relationship. This is an important consideration to bear in mind when, in the absence of express manifestation of intention by the parties, the determination of the applicable law becomes an imperative necessity.

SECTION I. THE DETERMINATION OF THE PROPER LAW OF LOAN CONTRACTS

I. EXPRESS STIPULATIONS OF APPLICABLE LAW

A. LOANS CONCLUDED BY PRIVATE PERSONS

1. *Loans Made by Private Lenders*

As a rule, the law expressly designated is either that of the lenders' country, in the case of direct loans, or that of the market in which funds are raised, in the case of bond issues.[8] Only France of all the leading financial markets does not appear to follow this general prac-

has been directed, both in France and abroad, against the French doctrine. See Mann, "The Proper Law", p. 49; see also text and notes 138 to 146 infra; Friedmann, op. cit., note 5 supra, p. 175.

[7] See in particular Jessup, op. cit., note 5 supra, at pp. 102-109; Lalive, "Contracts between a State or a State Agency and a Foreign Company, Theory and Practice: Choice of Law in a New Arbitration Case", 13 Int'l & Comp. L.Q. 987 (1964). But see, *Sereni,* at pp. 100-102.

[8] For reasons of professional confidence only those provisions which can be found in prospectuses or bonds publicly issued are quoted in the text or referred to in the notes. However, the reader may assume that similar provisions are found in loan contracts between bankers and foreign borrowers.

Though the statement in the text reflects the situation obtaining in the overwhelming majority of cases, it is nevertheless interesting to note the occasional exceptions to the general rule. An example is found in the prospectus relating to the International Standard Electric Corporation, New York 4¼% Loan of 1962 issued in *Switzerland* where the New York law was designated applicable.

Other illustrations are found in *England.* See e.g., In re Helbert Wagg

tice. That exception can probably be explained by the unique French doctrine of "international transactions," under which effect is given to the intention of the parties, as expressed in monetary clauses in international transactions, without regard to the principles of the conflict of laws normally applied by French courts in other types of cases.[9]

Although there may be some diversity in the forms of stipulation actually employed in the respective markets, most clauses found in loan agreements and bonds are precisely drafted and indicate clearly the matters which the parties intend to be governed by the designated law. A typical American example is as follows:

> "This Indenture, the Guarantee Agreement, the Debentures issued hereunder and the coupons appertaining thereto and the guarantee endorsed thereon, and all rights arising under any of the same shall be construed and determined in accordance with the laws of [e.g., New York], and the performance of each thereof shall be governed and enforced according to such law."[10]

Comparable clauses are commonly stipulated in loans negotiated in other countries such as the United Kingdom:

> "The construction and administration of the trusts under the

---

[1956] 1 All E.R. 129, in which the German law of the borrower rather than the English law of the lender was stipulated to be applicable. See also the following prospectuses regarding bonds issued in London (though primarily placed in Continental markets) by: (i) Autostrade Concessioni e Costruczioni Autostrade S.A., US $15 million 5½% Guaranteed Bonds 1972/78:
> "The Bonds and the Guarantees will be subject to Italian law and any dispute between the Company or IRI [i.e. Istituto per la Ricostruczione Industriale, the Guarantor] and any bondholder will be submitted to the Italian courts."
and (ii) The City of Copenhagen, Swiss Frs 60 million 5% External Loan 1974/1983:
> "The rights and obligations of the Bondholders and of the City will be governed by the provisions of Danish law."
But see the prospectus of the City of Turin, £5 million 6½% Sterling/ Deutsche Mark Bonds 1984:
> "The terms and conditions of the Bonds will be construed in accordance with English law."
a provision which is also found in the Republic of Austria, US $18 million 6% Bonds 1979/1984.
[9] See text and notes 138-146 infra.
[10] Bataafsche Petroleum Company 4½% Loan of 1927. This provision was given effect by the Supreme Court of the Netherlands in the case of Vereeniging voor den Effectenhandel v. Bataafsche Petroleum Mij., March 13, 1936, Nederlandsche Jurisprudentie No. 281 (1936); Rev. 1936, 733; 36 B.I.J.I. 315 (1936). Comp., the Indentures referred to in note 15 infra.

Trust Deed and the determination of the rights and duties of the parties thereunder will be governed by the law of England."[11]

or Germany:

"All rights and duties arising under this loan or in connection therewith shall be governed by the laws of the Federal Republic of Germany" (as translated).[12]

or the Netherlands:

"This Agreement and all rights and obligations arising thereunder shall be governed by Dutch law" (as translated).[13]

or Switzerland:

"This Loan and the obligations of the Guarantors shall be governed by Swiss law" (as translated).[14]

Not all forms of stipulations are so specific. A common type of clause provides that the loan agreement or the bonds:

---

[11] Nigerian Ports Authority, prospectus relating to an issue of £4.25 million 6% Sterling Guaranteed Loan Stock 1980/83. See also the following provision in the prospectus concerning the Wolfson Clore Mayer Co., Ltd. (an Israeli company), US $5 million 6½% Debenture Stock 1983/88:
"The Trust Deed is to be governed by and interpreted in accordance with English law."
See also the following provision reproduced in the case of Indian and General Investment Trust, Ltd. v. Borax Consolidated, Ltd. [1920] 1 K.B. 539:
"The presents shall be construed and the rights of all persons claiming hereunder shall be regulated by the law of England."
[12] Prospectus of the City of Oslo 5½% Bearer Bonds of 1959. See also the prospectus of the Oesterreichische Donaukrafwerke A.G. 6% Bearer Bonds of 1959 guaranteed by the Republic of Austria and two private companies:
"The Loan and the Guarantees shall be governed by German law" (as translated).
[13] Prospectus of the Naphtachimie, S.A. Paris 4¼% Loan of 1955. See also the following prospectuses regarding the Compagnie Internationale des Wagons Lits 4% Loan of 1955; the Anglo-American Rhodesian Development Co., Ltd. 4½% Loan of 1955; the Raffinerie Belge des Pétroles (RBP) S.A. 5% Loan of 1961.
[14] Prospectus of the Société Ferroviaire Internationale de Transports Frigorifiques (INTERFRIGO) 4½% Loan of 1959, guaranteed by a number of European railway companies. See also the prospectuses relating to the British Petroleum Company, Ltd. 4½% Loan of 1961; the Société Norvégienne de l'Azote et de Forces Hydro-Electriques 4½% Loan of 1959; the Electricity Supply Commission (ESCOM) Johannesburg 5% Loan of 1959; the California Texas Oil Corporation 4½% Loan of 1960; the Istituto Mobiliare Italiano (IMI) 4½% Loan of 1961; The Compagnie Française des Pétroles, Paris, 4½% Loan of 1963; the Rheinish-Westfälisches Elektrizitätswerk, A.G. 4½% Loan of 1964.

"shall be deemed to be a contract made under the laws of the State of New York and for all purposes, shall be construed in accordance with the laws of said State."[15]

Presumably, these provisions are intended to cover both matters of validity and matters of construction. They may be intended to cover matters of performance as well, but it cannot be said that they would inevitably be so understood. At any rate, they may be the source of controversies which a more precise language would eliminate. The English case *In Re Helbert Wagg & Co., Ltd.* is in point.[16] In 1924, English bankers made a loan to a German company. The loan, which was payable in London in sterling free from German taxes, was secured by a specific mortgage on coal fields in Germany owned by the borrower. In form, the loan agreement followed the English practice and so did the bonds which were to be issued thereunder. The agreement contained the following provision:

"This agreement shall be construed in accordance with German law. An English and German texts have been drawn up, but the parties agree that in the event of any conflict between the English and German texts, the English text shall prevail."

After 1933, the borrower attempted to discharge its obligations by making payment in the Konversionkasse in accordance with

---

[15] Indenture dated March 1, 1962 concerning the Société du Pipe-Line Sud-Européen 5½% Sinking Fund Debentures due 1982 (Section 15.05). Similar provisions are found in other indentures relating to the Mitsui & Co. Ltd. 6⅜% Convertible Sinking Fund Debentures due 1978 and the Montecatini, Società Generale per l'Industria Mineraria e Chimica Anonima 5½% Sinking Fund Dollar Debentures due June 15, 1979. Cf. an even more limited provision in an Indenture dated March 1, 1926, relating to the Roman Catholic Church in Bavaria, 25 year Sinking Fund Gold Bonds, Ser. A, Art. X, § 3:
"This indenture is written in the English language and shall be executed and delivered in the City of New York, State of New York, United States of America."
The following provision in recent Swiss prospectuses is clearly unhappily worded:
"The text of the bonds and/or the coupons shall be *interpreted* in accordance with Swiss law. Any dispute between the bondholders, on the one hand, and, on the other, Aktiebolaget Volvo arising in connection with the bonds and/or the coupons shall be *governed* by Swiss law . . ."
Aktiebolaget Volvo Göteborg (a Swedish corporation 4½% Loan of 1961, prospectus, clause 10 (as translated, underlining added). Similar provisions are found in governmental bond issues, such as the Commonwealth of Australia 4½% Loan of 1961 and the Kingdom of Denmark 4½% Loan of 1960. Most of the bonds issued in Switzerland, however, continue to follow the clear language quoted in the text above. See note 14 supra.
[16] [1956] 1 All E.R. 129.

German law. The question at issue was whether such payments operated as a valid discharge, which could be true only if German law was the proper law of the contract. Despite the rather peculiar wording of the above quoted provision, the court had no difficulty in holding that German law was the law intended by the parties:

> "for if an agreement is to be *construed* in accordance with German law it can scarcely be doubted that the parties contemplate that their rights will be *governed* by German law, for it would be strange indeed to construe an agreement by German law (although the English text is to prevail) and then to apply to the construction so reached rules of English law."[17] (underlining added)

This reasoning, which inspires other cases also,[18] deserves approval. There is little doubt that in the overwhelming majority of cases the use of the word "construed" rather than the word "governed" has no particular significance and that the difference between the two phrases is, in the minds of draftsmen at least, "merely verbal."[19] Although the possibility remains that the parties may wish to dissociate the two notions, this is so unlikely in the ordinary type of international transactions,[20] that such an intention cannot be attributed to them in the absence of convincing evidence to the contrary.

2. *Loans Made by Domestic Public Lending Agencies*

Domestic public lending agencies, when they deal expressly with conflicts-of-laws issues, which is not always the case,[21] usually follow the example of private lenders and provide for the applicability of

---

[17] Ibid., at p. 135. See also p. 136: "In my judgment the parties intended that German law was to govern their relationship, i.e. German law as it exists from time to time, and that it is the proper law of the loan agreement."

[18] See e.g., in the case of loans, Barcelo v. Electrolytic Zinc Co. of Australasia, Ltd. (1933) Vict. L. R. 94, 48 C.L.R. 391. Comp., dictum in Irving Trust Co. v. Deutsch Atlantische Tel., 22 N.Y.S. 2d 581 (1940).

Most cases concern shipping or other commercial contracts. See e.g., Vita Food Products v. Unus Shipping Co., Ltd. [1939] A. C. 277; Overseas Trading Company, S.A. v. United States, 159 F. Supp. 382 (Ct. Cl. 1958). But see, the Torni [1932] P. 78; Cass. March 3, 1924, The Produce Brokers Co. v. Société Maritime et Commerciale de France, S. 1924.1.252, Clunet 1926, 349.

[19] Vita Food Products v. Unus Shipping Co., Ltd. cited in the preceding note. See also Overseas Trading Company, S.A. v. United States, id. loc.

[20] See, however, infra text and notes 37 to 44.

[21] No provision designating the applicable law is normally found in loans made by the French Caisse Centrale. However, the Caisse takes care to provide for the jurisdiction of the French courts (specifically the Paris courts) and the many factors in its loan contracts connecting these contracts with France leave little doubt as to the solution of the conflict-of-laws issue.

the municipal law of their own country. In the United States the AID (following the practice of the former DLF), and in England the CDFC stipulate in their loan contracts that the law of the District of Columbia and English law, respectively, shall govern the rights and obligations of the parties.[22] In Japan, loans made by the Export-Import Bank currently provide for the applicability of the law of Japan.

B. LOANS CONCLUDED BY INTERNATIONAL PERSONS

1. *Direct Loans*

Loan contracts between international persons and bankers or other institutional investors rarely fail to contain stipulations of applicable law. Most frequently such stipulations, like those consistently contained in loan contracts with foreign private borrowers, provide that the law of the lenders shall govern the loan relationship. Typical examples are found in a loan made to the Republic of France by a group of American bankers:

"This Agreement and the notes issued pursuant thereto and all rights under this Agreement and said notes shall be construed and determined and may be enforced in accordance with the laws of the State of New York."[23]

Similar provisions are found in loans made by both national and international public lending agencies, the number of which is steadily increasing. Thus, agreements between the AID and foreign governments, acting as borrowers or as guarantors of loans made to private borrowers, currently provide that the law of the District of

---

[22] The provision currently used by the AID reads as follows:
"*Applicable Law.* This Loan Agreement shall be deemed to be a contract made under the laws of the District of Columbia, United States of America, and shall be governed by and construed in accordance with the laws of the District of Columbia, United States of America."
The provision used by the CDFC reads:
"This [agreement] shall be construed and have effect in all respects in accordance with the laws of England."
A similar provision is found in loans made by the CDC.
[23] Loan Agreement dated October 31, 1949, between the Republic of France, The Chase National Bank of the City of New York and other bankers, Section 10, para. 10.3. Similar stipulations are found in various loan contracts negotiated in other, including European, financial centers, the provisions of which the present writer is not authorized to quote. For an earlier American example, see Loan Contract between the Republic of Nicaragua and Brown Brothers & Co., etc., dated October 8, 1913, Article XV, reprinted in *Dunn*, at p. 378.

Columbia shall be the applicable law.[24] Although provisions of applicable law appear to be somewhat less frequent in loans made by the Export-Import Bank of Washington (Eximbank), the loan made by that institution to the United Kingdom in 1957 contemplates the applicability of the law of New York.[25]

Like private lenders, public lenders are usually attentive to the problem of the law governing the loan relationship. Public lenders, however, and in particular international lending organizations, do not necessarily insist that the choice be made in favor of the law in force at their headquarters.

A typical example is that of the investment agreements of the International Finance Corporation (IFC), whose headquarters are located in Washington, D.C. IFC, whose investment patterns are sometimes complex, originally stipulated that the law of New York should govern its investments in private foreign enterprises.[26] However IFC subsequently took the view that a reference to the law of New York would, in many cases, be ineffective unless accompanied by a specific submission by the parties to the New York courts. This additional provision was considered necessary because in many countries the courts would either refuse to apply New York law or apply New York law only to the extent that it was consistent with local law. However, IFC considered that it would not always be possible to insist upon a provision requiring submission to the New York courts and further, that any such submission might not be of much use in many cases since any award would ultimately have to be enforced in the foreign jurisdiction (unless the investment enterprise had assets in New York, which would not usually be the case). IFC finally

---

[24] See note 22 supra.

[25] Agreement dated February 25, 1957 (Cmnd. 104), Article XVI:

"All questions with respect to the execution and interpretation of this Agreement and the notes or with respect to performance or non-performance hereunder or thereunder shall be interpreted according to New York law."

See also, Townsend, "The Export-Import Bank of Washington: Organization and Operation", U. of Ill. Law Forum, Legal Problems of International Trade, 237 (1959 Spring Number); Sauer, "The Export-Import Bank and Private Investment", 19 Fed. Bar J. 327 (1959).

Loans made by the Export-Import Bank of Japan currently stipulate that Japanese law is the applicable law.

[26] See Nurick, "Choice of Law Clauses and International Contracts", Proceedings of the American Society of Int'l L. 56 (1960). The majority of IFC investments provide for the issuance of notes denominated in U.S. dollars and payable in New York. IFC takes care that these notes are in any case valid under the laws of New York.

took the position that since its ultimate remedies would normally lie in the courts of the country in which the investment enterprise is located, its investment documents should be prepared so as to be valid under the law of that country. For these reasons, most IFC investment agreements do not specify the applicability of any particular law.

In certain cases, submission to the law of the borrower's country may be motivated by other considerations. The organization involved, such as the ECSC, may wish to avoid the only likely alternative, namely having all its loan contracts governed by the law of the particular member country in which it is located.[27] On other occasions, as in the case of the European Investment Bank (EIB), it may reflect an understandable desire to facilitate the recovery and enforcement of a judgment against the borrower.[28]

A different situation is presented by IBRD loan agreements.[29] The IBRD, which is an international entity and a subject of international law, makes loans either directly to a member government or that are guaranteed by a member government. Leaving aside for the moment the nature of the relations between the IBRD and a borrower, whose loan is guaranteed by a member government, it would seem prima facie that, in the absence of express provision to the contrary, the relations between the IBRD and one of its members, *qua* borrower or guarantor, should be governed by international law, the law common to both parties. The IBRD loan documents are consistent with this conclusion.

Loan Regulations No. 3, which are applicable to direct loans to member governments and are incorporated by express reference into loan agreements with such governments, contain the following provision (Section 7.01):

---

[27] Blondeel and Vander Eycken, "Les Emprunts de la Communauté Européenne du Charbon et de l'Acier", 19 Revue de la Banque 249 (1955), at p. 274.

[28] Stein and Hay, "Legal Remedies of Enterprises in the European Economic Community", 9 Am. J. Comp. L. 375 (1960), at p. 407.

If the loan is guaranteed or secured and the guarantor belongs to a country other than that of the borrower or the security is located outside that country, the law of the guarantor or that of the situs may be stipulated applicable.

It is interesting to note that, in connection with its operations in countries associated with the European Economic Community (Greece, Turkey, Associated African States and Malagasi Republic), the EIB stipulates that Swiss law should be the applicable law and Swiss courts should have jurisdiction over possible loan disputes.

[29] The following discussion of these agreements is in large part based on the views developed in *Broches*, 316-353.

"The rights and obligations of the Bank and the Borrower under the Loan Agreement and the Bonds shall be valid and enforceable in accordance with their terms notwithstanding the law of any state, or political subdivision thereof to the contrary . . . "

This provision makes clear the intention of the parties that the terms and conditions of the loan agreement shall not be frustrated by conflicting domestic law. Since no agreement can exist in a legal vacuum, the conclusion is inescapable that the effect of this provision, although it is formulated in a negative fashion, is not only to remove the loan relationship from domestic law but to subject it to international law.[30]

Section 7.01 of Loan Regulations No. 4, applicable to guaranteed loans, is substantially similar to the corresponding provision of Loan Regulations No. 3.[31] In the case of guaranteed loans, however, the borrower usually a public or private entity created or operating within the guarantor's territories) is not a subject of international

---

[30] This conclusion is not impaired by the second sentence of Section 7.01 which reads as follows:

". . . Neither the Bank nor the Borrower shall be entitled in any proceeding under this Article to assert any claim that any provision of these Regulations or of the Loan Agreement or the Bonds is invalid or unenforceable because of any provision of the Articles of Agreement of the Bank or for any other reason."

This provision is justified by the following considerations. On the one hand, the Loan Regulations (Section 7.04) provide for the settlement of loan disputes by an arbitral tribunal. On the other hand, the Articles of Agreement of the IBRD (Article IX) stipulate that any question of interpretation of the Articles shall be submitted to the Executive Directors of the IBRD for their decision. In order to protect the Directors' jurisdiction to interpret the Articles, and insure that the arbitral tribunal not pass judgment upon issues involving the consistency of a loan transaction with the Articles, it was necessary to remove all such issues from the jurisdiction of the arbitral tribunal. This is the rationale of the provision under review. Far from making the Loan Agreement a self-supporting instrument or subjecting the loan relationship to the "internal law" of the IBRD (as suggested by *Salmon,* p. 230; but see, Adam, "Les Accords de Prêt de la Banque Internationale pour la Reconstruction et le Développement", Revue Générale de Droit International Public, 1951, 41, at pp. 55-56; Sereni, op. cit., note 5 supra, p. 160), this provision is intended only to avoid an adjudication by the arbitral tribunal of issues within the jurisdiction of the Executive Directors. With the exception of this type of issue, however, the arbitral tribunal is competent to settle any disputes arising between the IBRD and a borrowing member country, on the basis of international law. See *Broches,* pp. 362-373.

[31] "The rights and obligations of the Bank, the Borrower and the Guarantor under the Loan Agreement, the Guarantee Agreement and the Bonds shall be valid and enforceable in accordance with their terms notwithstanding the law of any state, or political subdivision thereof, to the contrary. . . ."

law.[32] Since a loan agreement between the IBRD and a borrower other than a member country cannot be regarded as an international agreement,[33] the question arises whether the loan, as distinguished from the guarantee, can be insulated from the effect of conflicting domestic law. It is submitted that the answer to this question is in the affirmative for the following reasons.

The tripartite relations arising under any guaranteed loan made by the IBRD are so interdependent that to consider them separately would ignore both the factual and the juridical considerations pertaining to the IBRD's lending operations. In many instances, the fact that the loan is made to an entity other than a member government is purely a matter of form without substantive significance: The lending process could be achieved with equal success were the loan made directly to the member concerned, subject to its making available the proceeds of the loan to the entity in charge of the project involved.[34] Also, from a juridical viewpoint, it is significant that the guarantor, by accepting the terms of the guarantee agreement, agrees to be bound "as a primary obligor," an undertaking which goes far beyond the ordinary concept of suretyship and in effect makes the guarantor a joint co-debtor.[35] Under the circumstances, it is apparent that the IBRD guarantee agreements give rise to a very unusual situation in which the guarantor's obligations are not merely accessory to those of the borrower, as in the case of ordinary guarantees including those obtained by such other international lending organizations as the EIB or the ECSC, but are in effect paramount to the borrower's undertakings.[36]

---

[32] Difficult questions may arise when the borrower is a dependent territory in a stage transitional to full independence. See *Broches,* p. 351.

[33] *Broches,* Id. loc.

[34] For examples, see *Broches,* pp. 352-353.

[35] See e.g., Guarantee Agreement dated February 17, 1959, between Japan and the IBRD (Section 2.01) relating to a loan made by the IBRD to the Japan Development Bank, 337 UNTS 205.

[36] See e.g., *Broches,* p. 352:

". . . the loan agreement is only one element—although obviously an important one—in the dealings on the international level between the Bank and its member, and partakes of the international character of these dealings. This is not the same as saying that the loan agreement itself thereby becomes an international agreement, and that it is governed by international law. But it does justify the internationalization of the loan agreement to the extent of insulating it from the effect of municipal law. It seems perfectly proper for the guaranteeing member and the Bank, both subjects of international law, to agree that this shall be so, and they do so agree by accepting Section 7.01 of Loan Regulations No. 4 as governing the transaction. To put it somewhat differently, while the borrower

In addition to the provisions of Section 7.01, the early agreements of the IBRD stipulated that:

> "The provisions of this Agreement and of the Bonds and of the Guarantee Agreement shall be interpreted in accordance with the law of the State of New York, as in effect at the date of this Agreement."[37]

It has been contended that, despite the language of Section 7.01 which always preceded this provision, it had the effect of subjecting loan agreements to New York law not only in regard to matters of interpretation but in respect to matters of substance also.[38] This contention is unacceptable. It is true that under ordinary circumstances, a reference in a contract to a specific law, even if apparently limited to matters of "interpretation," should be construed as implying subjection of the relationship to that law also.[39] However, there are instances in which such an inference would be improper because the law referred to, far from being the proper law of the contract, is merely incorporated to regulate some of its particular features.[40] The difficulty in distiguishing between these two situations is illustrated by the many controversies respecting gold or multiple currency clauses or maritime contracts.[41] It seems clear nevertheless that, in the case of the IBRD loan agreements, the distinction was particularly well spelled out, since it was expressly stated that the applicable New York law was the law *in force at the time of contracting*, a formula which

---

> could not contract itself out of the application of municipal law, the Bank and the guaranteeing member may do so in respect not only of their own relationship but also (with the borrower's consent evidenced by the borrower's acceptance of Section 7.01) of that between the Bank and the Borrower."

See also, Id. op., pp. 355-356; Adam, op. cit. note 30 supra, pp. 57-58.

[37] Loan Agreement between the IBRD and Crédit National pour faciliter la réparation des dommages causés par la guerre (guaranteed by the Republic of France) May 9, 1947, Article IX, Section 2 (152 UNTS 111).

A slightly different formulation is found in other Loan Agreements of the same period, such as the Agreement of August 18, 1949, between India and the IBRD, Article IX, Section 2 (154 UNTS 4):

> "The provisions of this Agreement and of the Bonds shall be interpreted in accordance with the law of the State of New York, *as at the time in effect.*"

[38] *Sereni*, op. cit., note 5 supra, p. 206; Mann, "The Proper Law", p. 38. See however note 42 infra.

[39] Re Helbert Wagg & Co., Ltd. [1956] 1 All E.R. 129, at 135.

[40] See text and notes 15 to 20 supra.

[41] See e.g., Batiffol, *Les Conflits de Lois en Matière de Contrats* (1938), pp. 151-155; Dicey, *Conflict of Laws* (7th ed. 1958), pp. 728-729; *Mann*, pp. 138-139.

by all relevant canons of interpretation cannot be construed as a choice of law provision.[42]

Under the circumstances, the reference to the law of New York, which was soon dropped from the IBRD loan agreements,[43] constituted merely one example of the kind of stipulations sometimes found in commercial or financial agreements concluded by international persons, which for the sake of precision incorporate into such agreements technical definitions borrowed from municipal law.[44]

Until now, the IDA credits have been extended only to member governments and the credit agreements in existence contain a provision similar to that of Section 7.01 of the IBRD's Loan Regulations No. 3.[45] However, it should be noted that the IDA is authorized to extend credits to public or private entities in the territories of members and, unlike the case of the IBRD, such credits need not be guaranteed by a member government and may be secured by any form of security. It is possible that in this last case conflict-of-laws issues might arise.

The IADB is authorized to embark upon financing operations similar to those of the IBRD, the EIB, the IFC and the IDA. In view of the variety of these operations, it is not unlikely that the IADB may find it convenient to resort alternatively to public and private international law. It is possible also that in the process of selection between the two systems of law, the use of public international law will be increased. It is indeed significant that loans made by the IADB to governmental entities with the guarantee of their respec-

---

[42] See Adam, op. cit., note 30 supra, p. 58; *Salmon*, pp. 228 9; *Broches*, p. 357. See also, Jenks, op. cit., note 4 supra, p. 180.

Dr. Mann ("The Proper Law", p. 38, note 2), bases his critical reasoning on the type of provision quoted supra note 37, which was avowedly less clear than that quoted in the text above. Dr. Mann agrees that the reference to the law of New York as in effect at a given time "would, indeed, involve a mere case of incorporation, not a choice of New York law". This construction is further reinforced by the unambiguous statement of Section 7.01 of the IBRD Loan Regulations.

[43] It is believed that the last time this provision was used was on the occasion of the July 7, 1950, Loan to Turkey (156 UNTS 75), which was the 28th loan made by the IBRD.

[44] See Mann, "Reflections on a Commercial Law of Nations", 33 B.Y.B.I.L. 20 (1957).

[45] See Development Credit Agreement dated May 12, 1961, between Republic of Honduras and IDA, Article VII, Section 7.01 (414 UNTS 179); Development Credit Agreement dated November 22, 1961, between India and IDA, incorporating by reference the provisions of Development Credit Regulations No. 1 of the IDA (427 UNTS 3).

tive governments, contain a provision substantially similar to that of
Section 7.01 of the IBRD's Loan Regulations No. 4.[46]

2. Bonds

The practices of lenders in leading financial markets vary considerably regarding conflict-of-laws provisions in bonds issued by international persons. Continental lenders usually stipulate, both in the
case of government bonds,[47] and bonds issued by international organizations,[48] that the rights and obligations of the parties shall be
governed by the law of the market of issue. Lenders in the United
States, the United Kingdom or Canada do not always insist on stipulating the applicable law in bonds issued in these countries by international entities.[49] However, it seems clear that they consider the
loan relationship to be governed by domestic law.[50]

[46] The relevant provision reads as follows:
"Los derechos y obligaciones establecidos en este Contrato son válidos y
exigibles de conformidad con los términos en él convenidos, inde-
pendientemente de cualquier legislación y, en consecuencia, ni el Banco
ni el Deudor podrán alegar la invalidez de ninguna de sus disposiciones."
[47] See e.g., in Switzerland, the prospectus of the Commonwealth of Australia 4½% Loan of 1960, reading as follows:
"Any dispute between the bondholders, on the one side, and on the
other side the Australian Government arising in connection with the
bonds or the coupons of this loan shall be governed by Swiss law and
shall be decided by the ordinary courts of the District [canton] of Bâle-
Ville, subject to appeal to the Federal Tribunal at Lausanne." (as
translated)
Similar provisions are found in other Swiss issues such as those regarding
the Belgian Congo Guaranteed 4% Loan of 1953; the Union of South Africa
4% Loan of 1952; or the Kingdom of Denmark 4½% Loan of 1959.
Comp., in Germany, the prospectus respecting: (i) Oesterreichische
Donaukraftwerke A.G. 6% DM Bonds of 1959, guaranteed by the Republic of
Austria and two power companies; (ii) Japan 6% Bonds of 1964; and (iii) the
Republic of Finland 6% Loan of 1964.
[48] See e.g., the following provision regarding the IBRD 5% Deutsche
Mark Bonds of 1959:
"All rights and duties arising out of or in connection with this issue
are exclusively determined in accordance with the law of the Federal
Republic of Germany. The place of performance and jurisdiction will
be in Frankfurt am Main for all parties concerned" (as translated).
Similar provisions are found in: (i) the IBRD: 4½% Swiss Franc Loan
of 1960; 4½% Netherlands Guilder Bonds of 1961; 5% Belgian Franc Bonds
of 1960; 5% Italian Lire Bonds of 1961; (ii) the ECSC 4¾% Dutch Guilders
Loan of 1962; (iii) the EIB 5¾% Dutch Guilders Loan of 1964; and (iv) the
IADB 5½% DM Bearer Bonds of 1964. Comp., the EUROFIMA 5½% DM
Bonds of 1964.
[49] For example, no conflict-of-laws provision is found in bonds issued in
the United States by the Kingdom of the Netherlands, the Italian Republic,

Apparently no attempt has ever been made by private lenders contracting with an international person to remove the loan relationship from the field of domestic law to that of international law. Dr. Mann has argued that such a removal was implicit in certain loans made by private lenders to foreign governments which provided for the settlement of loan disputes by the PCIJ or the ICJ.[51] This contention is open to the objection, acknowledged by Dr. Mann himself,[52] that since the jurisdiction of the Hague Court is limited to disputes between states, the Court would have had to refuse jurisdiction over disputes brought by the lenders against the debtor government.[53] Furthermore, since, in certain of these clauses, provision is made not only for the jurisdiction of the ICJ but also for that of domestic courts,[54] it is doubtful that the clauses in question were intended to

and the Kingdom of Norway in 1947 (and by the latter Government in 1961), the State of Israel in 1950, the Kingdom of Belgium in 1962, the Union of South Africa in 1955; Japan in 1963; New Zealand in 1962 and the Republic of Panama in 1958; or in bonds issued in Canada by the Commonwealth of Australia in 1962; or in bonds issued in England by the Danish Government in 1946, the Kingdom of Norway in 1951 and by New Zealand in 1961. But see: (i) in England, the prospectus of the Republic of Austria, US $18 million 6% Bonds 1979/84:

"The Bonds will be construed in accordance with English law," and (ii) in the United States, the prospectus of the Belgian Congo $15 million, Fifteen Year 5¼% External Loan Bonds of 1958, due April 1, 1973, which provides that:

"The Bonds will provide that the rights and obligations of the Government and the holders of the Bonds shall be governed by and construed in accordance with the laws of the State of New York."

Similar provisions are found in the Kingdom of Denmark 5½% Fifteen Year External Loan Bonds of 1959 and the Kingdom of Norway Fifteen Year 5¼% External Loan Bonds of 1963.

Bonds issued by the IBRD in the United States, Canada and the United Kingdom contain no stipulation of applicable law. Bonds issued by: (i) the High Authority of the ECSC (5⅜% Secured Bonds (Thirteenth Series) of 1960); and (ii) the EIB (6% Dollar Bonds of 1965, Due September 15, 1985) in New York are governed by the law of that State.

[50] See Sommers, Broches and Delaume, op. cit., note 4 supra, pp. 472-3.

[51] See e.g.: (i) PCIJ: the 5% 1932 and 1937 Bonds of the Czechoslovak Republic guaranteed by the Republic of France; the External Loan of the French Republic of 1939 issued both in Switzerland and the Netherlands. See Chapter IV text and note 74; and (ii) I.C.J.: the provision in bonds issued in Switzerland by the Régie des Télégraphes et Téléphones, guaranteed by the Belgian Government (External Loan 4% of 1947), quoted in Chapter IV text and note 76.

[52] "The Proper Law", p. 51.

[53] See Chapter IV text and notes 73-74; Sereni, op. cit., note 5 supra, pp. 223-224.

[54] Id. loc.

solve problems other than those respecting jurisdiction. Yet the habit
of lenders to couple jurisdictional clauses with provisions of applicable
law certainly lends support to Dr. Mann's contention. Had the parties substituted for an impossible forum an effective mean of international adjudication, e.g. by way of arbitration, it would seem that
Dr. Mann's view would be entitled to great weight.[55] Although provisions of the kind anticipated by Dr. Mann are viewed with increasing
favor in concessions and economic development agreements,[56] it
seems unlikely that they will be incorporated in international loan
documents in the near future. Recently, for example, on the occasion of lending operations undertaken jointly by private lenders and
international organizations, private lenders had several opportunities
to follow Dr. Mann's suggestion. Invariably, however, they failed
to do so.

3. Joint Operations

In an increasing number of instances, domestic and international
institutional lenders combine efforts to supply borrowers with the
funds needed for their operations or the development of their economy. Sometimes this cooperation, both from an economic and a legal
viewpoint, is rather a loose one: Each lender supplies separate funds
for a separate purpose.[57] On other occasions, the proceeds of all financ-
ings are applied to a single economic objective, such as the completion of a specific project.[58] In the latter case, the various loan agree-

---

[55] See McNair, "General Principles", p. 6.

Bonds issued in the United States by the High Authority of the ECSC
constitute an interesting exception to the maxim "qui elegit judicem elegit
jus". The Bonds indeed provide simultaneously for the jurisdiction of the
Court of Justice of the Community and for submission of the loan relationship to the law of New York. See Chapter IV text and note 71. But see ibid.,
text and note 72.

[56] See e.g., Hyde, op. cit., note 5 supra; Friedmann, op. cit., note 5 supra,
at p. 222; Haight, "The Choice of Public International Law in Development
Contracts with Foreign Governments", in McDaniels, p. 554. See also note
159 infra.

[57] Thus, in 1959 the Kingdom of Denmark concurrently borrowed $20
million in the New York market and contracted a loan from the IBRD for
the equivalent of $20 million. The proceeds of the bond issue were not
allocated to a specific purpose. The IBRD loan is intended to assist in the
financing of specific power projects. See Loan Agreement dated February 4,
1959, 328 UNTS 143, and the Prospectus of the 5½% Fifteen Year External
Loan Bonds of 1959, p. 3.

For other illustrations, see The World Bank, pp. 102-105.

[58] Thus, in 1959 Japan borrowed the equivalent of $40 million in a com-
bined operation consisting of public offerings of $30 million of bonds in New

ments normally contain provisions making the transactions mutually interdependent in regard to such matters as entry into force, disbursements, consultations, default, etc. Even in this type of situation, however, and *a fortiori* in the first type of operation described above, the private lenders generally specify domestic law as the law applicable to their agreements.

A concrete example is that of the 1957 loans made by several American commercial banks and the IBRD to finance the purchase of jet passenger planes by Air-India International, India's international airline. The relations between the bankers, the IBRD and the borrower (and India as guarantor) are defined in two sets of agreements. The IBRD Loan and Guarantee Agreements, which incorporate by reference several provisions of the Bankers' Agreement,[59] follow the ordinary pattern of IBRD agreements. They incorporate Section 7.01 of Loan Regulations No. 4 and provide for the arbitral settlement of disputes arising thereunder.

In view of the interdependence of the loans by the IBRD and the bankers, there was a perfect opportunity for the bankers to seek to "internationalize" their own agreements. No such attempt was made. Instead, the bankers chose to stipulate the applicability of the law of New York and the jurisdiction of the New York courts. It is believed that this example is significant. It shows that private lenders feel adequately protected as long as the loan relationship is brought within their own system of law and the jurisdiction of their own courts. Whether this feeling is justified is not the question; it explains, however, why private lenders have no compulsion to place their interests under the umbrella of international law, which is much less precise, in their opinion, than the domestic law with which they are familiar.

Other examples are worth mentioning also. Thus, in 1959 the Southern Italy Development Fund (Cassa per il Mezzogiorno) an agency of the Government of Italy, borrowed $70 million in a joint

---

York and a $10 million loan by the IBRD to the Japanese Development Bank, a government agency. The purpose of the borrowings was to provide part of the funds needed for a hydroelectric power project. See, Loan, Guarantee and Project Agreements dated February 17, 1959, 337 UNTS 205, and the Prospectus of the External Loan Bonds dated January 15, 1959, p. 4.

[59] Only the IBRD Agreements dated March 5, 1957 have been published. See 272 UNTS 201. See in particular, Section 5.02 of the Loan Agreement. The due execution of the Bankers' Agreement was a condition of effectiveness of the IBRD loan (Loan Agreement, Section 7.02 (b)), while the bankers' obligation to make loans under their Agreement was conditional upon the execution of the IBRD Loan Agreement.

operation consisting of two loans of $20 million each from the IBRD and the EIB, respectively, and of $30 million of bonds issued in the New York investment market. The lire equivalent of the proceeds of the IBRD and the EIB loans were used to finance a power project in Southern Italy and two industrial projects in Sicily, while funds borrowed from the market were applied to the general program of the Cassa.[60]

In order to coordinate the IBRD and the EIB's financing, the loan agreements between each of these two organizations and the Cassa were interrelated, the terms and conditions of both loans being substantially the same in regard to disbursements and repayment at or in advance of maturity.[61] Nevertheless;, while the IBRD loan is subject to the provision of Section 7.01 of the Loan Regulations, the EIB loan is governed by the law of Italy. No stipulation of applicable law is found in the bonds issued in the New York market.

In 1960, simultaneously with the signing of the Indus Water Treaty between India and Pakistan, an international agreement was executed by the IBRD and the governments of Australia, Canada, Germany, New Zealand, Pakistan, the United Kingdom and the United States. This agreement created an Indus Basin Development Fund equivalent in value to nearly $900 million to finance the construction of irrigation and other works in Pakistan. The Fund's resources were supplied by the participating governments, with a contribution payable by India under the Water Treaty, and another contribution payable by the IBRD (which also acts as Administrator of the Fund) under a Loan Agreement of even date with the Water Treaty and the Fund Agreement.[62] On the same date that

---

[60] See the preamble of the Loan Agreement dated April 21, 1959, between the IBRD and the Cassa per Opere Straordinarie di Publico Interesse Nell'Italia meridionale (Cassa per il Mezzogiorno) guaranteed by Republic of Italy (359 UNTS 191). See also, the Prospectus of the Southern Italy Development Fund, Guaranteed External Loan Bonds of 1959, pp. 3-4.

[61] IBRD Loan Agreement, Article II, Section 2.02 and Schedule 3 (d) (h) (i) and (k). Both loans also provided that the subsidiary loan agreements and other arrangements between the Cassa and the three beneficiary enterprises concerning the financing, construction and operations of the projects should contain provisions adequate to protect the interest of the Cassa and the two lending organizations, and could not be amended without the latters' consent (IBRD Loan Agreement, Article IV, Sections 4.01 and 4.03).

[62] Loan Agreement dated September 19, 1960. Indus Basin Development Fund Agreement, dated September 19, 1960 (444 UNTS 259, Supplemented in 1964, 503 UNTS 388); Water Treaty dated September 19, 1960 (419 UNTS 125).

these instruments were executed, the DLF agreed to make a $70 million loan to Pakistan, the proceeds of which were disbursed directly to the Fund and used for the purposes and in the manner specified in the Fund Agreement. While there is little question that the Water Treaty, the Fund Agreement and the IBRD Loan Agreement are subject to international law, the DLF Agreement, conforming to the usual practice of the DLF, provided that it was governed by the law of the District of Columbia.

II. THE RELEVANT RULES IN THE ABSENCE OF EXPRESS STIPULATION OF APPLICABLE LAW

A. LOANS BETWEEN PRIVATE PERSONS

In the absence of an express stipulation to the contrary, international loans are usually governed by the law of the lenders' country (in the case of loan agreements) or the market in which the funds are raised (in the case of bond issues). It is at that place that documents are signed and delivered;[63] that funds are received by the borrower; and, in most cases, that the funds are to be repaid.[64] The language of that country is usually used and its fashions in draftsmanship observed.[65] Where a trustee or a bondholder's rep-

---

[63] In the case of a bond issue, many instruments may be executed at or about the time of issue, such as underwriting and fiscal or paying agency agreements, trust indentures, etc. Frequently, these agreements also are governed by the law of the market involved, although on occasion a different solution may prevail. See e.g., Ehag Eisenbahnwerke Holding A.G. v. Banca Nationala A Romanei, 306 N.Y. 242, 117 N.E. 2d 346 (1954). See also, Sauser-Hall, *La Clause Or dans les Contrats Publics et Privés,* 60 Recueil des Cours 657 (1937), at p. 754.

[64] See e.g., Coghlan v. South Carolina R. Co., 142 U.S. 101, 12 S. Ct. 150 (1891); Lemaire v. Kentucky and Indiana Terminal RR. Co., 242 F. 2d 884 (1957). These cases should be distinguished from those applying the place-of-payment doctrine. See infra text and notes 69 to 74.

[65] Ordinarily, no special weight is attached to the language in which the loan documents are written, a practice which conforms to that generally prevailing with regard to other types of contracts. See e.g., Batiffol, *Les Conflits de Lois en Matière de Contrats* (1938), pp. 127-129. For a controversial decision, see also Cass. January 14, 1931, Bonnaud v. Ville de Tokio and Ville de Tokio v. Roussey, D.P. 1931.1.5; Rev. 1934, 537.

An agreement by the parties that the bonds be expressed in the language of the lenders' country, and drafted in a form generally used in that country would, in itself, be insufficient to override a statement in the loan documents that the loan relationship be governed by the law of another country. See e.g., Re Helbert Wagg & Co. Ltd. [1956] 1 All E.R. 129.

resentative is appointed, it will normally be a national and resident of the lenders' country. The same is true of fiscal agents, paying agents and registrars.[66] Further, the regulatory requirements of the market concerned, such as registration and listing, will have been complied with.[67] Thus, there is usually every reason to assume that:

> ".... in the absence of any express clause determining the proper law, the transaction should be governed by the law of the country of the lender. A borrower who come from a foreign country seeking a loan must expect to conform to the laws of the country to which he comes; for otherwise he is unlikely to get the loan."[68]

This presumption can be overcome, of course, if circumstances so warrant. However, attempts to remove the loan relationship from the law of the lenders' country or of the place of issue should be viewed with caution since they are usually inspired by considerations of convenience rather than by objective legal considerations.

Panamerican Securities Corporation v. Frederich Krupp A.G.[69] is a typical illustration of this remark. A German company had issued bonds payable at the option of the holder, either in Germany in Reichmarks, or in the Netherlands in Dutch guilders at the rate of exchange on Berlin. After the imposition of exchange restrictions in Germany, a bondholder sought payment in the Netherlands. The borrower demurred by invoking the German exchange restrictions which, in its opinion, were part of the proper law of the loan. An impressive number of considerations could be invoked in favor of the borrower's view including the following: the contract was expressed in the German language; a German bank had purchased the entire issue and had been appointed representative of the bondholders; the bonds were redeemable in Germany where the underlying security was also located; the period of prescription of the coupons and the procedure relating to the invalidation of lost bonds, were governed by German law; all notices were to be made in Germany; and reference was expressly made in the bonds to the German law of 1899

---

[66] See e.g., Guaranty Trust Co. v. Henwood, 307 U.S. 247, 59 S. Ct. 847 (1939); Supreme Court of the Netherlands February 11, 1938, Rotterdam Gold Bond Case, Annual Digest 1919-42, 26.

[67] See infra text and notes 191 to 194.

[68] Re United Railways of the Havana and Regla Warehouses, Ltd. [1960] 2 All E.R. 332, at p. 355 per Lord Denning. See also, T.F. October 9, 1962, Legerlotz v. Ville de Salzbourg, R.O. 88.II.283 (Summarized in Clunet 1965, 937).

[69] 256 App. Div. 955, 10 N.Y.S. 2d 205 (1939).

regarding the protection of bondholders. Despite these considerations, however, the court held that "the plaintiff by demanding payment in Holland fixed that country as the place of performance," with the consequence that Dutch rather than German law was applicable.

This and other cases[70] are subject to the fundamental objection that they remit the solution of the conflict-of-laws issue entirely to the discretion of the lender who, by demanding payment in one country or the other, has it in his power to change the law applicable to the loan or the bonds. "This is bad law."[71] Also, these decisions lead to a regrettable confusion between two categories of problems which should be carefully distinguished: those relating to the "substance" of the debt, which should be governed by the proper law of the contract; and those dealing with the "manner of performance," as to which the *lex loci solutionis* may be relevant.[72] The fact that a loan contract has some incidental contact with the law of the place of payment is, under normal circumstances, no justification for substituting that law for the law of the market with which the contract is most closely connected and in which the contract has its "center of gravity."[73] It is only in exceptional cases, such as those in which the parties have provided for an option of currency and agreed upon several places of payment, that the *lex loci solutionis* may be considered to determine

---

[70] Lann v. United Steel Works Corporation, 1 N.Y.S. 2d 951, 166 Misc. 465 (1938); Irving Trust Co. v. Deutsch Atlantische Tel., 22 N.Y.S. 2d 581 (1940).

These cases must be distinguished from those which, after correctly determining the proper law, refused to give effect to German exchange restrictions on the ground that they were not part of the proper law and could therefore be disregarded. See e.g., Barncs v. United Steel Works Corporation, 11 N.Y.S. 2d 161 (1939). See generally, *Mann,* pp. 367 et seq.

[71] *Nussbaum,* at p. 420.

[72] It has been contended that the P.C.I.J., in the Serbian and Brazilian Loans Cases, relied on the place-of-performance theory to determine the validity of a gold clause in the bonds (see *Nussbaum,* p. 418). However, a close reading of these cases discloses that this contention is unjustified. The Court actually ascertained the validity of the clause under the law of the respective borrowing governments and then proceeded to show, for the sake of argument, that even if the French law of the place of payment had been applicable, there would have been no obstacle in that law to the implementation of the clause (Series A, No. 20, p. 44, No. 21, p. 122). See *Mann,* pp. 261-262.

[73] Cf. British and French Trust Corporation v. New Brunswick Railway Company [1937] 4 All E.R. 516, aff'd on other grounds, [1939] A.C.1, and *Mann's* (p. 264) and *Nussbaum's* (p. 421) critical appraisal of this decision.

As to cases dealing with the revalorization of debts, see *Mann,* pp. 238-245; *Nussbaum,* pp. 357-359.

the substance, as well as the mode of performance, of the debt. Even then, great care should be exercised not to give to the factors involved more weight than was intended by the parties.[74]

Similar discretion is required in the case of secured loans, when one of the parties attempts to bring the entire loan relationship within the scope of the *lex situs,* presumably more favorable to the claimant's interests than the law of the lenders' country or that of the place of issue. The case of *Re United Railways of the Havana and Regla Warehouses, Ltd.*[75] is in point. An English company operating a railway in Cuba had issued equipment trust certificates in the United States. As part of a complex financial scheme, it had sold its rolling stock and equipment to a subsidiary incorporated for the occasion in the State of Delaware; and by a "lease," it had agreed to rent such stock and equipment from its subsidiary, the rent (corresponding to the installments payable under the certificates) being payable as to principal in Philadelphia, and as to interest in New York. At or about the same time, the subsidiary company had assigned its rights under the lease to the trustee, a Pennsylvania corporation.

A provision of the lease stipulated that the parties intended to execute the lease in accordance with the laws of Cuba "to the end" that the lease might be registered in that country. Provision was also made for submission to the jurisdiction of the Cuban courts.[76] The assignment between the subsidiary company and the trustee contained

---

[74] See Chapter VI text and notes 77 to 88.

[75] [1960] 2 All E.R. 332. See also [1957] 3 All E.R. 641 and [1959] 1 All E.R. 214, and comments in 9 Int'l & Comp. L. Q. 700 (1960) ; and 21 Modern L. Rev. 174 (1958) .

[76] These stipulations read as follows:

"Eleventh.—It is the intention of the parties to this lease to enter into and execute this lease in accordance with the provisions of the laws of the Republic of Cuba to the end that this lease may be deposited or filed and/or registered thereunder, and the railway company agrees to so deposit and/or register or file the same, and to record the same in such State or Territories of the United States as may be required by law, and to perform any other act required by law that may be necessary to protect the trustee's title. In case it becomes necessary that this lease be translated into the Spanish language in order that it may be filed and/or registered in the proper offices in the Republic of Cuba, then and in that event it is understood and agreed that the English text shall govern in case of any conflict between the English and Spanish texts.

"Twelfth.—The parties hereto submit themselves to the jurisdiction of the tribunals of the City of Havana, in the Republic of Cuba, for all notifications, summonses and other judicial or extra judicial formalities to which this lease shall give rise, with express renunciation of their own jurisdiction if different."

substantially similar provisions. The trust certificates themselves contained no stipulation of applicable law.

One of the questions in issue was whether the stipulations in the lease were intended only to cover matters affecting the security or whether they should be deemed determinative also in the selection of the proper law of the loan. All the judges who heard the case, with one exception, favored the first alternative which, both from the wording of the stipulations and the circumstances surrounding the overall financial transaction, was clearly the correct solution.[77]

---

[77] Unfortunately, the courts have not always been successful in making the proper distinction between the area of application of the proper law and that of the *lex rei sitae*. Thus, the case of Société Administratie Kantoor de Mas [or Maas] v. Syndic Société des Etablissements Ravel [or Bez] (Cass. May 24, 1933, S. 1935.1.258; Rev. 1934, 142), involved a loan contract between a Dutch and a French corporation, which contained a stipulation that German law, the *lex loci contractus*, would govern. The loan was secured by a "pledge" (a chattel mortgage equivalent) of property located in France, and it was agreed that the lender could forfeit the security if the borrower defaulted. Despite the reference to German law, it was held that the clause regarding forfeiture was governed by the French law of the situs, under which the clause was invalid.

In Montreal Trust Co. et al. v. Stanrock Uranium Mines Ltd., 53 D.L.R. 2d 594 (1965), it was held that the law of Ontario was the proper law of bonds sold for the most part in New York by an Ontario mining company and secured by a mortgage and a floating charge on the borrower's assets in Ontario. This decision, in its search for the "center of gravity" of the loan transaction, would seem to place somewhat excessive weight on the *lex situs*. In addition to other factors connecting the loan with Ontario, which are noted in the judgment, it is also noteworthy that the indenture contained the following provision:

"Section 20.09. This Indenture and the Bonds and coupons issued pursuant hereto shall, to the extent permitted by law, be construed under the laws of the Province of Ontario; provided, however, that with respect to the exercise, performance or discharge by the American Trustee within the United States of America of any of its rights, powers, duties or responsibilities hereunder, the provisions of this Indenture and of the Bonds and coupons issued hereunder shall, to the extent permitted by law, be construed in accordance with the laws of the State of New York and the laws of the United States of America applicable therein, except that the foregoing proviso shall not be applicable to any proceedings which may be brought or instituted by or on behalf of the Trustees, or either of them, in Canada for the enforcement of any rights or remedies hereunder."

The reference to the law of Ontario in the first sentence of this provision is perhaps not as specific as it should, especially in view of the restrictive language used in that sentence. It would seem, however, that, as a factor evidencing the parties' intention regarding the law applicable to the loan, this provision should have been the object of close attention. It is surprising to note that, in the determination of the proper law, no consideration appears to have been given to this stipulation.

This case is interesting also in another respect. In 1953, the borrowing company, then in default, sold its entire undertaking and assets in Cuba to the Cuban Government. As part of the transaction, the Government agreed to release the borrower from all responsibility in respect of certain liabilities, including those arising under the certificates. Subsequently, the borrower went into voluntary liquidation in England. In a dispute between the trustee and the liquidators, the liquidators argued that the transfer of the borrower's assets to the Cuban Government constituted a compulsory novation; and that, by analogy with the solution obtaining in regard to compulsory transfers of contractual rights,[78] the novation should be governed by the *lex situs* of the debt, i.e. in this instance the law of Cuba. The analogy between these two situations was rejected on the ground that novation, unlike a transfer of contractual rights, involves no transfer of property but rather implies that one debt is extinguished and another created; therefore its effect, at least insofar as the extinction of the original debt is concerned, must be governed by the proper law of that debt, which in this case was the law of Pennsylvania.

That the *lex situs* and the proper law of the loan may coincide is not, of course, impossible. Such was the case in *Re Helbert Wagg & Co., Ltd.*[79] in which German law, applied by the court as the proper law of a loan made by English lenders to a German corporation, was also applicable as the *lex situs* of the related security. In this connection, the case of *Chalmers v. Nederlandsch Amerikaansche Stoomvaart Maatschappij*[80] is worth mentioning also. The borrower, a Dutch corporation, had issued bonds in the Netherlands, of which some were sold to Dutch bankers and some to a New York banking firm for resale and distribution in the United States market. The bonds, which referred to a trust indenture between the borrower and a Dutch trustee for a full statement of the terms and conditions of the loan, were payable at the option of the holder in the Netherlands or at the office of the New York fiscal agent. In 1931, an association of bondholders was created in the Netherlands. Two years later, the association approved, by a majority vote taken in conformity with the provisions of the indenture, a scheme of reorganization subsequently

---

[78] See e.g., Arab Bank Ltd. v. Barclays Bank (Dominion, Colonial & Overseas) [1954] 2 All E.R. 226.

Comp. Federal Supreme Court of Germany February 18, 1957, Assignment of Debt (Eastern Sector of Berlin) Case, Int'l L. Rep. (Year 1957), p. 28; and July 11, 1957, Assignment of Confiscated Debt (Germany) Case, Ibid, p. 31.

[79] [1956] 1 All E.R. 129. See also supra text and notes 16-17.

[80] 36 N.Y.S. 2d 717 (1942).

carried out by the debtor corporation. In an action brought by a dissenting American bondholder, it was held that Dutch law governed and that all the bondholders were bound by the decision of the majority. In view of the congregation of factors connecting the transaction with the Dutch legal system, the outcome of the conflicts issue was hardly questionable. It is surprising, therefore, that the court felt compelled to base its decision on the so-called "principle" that the relations between bondholders and a borrowing corporation "must be regulated and controlled by the law of the jurisdiction in which the corporation is organized," in the absence of an express provision to the contrary.[81] This presumption, which has been challenged in the limited sector of the conflict of laws in which it has been formulated, (i.e. foreign compositions with creditors)[82] would be entirely unacceptable as a general rule of the conflict of laws. It is generally recognized that a corporation's internal affairs are governed by its personal law, i.e., by the law of its plan of incorporation or by that of its *siège social*. But it does not follow at all that the same law should be presumed to apply to the relations between a corporation and third parties.[83] In the particular case of loans, which are normally negotiated and performed outside the borrower's country, the alleged presumption would be completely unrealistic and contrary to the relevant judicial decisions as well as all the evidence which can be found in loan documents. Such a presumption would be even more objectionable than that which, in the case of governmental borrowing, has sometimes been invoked in favor of the law of the debtor government.[84]

B. LOANS CONCLUDED BY INTERNATIONAL PERSONS

1. *The Traditional Approach*

Traditionally, a distinction is made between loans involving international persons only and loans between international and private persons.

---

[81] Ibid. at p. 725.

[82] Canada Southern Ry. Co. v. Gebhard, 109 U.S. 527, 3 S. Ct. 363, 27 L. Ed. 1020 (1883). For a discussion of this and other cases, see Nadelmann, "Compositions—Reorganizations and Arrangements—in the Conflict of Laws", 61 Harv. L. Rev. 804 (1948) particularly at p. 833.

[83] See generally, Reese and Kaufman, "The Law Governing Corporate Affairs: Choice of Law and the Impact of Full Faith and Credit", 58 Col. L. Rev. 1118 (1958).

[84] See e.g., Adams v. National Bank of Greece and Athens [1960] 2 All E.R. 421. See also text and notes 180 to 182 infra.

Loans between international persons are normally governed by international law. This rule applies to intergovernment loans or credit arrangements,[85] government loans to international organizations (such as the United States Government loan to the ECSC,[86] or the Swiss Government loans to the IBRD);[87] and international organization loans to governments (such as those between the IMF and its members,[88] or those between the United Nations Development Programme/Special Fund and recipient governments).[89]

International persons sometimes specify municipal law as the law applicable, in toto or in part, to a loan transaction between them.

---

[85] See e.g., Mann, "Reflections on a Commercial Law of Nations", 33 B.Y.B.I.L. 20 (1957), at pp. 26-27; Jenks, op. cit., note 4 supra, p. 186; Boguslavski, "Legal Aspects of the Soviet Technical Aid Programme for Economically Under-Developed Countries", 8 Review of Contemporary Law (1961) 41, at p. 44.

[86] September 17, 1956, 340 UNTS 312. The view has been advanced that the Loan would be subject to "American" law (see Blondeel and Vander Eycken, op. cit., note 27 supra at pp. 273-4). It would seem that the better view is that the loan is governed by international law. See Mann, "The Proper Law", pp. 39-40; X......, "La Personnalité Juridique de la Communauté Européenne du Charbon et de l'Acier dans les Relations Internationales", *Annuaire Français de Droit International* 1959, 714, at pp. 722-3. De Soto, *Les Relations Internationales de la Communauté Européenne du Charbon et de l'Acier,* 90 Recueil des Cours, 29 (1956), at p. 59.

Sereni, op. cit., note 5 supra, is mistaken when he states that the loan is governed "by national law, although it was pre-arranged through an international agreement" (p. 162). This statement is based on the erroneous assumption that the Export-Import Bank acted on its own account rather than as agent for the United States Government. The agency relationship is clearly stated in Article I of the Loan Agreement.

See also, the United States Government loan to the United Nations for the construction of the headquarters building, March 23, 1948, 19 UNTS 43. Comp., the French Government Loan to UNESCO for the same purpose, analyzed by *Salmon,* pp. 114-120, 313-317.

[87] A first loan was made on September 17, 1956 (340 UNTS 312); see *Broches,* pp. 383-384. A second loan was made on October 23, 1961 (415 UNTS 395).

[88] Economically, these transactions are equivalent to short-term loans. Legally, however, they partake more of the nature of an exchange transaction than a loan. See Mann, *Money in Public International Law,* 96 Recueil des Cours, 7 (1959), pp. 23-25; see also, Tew, *The International Monetary Fund: its Present Role and Future Prospects,* Essays in International Finance, Princeton University No. 36, March 1961, pp. 16-17. Fawcett, "The Place of Law in an International Organization", 36 B.Y.B.I.L. 321 (1960) at pp. 339-340. Gold, "The Law and Practice of the International Monetary Fund with Respect to 'Stand-by Arrangements' ", 12 Int'l & Comp. L.Q. 1 (1963) at p. 2.

[89] See e.g., Agreement dated October 6, 1959, between the Fund and Iran, 342 UNTS 89; Agreement dated October 15, 1959, between the Fund and the Polish People's Republic, 344 UNTS 29.

Submission to domestic law occurs from time to time with respect to such matters as interpretation,[90] formalities,[91] performance[92] or the creation and enforcement of securities.[93] Such submission is not to be presumed, however. The mere use, in international loans and financial agreements, of terms like "tender," "gold value," "place of payment," or "trustee," which have technical meanings in domestic law, should not raise any presumption that domestic law is applicable. It is true that, in the present status of international law, the exact content of such terms may have to be ascertained by way of a comparative analysis of domestic legal systems. However, when the process of comparison is ended, the definition arrived at acquires an independent meaning which, like the agreement to which it applies, is effectively "international" in character.[94]

Domestic law, of course, is the law normally applicable to loans between private and international persons. Since governments do not usually lend to private foreign borrowers, and international organizations currently solve the issue of applicable law by express stipulation, the case which remains for discussion concerns loans between private lenders and international borrowers.

Since the various connecting factors noted above with respect to private loans are usually present also in this type of transactions, it would seem reasonable to apply the same general rule in both cases,

---

[90] See supra text and notes 37 to 44.

[91] See infra text and note 194.

[92] A provision of this type is found in the IBRD Loan Regulations. The IBRD, whose loans often involve repayment in several currencies and in several countries, incorporates in its loan agreements a special provision on exchange restrictions reading as follows:

"*Exchange restrictions.* Any payment required under the Loan Agreement to be made to the Bank in the currency of any country shall be made in such manner, and in the currency acquired in such manner, as shall be permitted under the laws of such country for the purpose of making such payment and effecting the deposit of such currency to the account of the Bank with a depository of the Bank in such country."

Comp., Agreement dated April 9, 1956, between Canada and France (Art. 8) 43 UNTS 43; Agreement dated May 13, 1959, between Japan and Viet-Nam (Art. 3, para. 3) 373 UNTS 149. See also the Loan Agreement dated March 30/April 15, 1957, between the Swiss Confederation and the ILO (40 ILO Official Bulletin 352 (1957) Article 3).

[93] See infra text and notes 205 to 212.

[94] See in particular the definition of "place of payment" in the decision of the Mixed Commission for the Agreement on German External Debts, November 7, 1956, in the case of Bodenkreditbank in Basel and the Swiss Confederation v. Gebrüder Rohrer GmbH. and the German Federal Republic, 25 Int'l L. Reports (year 1958 (I) p. 326). See also, Mann, "The Proper Law", at pp. 36-37.

i.e. make the loan agreement subject either to the law of the lenders' country or to that of the market of issue. Although no recent case involving direct loans seem to have been reported,[95] judicial decisions concerning publicly issued loans indicate that this expectation is justified.[96]

It should be noted that a different solution has been advocated in the case of privately financed governmental loans. It has been held that, failing any stipulation of applicable law in the loan contract or bonds, the parties should be presumed to have contracted under the law of the borrowing government. This presumption, which received its most publicized formulation in the *Serbian and Brazilian Loans Cases*,[97] has been relied upon also by some domestic courts. However, it is significant that in each of the domestic court decisions there were

---

[95] It seems fair to assume that this absence of judicial decision is due to the fact that most loan contracts between private lenders and foreign governments contain express stipulations of applicable law. See text and note 23 supra. Another possible explanation is that, should a dispute arise out of such transactions, the parties are likely to seek some sort of amicable settlement rather than resort to litigation.

The Italian case of Minister of Finance of Republic of France v. Italian Discount Bank in Liquidation (Cass. Ital. February 4, 1932, Rivista Italiana di Diritto Internazionale 1933, 386; summarized in Clunet 1933, 455, Annual Digest 1931-32, p. 36), which concerned a paying agency agreement between an Italian bank and the French Government in connection with a French bond issue in Italy, is in accord with the view stated in the text above.

Not much weight can be attached today to the old decision of a lower French court (Trib. Civ. Seine March 3, 1875, Etat Ottoman v. Comptoir d'Escompte, S. 1877.2.25), which held that a loan by French bankers to the Turkish government was governed by Turkish law. The view now prevails in France that state contracts are not necessarily governed by the law of the obligor government. See Cass. May 31, 1932, Carathéodory v. Etat Français (involving a contract of lease), Clunet 1933, 347.

[96] See text and notes 101, 102 infra.

[97] PCIJ, Series A, Nos. 21 and 22. Said the Court:

"The Loans in question are loans contracted by the State of Serbia [Brazil] under special laws which laid down the conditions relating to them. These laws are cited in the bonds; and it appears that the validity of the obligations set out in the said bonds is indisputable in Serbian law. The bonds are *bearer bonds* signed at Belgrade by representatives of the Serbian Government. *It follows from the very nature of bearer bonds* that, in respect of all holders, the substance of the debt is necessarily the same and that the identity of the holder and the place where he obtained it are without relevancy. *Only the individuality of the borrower is fixed: in this case it is a sovereign state which cannot be presumed to have made the substance of its debt and the validity of the obligations accepted by it in respect thereof, subject to any law other than its own.*" (Series A, No. 20, p. 42. See also No. 21, p. 121) (underlining added).

The reference in these judgments to the particular nature of bearer bonds and the need to achieve uniformity in the relations between the bondholders and the borrower, is also found in other cases involving government

other considerations supporting the application of the law of the
debtor government, such as the fact that this law coincided with the
lex loci contractus or the *lex loci solutionis*,[98] or the monetary system
presumptively intended by the parties,[99] or the law governing the
principal contract guaranteed by the debtor government.[100]

Most national tribunals have refused to follow the *Serbian and
Brazilian Loan Cases*. In several cases arising during the thirties, the
laws of places of issue were held applicable by national courts on the
basis of the same considerations which would be given weight in cases
of loans to private borrowers. For example, in the leading British
case, *Rex v. International Trustee for the Protection of Bondholders
A.G.*, the House of Lords held that dollar bonds issued in New York
by the British Government were subject to the American Joint Resolution of June 5, 1933, and that the gold clause in the bonds was,
therefore, unenforceable.[101] The same solution was reached by the
courts of a number of other countries.[102]

It is believed that this solution reflects the expectations of international lenders and borrowing governments. The omission of con-

---

bonds, although in such other cases it led courts to apply the law of the
market, rather than that of the debtor government. See e.g., Supreme Court
of Austria November 26, 1935 and July 10, 1936, Austrian Government Guaranteed Loans Cases, Rev. 1936, 717 and Clunet 1937, 334; Supreme Court of
Sweden January 30, 1937, Skandia v. National Debt Office, 36 B.I.J.I. 327
(1937).

[98] Hartman v. United States, 65 F. Supp. 397 (Ct. Cl. 1946).

[99] Bonython v. The Commonwealth of Australia [1951] A.C. 201; but see
National Mutual Life Association of Australasia Ltd. v. Attorney General for
New Zealand [1956] 1 All E.R. 721. See also Mann, "Free of Exchange", 19
Modern L. Rev. 424 (1956).

[100] Paris May 16, 1951, Trésor Public et Société Royal Bank of Canada v.
Schumann, J.C.P. 1952, II, 6887, Clunet 1952, 1228, affirmed on other grounds,
Cass. January 24, 1956, J.C.P. 1956, II, 9400; D. 1956, 317; Clunet 1956, 1012;
Paris June 2, 1959, Trésor Public v. Veuve Hermann, Gaz. Pal. 1959, II, 170,
affirmed Cass. October 29, 1964, Etat Français v. Veuve Hermann, Clunet 1965,
637.

Comp., Conseil d'Etat November 28, 1958, Langlois et Rolland de Chambaudoin d'Erceville, Clunet 1960, 444; Rev. 1959, 117; J.C.P. 1959, II, 10986;
D. 1959, 361.

[101] [1937] A.C. 500.

[102] See e.g., Supreme Court of Austria November 26, 1935 and July 10,
1936, note 97 supra; Supreme Court of Sweden January 30, 1937, note 97
supra; Supreme Court of Denmark January 30, 1939, Vereeniging voor den
Effectenhandel v. Ministère des Finances, 13 Zeit. fur Ausl. und Int. Privat.
825 (1942); Clunet 1954, 490; 40 B.I.J.I. 284 (1939); Supreme Court of
Norway December 8, 1937, Insurance Companies Minerva and Viking and
Stavanger Saving Bank v. The Norwegian Government, Clunet 1938, 935;
38 B.I.J.I. 71 (1938); Helsingfors City Court December 23, 1937, Amsterdam
Stock Exchange Committee v. Government of Finland, 38 B.I.J.I. 280 (1938).

flict-of-laws provisions from bonds issued by foreign governments is most frequently due to considerations of prestige rather than substance. A provision specifying that the applicable law is that of the lenders or the market is more likely to be acceptable to a borrowing government if the loan documents will receive limited distribution, as in the case of a direct loan; and less likely to be acceptable if such documents are subject to the widest publicity, as in the case of bonds. To infer from this that governmental bonds should be governed by the law of the borrower, in the absence of express agreement to the contrary, would be to place undue weight upon the governmental charter of the borrower, and attribute to the parties an intention which, in most cases, they did not have. Aside from considerations of prestige, there is little difference between the situation of a borrowing government and that of any other borrower, and it is somewhat difficult to see why financial transactions which are basically the same, and in which the connecting factors are substantially identical, should be subject to different rules of conflict of laws. Although a decision of the PCIJ is not to be disregarded, over three decades have now passed since the PCIJ judgments were rendered, and it is questionable how much weight still attaches to them. It is not inconceivable that, should the issue now be brought before the ICJ, the judges of the new Court would be impressed by the number and authority of the decisions contrary to the PCIJ judgments, and reach the same solution which prevailed in those decisions.[103]

At any rate, it is clear that the presumption is inapplicable to bonds issued by borrowers other than governments and, in particular, to bonds issued by international organizations. Such bonds are governed by the ordinary rules of the conflict of laws and will, in most

---

[103] The issue may be brought before the Court if the Norwegian-French dispute (which was dismissed on jurisdictional grounds in the Case of Certain Norwegian Loans (I.C.J. Reports 1957, p. 9)) is again submitted *au fond* for decision. In the reported Case, Judge Lauterpacht pointed out the unsettled status of the law in this field, but was inclined to consider that the law of Norway was the proper law of the loan (Reports 1957, at p. 40 and p. 36), a view which was shared by Judge Badawi (Reports 1957, at p. 30).

Another case raising the same issue (Association Nationale des Porteurs Français de Valeurs Mobilières v. The Norwegian Government, the Mortgage Bank of Norway and the Small Holding and Workers' Housing Bank), after argument before the lower Norwegian courts, was settled by the parties' admission that Norwegian law was applicable. See the judgment of the Supreme Court of Norway May 2, 1962, as summarized by Bahr, "The Norwegian Gold Clause Case", 12 Am. J. Comp. L. 1 (1963), at pp. 6-7; and Hambro, "L'Affaire des Emprunts Norvégiens devant les Juridictions de Norvège", Clunet 1965, 613.

cases, be subject to the law of the market even in the absence of a specific bond provision to that effect.

2. *The "Internationalization" of Loans between Private and International Persons*

With increasing frequency in recent years, the question has been raised, whether the presumption in favor of domestic law in the case of loan agreements between private and international persons should be abandoned, in all or in specific respects, so as to subject the transaction to international law.[104] Current legal thinking seems to favor the view that an international person must have the authority to contract under its own system of law rather than under the system of law of the private contracting party. Should the judge, therefore, in the absence of express statement of intention, be free to apply international law to the transaction? Or is this a case in which the choice between two systems of law is a process so substantially different from that which characterizes the daily administration of the conflict of laws, that the judge or the arbitrator should be denied his usual authority to select the applicable law? It is submitted that the difference, if any, is one of degree rather than substance. In an era in which the traditional distinction between domestic and international law is subject to considerable erosion, there can be little reason why judges should not be free to select either system as the proper law. If circumstances are such as to make it "impossible to assume that the parties intended to be governed by a national system of law",[105] courts should be authorized to adjudicate the issue on the basis of international law.

This situation is unlikely to arise frequently in the case of international loans, due to the practice of lenders to settle in advance the

---

[104] This idea is not entirely new. One of its early manifestations is found in the case of Etat Ottoman v. Comptoir d'Escompte (Trib. Civ. Seine March 3, 1875, S. 1877.2.25). As security for a loan, the borrowing government had pledged certain securities with French bankers and agreed that the security would be forfeited in the event of a default. Under French law, the forfeiture clause was invalid; it was apparently valid under Turkish law. The Court reached the unoriginal conclusion that the latter law was applicable, as the law of the debtor government. The court nevertheless remarked that if a state contracting with a foreign private person wished to avoid subjecting the contract to its law or to that of the private party, it might specify ". . . par la convention une loi particulière destinée spécialement à régir le contrat".

[105] Mann, "State Contracts", p. 21. See also Jessup, op. cit., note 5 supra, pp. 102-103; Jenks, op. cit., note 4 supra, pp. 150-151. The statement in Bowett, op. cit., note 4 supra, p. 299, note 15, that this writer's opinion is "contrary" to Dr. Mann's on this point, is incorrect.

issue of applicable law. Yet there are cases in which the difficulty is real and the proper determination far from easy. The Young Loan was one of these cases,[106] and another example is that of the "Act of Pledge" of November 28, 1954 between the High Authority of the ECSC and the Bank for International Settlements (BIS).[107] This instrument, which contains no stipulation of applicable law, is intended to secure the rights of present and future creditors of the High Authority, by a pledge of (a) the monetary claims for loans made by the High Authority to enterprises of the Community out of the proceeds of the High Authority's own borrowings, and (b) the notes constituting or evidencing such claims. The Act and Indentures supplemental thereto were executed in Luxembourg, where the seat of the Authority is located. The central place of business of the BIS is in Switzerland. One of the creditors, the first to make a loan to the Authority, is the United States Government; all other creditors are private investors in member countries of the Community, Switzerland and the United States. The Act is drafted in English and makes extensive use of American legal phraseology.

Although every commentator agrees that the Act, to achieve its purpose, must be governed by one and the same law as regards all creditors, they disagree on the selection of the proper law. Some writers suggest that "American" law should govern, thereby treating the Act of Pledge as an accessory to the first loan to the High Authority, which was made by the United States.[108] This view, whatever its somewhat doubtful original merits, is outdated because the security created by the Act now benefits also many private lenders in countries outside the United States. Other writers consider that Swiss law should be the applicable law, since the BIS, which is the basic pivot of all the relationships arising under the Act, is incorporated and operates in Switzerland.[109]

To avoid these controversies, Dr. Mann has submitted that "no solution other than the application of public international law would appear to be reasonable and practicable."[110] This is an interesting sug-

[106] Mann, op. cit., preceding note, id. loc. See T. F. May 26, 1936, Aktiebolaget Obligationinteressenter v. The Bank for International Settlements, R.O.62, II, 140. All the decisions, including those of the lower courts in this case have been reproduced in *League of Nations*, Doc. I.L. 18, Geneva, February 11, 1937.

[107] 238 UNTS 340.

[108] Blondeel and Vander Eycken, op. cit., note 27 supra, p. 274.

[109] *Salmon*, p. 293; Sereni, op. cit., note 5 supra, p. 163.

[110] Mann, "The Proper Law", p. 54.

gestion which makes due allowance for the international complex resulting from the Act of Pledge and the diversified borrowings of the High Authority. Yet a word of caution appears necessary since this solution, however appealing, may not correspond entirely to the parties' intention. In this connection, the cautious wording of applicable-law provisions in recent loans raised by the High Authority in various private markets may not be without significance. Thus, the prospectus of the $5\frac{3}{8}\%$ Secured Bonds (Thirteenth Series) of 1960, issued by the High Authority in the United States, provides that the Indenture and the Bonds:

> "shall be governed by the laws of the State of New York, except that any question with respect to the interpretation or application of the Act of Pledge hereinafter mentioned, or with respect to the security afforded thereby, shall be determined in accordance with the law which would otherwise be appropriate for such determination."[111]

This provision, although not conclusive, possibly implies that domestic, rather than international, law is the law contemplated by the parties, and that in the determination of the "proper law" the ordinary rules of the conflict of laws would be relevant. This last remark is, of course, tentative and has no purpose other than to show the complexity of the problem and the many factors a court would have to consider, should a judicial determination be required.

Bonds recently issued in the United States by the Republic of Panama raise an interesting problem, albeit a simpler one than that created by the Act of Pledge. The bonds, which contain no stipulation of applicable law, are payable in United States dollars at the New York Head Office of the First National City Bank of New York, the Fiscal Agent. The bonds are secured by an assignment of monies receivable by Panama from the United States pursuant to Treaty arrangements between the two countries. The terms of the security are set forth in specific provisions of the Fiscal Agency Contract, an agreement which provides that it shall be "construed" in accordance with the laws of New York. Pursuant to letters exchanged by the two

---

[111] Prospectus, p. 26. See also, the following provision in the prospectus relating to the High Authority $4\frac{1}{4}\%$ Loan of 1956 issued in Switzerland:

> "Le présent emprunt est régi par le droit suisse, sauf en ce qui concerne l'interprétation et l'application du Contrat de Nantissement qui reste soumis au droit qui lui est propre." (p. 4)

According to Zimmer, op. cit., note 4 supra, the absence of a stipulation of applicable law in the Act of Pledge was intentional. See pp. 270-271.

governments, which contain express reference to the Fiscal Agency Contract, the United States Government has agreed to pay annually to the Fiscal Agent a stated amount of the sums due under the Treaty. There is no doubt that the Treaty is governed by international law and that neither Panama nor the United States could alter its provisions by unilateral action so as to reduce the value of the security.[112] However it would seem, especially in view of the express reference to the Fiscal Agency Contract in the United States' undertaking, that domestic law (presumably the law of New York) is the applicable law as between the bondholder assignees and the United States.[113]

This last example illustrates the legal problems which arise when an international person's rights under an agreement with another international person are assigned to private persons. Financial agreements or loans between governments, or between international organizations and governments, not infrequently contemplate that the rights and obligations arising thereunder may be assigned or transferred, in toto or in part, to private persons. Should international law, applicable to the original transaction, continue to govern the post-transfer relationship or should the latter be governed by domestic law?

In most instances the loan or financial agreement is limited to authorizing the transfer,[114] for example by authorizing the creditor

---

[112] An issue of this kind arose in 1934. Pursuant to Article XIV of the Panama Canal Convention of 1903, it was agreed that the United States would pay to Panama: "the sum of ten million dollars in gold coin of the United States . . . and also an annual payment during the life of [the] Convention of two hundred and fifty thousand dollars in like gold coin . . ." After the devaluation of the American dollar and the abrogation of gold clauses in 1933, the United States tendered payment in depreciated dollars. Panama refused to accept this payment and demanded that payment be made on a gold basis. The matter was finally settled by a new treaty which increased the balboa amount of the annuities payable by the United States. Simultaneously the gold content of the balboa was reduced to that of the devalued U.S. dollar. See *Broches,* pp. 346-350. See also, Hackworth, 5 *Digest of International Law,* p. 630. The treaty of January 25, 1955 (243 UNTS 211) increased the amount of the anuities from $430,000 to $1,930,000.

[113] See Prospectus of the Republic of Panama 4.80% External Secured Bonds of 1958, containing as Appendix I the Fiscal Agency Contract, together with the form of bonds and the letters exchanged by the Panamanian and the United States Government.

The view expressed in the text is supported by the arguments exchanged by the representatives of Panama and, somewhat less clearly, by the United States representatives, in connection with the controversy between the two governments regarding the payment of the Canal annuity in devalued dollars. See *Foreign Relations of the United States* 1934, vol. V, pp. 612-623.

[114] Such is not always the case. Thus, the Agreement Concerning Polish Reconstruction Debts of March 14, 1935 (Hudson, 7 *International Legislation*

country to assign or otherwise transfer bonds or notes issued by the debtor. A concrete example, which has been extensively used by Dr. Mann,[115] is that of funding agreements entered into after the First World War which provided for the issuance of bonds by debtor governments which could be exchanged for marketable obligations at the creditor government's request. Some of the forms of bonds to be issued to the creditor governments state merely that the bonds are issued "pursuant to the agreement";[116] some other forms contain the additional statement that the bonds are "subject" to the agreement "to which reference is made for a further statement of [the] terms and conditions" of the bonds.[117]

Dr. Mann, noting that the different wording of these provisions, "presumably was intentional",[118] suggests that bonds in the first category, once assigned to private persons, would have been governed by domestic law; whereas bonds in the second class, i.e. bonds "subject" to the original agreement, would have remained governed, like the agreement itself, by international law.

The merits of this distinction are questionable. Indeed, the wording discrepancies noted by Dr. Mann in respect of bonds occur also in the provisions of the funding agreements regarding the execution

---

(1941), p. 39), providing for Poland's issuance of bonds to creditor countries, stipulated that the bonds would remain in the creditors' possession up to the date of their maturity (Article 5). Other agreements are silent on the subject of the assignability of bonds issued thereunder, thereby probably excluding any assignment (see e.g., Financial Agreement dated April 9, 1946, between Canada and France, Articles 6 and 9, 43 UNTS 43). On other occasions, assignments are subject to various restrictions and conditions. See, e.g., the Agreement of February 25, 1957, between the United Kingdom and the Export-Import Bank (Cmnd. 104), Article IV, Section 3:

"Eximbank agrees not to negotiate or transfer any note or notes issued hereunder nor to dispose of any participation in any of said notes unless the United Kingdom consents in writing to such transfer or participations."

See also, the Loan Agreement dated September 7, 1949, between Belgium and France, Articles 5 and 6 (123 UNTS 14); Loan Agreement dated September 7, 1949, between the United Kingdom and Belgium, Articles 5 and 6 (106 UNTS 61). See also, Mann, "The Assignability of Treaty Rights", 30 B.Y.B.I.L. 475 (1953).

[115] Mann, "State Contracts", pp. 28-31; "The Proper Law", pp. 56-57.

[116] See e.g., the Government of the United Kingdom 62 Year 3-3½% Gold Bond quoted by Mann, "State Contracts", pp. 28-29; The Roumanian Bond issued to the British Government, ibid., p. 30.

[117] See e.g., The Finnish Bond issued to the United States Government, Ibid., p. 29; The French Bond issued to the United States Government, reproduced in Petit, Le Règlement des Dettes Interalliées (1919-22) (1932), p. 676.

[118] Mann, "State Contracts", p. 31.

of the marketable obligations for which the bonds could be exchanged, but the latter discrepancies do not support his opinion. Thus, while certain agreements provide that such obligations shall conform to the bonds "in all respects,"[119] other agreements limit the conformity of the bonds and obligations to the most essential provisions and leave room for different or additional stipulations in the obligations (which might well have been stipulations of applicable law if they made the obligations more "suitable for sale to the public").[120] The curious thing, however, is that the latter provisions occur in those agreements in which the form of bonds is made expressly "subject" to the terms of the agreement, a kind of bond which, according to Dr. Mann, would retain an international character even after being assigned to private persons. The former type of provision, paradoxically enough, is found in agreements relating to bonds which, not being expressly "subject" to the terms of the agreement, would allegedly be governed by domestic law, once in the hands of private holders. It would seem, therefore, that these discrepancies represent no more than mere drafting variations with which all lawyers, particularly in the international field, are familiar.

Under the circumstances, it is believed that bonds held by private persons would have been governed by domestic law.[121] Dr. Mann is perfectly right, of course, in pointing out that this solution leaves undetermined the question of the applicable domestic law. This is, however, an altogether different problem, which might have been settled at the time of execution of the marketable obligations (at least to the extent that the form of such obligations could differ from that of the original bonds), or resolved under the relevant rules of conflict of laws.

In this connection, reference should be made to the practice of the IBRD regarding sales from its loan portfolio. The IBRD frequently transfers to private investors portions of loans made by it.

---

[119] See e.g., the Agreement dated October 19, 1925, between Roumania and the British Government, Article 5, 123 State Papers (1926), Part I, p. 562. On the other hand, the Agreement dated June 18, 1923, between Great Britain and the United States relating to the bonds referred to in note 116 supra, (reprinted in Fischer Williams, *Chapters on Current International Law and the League of Nations* (1929), pp. 361-370, Article 9), conforms to the text of the Agreement between France and the United States referred to in the following note.

[120] See e.g., the Agreement dated April 29, 1926, between France and the United States, Article 7, reprinted, in Petit, op. cit. note 117 supra, at pp. 671, 674-5.

[121] See also, Sereni, op. cit., note 5 supra, p. 164.

Such transfers may be accomplished through different techniques. Sometimes the transfer takes the form of an agreement between the IBRD and the investor, under which the IBRD undertakes to pay to the investor the principal and all or part of the interest and other charges which it receives on the account of the portion of the loan "sold" to the investor. Such an agreement typically contains a provision to the effect that all matters relating to the administration and enforcement of the loan shall be administered solely by the IBRD, thereby making it clear that there is no privity of contract between the investor and the borrower and/or guarantor; and that the contractual relationship created by the agreement is one solely between the IBRD and the participant. Under this arrangement, it can be argued that no issue of applicable law can arise, except as between the IBRD and the participant.

A different situation is presented when the IBRD requests a borrowing government to issue bonds in representation of the loan, which are sold to private investors.[122] Such bonds establish a number of rights and obligations, like those regarding payment of principal and interest, exemption from taxation or exchange restrictions, which exist directly between the borrowing government and the bondholders. The bonds state that they are issued under the loan agreement between the borrower and the IBRD, and that:

> "No reference herein to the Loan Agreement shall confer upon the holder hereof any rights thereunder . . . ."

This stipulation is the counterpart of a provision of the Loan Regulations which provides that:

> "No holder (other than the Bank) of any Bond shall, by virtue of being the holder thereof, be entitled to exercise any rights under the Loan Agreement or be subject to any of the conditions or obligations imposed upon the Bank thereby. The provisions of this Section shall not impair or affect any rights or obligations under the terms of any Bond." (Section 6.17)

These provisions make clear that, as a consequence of the sale of bonds, there is not only a legal relationship between the borrower and the IBRD under the Loan Agreement but likewise a legal relationship between the borrower and the bondholders. This latter relationship is governed by domestic law.[123] So far, no attempt has

---

[122] See *Broches,* pp. 359-362.
[123] Ibid., at pp. 361-362. See also, *Salmon,* p. 232.

been made to stipulate in the bonds the particular law applicable thereto, and the determination of the proper law may not be free from difficulty.[124] It is not inconceivable, however, that the occasion may arise which would make it desirable to include an express stipulation in the bonds of the applicable law.

Notes issued to the AID by its borrowers are substantially similar to the bonds issued to the IBRD; the AID, however, has thought it appropriate to solve the conflict-of-laws issue by providing that these Notes, like the Loan Agreement under which they may be issued, shall be governed by the law of the District of Columbia.

III. THE SPECIAL CASE OF GUARANTEED LOANS

What law governs contracts of suretyship or guarantee is still the subject of controversy. Even in the simplest case of private loans, there is considerable difference of opinion as to whether the guarantee should be governed by its proper law or by the law applicable to the principal debt.[125] Cases in leading countries are about equally divided between the first[126] and the second[127] alternatives. Similar variations,

---

[124] *Broches* (pp. 361-362) lists the following relevant elements:
"The loan and guarantee agreements under which the bonds are issued are generally signed in Washington; the bonds may be executed and delivered in Washington, in the borrowing country or in the country in which they are payable; and the bonds (or the guarantees thereon) are obligations of sovereign governments. Moreover, the Bank frequently disburse more than one currency under a loan. Since the borrower must repay the loan in whatever currencies are loaned, most of the Bank's loans are repayable in more than one currency; that is to say, different portions of the loan are repayable in different currencies. And the same is true of the bonds which the Bank is entitled to receive. Furthermore, the several bonds issued under a loan agreement with the Bank are payable in the several countries in whose currencies they are payable. The points of contact with different jurisdictions are therefore likely to be more numerous than in the usual kind of international financial transactions, which normally involve only two jurisdictions, those of the lender and the borrower. This is likely to complicate the resolution of conflict of laws problems."

[125] See e.g., Batiffol, *Les Conflits de Lois en Matière de Contrats* (1938), pp. 423 et seq.; Domke, "Les Garanties de Tiers dans les Emprunts Internationaux", 34 Revue de Science et de Législation Financières 1936, 598.

[126] See e.g., Supreme Court of Austria September 5, 1934, Rechtsprechung 1934, 178, Clunet 1935, 190; T.F. September 18, 1934, Nathan Institut A.G. v. Schweizerische Bank fuer Kapitalanlagen, R.O. 60, II, 294, J.T. 1935, 72, Clunet 1935, 1096. Comp., T.F. February 28, 1950, Inleyman v. Tungsram Elektrizitaets, A.G., R.O. 76, II, 33; Cie Générale de Fourrures et Pelleteries v. Simon Herzig & Sons Co., 153 N.Y.S. 717, 89 Misc. 573 (1915).

[127] See e.g., T.F. June 19, 1935, Ruetz v. Ettlinger, R.O. 61, II, 181, Clunet

due undoubtedly to the circumstances of each case rather than to a systematic preference for one or the other solution, are apparent from express stipulations of applicable law in private loans and guarantee agreements.[128]

In the case of guaranteed loans involving both private and international persons, the difficulty is increased. A good example is that of the Austrian Guaranteed Loans. Let us assume, merely for the sake of agreement, that government contracts with private persons are

1936, 709, S.1936.4.15, Rev. 1936, 692; Supreme Court of Austria April 24, 1936, Nouvelle Revue de Droit International Privé 1936, 608 and Clunet 1937, 333; Supreme Court of Denmark May 22, 1940, Nicolaysen v. Weiss, Clunet 1954, 496. Comp., Cass. October 27, 1943, Société des Grandes Minoteries Bassot et Cie v. Crédit Foncier d' Algérie et de Tunisie, S.1946.1.17; National Bank of Greece and Athens, S.A. v. Metliss [1958] A.C. 509. See also Article 501, para. 4 of the Swiss Code of Obligations authorizing a surety domiciled in Switzerland to invoke the benefit of the foreign law applicable to the principal debt.

[128] Most stipulations making the law of the principal debt applicable also to the guarantor's obligations are found in contracts providing for a joint and several guarantee. When the guarantee is merely joint, the law governing the guarantee is frequently different from that applicable to the principal debt.

Examples of the first category of stipulations are found in the following prospectuses respecting bond issues in (i) Switzerland: Anglo-American (O.F.S.) Housing Company Limited, Johannesburg, 4½% Loan of 1955; California Texas Corporation (Caltex) 4½% Loan of 1955; Aktieselskabet Dansk Svovlsyre og Superphosphat-Fabrik Copenhague, 4½% Loan of 1961; A.S. Vaksdal Mølle, Bergen (Norvège) 4½% Loan of 1961; which are all governed by Swiss law; (ii) The Netherlands: Naphtachimie S.A. Paris, 4½% Loan of 1955 (Dutch law applicable); (iii) Germany: Prefecture and City of Osaka 6½% DM Bonds of 1962 (German law applicable); and (iv) England: Mobil Oil Holdings, S.A. 5¾% Sterling/DM Guaranteed Bonds 1980 (English law applicable).

Examples of the second kind of stipulations are found in a 1953 indenture involving an American trustee, a German borrower and a German guarantor (law of New York applicable to the loan; German law applicable to the guarantee), and in a 1954 indenture involving a Canadian trustee, a Canadian borrower and a New York guarantor (law of Ontario applicable to the loan; law of New York applicable to the guarantee).

That broad generalizations are nevertheles dangerous is sufficiently illustrated by the fact that joint and several guarantees have sometimes been considered subject to a law other than that applicable to the principal debt (Schering, Ltd. v. Stockholms Enskilda Bank Aktiebolalt [1946] 1 All E.R. 36, German law applicable to the principal debt, English law applicable to the guarantors' obligations) while the latter law has been held to govern also, or has been made contractually applicable to the guarantor's obligations in the case of joint guarantees. See e.g., Indian and General Investment Trust Limited v. Borax Consolidated, Limited [1920] 1 K.B. 539 (English law applicable); Aktieselkapet Union (Union Co.) Oslo, 4¼% Loan of 1956 (Swiss law applicable). Société Ferroviaire Internationale de Transports Frigorifiques (INTERFRIGO), Bruxelles, 4½% Loan of 1959 (Swiss law applicable).

governed by the law of the obligor government, and that the proper law of a guarantee relationship is not necessarily the same as that of the principal debt. It would then follow that in the Austrian case, nine different municipal laws would govern the respective relations between the lenders, Austria and the several guarantors, while international law would govern the relations among the guarantors, and between any one of them and Austria.[129] This solution is further complicated by the fact that, as a consequence of the implementation of the guarantees, the guarantors are expressly subrogated to the rights of the bondholders.[130]

The best way to avoid such complex situations, of course, is to specify the applicable law or system of law at the time of the loan, and it is not surprising that provisions of applicable law have become increasingly popular in recent international loan instruments. These provisions currently reflect the desire of the parties to simplify the legal status of their relations as much as possible by bringing both the loan and the guarantee under a single system of law. Such is the obvious intent of Section 7.01 of the IBRD Loan Regulations and of provisions designating the applicable domestic law in government-guaranteed loans issued in the private market, and in guaranteed loans made to private borrowers by international organizations. The law selected may be that of the lenders,[131] of the market of issue,[132] or of the guarantor.[133]

---

[129] See e.g., Schmitthoff, "The International Government Loan", 19 J. Comp. Leg. & Int'l L. (3d Series) 179 (1937), at p. 193; Mann, "State Contracts", p. 32.

The Austrian Debt Settlement Plan reached at the 1952 Rome Conference would seem to support the view that the relations between Austria and the bondholders, on the one hand, and Austria and the Guarantor Governments, on the other, were governed by two different systems of law: The two sets of relations, although part of an overall settlement plan, were the object of separate understandings. See Annex I regarding the claim of the guarantor governments against the Austrian Government and Annex II concerning the agreement between Austria and the representative of the bondholders. It should be noted, however, that Annex I (para. 7) expressly provides that the guarantors "assume the rights of the bondholders" until the undertakings of the Austrian Government to the guarantors are finally discharged.

[130] See the preceding note. See also, Sir John Fisher Williams, La *Convention pour l'Assistance Financière aux Etats Victimes d'Agression* 34 Recueil des Cours 81 (1930), at pp. 137-138; Mann, "State Contracts", at pp. 32-33.

[131] Provisions to that effect are most frequent in direct loans between private lenders, e.g. in the United States or Switzerland, and foreign private or public entities when the loan is guaranteed by the borrower's government.

The AID also extends to the case of government-guaranteed loans the pro-

As a rule, however, such stipulations are limited in scope; while they specify the law governing the lender-borrower and lender-guarantor relationships, they normally contain no indication regarding the law applicable to the relations between the guarantor and the borrower, or the right of contribution between guarantors. To preserve the simplicity of the juridical status intended by the parties, it would seem reasonable to bring the ancillary consequences of the guarantee within the scope of the law specified in the loan instruments. In view of the uncertainty of the law in this field, it cannot be said, nevertheless, that this solution will always prevail.

SECTION II. THE SCOPE OF THE PROPER LAW
I. MATTERS WITHIN THE SCOPE OF THE PROPER LAW

A. Loans Governed by Domestic Law

1. *The Ordinary Rules of the Conflict of Laws*

It is generally agreed that the proper law "because it sustains, may also modify or dissolve, the contractual bond".[134] In other words, once the proper law has been determined, that law applies as it exists from time to time and not merely as it stood at the time of the contract.

---

vision ordinarily stipulated in its loan agreements that the law of the District of Columbia shall be applicable.

[132] See e.g., in Germany: (i) the prospectus of the Oesterreichische Donaukraftwerke A.G. 6% Bearer Bonds of 1959, guaranteed by the Republic of Austria and two private companies and (ii) Suomen-Teolliscuus-Hypotheeki-panki Oy (Industrial Mortgage Bank of Finland) 6¼% DM Loan of 1964; and the prospectuses relating to the following bonds issued in Switzerland by: (i) the Belgian Congo (Guaranteed Loan 4% of 1952), the Régie des Télégraphes et Téléphones (Guaranteed Loan 4% of 1947), the Société Nationale de Crédit à l'Industrie (Guaranteed Loan 4% of 1950), the Société Nationale des Chemins de Fer Belges, Bruxelles (Guaranteed Loan of 1961), all guaranteed by Belgium; (ii) the Société Concessionnaire Française pour la Construction et l'Exploitation du Tunnel Routier sous le Mont-Blanc (Guaranteed Loan of 1961), guaranteed by France; and (iii) the Cassa per il Mezzogiorno, Rome (Guaranteed Loan of 1961), guaranteed by Italy.

[133] Such is the case of most guaranteed loans made by the EIB and the High Authority of the ECSC, since the law declared applicable is common to both the borrower and the guarantor. However, a different solution may obtain if the borrower and the guarantor belong to different countries. See note 28 supra.

[134] Kahler v. Midland Bank [1949] 2 All E.R. 621, at p. 641.

This general rule, which has been relied upon in cases involving foreign loan disputes,[135] has been subjected in France to an important limitation. Although French courts normally acknowledge the existence of the rule,[136] they have refused to apply it to contracts involving "international" payments and in particular to gold and currency clauses in foreign loans. Pursuant to the French doctrine of "international" payments, gold and currency clauses in foreign loans are deemed enforceable in accordance with their terms, any provisions of the proper law to the contrary notwithstanding. A typical illustration follows.[137] A French shipping company, issued gold Canadian dollar bonds in Canada and the Netherlands. The bonds, which were guaranteed by the French Government, contained no stipulation of applicable law. The bonds of the Canadian issue were payable in Canada; the bonds of the Dutch issue were payable in dollars in Canada or in guilders in the Netherlands at the current rate of exchange for the Canadian dollar.[138] Following the 1937 abrogation of gold clauses in Canada, the borrower offered payment in depreciated Canadian currency or its equivalent in Dutch guilders. The bondholders objected and sought to enforce the gold clause. Under normal circumstances, the resolution of the controversy would have depended

---

[135] See e.g., Supreme Court of Austria November 26, 1935 and July 10, 1936, Austrian Government Guaranteed Loans Cases, Rev. 1936, 717, Clunet 1937, 334; Supreme Court of Denmark January 30, 1939, Vereeniging voor den Effectenhandel v. Ministère des Finances, 13 Zeit. fur Ausl. und Int. Privatrecht 825 (1942), Clunet 1954, 490, 40 B.I.J.I. 284 (1939); Supreme Court of Norway December 8, 1937. Insurance Companies Minerva and Viking and Stavanger Saving Bank v. The Norwegian Government, Clunet 1938, 935, 38 B.I.J.I. 71 (1938); International Trustee for the Protection of Bondholders A.G. v. The King [1937] A.C. 500. See also, Mann, p. 266; Nussbaum, p. 416; Batiffol, Les Conflits de Lois en Matière de Contrats (1938), p. 68; Mann, "Time Element in the Conflict of Laws", 31 B.Y.B.I.L. 217 (1954); Spiro, "The Incidence of Time in the Conflict of Laws", 9 Int'l & Comp. L. Q. 357 (1960).

[136] Gavalda, Les Conflits dans le Temps en Droit International Privé (1955), pp. 360-362, 385-389.

[137] Cass. January 1, 1950, Etat Français v. Comité de la Bourse d'Amsterdam, Rev. 1950, 609; S.1951.1.1; D. 1951, 749; J.C.P. 1950, II, 5812.

[138] Only the prospectus of the Dutch issue referred to payment in Holland; the bonds themselves referred to payment in Canada only. The Court of Appeals of Paris (April 24, 1940, S.1942.2.29), whose judgment was affirmed by the Supreme Court in the decision cited in the preceding note, held that the provisions of the prospectus were controlling since the bondholders had subscribed on the basis of the propectus and the bonds had been delivered to the subscribers at a later date.

upon whether the Canadian law, or some other law, was applicable. In the first instance, and subject to public policy,[139] effect should have been given to the Canadian Act; in the second instance, e.g. if the French law of the borrower and guarantor governed the substance of the debt,[140] the gold clause would have remained enforceable. This, however, was not the line of reasoning used by the French Supreme Court in this particular case.

Although the Court stated, by what may be called a "magnificent dictum", that the bonds were "necessarily governed by the law of some country", it failed to determine the law in question and held that, whatever that law might be, even the imperative provisions of that law would not bind the parties since:

> "the parties to such a contract may, any imperative provision of the domestic law applicable to their convention to the contrary notwithstanding, stipulate a gold value clause [in the contract] . . . " (as translated).

It is apparent that there are in this judgment two contradictory propositions. The first is that an "international" transaction, like any other contract, must be governed by some domestic law. The second is that the parties may ignore the provisions of domestic law merely because the relationship involved is "international" in character.

Perhaps these two statements could be reconciled if the Court, *after* determining the proper law, had held that law contrary to French public policy. However, as the Court failed to determine the proper law, it is difficult to see how French public policy could have been relied upon, unless the Court intended to give to French public policy a world-wide application, obviously an over-simplification of the problem.

The doctrine of "international" payments upheld in this and similar French judgments[141] has been criticized both in and outside

---

[139] See, in respect of the Dutch issue of the loan, Supreme Court of the Netherlands April 28, 1939 Prins et Van der Linde v. Société des Services Contractuels des Messageries Maritimes, S.1939.4.20, Annual Digest 1919-42, 28.

[140] See, in respect of the Canadian issue of the loan, Paris May 16, 1951, Trésor Public et Société Royal Bank of Canada v. Schumann, Clunet 1952, 1228; J.C.P. 1952, II, 6887 (affirmed on other grounds, Cass. January 24, 1956, J.C.P. 1956, II, 9400; D. 1956, 317; Clunet 1956, 1012); Paris June 2, 1959, Trésor Public v. Veuve Hermann, Gaz. Pal. 1959, II, 170, affirmed Cass. October 29, 1964, Etat Français v. Veuve Hermann, Clunet 1965, 637.

[141] Cass. November 4, 1958, Amar v. Veuve Rahmy bey Arslan, Clunet 1960, 440: J.C.P. 1959, II, 10986.

France,[142] and there are indications in recent French Supreme Court decisions that this doctrine may be on the wane.[143]

Sometimes lenders have attempted to achieve by means of contractual stipulations, results similar to those obtained in France by way of judicial determination. Thus, American indentures of the nineteen-twenties, and especially those concerning German industrial loans of that period, not infrequently contained an agreement by the borrower to waive the benefit of any defenses derived from either American or some other (e.g. the borrower's) law, present or future, which would prevent the trustee from exercising the powers of the trust.[144] The validity of these provisions was extremely doubtful at best. Probably for that reason, they have apparently been the

---

[142] See e.g., Batiffol, *Traité Elémentaire de Droit International Privé* (3d ed. 1959), p. 681; Delaume, "L'Autonomie de la Volonté en Droit International Privé", Rev. 1950, 321; Pédamon, "Le Régime Contemporain des Clauses Monétaires", D. 1958, Chronique XVIII, p. 102; Mann, "State Contracts and State Responsibility", 54 Am. J. Int'l L. 572 (1960).

[143] See Cass. January 12, 1960, Normand v. Buzier, Rev. 1960, 573; Cass. April 27, 1964, Monballiu v. Desmyter-Caron, Clunet 1964, 819; Rev. 1965, 346. Cass. October 29, 1964, Etat Français v. Veuve Hermann, Clunet 1965, 637. But see Cass. May 4, 1964, Coopérative de Stockage v. Etab. Deutsche Tradax, Rev. 1965, 348; Clunet 1965, 126; Cass. December 22, 1964, Mousset v. Héripret, J.C.P. 1965, II, 14290; Cass. March 3, 1965, Diamantidi v. Raneilo, J.C.P. 1965, II, 14466.

[144] The following provision is typical:
'The Company, for itself and its successors and assigns, hereby agrees to waive, and does hereby absolutely and irrevocably waive and relinquish, the benefit and advantage of any and all valuation, stay, appraisement and extension law or laws now existing, or which may hereafter be passed either in Germany or in the United States of America, which, but for this provision, agreement and waiver, might be applicable to any sale made hereunder or under the judgment, order or decree of any court or courts, based on the Bonds or on this Indenture; and the Company hereby agrees that it will not in any manner set up, or attempt to take any benefit or advantage of, any such present or future valuation, stay, appraisement, extension or redemption law, to prevent, hinder or delay such absolute and irrevocable sale of the mortgaged property, or any part thereof, as might, but for such law, be directed or decreed by a court of competent jurisdiction; and the Company, for itself and its successors and assigns, hereby agrees to waive, and does hereby absolutely and irrevocably waive any and all rights of redemption which it, they or any of them might or could otherwise have, or be entitled to under any present or future laws of the United States of America or of Germany, upon or after, or in respect of any such sales of the mortgaged property, or any part thereof."
Comp., the following provision in a commercial contract between the United States and a buyer of government surplus property in Belgium:
"D.C. Law to Govern: This contract shall be governed by and construed in accordance with the law *now* prevailing in the District of Columbia, United States of America.

object of very little litigation.[145] In any event, these provisions proved, in the light of subsequent events, to be totally ineffective. They seem to have completely disappeared from contemporary loan documents.

2. *The Special Case of Governmental Loans.*

The ordinary rules of conflict of laws apply to all kinds of loans, including loans to foreign governments. Under these rules, the original exceptions of the lender may be defeated by changes in the content of the applicable local law regardless of whether this local law is that of the debtor government or of some other state.[146] There is a question, however, whether a change in the applicable local law may result in a violation of public international law. It seems clear that there will be no such violation in a situation where the applicable local law is not that of the debtor government. Otherwise, the debtor government would in effect be held responsible for the actions of another state over which it has no control.[147]

Should the same result be reached if the contract is governed by the law of the debtor state and the debtor, by its own action, interferes with or terminates its contractual undertakings? More precisely, in the absence of any arbitrary or tortious action by the debtor government such as discrimination or outright repudiation, can the debtor government successfully invoke a change in its own law, to justify

---

(Emphasis added. Overseas Trading Company S.A. v. United States, 159 F. Supp. 382 (Ct. Cl. 1958)).

[145] The only case which has been found in which a provision similar to that first quoted in the foregoing note was discussed, is Goodman v. Deutsch-Atlantische Telegraphen Gesellschaft (2 N.Y.S. 2d 80, 166 Misc. 509 (1938)), following the imposition of exchange restrictions in Germany. The court held, however, that the law of New York was the proper law of the loan and that under the circumstances, "the conclusion was irresistible" that the parties had intended "that future governmental law or act of Germany was not to limit the promise to pay" (2 N.Y.S. 2d at p. 83).

See generally, Hamel, "L'Application des Lois Monétaires Annulant les Clauses-Or et les Principes des Conflits de Lois", Nouvelle Revue de Droit International Privé 1938, 499, at p. 509; *Mann,* p. 266.

[146] See note 135 supra.

[147] Query, if the proper law were discriminatory or otherwise contrary to international law, whether the borrower by invoking the benefit of its provisions would not commit a tortious act? No international precedent is known, but see, in respect to the German law of June 26, 1936, T.F. February 1, 1938, Allgemeine Elektrizitätsgesellschaft, Berlin and Siemens & Halske A.G., Berlin v. Journaliag A.G., Glarus R.O. 1939.III.65, Annual Digest 1938-1940, p. 155.

See also the Draft Convention on the International Responsibility of States (hereinafter called the Harvard Draft), comment to article 12, sub-paragraph 1 (c), in Sohn and Baxter, "Responsibility of States for Injuries to the Economic Interests of Aliens", 55 Harv. L. Rev. 545 (1961), at p. 572.

non-performance? For example, suppose that a state, after having issued foreign gold bonds, enacts a law invalidating gold clauses in all contracts, and refuses to pay more than the nominal amount of the bonds or coupons in depreciated currency. Under the rules of private international law, such an enactment, presumably made by constitutional means, would not constitute a breach of contract. Can it nevertheless be treated as such for the purposes of public international law?

This question, which may arise in connection with state contracts, other than foreign loans, was brought before the ICJ in the *Case of Certain Norwegian Loans*.[148] This case involved a dispute between Norway and French holders of Norwegian bonds over the existence, and the subsequent invalidation by Norway, of a gold clause in the bonds. France, which had espoused the claims of the French bond-holders, argued that the abrogation of gold clauses by Norway constituted a "breach of contract." In this case, however as in the other cases in which the argument had been made before the Hague Court,[149] the question was left undecided.

The confusion of the international doctrine in this particular sector of the law of state responsibility is particularly great, and the extreme positions taken by some writers have done little to bring us closer to a solution of the problem. While a trend toward an objective reappraisal of the basic factors in issue is clearly discernible in the views expressed by an increasing number of publicists,[150] it must be acknowledged that "in this area we [are] still, in large measure . . . groping towards the future".[151]

One extreme opinion, which is said to be based on the "teachings of private international law", contends that:

> "If . . . the debtor relies on changes in the proper law, he does what he is entitled to do and cannot be charged with a breach of contract, his undertaking being limited to perform in accordance

---

[148] I.C.J. Reports 1957, p. 9. For statements of the French argument, see I Pleadings p. 34 and p. 404, II Pleadings, p. 61. For the Norwegian reply, see I Pleadings, pp. 485 et seq; II Pleadings, pp. 134 et seq.

[149] See e.g., the Losinger and Company Case, PCIJ, Series C, No. 78 (1936); The Anglo-Iranian Oil Company Case, I.C.J. Reports 1952, p. 93.

[150] This is particularly apparent from the comments appended to the Harvard Draft, 55 Harv. L. Rev. 545 (1961), at pp. 567-574) and the relevant provisions (articles 198 to 200) of the American Law Institute's Restatement of the Law, The Foreign Relations Law of the United States (Proposed Official Draft, May 3, 1962, hereinafter called Restatement).

[151] Jenks, *The Common Law of Mankind* (1958), p. 152.

with the terms of the contract as sanctioned by the provisions of the proper law . . .

These rules of private international law demand the rejection of any idea of 'breach' of contract also in the case in which the state enacting the new law of general impact is itself a party to the contract."[152]

If therefore, or so the argument runs, under the proper law no breach of contract occurs, "it is not open to public international law to assert the contrary".[153]

In other words, if a private person contracts with a foreign government and fails to specify an applicable system of law other than that of the contracting state,

"by implication the contract concedes to the state the power of interference and if the exercise of such power is not subject to criticism, international law ought not to impose responsibility for what is not tortious."[154]

It is submitted that this conclusion is unacceptable for the following reasons. First of all, the real issue is not whether, in the formulation of international-law norms, the teachings of private international law may be relevant, as they may well be on occasion.[155] Rather, the issue is whether a change in the proper law, as designated by the rules of private international law, can be reconciled with the international obligations of the contracting state. The problem is not whether the exercise by the state of its "power of interference" can be justified under the proper law, but whether the proper law, to the extent that it is changed to interfere with the state's contractual undertakings, is consistent with international law. Clearly, this is a problem of international law[156] and to remit the solution to the proper law is to beg the question at issue.

---

[152] Mann, "State Contracts and State Responsibility", 54 Am. J. Int'l L. 572 (1960), at p. 581.

[153] Ibid., at p. 582.

[154] Ibid., at p. 588.

[155] See e.g., Hambro, *The Relations between International Law and Conflict of Law,* 105 Recueil des Cours 1 (1963) ; Wortley, *The Interrelation of Public and Private International Law to-day,* 85 Recueil des Cours 254 (1954) ; Jenks, op. cit. note 151 supra, pp. 51-54; Stevenson, "The Relationship of Private International Law to Public International Law", 52 Col. L. Rev. 561 (1952).

[156] "The question of conformity of national legislation with international law is a matter of international law. The notion that if a matter is governed by national law, it is for that reason at the same time outside

The second objectionable feature of the proposed theory is its
assumption that the failure to specify an applicable system of law
other than that of the debtor necessarily implies a concession by the
private contracting party which is tantamount to an anticipated aban-
donment of contractual rights. This ignores the other considerations
which might produce a failure to specify the applicable law.[157] Further,
this theory produces a result which is probably far remote from the
expectations of the parties, since if the parties did not contract in
the expectation of performance, there would of course be no contract.
In effect, the theory under review, by implying in the contract a
complete surrender to the debtor's "power of interference", leads, in
a circuitous way, to substantially the same results as those which would
be reached if, as it has sometimes been contended, there were in every
state contract an implicit sovereign "right" of unilateral termination.
In both cases, therefore, we arrive at the same "anomaly" as that
exposed by Sir John Fischer Williams in his critical analysis of the
Drago and related doctrines:

> "namely a unilateral decision by an interested party which is
> to be binding upon the other. Such a solution cannot be accepted
> as a solution of international law."[158]

---

the sphere of international law is both novel, and if accepted, subversive
of international law. It is not enough for a state to bring a matter under
the protective umbrella of its legislation, possibly of a predatory character, in order to shelter it effectively from any control by international
law. There may be little difference between a government breaking un-
lawfully a contract with an alien and a government causing legislation to
be enacted which makes it impossible for it to comply with the contract."
(See Hersh Lauterpacht, separate opinion in the case of Certain Norwegian
Loans, I.C.J. Reports 1957, p. 9, at p. 37). See also, Jennings, "State Contracts in International Law", 37 B.Y.B.I.L. 156 (1961), at pp. 162-163.

[157] The fact that, contrary to the prevailing practice of lenders, stipulations of applicable law are sometimes omitted from foreign loan contracts,
and especially from bonds publicly issued, is not necessarily relevant. This
omission may be attributable simply to considerations of prestige: A government may be reluctant to agree, in documents that are to be widely published, that it will comply with the laws of another sovereign. Such considerations may well disappear if the loan documents are to be seen only by a few
banking or lending institutions. It is significant that, in several cases in which
public bonds contain no stipulation of applicable law, such provisions are
nevertheless found in the related underwriting, fiscal agency or other agreement with bankers or underwriters. For a concrete example, see Supreme
Court of Sweden, January 30, 1937, Skandia v. National Debt Office, 36
B.I.J.I. 327 (1937), Annual Digest 1935-1937, p. 20. This method has been
employed in several contemporary loan documents which this writer is not
at liberty to identify.

[158] *International Law and International Financial Obligations Arising*

If the proper law, in its splendid isolation, does not supply an answer to the problem, what then are the rules of public international law which may be relevant to determine the consequences of state measures affecting the contractual rights of aliens? As a matter of international law, should it be held that any change in the proper law, contrary to the state's contractual undertakings, should automatically constitute a "breach of contract"? Or should such a result be reached only in the case of certain state measures which are particularly undesirable because of the motivation involved or the circumstances in which they take place? As yet there is no definite answer to this question.

The usual rule is that legislative interference with the rights of aliens under a state contract does not *per se* constitute, for purposes of public international law, a "breach of contract" giving rise to responsibility. Responsibility, to the extent that it may exist, arises only when the state's action, by reason of the circumstances in which it occurs, can be characterized as an international tort or delict (such as a denial of justice following the exhaustion of all available remedies) distinct from any concept of breach of contract.[159]

It is now argued that this view is obsolete. It may have been acceptable when international law was confined to the relations between states and their duties to one another. However, this view does not correspond to present legal and economic realities and can no longer satisfy the requirements of contemporary economic relations between states and aliens. The development of these relations call for a complete reconsideration of the traditional position, and the adoption of new rules capable of giving an adequate legal framework to the many transnational relations arising from the financial, commercial and economic activities of states.

If this objective is clear, however, the means proposed to achieve it vary considerably. Certain publicists take the position that state contracts with aliens, though not identical to treaties or other agreements between international persons, are sufficiently rooted in international law to justify the extension to them of the principle *pacta*

---

from Contract (Bibliotheca Visseriana 1924), p. 23. See also, Verzil, "The Relevance of Public and Private International Law Respectively for the Solution of Problems Arising from Nationalization of Enterprises", 19 Zeitschrift für Ausländisches Öffentliches Recht und Völkerrecht 530 (1958), at p. 535.

[159] For a review of the traditional doctrine, see e.g., Fatouros, *Governments Guarantees to Foreign Investors* (1962), pp. 244 et seq.; Garcia Amador, *International Responsibility.* Fourth Report, U.N. Doc. A/CN.4/119, paras. 121 et seq.

sunt servanda. According to this opinion, any action taken by a state in contradiction of its contractual commitments to aliens, whatever the form or purpose of such an act, would be contrary to international law and make the state liable for the consequences of its own act.[160]

This theory has been criticized on the ground that it is based on an erroneous assimilation of state contracts to genuine international agreements Other writers, without questioning the principle *pacta sunt servanda,* or the possibility of "internationalizing" state contracts by subjecting them directly to international law, have pointed out that the proposed theory, in the particular circumstances to which it refers, is unrelated to the facts of the case. For the facts of the case are that, either expressly or by implication, the parties have agreed to submit the contract to a proper law which is municipal law, and that under the proper law there is no "breach of contract" or, so it may be said, "no breach whatever of the principle *pacta sunt servanda*".[161]

It is therefore argued that an attempt should be made to find a reasonable equilibrium between the protection of the contractual rights of aliens and the *reasonable* exercise by the state of its power of legislation; and that such an equilibrium cannot be found either in the theory under consideration (which would uphold the interests of aliens in all cases, regardless of the circumstances), or the "proper law" doctrine discussed earlier (which would uphold the interests of states in all cases, regardless of the circumstances).

It has been suggested that the doctrine of acquired rights, because of its flexibility, might afford a useful basis for the achievement of this equilibrium.[162] Respect for the acquired rights of aliens undoubtedly "forms part of generally accepted international law".[163]

[160] See e.g., The Losinger and Company Case, P.C.I.J., Pleadings, Oral Statements and Documents, Series C. No. 78, p. 32; Brandon, "Legal Aspects of Private Foreign Investments", 18 Fed. Bar J. 298 (1958), at pp. 337-40; Ray, "Law Governing Contracts between States and Foreign Nationals", 2 *Institute on Private Investment Abroad* 847 (1960), at pp. 40 et seq.

[161] Jennings, op. cit., note 156 supra, at p. 176.

[162] See e.g., McNair, "The General Principles", at pp. 16-18; Draft Resolution, Int'l Law Ass. Report, 48 Conference (New York 1958), pp. 144-145; Schwarzenberger, "The Protection of British Property Abroad", 5 *Current Legal Problems* 294 (1952), at pp. 312-315; Domke, "Foreign Nationalizations", 55 A.J.I.L. 585 (1961), at pp. 596-598. See also, Hyde, op. cit., note 5 supra, at pp. 317-319 and 322-323; Jennings, op. cit., note 156 supra, at pp. 173-177.

[163] German Interests in Polish Upper Silesia Case, P.C.I.J., Series A, No. 7, p. 42 (1926). See also, Garcia Amador, op. cit., note 159 supra, para. 5; Rousseau, *Principes Généraux du Droit International Public* (1944), p. 95; Ripert, *Les Règles de Droit Civil Applicables aux Rapports Internationaux,*

However, the principle, as an abstract concept, does not necessarily supply an answer to the many varied and complex situations which, in concrete cases, may require determination. Suppose, for example, that a foreign banking institution makes a loan to a government to finance the purchase of goods and services supplied by foreign manufacturers and consultants for the completion of an economic development project carried out in the borrower's territories by a foreign firm operating under a concession or similar arrangement with the debtor government. In a situation like this, which is far from theoretical, the acquired rights of the lender may not be co-extensive with those of the concessionaire, the manufacturers or the consultants. Should a dispute arise, the international judge might, in the one case, have to take into consideration factors substantially different from those relevant for the determination of the other cases. The principle of acquired rights, therefore, however useful it may be, cannot:

> "be regarded as being necessarily absolute or unconditional in its application. As so often in law it is a question of drawing limits and defining exceptions. Whether or not an alleged 'breach' of contract amounts to a breach of international law may depend upon a number of variants such as the circumstances, or even the motives of the state action with respect to the contract; as also on the nature of the contract itself and the terms in which it is drafted."[164]

---

44 Recueil des Cours 569 (1933), at p. 636. See specifically, in the case of foreign loans, the Lighthouses Concession Case (Award dated July 24-27, 1956, *Reports of Int'l Awards*, vol. XII, p. 155, p. 236).

[164] Jennings, op. cit., note 156 supra, p. 177. It has sometimes been proposed that a distinction should be made between those contracts which contain an express promise of non-interference by future legislation and those in which such a promise is absent. The doctrine of acquired rights would be applicable, of course, to both types of contracts. The addition of a non-interference guarantee, "plainly intended to produce a situation other than that which would exist if it were not inserted", would have:

> "the effect of rendering cancellation [presumably also modification or suspension] illegal in *all* circumstances, including those in which, apart from the explicit undertaking, cancellation would be legal" (Anglo-Iranian Oil Co. Case, *Pleadings*, p. 89).

As a general proposition, however, this statement would certainly require some qualification. It is clear, for example, that the imposition of war-time transfer restrictions or genuine exchange-control regulations would not necessarily give rise to responsibility even though similar measures, taken in another context, would be objectionable. See e.g., In Re Helbert Wagg & Co. Ltd. [1956] 1 All E.R. 129, at p. 144; In Re Fried Krupp Aktiengesellschaft [1917] 2 Ch. 188. Similar problems may arise in connection with the manipulation of currency and gold-clause legislation. See e.g., in addition to the

This, it is believed, is the correct approach. The pertinent provisions found in contemporary state contracts have gained much in comprehensiveness and precision. Under the circumstances, a comparative analysis of the particular situations which produced them or required their subsequent amendment, and the judicial adjudication of disputes arising thereunder, is likely to prove most useful in the delineation of legal trends in this area. It is believed that such an approach is preferable to the mere assertion of categoric abstractions which, if they were to prevail, might prove more detrimental than helpful to the development of international economic relations.[165]

B. LOANS GOVERNED BY INTERNATIONAL LAW

Since loans are essentially contracts, regardless of the system of law applicable to them, it would seem reasonable to expect that international law, when applicable, would perform substantially the same function as that performed by the "proper law" in the case of contracts governed by domestic law. This expectation is generally justified. Nevertheless, it is only too evident that international financial law, because it is still in a relatively early stage of development, does not always supply answers as precise or as positive as those which can be found in domestic law.

This last remark applies to both the essential validity and the

---

arguments developed by France and Norway in the Case of Certain Norwegian Loans, note 148 supra: P.C.I.J. Judgments No. 14 (at p. 44) and No. 15 (at p. 122) in the Serbian and Brazilian Loans Cases; T.F. February 1, 1938, cited note 147 supra; Mann, *Money in Public International Law*, 96 Recueil des Cours 7 (1959), at pp. 85-86, 95, 97-98; Jèze, *Les Défaillances d'Etat*, 53 Recueil des Cours 381 (1935), at p. 392; Dupuis, *Règles Générales du Droit de la Paix*, 32 Recueil des Cours 5 (1930), at p. 164; Bindschedler, *La Protection de la Propriété Privée en Droit International Public*, 90 Recueil des Cours 173 (1956), at pp. 226-227; *Nussbaum*, pp. 443-445; I *Borchard*, p. 134, note 29.

The possible severance of guarantee clauses (governed by international law) from the stipulations (governed by municipal law) found in state contracts was admitted in the Lena Goldfields, Ltd. Arbitral Award (see Nussbaum, "The Arbitration between the Lena Goldfields, Ltd. and the Soviet Government", 36 Cornell L.Q. 31 (1950), at pp. 42-53, para 22 at p. 50). See also Mann, "The Proper Law", at pp. 55-56; Wilner, "Contract Guarantees in International Law", 3 The Indian J. of Int'l L. 278 (1963), particularly at pp. 282-292. The Saudi Arabia v. Aramco Award (Rev. 1963, 272; 27 Int'l L. Rep. 117) is not in point. See Fatouros, op. cit., note 159 supra, pp. 292-293.

[165] See also Fatouros, op. cit., note 159 supra, p. 283, Hyde, op. cit., note 5 supra, p. 331; *Harvard Draft*, Explanatory Note pp. 569-570.

effects of international financial agreements. As a practical matter, however, questions involving the validity of these agreements are unlikely to create difficulty. International persons, under normal circumstances, do not intentionally contravene cogent rules of international law or deliberately violate international public policy in the pursuit of financial objectives.[166] When violations of international obligations do occur, which is relatively rare, they are usually the result of oversight, such as the inadvertent contracting by the borrower of conflicting undertakings toward different lenders. For example, the borrower may attempt to create a lien on its assets or revenues as security for a new loan, in contravention of a negative-pledge covenant in an existing loan contract; or the borrower may fail to comply with a clause requiring it to inform, or seek the consent of, an old creditor or guarantor before contracting new debts. In all these cases, however, it is clear that the difficulty arises from a conflict between two contracts rather than from an incompatibility between the terms of a contract and a rule of international law.[167]

Under the circumstances, therefore, controversies are most likely to occur in connection with the termination or discharge of international financial obligations. This is the case when one of the parties, usually the borrower,[168] invokes doctrines like *force majeure,* or *rebus sic stantibus,* as an excuse for the non-performance or termination of its obligations.

International courts, on several occasions, have acknowledged that a plea of impossibility of performance based on *force majeure* is admissible in international as well as domestic law. Thus, the *Russian*

---

[166] "It is perhaps easier to suggest that there exist in international law these possibilities of a limitation on perfect freedom of contract than to suggest instances of possible provisions in financial agreements which might be obnoxious to the rule."
Sir John Fischer Williams, *Chapters on Current International Law and the League of Nations* (1929), p. 334. See also *Broches,* pp. 362-370. One may conceive that in exceptional circumstances the realization that a proposed loan transaction would violate international law might not deter the parties from proceeding with the operation. Such would be the case of a loan made to a belligerent by a neutral government sympathetic to the cause of the borrower. See Harvard Research in International Law, *Draft Convention on Rights and Duties of Neutral States in Naval and Aerial War,* 33 Am. J. Int'l L., Supp. (1959), Article 5 at pp. 235-245.

[167] Comp. the Saudi Arabia v. Aramco Award, referred to note 164 supra.

[168] See infra text and note 173. On occasions, lenders, although not formally invoking *force majeure,* may simply suspend disbursements if it appears that circumstances, e.g. war or enemy occupation, are such as to defeat the purpose of the loan.

Indemnity Case[169] involved a default by Turkey in the payment of the indemnity due Russia under the peace treaty of 1879. Turkey sought to prove that, from 1881 to 1902, she had been prevented from discharging her obligations by financial difficulties of the utmost gravity, increased by insurrection and foreign war, which had forced her to undergo foreign control over part of her financial resources and delay the fulfillment of her obligations. Although these facts were sufficiently established, it nevertheless appeared that during the same period Turkey had been able to obtain loans at favorable rates, redeem other loans, and pay off a substantial part of her public debt. Under the circumstances, it was found that:

> "It would clearly be exaggeration to admit that the payment (or obtaining of a loan for the payment) of the comparatively small sum of about six million francs due the Russian claimants would imperil the existence of the Ottoman Empire or seriously compromise its internal or external situation."[170]

Consequently, the plea of *force majeure* was denied.

A similar conclusion was reached by the P.C.I.J. in the *Serbian and Brazilian Loans Cases*[171] in which the debtor governments contended that, due to the economic disequilibrium following World War I, they were no longer able to fulfill their obligations. The Court rejected this contention on the ground that war, as such, does not necessarily constitute an event of *force majeure*; and that the debtor is not discharged merely because, as in these cases, war renders performance more difficult for the debtor than had been anticipated.[172]

---

[169] Award of November 11, 1912, Scott, I *The Hague Reports,* p. 297; U.N. Reports of International Arbitral Awards, vol. XI, p. 421.

[170] Scott, at pp. 317-318.

[171] P.C.I.J. (1929) Series A No. 20, at pp. 39-40 and No. 21 at p. 120.

[172] Comp., the Case Concerning the Société Commerciale de Belgique (PCIJ 1939, Series A/B No. 78) in which the Court did not pass judgment on the isue of *force majeure* raised by the Greek Government because "the question of Greece's capacity to pay [was] outside the scope of the proceedings before the Court", (pp. 177-8 (21/22)).

Comp., the Alsing case (Award of December 22, 1954, Int'l Law Reports (Year 1956), p. 633) in which the arbitrator refused to rule that the imposition of a moratorium and the complete suspension of loan service by Greece constituted circumstances "unforeseeable" by the plaintiffs because:

> "Greece is not a country which enjoys great natural resources. It had already experienced serious financial crises. At the time of the contracts the administration of its public debt was run by an international financial Committee . . . To this add that in long-term contracts, the parties should reckon with rather considerable fluctuations due to troubles of which the origin cannot be foreseen . . . If the lender and supplier could

Until recently, contractual provisions dealing with the problem were practically non-existent in international agreements which primarily involved interstate relations. With the creation of new lending organizations, the situation has changed. Thus, it is a standard provision in the Loan Regulations of the IBRD that this organization may suspend disbursements on a loan if:

> "an extraordinary situation shall have arisen which shall make it improbable that the Borrower will be able to perform its obligations under the Loan Agreement."[173]

This and similar provisions in agreements concluded by other organizations, like the IADB, admittedly fall short of giving a final answer to the problem, since the characterization of the event giving rise to suspension is formulated in such general terms as to leave room for interpretation. Nor can the fact be ignored that, in making the necessary determination, the organization involved enjoys a large margin of discretion. These objections, however pertinent, must nevertheless be weighed with caution. It will be recalled that international lending organizations maintain a continuous relationship, throughout the life of the loan, with their respective borrowers (and guarantors, in the case of guaranteed loans). Under the circumstances there is good reason to believe that corrective measures will be taken before conditions are allowed to deteriorate to such an extent as to put in question the borrower's (or guarantor's) ability to meet its commitments. It seems reasonable to expect, therefore, that the scope of the provision under consideration will be limited to events of major proportion so sudden or severe as to leave little question of the borrower's inability to perform its obligations. Conceivable examples are natural calamities, like an earthquake or flood, wiping out the site of a project or making its completion useless or economically or financially unsound; or political upheavals, like war or revolution, having a direct bearing upon the borrower's or guarantor's ability to perform its obligations.

It should also be remembered that if the organization avails itself of the provision, and the borrower or the guarantor contests the validity of the organization's decision, the borrower or guarantor has the right to request that the dispute be submitted to arbitration in

---

not foresee the events of the 1939-1945 war, he should, however, expect that in the course of the 28 years of the contract, more or less serious difficulties would arise as a result of internal or external events." (p. 655)
[173] Section 5.02 (d) .

accordance with the procedure set forth for the settlement of controversies between the parties.[174] Therefore, in addition to the fact that the cooperative character of these organizations is a valuable assurance against arbitrary or capricious decisions on their part, the right of the borrower and/or guarantor to arbitrate any contested decision is an important safeguard against any misuse of the provision by the lending organization.

In contrast with the above, loan or similar agreements between states frequently make no attempt to anticipate the effect of future events upon the transaction.[175] It cannot be assumed that governments are unaware of the various factors which, during the more or less protracted life of a loan or similar financial agreement, might interfere with their original expectations. This omission must therefore be substantiated by other reasons. One reason may be the repugnance of governments, based on considerations of prestige, to cast the faintest shadow of doubt upon the debtor's ability to honor its obligations. Another consideration may be the conviction of the parties that, should an unexpected difficulty occur, the issue would be the object of consultation normally resulting in a mutually acceptable adaptation of the agreement. Either explanation is plausible, although the latter is perhaps more important, since in an increasing number of cases, governments have no hesitation in approaching the problem directly. An example is the London Agreement on German External Debts of February 27, 1953 (article 34), which provides for consultation between the parties in a number of instances, including "a situation in which the Federal Republic of Germany finds that it is faced with difficulties in carrying out its external obligations."[176]

This and certain other agreements.[177] are interesting also in an-

---

[174] See Chapter IV text and note 79.

[175] See e.g., the following agreements between: Canada and (i) Belgium (October 25, 1945, 230 UNTS 127; as revised on May 2, 1946, Ibid. p. 140); (ii) France (April 9, 1946, 43 UNTS 43; as revised on August 20, 1947, Id. loc.); India and Burma (March 12, 1957, 312 UNTS 131); the United Kingdom and (i) Belgium (April 23, 1959, 343 UNTS 271); (ii) Greece (May 21, 1959, 344 UNTS 3); (iii) Jordan (May 7, 1958, 312 UNTS 379); the United States and Pakistan (September 17, 1952, 227 UNTS 77); the USSR and (i) Communist China (February 14, 1950, 226 UNTS 21); (ii) Finland (February 6, 1954, 221 UNTS 143); (iii) Yugoslavia (February 2, 1956, 259 UNTS 111); Switzerland and the United Kingdom (October 20, 1961, 431 UNTS 29).

[176] 333 UNTS 3.

[177] See e.g., the February 27, 1953 Agreement between the United Kingdom and the Federal Republic of Germany (330 UNTS 217, Article 8); the March

other respect. They confirm the fact that governments, although prepared to acknowledge in the agreement the conceivable need for its revision, do not consider any such revision possible except by mutual consent. In other words, although states may accept the principle of a consensual readjustment of their respective rights and obligations, they show no inclination to subscribe to doctrines like *rebus sic stantibus*, to the extent that these doctrines would appear to condone a unilateral termination of contractual obligations. This remark finds additional support in the protests voiced by creditor governments against unilateral repudiations of debts allegedly based on changed conditions;[178] and also in the provisions now found in the charters of certain international organizations authorizing these organizations to "agree" to a relaxation or modification of the terms of their financing.[179] The language of these provisions makes abundantly clear the

---

6, 1946, Financial Agreement between Canada and the United Kingdom (20 UNTS 13, Articles 4 and 8); the March 21, 1957, Economic Cooperation Agreement between the United States and Burma (8 UST 1862, Article VII, 2); the September 7, 1949 Agreement between the United Kingdom and Belgium (106 UNTS 61, Article 9); the January 11, 1962, Agreement between the United States and the Dominican Republic (433 UNTS 133, Article VII, para. 4).

Provisions for consultation are normally found in Agricultural Commodities Agreements between the United States and other governments, such as: (i) India (Agreement of August 29, 1956 (Article V), 7 UST 2803); (ii) Brazil (Agreement of December 31, 1956 (Article V), 7 UST 3475); (iii) Greece (Agreement of August 8, 1956 (Article V), 7 UST 2459); or (iv) Finland (Agreement of August 14, 1961 (Article V), 418 UNTS 19).

[178] See e.g., in respect of the repudiation of the public debt of Russia by the Soviet, Marek, *Identity and Continuity of States in Public International Law* (1954), pp. 34-38. France also partly relied upon the doctrine *rebus sic stantibus* in its negotiations with the United States Government, following the Hoover moratorium and the quasi-total renunciation by European Powers to German reparations after the Lausanne Conference. However, the French contention was also based on the argument that by imposing the moratorium, the United States Government was "estopped" from seeking payments on inter-allied war debts as they existed before the moratorium. This view was objected to by the United States Government before the final suspension of war debt payments in 1932-1933. See Rousseau, *Principes Généraux du Droit International Public* (1944), pp. 609-612; Witenberg, "Vers l'Arbitrage? Un Aspect Juridique du Problème des Créances Américaines", Clunet 1932, 1201 and "L'Estoppel", Clunet 1933, 529; Holohan, "Legal Aspects of the Inter-Allied Debt", 14 Boston L. Rev. 47 (1934). See also, Dept. of State, Papers Concerning Intergovernmental Debts November-December 1932 (1933).

[179] See e.g., IBRD, Articles of Agreement, Article IV, Section 4 (c), reading as follows:

"If a member suffers from an acute exchange stringency, so that the service of any loan contracted by that member or guaranteed by it or by one of its agencies cannot be provided in the stipulated manner, the member concerned may apply to the Bank for a relaxation of the condi-

intention of the drafters that the terms originally agreed upon should stand unless the organization in question is satisfied that a relaxation or modification thereof is warranted by the circumstances.

II. MATTERS OUTSIDE THE SCOPE OF THE PROPER LAW

A. CAPACITY

It is generally recognized that the capacity or authority of a corporate, governmental or other juridical entity to contract loans and issue bonds is governed by its personal law, i.e. by the law of the borrower itself, if it is a government; by the law of the state of incorporation or by the *siège social* if it is a corporate entity; or, if the borrower is an international organization, by its charter, statutes or articles of agreement.[180] Stipulations such as the following:

" . . . all corporate proceedings of the Company relating to the authorization, execution and validity of this Indenture and the Debentures shall be governed by the laws of Italy."[181]

which are sometimes found in loan documents, can be considered, therefore, as merely declaratory of a universal rule of conflict of laws.

In most cases, international loans deal with the issue by direct reference to the particular resolution, statute or other source of au-

---

tions of payment. If the Bank is satisfied that some relaxation is in the interests of the particular member and of the operations of the Bank and of its members as a whole, it may take action under either, or both, of the following paragraphs with respect to the whole, or part, of the annual service:

   (i) The Bank may, in its discretion, make arrangements with the member concerned to accept service payments on the loan in the member's currency for periods not to exceed three years upon appropriate terms regarding the use of such currency and the maintenance of its foreign exchange value; and for the repurchase of such currency on appropriate terms.

   (ii) The Bank may modify the terms of amortization or extend the life of the loan, or both."

See also, IDA, Articles of Agreement, Article V, Section 3. Comp., IMF, Articles of Agreement, Article V, Section 4. See also, Scott, op. cit., note 4 supra, p. 193.

[180] See e.g., *Van Hecke,* pp. 90 et seq.; *Salmon,* pp. 146 et seq. See also, *L.N. Report,* § 73.

[181] Indenture dated May 29, 1959, between Montecatini Società Generale per l'Industria Mineraria e Chimica Anonima and Morgan Guaranty Trust Company of New York, Section 15.12. Similar provisions are found in other indentures such as those referred to in note 15 supra.

thority under which the borrower purports to act.[182] It is only in exceptional cases, attributable mostly to drafting deficiencies or the existence of an abnormal set of circumstances, that the issue may raise difficulty. Two cases are in point. In *Goodman v. Deutsch-Atlantische Telegraphen Gesellschaft*,[183] a deed of trust on properties of a German company securing bonds sold in New York provided that the obligations of the borrower were "covered" by German law, although the relations between the parties were generally "governed" by the law of New York. Despite the ambiguous wording of these stipulations, the court had little difficulty in concluding that the reference to German law should be restricted to matters such as corporate action and authority to enter into the deed of trust; and that in all other respects the rights and obligations of the parties were governed by the law of New York.

Adams v. National Bank of Greece and Athens[184] presented a more difficult situation. In 1927, the National Mortgage Bank of Greece had issued bonds in England; the bonds were guaranteed by the National Bank of Greece; the bonds and the guarantee were governed by English law. No interest had been paid on the bonds since 1941. In 1953, as a result of a Greek statute, the National Bank of Greece was amalgamated with the Bank of Athens into one new company, the National Bank of Greece and Athens. The statute provided that the new company became the "universal successor" to the rights and obligations of the amalgamated companies. In an action by a bondholder against the new bank, the House of Lords held that the question of succession and juridical personality of the dissolved and new companies was governed by Greek law and that since the new company was, under that law, successor to the obligations of the amalgamated companies, the action must be entertained.[185]

Pending these proceedings, the Greek Government enacted a new statute, retroactive in effect, excepting from the obligations transferred to the new bank those which the original companies had incurred as guarantors of foreign bonds.[186] In a new action against the bank, it was first held that effect would be given to the new statute,

---

[182] See Chapter I text and notes 7, 8, 12, 17, 18, 28 and 39.

[183] 166 Misc. 509, 2 N.Y.S. 2d 80 (1938).

[184] [1960] 2 All E.R. 421.

[185] National Bank of Greece and Athens v. Metliss [1957] 3 All E.R. 608; Int'l Law Reports (1959) II, 6. See Mann, Case Annotation, (1958) 7 Int'l & Comp. L. Q. 370.

[186] The statute was enacted four days after the first decision. See [1960] 2 All E.R. 421, at p. 423.

and the action was dismissed.[187] On appeal, however, that decision was reversed: the House of Lords held the respondent bank liable as successor to the original guarantor, the new statute to the contrary notwithstanding.[188] The whole issue depended on a question of characterization. If the Greek statute was regarded as an attempt to discharge the guarantor from its contractual liabilities, it was clear that the English courts were free to disregard its provisions, inasmuch as the contract was governed by English, rather than Greek, law. If, however, the statute was characterized as affecting the status of the bank, which was governed by Greek law, it would have to be enforced unless it was found contrary to English public policy, for example because the statute was either confiscatory or discriminatory in character. While the second characterization underlies the judgment of the Court of Appeals, the first characterization was given much attention by the Law Lords. Their decision, however, is also based on the consideration that the exclusion attempted by the retroactive statute constituted such an unusual exception to the concept of amalgamation, as that concept exists in English law, that the English courts were not bound by any rule of comity to give it effect.[189]

An altogether different question, which should be noted for the sake of completeness, is that of the applicability of local regulations which require that loans to foreign borrowers be approved by governmental or other authorities. These regulations, which may limit the "ability" of a borrower to raise funds locally, in no way affect its "capacity" to borrow. They merely form part of the mandatory provisions of the law of the particular market involved. Specific mention in the loan documents of the fact that the borrower has complied with both the provisions of its personal law and those of the law of the place of issue, therefore, constitute merely a formal assurance that the applicable legal requirements have been satisfied.[190]

---

[187] [1959] 2 All E.R. 362. See, Keenan, "Adams v. National Bank of Greece and Athens", (1959) 22 Modern L. Rev. 556; see also comment: "Conflict of Laws: Greek Bank and Sterling Bonds", (1959) 228 The Law Times 269.

[188] See note 184 supra.

[189] This judgment is of foremost significance not only because of the relative scarcity of authoritative decisions dealing with the effects of retroactivity in this field of the law (see e.g. Rabel (4 *The Conflict of Laws* (1958), p. 503; Gavalda, *Les Conflits dans le Temps en Droit International Privé* (1955), pp. 380 et seq.), but also because it illustrates the importance of specifying an applicable law other than that of the debtor government.

[190] See e.g., the following provision in an indenture dated January 1, 1953, between Rheinish Westfälisches Elektrizitätswerk A.G. and the First National City Bank of New York and Treuhand-Vereinigung A.G., Trustees (Article VI, Section 6.02) :

B. Formalities

A similar remark can be made in regard to stipulations respecting the formal validity of the loan or bonds, such as the following:

> "The bonds for the issuance of which provision is made in this agreement shall be issued in the United States of America and shall therefore be issued in accordance with the laws and with the legal and commercial practice in force in the United States of America."[191]

Indeed, especially in the case of bond issues, the borrower would be ill-advised to try to sell bonds in a form with which potential investors are not familiar. Of necessity, the borrower must give due consideration to the usages obtaining at the place of issue. In light of this practical consideration, a discussion of the character, binding or optional, of the old maxim *locus regit actum* would be, in most cases, an entirely gratuitous exercise. This is particularly true since the *lex loci actus* frequently governs matters of formal validity. In many instances, compliance with legal requirements in force at the place of issue is an essential condition to the validity of the bonds. Although the applicability of the *lex loci actus* is based on considerations of a character different from those which inspire the old rule *locus regit actum*, the practical solution in each case is nevertheless identical. It is therefore not surprising that the typical loan documents contain no stipulation of applicable law as to this issue, and simply requires the borrower to satisfy the lenders that all steps necessary to perfect the validity of the bonds or the loan have been taken. This procedure acknowledges implicitly, rather than expressly, the applicability of the *lex loci actus* in determining the formal validity of the loan relationship.[192]

Despite the absence of any real legal problems in this connection, lenders sometimes insist on including in the loan documents express provisions regarding the form of the bonds issued thereunder or in

---

"The Company is duly authorized and empowered under all applicable provisions of law in the United States of America and in the Federal Republic of Germany to create and issue the Bonds and coupons and to execute this Indenture; and all action on its part for the creation and issue of the Bonds and coupons and the execution of this Indenture has been duly and effectively taken and all Bonds and coupons, when executed and authenticated as herein provided and issued, will, in the hands of holders thereof, be the valid and legally enforceable obligations of the Company in accordance with their terms and the terms of this Indenture."

[191] Provision found in a nineteen 'twenties indenture between an American trustee and an Italian company.

[192] See note 190 supra.

pursuance thereto. This practice should not be construed, however, as an example of exceeding caution on their part. If it is not known, at the time of the original loan negotiations in which markets the bonds will be issued, or if the loan is to be issued in several "tranches" in a number of markets, a statement in the basic loan instrument that the bonds will have to satisfy the formal requirements of each place of issue serves as a useful reminder of the particular features of the proposed operation. A good illustration of this remark is found in the General Bond of the Young Loan which provided:

" . . . The form of [the] Bonds shall be in accordance with the requirements of the Stock Exchange Regulations of the country of issue and subject thereto shall be such as the Bank approves or prescribes, the Bank cooperating with the Reich Debt Administration and the respective issuing bankers with regard to the form of the Definitive Bonds. (Article XX) [193]

Similar stipulations are found in the Loan Regulations of the IBRD. The Regulations provide that bonds issued in representation of a loan made by that organization, although substantially in the standard form appended to the Regulations, shall contain such modifications as the IBRD shall reasonably request to conform to the laws or financial usages of the place where they are payable.[194]

Conflict-of-laws rules regarding the transfer of bonds are also well settled. It is generally agreed that the transfer of bearer bonds is governed by the law of the country in which the transfer takes place, while the transfer of registered bonds is normally governed by the law of the place in which the register is kept.[195] Indeed, these rules are so well established that most of the relevant judicial decisions are concerned less with the implementation of the rules than with particular situations, such as those involving the transfer of lost or stolen bonds, in which the rules may admit of several limitations.[196]

---

[193] See also the General Bond of the Austrian Guaranteed Loan 1923-1943 (Article 23 (c)) and of the Austrian Government International Loan of 1930 (Article XXX) which stated that the form of the definitive bonds would have to be approved by the Trustee and the Issuing Bankers.

[194] Section 6.07. See also Sections 6.08, 6.14 and 6.18 of the Regulations.
Loan Agreements between the High Authority of the E.C.S.C. and borrowing enterprises provide that conflict-of-laws questions regarding notes issued by such enterprises under the loan shall be settled in accordance with the rules set forth in the Geneva Convention of June 7, 1930.

[195] This last solution would apply also to the conversion of registered bonds into bearer bonds.

[196] See e.g., Loussouarn, *Les Conflits de Lois en Matière de Sociétés* (1949), pp. 345-368.

C. SECURED LOANS: MATTERS AFFECTING THE SECURITY

It is generally agreed that if a loan is secured by a mortgage or similar lien on assets of the borrower, the *lex situs* governs the validity of, and the rights of the lenders in, the security.[197] It might therefore appear that there is no reason to spell out this general rule in provisions of secured loan contracts. However, such provisions are commonly found in American indentures: For example:

"Except as herein otherwise provided, this Obligation and the rights of the Obligees hereunder shall for all purposes be governed by the laws of the State of New York, United States of America, and shall be construed and enforced in accordance with such laws; provided, that this provision is without prejudice to any mandatory provision of German law applicable either (a) to the creation of mortgages or the foreclosure thereof or other proceedings relative to real estate or fixed property or (b) to any proceedings which may be brought or instituted by the Obligees or either of them in Germany for the enforcement of this Obligation or any one or more of the provisions, covenants or agreements herein contained."[198]

Such provisions are also frequently included in English trust deeds. For example:

"[The Borrower shall create a mortgage] in accordance with the laws of [Country X] and do all such further things as shall be required by law to validate and give full effect to such mortgage and duly comply with all other requirements of [Country X's] law."

The practical usefulness of these provisions should not be underestimated. In the first place, the scope of the relevant legal provisions vary from country to country: Some domestic laws regulate only those matters concerning the validity and enforcement of the security, or the

---

[197] See e.g., the following cases dealing with loan transactions: Casey v. Cavaroc, 96 US 467, 24 L. Ed. 779, 6 Otto 467 (1878); Hockey v. Mother of Gold Consolidated Mines Ltd. (1903) 9 Austral. L.R. 163, 29 Vict. L.R. 196; Arbitral Award June 15, 1936, Société des Cimenteries et Briqueteries Réunies v. Union des Banques Suisses, Zurich, Clunet 1936, 834. Comp., the Award of July 5, 1901 of the French-Chilean Tribunal in the case of the Peruvian Guano Loans, Descamps et Renault, *Recueil International des Traités du XXème Siècle*, 188 (1901).

[198] Form of Obligation issued by the Liquidation of United Steel Works Corp. (Vereinigte Stahlwerke A.G.) pursuant to a Declaration and Agreement of Deposit, dated January 1, 1953 (Article XX).

characterization of chargeable assets;[199] others go further, to establish standards regarding the capacity of the borrower or the authority of its agents to create the security in question,[200] or the formal or substantial validity of ancillary instruments.[201] Furthermore, a single

[199] See e.g., the following provision in an indenture between an American trustee and a German company stipulating that the property to be covered by a German mortgage:

". . . shall mean property . . . of the character and defined by the laws of Germany as real property, situated within the German Reich."

In view of the variations among leading systems of law in regard to the definition of real property, provisions such as the above may be extremely useful. The danger, of course, is that if the role of the *lex situs* is not limited to relatively narrow matters of characterization, the whole concept of security may become obscure and the existence of the security itself questionable (see Chapter V text and note 2).

On the general question of characterization of property, see Lalive, *The Transfer of Chattels in the Conflict of Laws* (1955), pp. 14 et seq.; Robertson, *Characterization in the Conflict of Laws* (1940), pp. 190 et seq.

[200] See e.g., the Hockey Case cited supra note 197. In regard to the authority of agents, see Supreme Court of Germany October 18, 1935, RGZ 149, 93, 3; Nouvelle Revue de Droit International Privé 1936, 149, holding that the applicable law was the German law of the situs of the mortgaged property rather than the Belgian law applicable to the agency contract.

An altogether different question is whether the borrower, without prior governmental consent, can create an effective charge on its local assets in favor of alien creditors or their representatives. As a rule, loan contracts solve the question either by stating that all consents have been duly obtained or by making such consents a condition to effectiveness of the loan.

[201] An old French case (Cass. July 5, 1827, Etchegoyen v. Leray, D.P. 1827.1.295; S.1828.1.105) held that a power of attorney giving an agent authority to mortgage real property in France must comply with the provisions of the *lex situs*. However, the opposite conclusion was reached in a Dutch decision upholding the validy of a power of attorney executed in accordance with the provisions of the *lex loci actus* (California) rather than with those of the situs of the mortgaged property (the Netherlands) (Supreme Court of the Netherlands November 21, 1952, Nederlandse Belegging Maatschappij, S.A. v. Kaufman, Rev. 1958, 512; Clunet 1955, 896).

In view of these difficulties of characterization, which exist also in common-law countries, it is not surprising that legal advisers to lenders are careful to stipulate precise and adequate provisions in the loan documents. Thus, an indenture between an American trustee and two Italian companies, after stipulating for the creation of a mortgage on real property in Italy, owned by the guarantor company, provides that:

"**. . . the Company and the Guarantor jointly and severally covenant** that prior to the authentication and delivery by the Trustee of any bonds under this Indenture they will enter into a contract with the Trustee before a Notary in strict compliance with the Code of Civil Procedure and all other applicable provisions of the laws of the Kingdom of Italy in the form of contract (herein sometimes called the Notarial Act) a copy of which in the Italian language together with a certified English translation is annexed hereto . . ."

loan transaction may be secured by several types of assets located in various countries. This is true in the case of a loan secured by a mortgage and a pledge of assets owned by the borrower in various countries;[202] a mortgage of the borrower's real property coupled with an assignment of industrial or commercial contract between the borrower and third parties;[203] or as it is most common in England, a mortgage and a floating charge on the Borrower's assets.[204] In all these cases, the lender's attempt to settle the conflicts issue in the loan documents is entirely justified.

Sometimes, lenders supplement applicable-law stipulations with provisions requiring the borrower to perform all acts which the lenders consider appropriate to preserve their rights in the security. The obligation thus imposed may exceed the strict requirements of the applicable law. Thus, in the case of a loan secured by an assignment of the borrower's rights under contracts with third parties, the lender generally wants to be sure not only that the assignment is valid under its proper law, but also that all consents or notices necessary to make it enforceable against the third parties have been duly effected. A good illustration is found in a trust deed between an English trustee and a continental power company in country A, involving a loan secured by an assignment of power contracts between the borrower and purchasers of electricity in country A and another continental country (B):

"The [Borrower] will forthwith assign to the Trustees the benefit of [the power contracts]. . . . and will give all such notices and directions and procure all such acknowledgements and do all such

Comp., the following provision in a Trust Deed between an English Trustee and an Austrian company, stating that the mortgage to be created upon Austrian assets of the borrower:
"[shall] be in such form and [shall] be completed in such manner as the Trustees or their legal advisers may require . . ."

[202] Thus, an Indenture between a Canadian company and a Canadian trustee providing for the creation of: (i) a mortgage of real estate owned by the borrower in a foreign country; and (ii) a pledge of securities held in Canada by the borrower and deposited with the trustee, stipulates that the law of the Province of Ontario shall govern the rights of the Trustee in the pledged securities, while the *lex situs* will govern the trustee's rights in the mortgaged assets.

[203] See e.g., Irving Trust Co. v. Deutsch-Atlantische Tel., 22 N.Y.S. 2d 581 (1940) ; Royal Exchange Assurance v. Brownell, 146 F. Supp. 563 (1956), aff'd 257 F. 2d 582 (1958).

[204] See e.g., Pennsylvania Co. for Insurance on Lives and Granting Annuities v. United Railways of Havana & Regla Warehouse, Ltd., 26 F. Supp. 379 (D.C. Me 1939).

other acts and things as may in the opinion of the Trustees or
their legal advisers be necessary or proper to ensure that such
assignment shall be valid and enforceable by the Trustees as
against [the purchasers of electricity in countries A and B] and
each of them . . . "

The indenture and the assignment itself were governed by English law.

Similar provisions are found in loans made by public lenders. For
example, the 1955 IBRD loan to the Vorarlberger Illwerke Aktien-
gesselschaft, an Austrian company, is secured both by a mortgage and
an assignment of revenues received by the borrower from its sales of
power to German companies.[205] The assignment is defined as "an
assignment on account of payment (abtretung zahlungsbalber) within
the meaning of the laws of the guarantor [i.e. Austria]." The loan
agreement provides, among other conditions of effectiveness, that the
borrower must establish, to the satisfaction of the IBRD, the validity
of the assignment and the notification by the German companies ("in
form and substance satisfactory to the Bank") of their consent to the
assignment.

This loan deserves attention in another respect also. It illustrates
the fact that, although under Section 7.01 of the IBRD Loan Regulations the loan relationship (including the borrower's obligation to
create and maintain the security) is insulated against conflicting
domestic law, the security itself remains subject to municipal law.
The distinction between the law governing the loan transaction and
that governing the related security arrangements, already noted in
connection with private loan contracts,[206] is thus present also in the

---

[205] Loan Agreement dated June 14, 1955, 221 UNTS 375. See especially,
Sections 5.03, 5.04, 5.09, 5.10, 7.01 and 7.02 of the Agreement.

[206] See supra text and notes 75 to 77. See also the award of June 15, 1936,
in the case of Société des Cimenteries et Briqueteries Réunies, Anvers v. Union
des Banques Suisses, Zurich, Clunet 1936, 834. In that case, a Belgian company had issued bonds in Switzerland. The bonds were denominated in Swiss
francs of the weight and fineness existing at the time of issue, bore interest
at the rate of 7% per annum and were payable in Switzerland. The loan was
secured by a mortgage on real property located in Belgium; and the sum
recorded in the Belgian register of mortgages, expressed in Belgian currency,
was the equivalent of the Swiss franc amount of the loan.

In 1935, a Belgian statute was enacted to provide that the rate of interest
on mortgage loans should not exceed 5% per annum. The question at issue
was whether the borrower could invoke the benefit of the new statute or
was still bound to pay interest at the original contractual rate. The parties
agreed to submit the matter to arbitration. In a carefully weighed award,
which emphasized the conflict-of-laws aspects of the problem, the arbitrator

case of secured loans between the IBRD and private borrowers.[207]

Secured loans between the IBRD and a borrowing member government present a different picture: Since both parties are international persons, international law normally governs both the loan agreement and the lender's rights in the security.[208] A concrete example is a loan made by the IBRD to Yugoslavia, which provided that payments due Yugoslavia by timber importing countries, pursuant to agreements between each importer and Yugoslavia, were to be made to, or on the order of, the IBRD.[209] Both the loan and the security arrangement were governed by international law. The same principle applies to the several agreements between the IBRD and member governments which provide for security in the form of oil

---

held: (i) since the bonds were governed by Swiss law, the contractual rate of interest should be maintained, but (ii) since the mortgaged property was situated in Belgium, the Belgian statute in force at the situs determined the maximum amount of interest actually secured by the mortgage. In Belgium, therefore, the contractual rate of interest was secured up to 5% only; as to the remaining 2%, the bondholders were for the future deprived of any specific security and should rely exclusively on the borrower's solvency.

Regarding the determination of the law applicable to the Act of Pledge between the ECSC and the BIS, and the law applicable to actual pledges of enterprises obligations, see Zimmer, op. cit., note 4 supra, pp. 270-271.

[207] See also, among others, the following loans made by the IBRD to: (i) Corporación de Fomento de la Producción and Compania Carbonífera e Industrial de Lota (July 14, 1957, 228 UNTS 139, Article V, Section 5.03) secured by: "a hipoteca y prenda industrial of the first grade under the laws of the Republic of Chile"; (ii) several Dutch Shipping Companies (July 15, 1948, 153 UNTS 211, 259, Article VII, Section 1) secured by: "a ship mortgage in accordance with the laws of the Kingdom of the Netherlands"; (iii) K.L.M. Royal Dutch Airlines (March 20, 1952, 159 UNTS 207, Article VI, Section 6.01) secured by a chattel mortgage on aircraft "executed in accordance with the laws of the respective states of the United States hereinafter specified [California and New York]"; and (iv) Compagnie Algérienne du Méthane Liquide, "CAMEL" (May 14, 1964, Article V, Sections 5.10 and 5.12, 3 Int'l Legal Materials 821 (1964) registered with the United Nations Secretariat under No. 7552) secured by an assignment (délégation) of a purchase contract by "a hypothèque and nantissement de fonds de commerce of the first grade in accordance with the laws of the Republic of Algeria".

[208] See e.g., the Agreement dated March 19, 1936, between Italy and Albania (Article 3), 173 LNTS 83 (secured on the revenues of the Albanian Tobacco monopoly); the Agreement Regarding the Relief of Debts Contracted by the Kingdom of the Serbs, Croats and Slovenes, towards Australia, Denmark, France, Great Britain, the Netherlands, Norway, Sweden and Switzerland, dated August 8-12, 1927 (Article 6), 101 LNTS 483 (secured by a first charge on the receipts of war indemnities accruing to the debtor government).

[209] October 17, 1949, 155 UNTS 3.

royalties or other revenues accruing to the borrowing government.[210]

A different situation was presented by a loan from the IBRD to Iraq.[211] The loan was secured by an assignment of oil royalties due Iraq by three British oil companies, and the IBRD had the right to receive direct payment from the oil companies. As between the IBRD and Iraq, the assignment was governed by international law. However, the IBRD's claim to payments from the oil companies would have had to be enforced in accordance with the applicable domestic law.[212]

III. A BORDERLINE CASE: THE STATUTE OF LIMITATIONS

Statutes of limitations (called "prescription" in the civil law) exhibit considerable variations from country to country. In most countries the general rules regarding limitation of contractual claims are applicable to causes of action under loan contracts, bonds or coupons, and the periods of limitation may be relatively short,[213] or extend over several decades.[214] In an increasing number of countries, however, specific statutes have been enacted which shorten the period of limitation applicable to bonds and coupons.[215]

---

[210] Loan Agreement dated January 22, 1957, between Iran and the IBRD, 317 UNTS 129 (oil revenues) ; Loan Agreement dated September 9, 1960, between Israel and the IBRD, 406 UNTS 3 (port revenues).

[211] Loan Agreement dated June 15, 1950, 155 UNTS 267 and Annexed Indenture of Assignment (Articles II and V).

[212] See also, *Broches,* p. 358.

[213] See e.g., New York, City Practice Ace § 48 (1) (six years) ; Switzerland, Code of Obligations, Arts. 127-128 (ten years for the payment of principal, five years for the payment of interest) ; Italy, Civil Code, Arts 2947-2948 (same as Switzerland); Japan, Commercial Code, Art. 316 (same as Switzerland). For a recent Swiss decision regarding the possible effect of force majeure as an event tolling the statute of limitations, see T.F. October 9, 1962, Legerlotz v. Ville de Salzbourg, R.O. 82.II.283 (summarized in Clunet 1965, 937).

[214] See e.g., France, Civil Code, Arts. 2262 and 2277 (thirty years as to principal and five years as to interest) ; Belgium, Civil Code, Arts. 2262 and 2277 (same as France) ; the Netherlands, Civil Code, Arts. 2004 and 2012 (same as France) ; Germany, BGB, Arts. 195, 197 and 801 (thirty years and four years, respectively).

[215] See e.g., Chile, Law No. 4657 on the Issuance of Bonds by Corporations of September 25, 1929, Art. 76 (five years from the date of maturity) ; Mexico, Law of Negotiable Instruments of August 26, 1932, Art. 227 (five years as to principal, three years as to interest).

Sometimes governmental debts have been the object of special attention. For example the French statute of January 29, 1831 (as amended) provides that claims against the government, political subdivisions thereof, or agencies of the government or such subdivisions, are:

> " . . . barred and definitely extinguished . . . within four years following the fiscal year in which they were payable, if the creditors are domiciled in Europe, and within five years if the creditors are domiciled outside the European territory."

A recent application of this statute is found in the case of *Trésor Public v. Veuve Hermann*,[216] involving a dispute between the French government and a holder of Canadian bonds of the French Messageries Maritimes issued in 1927 with the guarantee of the French Government.

Another complicating factor is the different view which obtains in common-law and civil-law countries, respectively, regarding the "procedural" or "substantial" nature of the statute of limitations. The traditional view in civil-law countries is that "prescription" is a substantive matter governed by the proper law of the cause of action.[217] Therefore, specific reference in the loan documents to the period of limitation may appear unnecessary, to the extent that these documents clearly define the applicable law. This is the view apparently adopted by German lenders, who seem to rely on stipulations of applicable law to resolve the incidental issue of limitation.[218] In other markets,

---

[216] Paris June 2, 1959, Gaz. Pal. 1959, II, 170.

[217] In France, until recently, the courts favored the applicability of the law of the debtor's domicil rather than of the proper law of the contract. This view is now outdated and the French courts have joined other continental courts in deciding that "prescription" is governed by the *lex contractus*. See Cass. March 28, 1960, Estarella Vincensini v. Aubaniac, Clunet 1961, 776; Rev. 1960, 202. For earlier judgments of the French Supreme Court, see Cass. January 31, 1950, Banque Internationale de Commerce de Pétrograd v. Bergens Privatbank, S. 1951.1.121; D. 1950, 261; Rev. 1950, 415; and Cass. January 20, 1954, Ramassamipoulle v. Soubramanayer, Recueil Penant 1956, 265.

[218] See e.g., the prospectuses concerning the: (i) Oesterreichische Donaukrafwerke A.G. 6% DM Bonds of 1959, guaranteed by the Republic of Austria and two power companies; (ii) City of Oslo 6% DM Bearer Bonds of 1964; (iii) Japan 6% DM Bonds of 1964; (iv) Republic of Finland 6% DM Bonds of 1964; (v) IBRD 5½% DM Bonds of 1965; (vi) EIB 5½% DM Bonds of 1964; (vii) IADB 5½% DM Bearer Bonds of 1964; and (viii) EUROFIMA 5½% DM Bonds of 1964.

however, such as those in Switzerland[219] or the Netherlands,[220] stipulations of applicable law are consistently supplemented by specific provisions regarding the period of limitation, even though the period so specified is usually that found in the relevant provisions of the proper law.[221]

In common law countries, on the other hand, the statute of limitations is generally regarded as a "procedural" matter. In the absence of statutory provision to the contrary,[222] therefore, a foreign cause of action is not allowed if the action is barred by the *lex fori*, even though the period of limitation has not expired under the foreign law. Conversely, such an action is admissible as the forum if the local time limit has not expired, even though it may be barred by the foreign law. From the creditors' viewpoint, of course, the common law approach is particularly advantageous. It enables him to vary the period of limitation by "shopping around" for the most convenient forum. This may explain why lenders in common-law countries often omit provisions specifying the applicable statute of limitations in loan contracts with foreign borrowers[223]

---

[219] See e.g., the prospectuses concerning the: (i) Cardbury Brothers Limited (an English company) 4½% Loan of 1963; (ii) Société Electrique de l'Our, SEO, Luxembourg, 4½% Loan of 1963; (iii) International Standard Electric Corporation, New York, 4¼% Loan of 1962; (iv Union Sidérurgique du Nord de la France, USINOR, Paris, 4½% Loan of 1964; (v) City of Quebec 4½% Loan of 1960; (vi) City of Oslo 4½% Loan of 1955; (vii) Kingdom of Denmark 4½% Loan of 1962; (viii) Republic of Finland 5% Loan of 1961; (ix) Commonwealth of Australia 4½% Loan of 1961; (x) IBRD 4½% Bonds of 1959; and (xi) ECSC 4¼% Bonds of 1956.

[220] See e.g., the prospectuses concerning the: (i) Kraftlaget Opplandskraft (Electric Supply Company), Norway, 5¼% Bonds of the 1962 Series; (ii) Sabena (the Belgian Airline) 4¾% 20 Year Bearer Bonds; (iii) City of Oslo 5% Loan of 1961; (iv) Commonwealth of Australia 5% 20 Year Bonds of 1961; (v) IBRD 4½% Bonds of 1961; and (vi) EIB 5¾% 20 Year Bonds of 1964.

[221] It is only in exceptional circumstances that the period of limitation stipulated in loan documents differs from that found in the proper law. An example is the International Standard Electric Corporation, New York, 4¼% Loan of 1962 issued in Switzerland. Clause 8 of the prospectus contains the usual stipulation that the bonds and the coupons shall cease to be enforceable 10 and 5 years, respectively, after the respective dates on which they become payable (a typical incorporation into the bonds of the provisions of the Swiss Code of Obligations); clause 11, however, provides that the indenture the bonds and the coupons are subject to the law of New York (except for the periods of limitation).

[222] New York Civil Practice Act, § 13.

[223] (a) A relatively rare example of such a provision in the United States market is found in a 1930 indenture between a German company and an

American and German trustee which, after stipulating that the applicable law was that of New York, provided that:

"the laws of the State of New York concerning limitations of actions are hereby waived to such extent that actions may be commenced for the enforcement of the principal of, or premiums on, any of the Debentures at any time within thirty (30) years after the date upon which such principal or premiums shall become due and payable and that actions may be commenced for the enforcement of interest upon any of the Debentures and all other payments upon any of the Debentures at any time within six (6) years from the date upon which such interest or other payments shall become due and payable."

Another example is found in the 6% guaranteed Dollar Debentures issued in 1965 by Kockums Mekaniska Verkstads Aktiebolag and Aktiebolaget Götaverken, respectively, and guaranteed by Sweden. These debentures provide that:

"Interest and principal and premium (if any) on this Debenture will cease to be payable after the expiration of whichever is the longer of the following periods:

(a) four years (in the case of a coupon) from the interest payment date shown thereon and six years (in the case of principal or premium) from the date on which the Debenture becomes due and payable; or

(b) four years (in the case of a coupon) and six years (in the case of principal or premium) from the date on which the amounts in U.S. dollars required to pay such coupon, principal or premium were paid to the Fiscal Agent in accordance with this Debenture.".

These transactions present other interesting features, which, according to the information given to this writer, were made necessary by certain peculiarities of Swedish law. As this writer understands it, under Swedish law, obligations cease to be payable ten years after the date of issue although they may be extended if, before the end of this period, the Obligor is notified of the existence of the debt. In order to account for this solution, which is probably unique, the Fiscal Agency Agreement provides that, at some time during the five years preceding the end of the tenth year following the date of issue, the Fiscal Agent will "notify the National Debt Office of Sweden in writing of the existence of the obligations of Sweden under its guarantee of the Debentures".

Notwithstanding the general absence of time-limit provisions in loan contracts between American bankers and foreign borrowers or in foreign bonds issued in the United States, it is not infrequent to find stipulations in American Fiscal Agency Agreements to the effect that any monies paid by the borrower to the Fiscal Agent to service the loan which remain unclaimed at the end of six years after the due date shall be repaid to the borrower, such repayment terminating the liability of the Fiscal Agent in respect to these monies, although not necessarily discharging the borrower from its obligations to the bondholders.

(b) References to specific periods of limitation, though not always found in bonds issued in England, have recently appeared in bonds issued by such Continental borrowers as: (i) the City of Turin 6½% Sterling/DM Bonds 1984:

"Prescription. Bonds and coupons will become void unless presented for payment within a period of 6 years from the due dates of payment or the dates on which S. G. Warburg & Co. Limited receives the full amount of the moneys payable thereon, whichever is the later."

An interesting question is presented in the case of intergovernmental loans or loans between governments and international organizations which contain no reference to municipal law:[224] When international law governs the transaction, does the principle of limitation or prescription apply? As yet, in view of existing doctrinal controversies, there is no clear answer to this question,[225] and the loan

---

and (ii) the City of Cophenhagen Swiss Frs. 5% External Loan 1974/1983:
"*Prescription.* Coupons will be paid on presentation on or at any time after the interest payment date shown thereon and the principal of and premium (if any) on the Bonds will be paid on presentation on or at any time after the due date of redemption thereof provided that a coupon will cease to be payable and will not be paid and principal and premium (if any) will cease to be payable and will not be paid after the expiration of whichever is the longer of the following periods calculated from the relevant interest payment date or due date of redemption as the case may be: (a) five years (in the case of a coupon) from the interest payment date shown thereon and ten years (in the case of the principal or or premium (if any) on a Bond) from the due date of redemption thereof; or (b) five years (in the case of a coupon) and ten years (in the case of principal or premium) from the date on which the amounts in Swiss Francs necessary to pay such coupon, principal or premium (as the case may be) were placed at the disposal of Morgan Grenfell & Co. Limited as principal Paying Agent. Upon any coupon, principal or premium ceasing to be payable under the foregoing provisions of this paragraph, Morgan Grenfell & Co. Limited will pay over to the City the moneys in its hands corresponding thereto."
In these cases, however, the bonds were intended to be placed primarily with Continental investors and this consideration may explain the departure from the prevailing English practice. An additional consideration in the case of the City of Copenhagen Bonds is that the law stipulated applicable is the law of the borrower rather than English law.
For a criticism of this type of provision, in light of an English decision giving them effect (see U.G.S. Finance Ltd. v. National Mortgage Bank of Greece, The Times July 3, 1963), see Mann, "New Light on the Law of Bearer Bonds", 113 The Banker 697 (1963).
[224] An example of a limited reference to municipal law is found in the Agreement of June 30, 1958, between Norway and the Netherlands regarding compensation for Norwegian bonds lost by Dutch owners during World War II (346 UNTS 217). This agreement provides that the Dutch Government shall "guarantee" any loss which the borrowers might sustain as a result of payments made to owners of bonds, and provides further that:
"The Netherlands Government's guarantee shall apply until the bonds and the coupons which are covered by the present Agreement are prescribed according to the Norwegian legislation in force at any time. However, when the bonds have face values in several currencies or in a currency other than Norwegian crowns, the guarantee shall also apply until prescription has come into force in conformity with the general regulations which the debtor in question applies in relation to foreigners" (Article I, Section 4).
[225] See e.g., the Gentini Case, Venezuelan Arbitration of 1903, *Ralston's Report* (1904), pp. 724-730; Mixed (Greek-Bulgarian) Arbitral Tribunal February 14, 1927, Sarropoulos v. Etat Bulgare, VII *Recueil des Décisions,*

agreements in question are usually silent on this point. Even if it were concluded, as it seems reasonable, that some period of limitation should be applied, it would be impossible to fix any precise time limit in the absence of a specific provision in the loan agreement.

SECTION III. THE EFFECTIVENESS OF STIPULATIONS OF APPLICABLE LAW; PROSPECTS.

The widespread practice of including applicable-law stipulations in international loan documents reflects the general belief of financiers and their legal advisers that this is the best method of avoiding disputes as to the applicable law.

On the whole, this belief appears justified. A stipulation of applicable law in a loan contract, even if it merely confirms existing conflicts rules, has the great merit of clarity. A contractual choice of the applicable law *pro tanto* excludes any doubt or argument as to the applicability of other legal systems with which the transaction may have contact. In this, as in the case of jurisdictional clauses with which conflict-of-laws clauses are usually combined,[226] an appropriate stipulation in the loan documents may considerably reduce the chance of future controversies, or at least make their outcome reasonably predictable. Thus, of the reported conflicts cases concerning international loans, only a few involved disputes over the meaning or scope of an express stipulation of applicable law, and in most instances the stipulation was given effect.[227]

---

p. 47; The Pious Fund Case of 1902, 1 *Hague Court Reports* (1916), p. 429; the Ambatielos Case (Greece v. United Kingdom) March 6, 1965, 50 Am. J. Int'l L. 674 (1956).

See also, Bin Cheng, *General Principles of Law* (1953), pp. 373-386; Schwarzenberger, I *International Law* (3d ed. 1957), pp. 565-570; Lauterpacht, *Private Law Sources and Analogies of International Law* (1927), pp. 273-5; Rousseau, I *Principes Généraux du Droit International Public* (1944), pp. 907-8; Pinto, *La Prescription en Droit International,* 87 Recueil des Cours 390 (1955), pp. 438-449; Jenks, *The Prospects of International Adjudication* (1964), pp. 538-540.

[226] See Chapter IV.

[227] See e.g., T.F. July 7, 1942, Rheinisch-Westfaelische Elektrizitaetswerk, A.G. v. Anglo-Continentale Treuhand, R.O.68.II.203; Clunet 1946-49, 208. In that case, a German corporation had issued gold-dollar bonds payable in New York and "collectible" in various countries, including Switzerland. The bonds provided that the law of New York should govern. A bondholder, attempting to avoid the consequences of the Joint Resolution of Congress of 1933 abrogating gold clauses, demanded payment in Switzerland, where gold clauses remained valid. The Court ruled against the bondholder:

"It is inadmissible that the law designated once and for all be ignored because of a unilateral act of a creditor and that such a creditor be given—

However, over-confidence in the merits of stipulating the applicable law would be misplaced. Though it may designate a set of legal rules which have a direct impact upon the rights and obligations of the parties, a contractual choice of law can never substitute for a clear and precise expression of the parties' intent as to the particulars of the loan transaction. For example, matters concerning performance, the lenders' remedies, or the borrower's defenses should be expressly provided for, whether or not an applicable-law provision is included. Otherwise, in the event of a dispute, the matter in issue may be given a characterization which removes it from the scope of the law stipulated applicable.[228]

Furthermore, there are certain areas in which the applicable law cannot be effectively stipulated by the parties.[229] For example, ex-

---

since he can select the place of payment—the unilateral power of designating the applicable law. If this were possible, the juridical uncertainty, which it was precisely the object of a stipulation of applicable law to remove, would be increased in an intolerable manner" (as translated).

See also, Barnes v. United Steel Works Co., 11 N.Y.S. 2d 161 (1939); In Re Helbert Wagg & Co., Ltd. [1956] 1 All E.R. 129; Cass. Belgium February 24, 1938, Société Antwerpia v. Ville d'Anvers, Rev. 1938, 661, Clunet 1939, 413; Supreme Court of the Netherlands March 13, 1936, Vereeniging voor den Effectenhandel v. Bataafsche Petroleum Mij., Nederlandsche Jurisprudentie No. 281 (1936), Rev. 1936, 733, 36 B.I.J.I. 315 (1936); Helsingfors City Court December 23, 1937, Amsterdam Stock Exchange Committee v. Government of Finland, 38 B.I.J.I. 280 (1938).

But see, Supreme Court of the Netherlands May 13, 1936, Royal Dutch Case, 36 B.I.J.I. 304 (1936). This case involved gold-dollar bonds issued by the Royal Dutch Company, payable in New York and collectible in Amsterdam. The bonds provided that they were to be governed by the laws of the State of New York. Despite this stipulation of applicable law, it was held that the "collection" clause providing for payment in Amsterdam had brought the loan relationship "within the sphere of Dutch interests", and that the Joint Resolution of Congress could not affect the substance of an obligation to be performed in the Netherlands. This decision, clearly based on a misconstruction of the facts of the case, belongs to that series of decisions which imputed into bonds or loan contracts an "option de change" where only an "option de place" had been intended. See Chapter VI, text and notes 77-80.

[228] Difficulties of characterization are not rare. See e.g., in connection with: (a) the powers of trustees, Chapter II, text and notes 95, 99 to 106; (b) corporate matters, text and notes 183-189 supra; (c) formalities, text and note 201 supra; or (d) the statute of limitation, text and notes 217 to 223.

[229] See generally, Yntema, " 'Autonomy' in Choice of Law", 1 Am. J. Comp. L. 341 (1952); Schmitthoff, "Conflict Avoidance in Practice and Theory", 21 Law & Cont. Problems 429 (1956); Maw, "Conflict Avoidance in International Contracts", in *International Contracts: Choice of Law and Language* (Parker School 1962), pp. 23 et seq.; Nurick, op. cit. note 4 supra; Restatement Second, Conflict of Laws, Draft No. 6, Section 332a.

The question of whether there are legal obstacles to stipulating the law

change contracts, including loans, which fall within the scope of the IMF Articles of Agreement and the exchange regulations maintained by members of the IMF, must now comply with the particular regulations involved,[230] regardless of any stipulation as to applicable law.[231]

Other examples are easy to find. Thus, a stipulation in a trust indenture that it is to be governed by the laws of country A will be of little help if the trustee attempts to discharge his duties in country B, and the concept of trust is foreign to, or contrary to the public policy of, B.[232] Similar problems might arise in the case of bonds issued in several countries, including France, if the bonds provide that they are to be governed by the law of country X, which gives bondholders' communities greater powers than those recognized by French law: This provision may prove to be of no effect if French bondholders, in a French forum, challenge a majority resolution which is valid under the proper law, but invalid under the law of France.[233]

The considerations indicated above lead careful practitioners to make certain that the loan contract is valid not only under the law stipulated applicable, but also under the laws of any other country with which the transaction or some of its most important features may be connected.[234]

Compliance with all conceivably applicable laws, however, does not necessarily eliminate all problems. In the case of long-term contracts (which most international loans are), the possibility is great that changes will occur in the law or laws stipulated applicable or complied with, defeating the original expectations of the parties. Thus, a stipulation of "United States" law by an American foreign lender in the nineteen-twenties would have encouraged foreign courts to apply the Joint Resolution of Congress of 1923 which invalidated

---

of a country which has no contact with the transaction involved appears moot, for practical purposes, in the field of international loans. Stipulations of applicable law in loan documents invariably refer to the law of the lender, the market of issue, the borrower, the guarantor, or the country where the loan is payable or the security is located. In all these cases, it is clear that there is a substantial connection between the transaction and the applicable law.

It may be noted also that "usury cases" such as those referred to by Rabel (2 *The Conflict of Laws* (2d ed. 1960), pp. 412 et seq.) are foreign to international loan transactions.

[230] See Chapter VII, text and notes 4 to 19.
[231] Ibid., text and notes 20 to 22.
[232] See Chapter II, text and notes 62, 105; Chapter V, text and note 77.
[233] See Chapter II, text and note 90.
[234] See supra, text and notes 181-182, 191, 193-194, 198 to 207. See also Chapter I, text and notes 95 to 107.

gold clauses, thereby frustrating the lender's objective.[235] The same result would follow in the case of a stipulation of the borrower's law, if the borrower's country subsequently imposed exchange regulations, moratoria or similar measures.[236]

In the absence of an appropriate stabilization device in the loan documents, these are risks the parties must accept.

Stabilization devices purporting to insulate the loan transaction from subsequent changes in the content of the applicable law are not frequently found in loan documents, and none are known to have been included in post-World War II loan contracts.[237] In the case of loans between private persons, such devices would probably be invalid or ineffective, except under the French doctrine of international payments.[238]

The situation might be different in the case of loans made by private lenders to foreign governments. Thus it is well known that, concessions or other arrangements between host governments and foreign investors frequently contain provisions intended to stabilize, as of the time of the arrangements, the relations between the parties and the investor's status in the host country.[239] *A priori*, there is no cogent reason why this type of stipulation could not be used also in connection with international loan transactions. In order to be effective, however, such a stipulation would have to be limited to future changes in the law of the borrowing government. This would require a willingness on the part of lenders to submit to the borrower's law, and forego the protection they seek to achieve by bringing loan contracts within the scope of their own law. Whether lenders would be willing to accept this radical departure from established con-

---

[235] Cf., T.F. July 7, 1942, Rheinish-Westfaelische Elektrizitaetswerk, A.G. v. Anglo-Continentale Treuhand, R.O.68.II.203; Clunet 1946-49, 208; Cass. Belgium February 24, 1938, Société Antwerpia v. Ville d'Anvers, Rev. 1938, 661, Clunet 1939, 413; Supreme Court of the Netherlands March 13, 1936, Vereeniging voor den Effectenhandel v. Bataafsche Petroleum Mij., Nederlandsche Jurisprudentie No. 281 (1936), Rev. 1936, 733, 36 B.I.J.I. 315 (1936); Helsingfors City Court December 23, 1937, Amsterdam Stock Exchange Committee v. Government of Finland, 38 B.I.J.I. 280 (1938).

[236] See e.g., In Re Helbert Wagg & Co., Ltd. [1956] 1 All E.R. 129.

[237] See text and notes 144-145 supra.

[238] See text and notes 136 to 143 supra. See also Van Hecke, "Choice-of-Law Provisions in European Contracts" in *International Contracts: Choice of Law and Language* (Parker School 1962), p. 49.

[239] See e.g., Kahn, "Problèmes Juridiques de l'Investissement dans les Pays de l'Ancienne Afrique Française", Clunet 1965, 338, at pp. 370-372; Nwogugu, *The Legal Problems of Foreign Investment in Developing Countries* (1965), pp. 169-171.

tractual practices is somewhat doubtful at the present. Yet in the case
of loans to responsible borrowers, submission to the borrower's own
law, supplemented by a stabilization device, might afford lenders a
protection substantially greater than that obtained under a stipulation
designating their own laws as applicable: A reappraisal of the fundamental issues involved perhaps is a matter worth of consideration.

Another alternative, suggested by a further comparison between
international loan transactions and other types of investment agreements, would be to remove the loan relationship from domestic law
and make it subject to international law. As yet, this solution has
found no favor with private lenders. This may be due to a natural
disinclination to deviate from established patterns of transacting business, or the fear that international law, as it now stands, is too rudi-
mentary to supply all the answers to complex financial schemes. The
most important factor, however, may be the belief that in the absence
of a truly international forum having jurisdiction over loan disputes between private and international persons, submission to international law would be a perilous exercise. If such a forum were available, as it soon may be, upon the effectiveness of the Convention on
the Settlement of Investment Disputes between States and Nationals
of other States,[240] it is possible that the attitude of lenders toward international law might change. In this respect, Article 42 of the Convention is of direct interest to lenders. This Article provides that if an
investment dispute is brought before an arbitral tribunal constituted
in accordance with the provisions of the Convention, the tribunal:

> ". . . . shall decide [such] a dispute in accordance with such
> rules of law as may be agreed by the parties. In the absence of
> such agreement, the Tribunal shall apply the law of the Con-
> tracting State party to the dispute (including its rules on the
> conflict of laws) and such rules of international law as may be
> applicable."

The conflicts rules contained in this provision are clear. The

---

[240] The text of the Convention and the Accompanying Report of the
Executive Directors, dated March 18, 1965 can be obtained from the IBRD.

For comments on the Convention, see e.g., Delaume, "La Convention pour
le Règlement des Différends Relatifs aux Investissements entre Etats et
Ressortissants d'autres Etats", Clunet 1966, 26; Hynning, "The World Bank's
Plan for the Settlement of International Investment Disputes", 51 Am. Bar
Assoc. J. 558 (1965); Sirefman, "The World Bank Plan for Investment Dis-
pute Arbitration", 20 Arb. J. 168 (1965). Sassoon, "The Convention on the
Settlement of Investment Disputes between States and Nationals of Other
States", 1 Israel Law Rev. 27 (1966).

arbitral tribunal must apply the "rules of law" stipulated by the parties; or, failing any such stipulation, the law of the Contracting State party to the dispute; or such other law as may be designated by the conflicts rules of that state.[241] The arbitral tribunal must also apply international law to the extent that it may be relevant to the solution of the dispute.

The question, however, is whether the parties, in selecting the "rules of law" applicable to their relations, are free to designate international law as the applicable law, or whether their choice is limited to some domestic system of law. Though the Convention is not explicit on this point, the former interpretation seems proper. It would seem illogical to deny to the parties the power to specify the applicability of a system of law which might ultimately be held applicable by an arbitral tribunal. If this is the correct approach, then the choice of law rule contained in the Convention offers great possibilities. What use will be made of them by lenders remains to be seen.

[241] The reference to the law of the Contracting State cannot be construed as an endorsement of the presumption that loans to governments, in the absence of agreement to the contrary, are governed by the borrower's own law (see text and notes 97 to 100 supra). On the contrary, the fact that the tribunal must take into consideration the conflicts rules of the state party to the dispute should, according to the rules of most countries, lead to the application of laws other than that of the borrower. Usually, the applicable law will be that of the market of issue (see text and notes 101-102 supra).

Chapter IV

The Quest For A Forum

The current practice of including applicable-law stipulations in loan documents would be of little value if no solution were sought to corresponding jurisdictional problems. To a large extent the two questions are interdependent, and determining the "proper forum" is certainly a matter no less essential to the protection of lenders' interests than the selection of the "proper law." It is therefore not surprising that lenders generally insist on supplementing stipulations of applicable law with jurisdictional clauses designed to facilitate the enforcement of their rights against borrowers.

Lenders usually prefer that both the forum and the system of law be that of the same country, generally their own.[1] "One judge, one law, preferably my own" seems to be the credo of international lenders. This remark applies equally to private loans and loans concluded by international persons. However, the function and effectiveness of jurisdictional clauses are not necessarily identical in the two types of loans.

In the case of private loans, the many grounds for the jurisdiction of domestic courts found in jurisdictional conflicts law provide lenders with a wide choice of forums. Lenders are generally in a position to bring suit in the courts of their own country or that of the borrower, either because the borrower is domiciled or incorporated,[2] or owns

---

[1] Practical or policy considerations sometimes lead certain lending organizations, like the EIB or the IFC, to depart from this general rule. See infra text and note 62.

[2] In addition to the standard textbooks on the subject of jurisdictional-conflicts law, valuable information can be found in the following Parker School Bilateral Studies in Private International Law: (1) Nussbaum, *American-Swiss Private International Law* (2d ed. 1958, hereinafter American-Swiss P.I.L.); (2) Delaume, *American-French Private International Law* (2d ed. 1961, hereinafter American-French P.I.L.); (3) Kollewijn, *American-Dutch Private International Law* (2d ed. 1961, hereinafter American-Dutch P.I.L.);

property,[3] or maintains an agent[4] within the jurisdiction; or because the loan contract was made or is to be performed there;[5] or because

(4) Domke, *American-German Private International Law* (1956, hereinafter (American-German P.I.L.) ; (5) Eder, *American-Colombian Private International Law* (1956, hereinafter American-Colombian P.I.L.) ; (6) Ehrenzweig, Fragistas and Yiannopoulos, *American-Greek Private International Law* (1957, hereinafter American-Greek P.I.L.) ; (7) Philip, *American-Danish Private International Law* (1957, hereinafter American-Danish P.I.L.) ; (8) Cowen, *American-Australian Private International Law* (1957, hereinafter American-Australian P.I.L.) ; (9) Garland, *American-Brazilian Private International Law* (1959, hereinafter American-Brazilian P.I.L.) ; (10) Etcheberry, *American-Chilean Private International Law* (1960, hereinafter American-Chilean P.I.L.) ; (11) Seidl-Hohenveldern, *American-Austrian Private International Law* (1963, hereinafter American-Austrian P.I.L.) ; (12) Ehrenzweig, Ikchara and Jensen, *American-Japanese Private International Law* (1964, hereinafter American-Japanese P.I.L.) ; (13) Nial, *American-Swedish Private International Law* (1965, hereinafter American-Swedish P.I.L.) ; (14) Lombard, *American-Venezuelan Private International Law* (1965, hereinafter American-Venezuelan P.I.L.) .

In connection with current efforts to improve the jurisdictional rules of countries within the European Common Market, see also Weser, "Bases of Judicial Jurisdiction in the Common Market Countries", 10 Am. J. Comp. L. 323 (1961) ; and "Les Conflits de Juridiction dans le Cadre du Marché Commun", Rev. 1959, 613—1960, 21, 151, 313, 533,—and 1961, 105.

[3] See e.g., Article 23 of the German Code of Civil Procedure; Article 764 of the Dutch Code of Civil Procedure; Article 25 of the Code of Civil Procedure of the Swiss Canton of Bern; Article 248 of the Code of Civil Procedure of Denmark; Article 17 of the Code of Civil Procedure of Japan. See also, Nadelmann, "Jurisdictionally Improper Fora", *XXth Century Comparative and Conflicts Law* (1961) , p. 321; Millar, "Jurisdiction over Absent Defendants: Two Chapters in American Civil Procedure," 14 Louisiana L. Rev. 321 (1954) .

This jurisdictional ground is particularly important in the case of loans by bankers to foreign borrowers which are secured by a pledge of assets, such as gold or securities, within the jurisdiction.

[4] Ordinarily this will be a special agent appointed to make and accept service of process within the jurisdiction. As a rule, international borrowers are not "doing business" in the country of the forum, and the mere fact of issuing bonds within the jurisdiction cannot normally be characterized as falling within the scope of that jurisdictional concept. See e.g., Wahl v. Vicana Sugar Company, 144 N.Y.S. 2d 613 (1955) affirmed 2 App. Div. 248, 156 N.Y.S. 2d 993; Grossman v. Sapphire Petroleums Limited, 195 N.Y.S. 2d 851 (1959) ; Robbins v. Ring, 166 N.Y.S. 2d 483 (1957) ; Badcock v. Cumberland Gap Park Company (1893) 1 Ch. 362. But see Actiesselskabet Dampskib "Hercules" v. Grand Trunk Pacific Railway Company (1912) 1 K.B. 222; Sullivan v. Kilgore Mfg. Co., 100 F. Supp. 983 (1951) . As to Indian law, see Devadason, "Indian Law as Applicable to Corporations Incorporated outside India", 16 The Business Lawyer 1070 (1961) , at 1071.

Specific statutory enactments sometimes provide that the local courts shall have jurisdiction over foreign issuers in respect to causes of actions arising out of bonds issued within the jurisdiction. See the following note and note 39 infra.

[5] See, New York Business Corporation Law § 1314 (b) (1) ; Maryland,

one of the parties is entitled to some jurisdictional privilege based on such considerations as nationality,[6] domicile,[7] or residence.[8] Under the circumstances, the absence of a jurisdictional clause in the contract is unlikely to deprive lenders of a forum. However, it may expose lenders to the inconvenience and expense of foreign litigation. Jurisdictional clauses, therefore, in addition to importing a desirable precision into the relations of the parties, may enable lenders to avoid the jurisdictional pitfalls set by foreign legal systems, and prevent, or at least reduce the intensity of, future disputes regarding the jurisdiction of the stipulated forum. A few examples will illustrate this remark.

Under articles 14 and 15 of the French Civil Code, the French nationality of the plaintiff or defendant is a sufficient basis for the jurisdiction of French courts. Under article 59 of the Swiss Constitution, Swiss courts have *in personam* jurisdiction in the case of a solvent debtor domiciled in Switzerland. In either case a clear submission, in the loan contract or the bonds, to foreign arbitration or the jurisdiction of a foreign court will normally operate as a waiver by the interested party of his jurisdictional privilege.[9] Such a submission

---

Annotated Code (1957), Art. 23, § 92 (d). See also in England, Order XI, Rule I (f) (i) and (iii), and (g) of the Rules of the Supreme Court according to which English courts may assume jurisdiction when the contract "was made within the jurisdiction" or is "by its terms or by implication governed by English law" or when the action is brought in respect of a breach "committed within the jurisdiction." This extension of the jurisdiction of the English courts is particularly important in the field of international lending because of the English practice to stipulate in trust deeds or other loan documents that English law shall be applicable. Several civil-law countries also give jurisdiction to the *forum contractus*. See e.g., Article 420 of the French Code of Civil Procedure; Belgian law of March 25, 1876, Article 2, para. 3; German Code of Civil Procedure, Article 29. See also, Nussbaum, *American-Swiss P.I.L.*, p. 30; Delaume, *American-French P.I.L.*, pp. 152-153; Philip, *American-Danish P.I.L.*, p. 25; Ehrenzweig, Fragistas and Yiannopoulos, *American-Greek P.I.L.*, pp. 30 and 35; Garland, *American-Brazilian P.I.L.*, p. 85; Etcheberry, *American-Chilean P.I.L.*, p. 79; Ehrenzweig, Ikehara and Jensen, *American-Japanese P.I.L.*, p. 27; Seidl-Hohenveldern, *American-Austrian P.I.L.*, p. 100; Lombard, *American-Venezuelan P.I.L.*, p. 92.

    [6] See Articles 14 and 15 of the French Civil Code. See also, Delaume, *American-French P.I.L.*, pp. 143-148; Nedelmann, op. cit., supra note 3, pp. 321-328.

    [7] See Article 59 of the Swiss Constitution; Nussbaum, *American-Swiss P.I.L.*, pp. 49-50.

    [8] See New York Business Corporation Law § 1314 (a). See also, Delaume, *American-French P.I.L.*, pp. 148-149.

    [9] See Nussbaum, op. cit., supra note 7, id. loc.; Delaume, op. cit., preceding note, pp. 146-148.

may have the additional advantage of binding successors or assigns.[10]
This consideration is particularly important in the case of bonds.
Under English law, submission to foreign adjudication prevents the
English courts from assuming jurisdiction in cases involving a loan
agreement, with foreign elements, "made" or "broken" in England.[11]
Under Dutch law, submission to foreign adjudication may have the
added benefit of facilitating the enforcement in the Netherlands of
judgments rendered by the forum in question.[12]

Considerations like these explain the consistent use of jurisdictional clauses and (to a lesser extent) provisions for the arbitral settlement of disputes, in loans between private persons. It must be noted,
however, that party autonomy is subject to several limitations. Thus,
it is well settled that no agreement can extend the jurisdiction of a
court over subject matters outside its jurisdiction. All that is permitted
is the selection of a forum with jurisdiction over the subject matter
of the dispute, which may be convenient for the parties. Furthermore,
although submissions to the jurisdiction of a particular forum are ordinarily enforced by that forum, even though it may enjoy some discretion in accepting jurisdiction, an attempt to oust a court from its
jurisdiction may be unsuccessful if it conflicts with statutory prohibitions or the public policy of the ousted forum.

In this last respect, however, party autonomy has made considerable progress in recent years. Following developments in various countries,[13] including the United States,[14] forum-selecting clauses are
viewed with increased favor.[15] The exact scope of party autonomy

---

[10] Cass. July 12, 1950, Montané v. Cie des Chemins de Fer Portguais, Rev.
1952, 509; Clunet 1950, 1206; S.1952.1.41.

[11] Whether a contract is "made" or "broken" in England is decided in
accordance with English concepts. See, Webb, "Some Thoughts on the Place
of English Law as the Lex Fori in English Private International Law", 10
Int'l & Comp. L. Q. 818 (1961). See also, Plugmay Limited v. National
Dynamics Corporation, 266 N.Y.S. 2d 240 (1966).

[12] 2Kollewijn, *American-Dutch P.I.L.*, p. 35. See also, Ropers, "La Recon-
naissance et l'Exécution Réciproque des Décisions de Justice à l'Intérieur du
Marché Commun", J.C.P. 1962.I.1679.

[13] See e.g., Garland, *American-Brazilian P.I.L.*, pp. 89-93. See also Schwind,
"Derogation Clauses in Latin-American Law," 13 Am. J. Comp. L. 167 (1964);
Straus, "Inter-American Commercial Arbitration," 21 The Business Lawyer
43, 51 (1965).

[14] See e.g., Reese, "The Contractual Forum: Situation in the United
States", 13 Am. J. Comp. L. (1964); Ehrenzweig, *Conflict of Laws* (1962),
pp. 148-159; Lenhoff, "The Parties' Choice of a Forum: 'Prorogation Agreements' ", 15 Rutgers L. Rev. 414 (1961), at pp. 430-439.

[15] Lenhoff, op. cit., preceding note, pp. 419-430; Perillo, "Selected Forum
Agreements in Western Europe", 13 Am. J. Comp. L. 157 (1964); Eek, "The

may remain subject to certain limitations, such as "fairness" or "reasonableness," which leave ample room for the exercise of judicial discretion. However, in the particular field of international lending, such limitations should not be of great concern to lenders. As a rule, jurisdictional clauses in international loans, like stipulations of applicable law, have enough contacts with the forum to make the choice reasonable. The fact that lenders may have sufficient bargaining power to dictate choice of the forum would normally not justify striking down the forum-selecting provision.

Loans concluded by international persons present an altogether different picture. Whereas jurisdictional clauses in private loan agreements frequently serve the purpose of eliminating forums considered inconvenient by the parties, jurisdictional clauses in loans involving international persons are generally designed to vest in a specific forum jurisdiction which would otherwise be lacking.

The case of governmental loans is typical. The number of successful pleas of immunity reported in creditor countries indicates that the situation of creditors of foreign governments is difficult.[16] True,

---

Contractual Forum: Scandinavia", Ibid., 173; Cowen and Mendes da Costa, "Contractual Forum: Situation in England and the British Commonwealth", Ibid., 179; Bülow, "Effets de la Prorogation Internationale de Juridiction en Matière Patrimoniale", 9 Nederlands Tijdschrift voor Internationaal Recht 1962, p. 89; Blackney, "Legal Aspects of Private Investment in Japan", *Proceedings of the 1961 Institute on Private Investments Abroad and Foreign Trade* (1961), p. 263, at p. 285; Gaudemet-Tallon, *La Prorogation Volontaire de Juridiction en Droit International Privé* (1965).

See also, Nadelmann, "The Hague Conference on Private International Law and the Validity of Forum Selecting Clauses", 13 Am. J. Comp. L. 157 (1964).

But see, in Canada, National Gypsum Co. Inc. v. Northern Sales Ltd. [1964] 43 D.L.R. 2d 235; and in Venezuela, Lombard, *American-Venezuelan P.I.L.*, p. 93.

[16] See e.g., *United States:* Frazier v. Hanover Bank, 119 N.Y.S. 2d 319, aff'd 119 N.Y.S. 2d 918, 281 App. Div. 861 (1953), reargument and appeal denied 127 N.Y.S. 2d 815, 283 App. Div. 655. See also, Frazier v. Foreign Bondholders Protective Council, 125 N.Y.S. 2d 900, 283 App. Div. 44 (1953); Frazier v. Foreign Bondholders Protective Council, 133 N.Y.S. 2d 606 (1954); Anderson v. Spyers, 115 N.Y.S. 2d 132 (1952); Lamont v. Travelers Insurance Co., 24 N.E. 2d 81, 281 N.Y. 362 (1939); *England:* Wadsworth v. Queen of Spain (1851) 17 Q.B. 171; Twycross v. Dreyfus (1877) 5 Ch. D. 605; *France:* Cass. January 22, 1849, Lambèze et Pujol, D.1849.1.10; November 5, 1934, Gouvernement du Maroc v. Laurans, Rev. 1935, 795, S.1935.1.31. See also Trib. Civ. Seine November 14, 1934, Huttinger v. Société des Chemins de Fer du Congo, Clunet 1935, 623, involving a suit against the Belgian Government as guarantor of bonds issued by the Congo Railways Company; Paris October 31, 1956, Congo Belge v. Montéfiore, J.C.P. 1956, II, 9605; Int'l L. Reports, Year 1956, p. 191 (reversed, Cass. November 21, 1961, Monefiore v. Associa-

the situation of lenders improves as the doctrine of relative immunity progressively supersedes that of absolute immunity. Thus, in those countries which make a distinction between acts *jure imperii* and acts *jure gestionis*, the outcome of a suit against a foreign government depends on the characterization of governmental borrowing. If borrowing is characterized as an act *jure gestionis*, the action will normally be allowed to proceed[17], even if subject to certain conditions.[18] If borrowing is regarded as an act *jure imperii*, the plea of immunity is likely to be successful.[19] Nevertheless, due to the somewhat hazy

tion Nationale des Porteurs de Valeurs Mobilières, J.C.P. 1962, II, 12521; Rev. 1962, 329; Clunet 1962, 686) ; Trib. Civ. Seine May 24, 1961, Association des Porteurs Français de Scripts Lombards v. Etat Italien et Comité des Obligataires de la Compagnie des Chemins de Fer Danube-Save-Adiatrique, J.C.P. 1961, II, 12196; Clunet 1962, 418 (aff'd Paris December 11, 1962, J.C.P. 1963, II, 13167; aff'd Cass. October 5, 1965, D. 1966, Sommaires, p. 7). These views have been endorsed by the Institute of International Law in 1954. See 46th Session, Resolutions, Article 4:

"The courts of a state cannot entertain actions against a foreign state relative to debts incurred by that state through a public loan in the territory of the state whose courts are seized of such actions." 46 Am. J. Int'l L. 80 (1955).

Comp. Harvard Draft Convention Article 11, 26 Am. J. Int'l L., Supp 597 (1932).

[17] See e.g., In *Italy*, Court of Appeals of Lucca March 14, 1887, Hamspohn v. Bey di Tunisi, Foro Italiano 1887.1.474.

In France, a lower court held that "a loan floated in France by a foreign government cannot be regarded as an act *jure imperii* beyond the jurisdiction of the French courts". Trib. Civ. Seine February 16, 1955, Montefiore v. Congo Belge, J.C.P. 1955, II, 8580. However, this judgment was reversed. See the Montéfiore case cited supra, note 16. A more recent decision (see Rouen February 10, 1965, Société Bauer-Marchal v. Ministre des Finances de Turquei, Clunet 1965, 655) characterizes Turkey's guarantee of a loan issued in France by the City of Constantinople as an *act jure gestionis* (see note 143 infra). See also, in *Belgium:* Brussels May 24, 1933, Mahieu et al v. République Hellénique, Clunet 1935, 1034; Trib. Civ. Brussels April 30, 1951, Socobelge et Etat Belge v. Etat Hellénique, Journal des Tribunaux 1951, 298; Clunet 1952, 244; S.1953.4.1; 18 Int'l L. Reports (Year 1951) p. 3.

[18] Thus in Switzerland, even in regard to acts *jure gestionis,* no jurisdiction is acknowledged unless the transaction is somehow connected with Swiss territory, e.g. either because the loan contract was made, or the bonds were issued, or payment is to be made in that country. See T.F. March 18, 1930, République Hellénique v. Walder, R.O. 56.I.237, and June 6, 1956, Royaume de Grèce v. Banque Julius Bär et Cie, R.O. 82.I.75; Int'l L. Reports, Year 1956, p. 195. But see, T.F. March 13, 1918, K.K. Oesterreichisches Finanzministerium v. Dreyfus, R.O. 44.I.49. Comp., T.F. February 10, 1960, République Arabe Unie v. Dame X...., R.O. 86.I.23; Clunet 1961, 458; 55 Am. J. Int'l L. 167 (1961).

[19] This characterization, together with the fact that the transaction involved presented no contact with the Swiss territory, may underlie the judgment of the Swiss Federal Tribunal of March 18, 1930 cited supra, note 18. See also text and notes 157 to 162 infra.

character of this distinction, it remains difficult to forecast the outcome of any particular proceedings against a foreign sovereign.

The difficulty is further increased by the fact that it is not entirely clear, in the present state of the law, which persons can successfully invoke the benefit of sovereign immunity. The only rule as to which there seems to be general agreement is that immunity from suit, when it does exist, benefits not only the borrower but also bankers or other persons acting as agents for the borrower. Although bankers as private persons have no immunity, an action usually cannot be maintained against them if it would require adjudication of a claim against the foreign sovereign they represent.[20] This, of course, is a case of "borrowed immunity" which leaves intact the basic problem of determining whether the principal itself enjoys immunity. On this point,

---

[20] See e.g., *United States:* Gledhill v. Schiff, 224 N.Y. 593, 120 N.E. 863 (1918) ; Frazier v. Hanover Bank, 119 N.Y.S. 2d 319, aff'd 119 N.Y.S. 2d 918, 281 App. Div. 861 (1953), reargument and appeal denied 127 N.Y.S. 2d 815, 283 App. Div. 655. See also Frazier v. Foreign Bondholders Protective Council, 125 N.Y.S. 2d 900, 283 App. Div. 44 (1953) ; Frazier v. Foreign Bondholders Protective Council, 133 N.Y.S. 2d 606 (1954) ; Lamont v. Travelers Insurance Co., 24 N.E. 2d 81, 281 N.Y. 362 (1939) . Comp., Ehag Eisenbahnwerke Holding A.G. v. Banca National a Romanei, 306 N.Y. 242, 117 N.E. 2d 346 (1954) ; *England;* Smith v. Weguelin (1869) L.R. 8 Eq. 198; Twycross v. Dreyfus (1877) 5 Ch. D. 605; United States of America v. Dollfus Mieg et Compagnie S.A. [1952] 1 All E.R. 572 (in part), Annual Digest 1949, 103; Rahimtoola v. The Nizam of Hyderabad and al. [1957] 3 All E.R. 441; *France:* Cass. August 14, 1878, Dreyfus v. Dreyfus et Compagnie, S.1878.1.345; Cass. April 21, 1886, Bernet v. Herrau, Dreyfus, S.1889.1.459, D.P. 1886.1.393, and the following decisions of lower courts: Trib. Comm. Seine April 11, 1867, Cavour Canal Company case, D.P. 1867.2.49; Trib. Civ. Seine August 12, 1895, Reilhac et Chabot v. Comptoir National d'Escompte, Gazette des Tribunaux 1902.2.270; Trib. Civ. Seine August 12, 1895, De Villaines v. Comptoir d'Escompte, Clunet 1909, 144 (aff'd Paris June 26, 1908, Id. loc.) ; Aix December 30, 1929, Gouvernement du Maroc v. Laurans, S.1930.2.153; Trib. Civ. Seine December 30, 1930, Banque Ottomane v. Philippe, Clunet 1931, 1040. See however, Paris April 2, 1936, Viel v. Crédit Lyonnais, Rev. 1936, 787.

This "borrowed immunity" will not be upheld, however, if the action against the agent is not directed again him *qua* agent but relates, for instance, to his fraudulent acts or misrepresentations. See e.g., Brussels August 4, 1877, Dreyfus, Pasicrisie 1877.II.307; Pilger v. U.S. Steel Co., 97 N.J. Eq. 102, 127 Atl. 103 (1925) and on appeal 98 N.J. Eq. 665, 130 Atl. 523. See also, Cass. August 14, 1878 (dictum) , and United States of America v. Dollfus Mieg et Compagnie S.A. (in part) cited above.

As to disputes between borrowing governments and their own agents, brokers, etc., see Brussels November 22, 1907, Feldman v. Etat de Bahia, Pasicrisie 1908.II.55; Clunet 1908, 210; Cass. Italy February 4, 1932, Minister of Finance of the Republic of France v. Italian Discount Bank in Liquidation, Rivista Italiana di Diritto Internazionale 1933, 386; Clunet 1933, 455; Annual Digest 1931-32, p. 36. Comp., the judgment of the latter court of July 14, 1953, Order of Malta v. Soc. An. Commerciale Commissionnaria, 4 Int'l & Comp. L. Q. 486 (1955) ; Rev. 1955, 159.

opinions differ. Thus, whereas it has been held in the United States that a state member of the Brazilian Federation could plead immunity,[21] the contrary view has prevailed in similar cases decided by the French courts.[22] Again, while a certain similarity is noticeable among recent decisions of courts in the United States and Continental Europe regarding the treatment of governmental agencies engaged in commercial activities,[23] there remain substantial differences between the two legal systems, as well as between them and the law of England.[24]

There is no uniform agreement as to the immunity of government-owned corporations. This is an important issue, because government-owned banks, such as central banks, mortgage banks or other credit institutions, often play an important role in international borrowing operations. It would appear that the general trend in Continental countries is to deny immunity to such organizations.[25] However, especially in the case of central banks which may act in different capacities, the decision may turn on whether the defendant's function, in the particular transaction was governmental or commercial in nature.[26] This last distinction may bring Continental law closer to

[21] Sullivan v. State of Sao Paulo, 36 F. Supp. 503 (1941).

[22] Cass. October 24, 1932, Etat de Céara v. Dorr, Clunet 1933, 644, D. 1933.1.196. See also Trib. Civ. Seine December 11, 1922, Crédit Foncier d'Algérie et de Tunisie v. Restrepo et Département d'Antioquia, Clunet 1923, 857; Trib. Civ. Seine March 2, 1948, Dumont v. Etat de l'Amazone, D. 1949, 428; Comp., Brussels November 22, 1907, Feldman v. Etat de Bahia, Pasicrisie 1908.II.55; Clunet 1908, 210.

However, it appears that under both American and French law, cities or municipalities cannot plead immunity. See e.g., Schneider v. City of Rome, Italy, 83 N.Y.S. 2d 756, 193 Misc. 180 (1948), 43 Am. J. Int'l L. 382 (1949); Paris June 19, 1894, Ville de Genève v. De Civry, D. 1894.2.513. Cass. January 14, 1931, Bonnaud v. Ville de Tokio and Ville de Tokio v. Roussey, D. 1931.1.5; Rev. 1934, 537 (implicit).

[23] See e.g., Brandon, "Sovereign Immunity of Government-Owned Corporations and Ships", 39 Cornell L. Q. 425 (1954).

[24] Wedderburn, "Sovereign Immunity of Foreign Public Corporations", 6 Int'l L. Q. 290 (1957); McLeod Hendry, "Sovereign Immunity from the Jurisdiction of the Courts", 36 Can. Bar. Rev. 145 (1958).

[25] See e.g., France: Trib. Civ Seine June 16, 1955, Passelaigues v. Banque Hypothécaire de Norvège, D. 1956, Sommaires, p. 39, col. 1; Gaz. Pal. July 23-26, 1955, reproduced as Annex II to the French Memorial in the Case of Certain Norwegian Loans, I Pleadings, pp. 72-84; Egypt: Trib. Civ. Alexandria 1926 Borg v. Caisse Nationale d'Epargne Française, Annual Digest 1925-26, 171; Switzerland: see Guggenheim, I Traité de Droit International Public (1953) p. 186.

[26] See e.g., Amsterdam June 26, 1958, Krol v. Bank of Indonesia, NJ 1959, No. 164; Clunet 1964, 636; Comp., Cass. November 3, 1952, Martin v. Banque d'Espagne, Rev. 1953, 425; Clunet 1953, 654. See also, van Panhuys, "In the

that of the United States, but does not mean that the two laws are coextensive. In the United States, the deciding consideration seems to be not the type of activity carried out by the defendant, but rather whether the defendant is a separate entity or is indistinguishable from the foreign government which owns it or controls its operations.[27]

It is apparent, therefore, that the doctrine of immunity may prevent lenders from enforcing their rights against foreign governments in any court other than those in the borrower's country. Lenders generally do not regard a right to sue in these courts as a satisfactory remedy; and they cannot safely rely on the borrower's willingness to waive its immunity in the courts of the lender's country at the time of an actual dispute.[28] Lenders therefore often turn to other devices. One device is to stipulate in the loan agreement that the borrower submits to the jurisdiction of a designated forum and waives any right to sovereign immunity with respect to its obligations under the agreement. Provisions such as these are enforced in the courts of Continental countries.[29] They may prove extremely valuable also in

---

Borderland between the Act of State Doctrine and Questions of Jurisdictional Immunities", 13 Int'l & Comp. L. Q. 1193 (1964), at pp. 1198-1200.

[27] In the first instance mentioned in the text there is no immunity. See e.g., Ulen & Co. v. Bank Gospodarstwa Krajewo, 261 App. Div. 1, 24 N.Y.S. 2d 201 (1940) ; Koster v. Banco Minero de Bolivia, 307 N.Y. 831, 122 N.E. 2d 325 (1954), 283 App. Div. 927, 130 N.Y.S. 2d 870. There is immunity in the second instance. See Kingdom of Sweden v. New York Trust Co., 96 N.Y.S. 2d 779, 197 Misc. 431 (1949). But see Mirabella v. Banco Industrial de la Republica Argentina, 237 N.Y.S. 2d 499 (1963).

[28] In an action by bondholders against the French agents of a foreign government, a French court held that the mere fact that the foreign government intervened in the proceedings to plead immunity amounted to a waiver of the same. This is a rather puzzling decision. See Paris April 2, 1936, Viel v. Crédit Lyonnais et Banque de Paris et des Pays-Bas, Rev. 1936, 787. In England, see e.g., High Commissioner for India and others v. Ghosh [1959] 3 W.L.R. 811; [1959] 3 All E.R. 659. See also, Simmonds, "Implied Waiver of Immunity: Permissible Counterclaims against a Sovereign Plaintiff", 9 Int'l & Comp. L.Q. 334 (1960).

[29] See e.g., France: Trib. Civ. Seine April 10, 1888, Rochaid-Dabdah v. Gouvernement Tunisien, Clunet 1888, 670; comp., Trib. Civ. Casablanca March 10, 1955, Ministère de l'Education Publique du Portugal v. Di Vittorio, Rev. 1955, 534; Germany: Heizer v. Kaiser Franz-Josephs-Bahn A.G. (1885) Beilage I, 1, 20-21; Switzerland: T.F. October 7, 1938, Etat Yougoslave v. S.A. Sogerfin, 61 La Semaine Judiciaire 327 (1939).

Note also that Continental courts construe as implicit waivers of immunity a number of acts done by the defendant within the jurisdiction. Thus, an implied waiver of immunity has been found when the defendant deposited funds with a local bank for the service of, or as a security for, the loan (see e.g., Court of Conflicts, Prussia May 29, 1920, X . . . . v. Tuerkischen Militaerfiskus, Juristische Wochenschrift, L (1921) II, 773). This solution also prevailed in France in the case of Cosson v. Etat de Céara, Colmar June 27, 1928,

countries like the United States,[30] in which it is not clear whether waivers of immunity are irrevocable. In view of the relatively close world of the lending community, the borrower might experience embarrassment if it attempted to escape a commitment to submit to jurisdiction.

Another device is to provide for the arbitral settlement of loan disputes. In the case of loans to international persons, this solution is particularly appropriate when a waiver of immunity is objectionable for reasons of prestige, or when the binding effect of such a waiver is questionable.[31] Unfortunately, submission to arbitration of governmental loan disputes is sometimes prohibited by statutory limitations upon the arbitrability of controversies arising out of state contracts.[32]

Arbitration, in one form or another, is frequently resorted to by governments and international lending organizations.[33] This pre-

Clunet 1929, 1040. See also a dictum in Aix December 30, 1929, Gouvernement du Maroc v. Laurans, S. 1930.2.153. But see Trib. Civ. Seine December 30, 1930, Banque Ottomane v. Philippe, Clunet 1931, 1040. The same result was reached on the bases of the defendant's issuance of bonds and promise of repayment within the jurisdiction (see e.g., T.F. March 13, 1918, K.K. Oesterreichisches Finanzministerium v. Dreyfus, R.O. 44.1.49).

[30] See e.g., De Simone v. Transportes Maritimos de Estado, 199 App. Div. 602, 191 N.Y.S. 864, 867 (1st Dep't 1922) (dictum), aff'd on rehearing, 200 App. Div. 82, 192 N.Y.S. 815 (1st Dep't 1922); Lamont v. Travelers Ins. Co., 281 N.Y. 362, 370, 24 N.E. 2d 81 (1939) (dictum), reversing 254 App. Div. 511, 5 N.Y.S. 2d 295 (1st Dep't 1938); Fields v. Predionica I Tkanica A.D., 265 App. Div. 132, 37 N.Y.S. 2d 874, 883 (1st Dep't 1942) (dictum), reversing 35 N.Y.S. 2d 408 (Sup. Ct. 1942); United States of Mexico v. Schmuck, 293 N.Y. 264, 56 N.E. 2d 577 (1944). But see, Pacific Molasses Company v. Comite de Ventas de Mieles de la Republica Dominicana, 219 N.Y.S. 2d 1018 (Sup. Ct. 1961); and Hannes v. Kingdom of Roumania Monopolies Institute, 260 App. Div. 189, 20 N.Y.S. 2d 825 (1st Dep't 1940); Victory Transport, Inc. v. Comisaria General de Abastecimientos y Transportes, 336 F 2d 354 (2d Cir. 1964) petition for certiorari filed, 33 U.S. Law Week 3233 (U.S. Jan. 7, 1965, No. 815). See also, Harvard Draft Convention, Art. 8 (c) 26 Am. J. Int'l L. Supp. 451 (1932); Note, "Sovereign Immunity—waiver and Execution: Arguments from Continental Jurisprudence", 74 Yale L. J. 887 (1965); Petition of Petrol Shipping Corporation, 360 F. 2d 103 (1966).

[31] In England, for example, waivers of immunity are revocable. See e.g., Duff Development Co. Ltd. v. Government of Kalatan (1924) A.C. 797; Kahan v. Pakistan Federation (1951) 2 K.B. 1003.

For an example of an arbitration clause in bonds issued in England, see e.g., the General Bond of the State of Sau Paulo 7% Coffee Realization Loan of 1930.

[32] Whether these limitations apply only to domestic contracts or also to international state contracts has been the object of much controversy in France in recent years. See text and notes 84-85 infra.

[33] Sometimes, as in the case of intergovernmental loans or loans made by the IBRD or the BIS, the classical pattern of arbitration is provided for; i.e.

ference for arbitral rather than judicial adjudication is partly due to the fact that arbitration is simple, rapid and without publicity; and also to the consideration that no international tribunal might otherwise be available. This remark is particularly relevant in the case of loans concluded by international organizations, since the ICJ by its Statute, has jurisdiction only over disputes between states.[34]

The recent trend appears to be toward an increased us of arbitration as a means of settling disputes between international and private persons as well as disputes between international persons.

SECTION I. JURISDICTIONAL CLAUSES

A. LOANS CONCLUDED BY PRIVATE PERSONS

1. *Loans Made by Private Lenders*

Lenders in the leading financial markets of the world insist on jurisdictional provisions in loan agreements with foreign borrowers, or in bonds and related documents issued by foreign issuers. In most cases the courts designated are those of the lender's country. On a number of occasions, however, such a jurisdictional provision is coupled with stipulations conferring jurisdiction also in the courts of a second country, generally that of the borrower or of the situs of the property pledged or mortgaged as security. For the purpose of convenience, it is proposed that the first type of stipulation be hereafter referred to as "exclusive-jurisdiction clauses," and the second as "multiple-jurisdiction clauses."

(a) EXCLUSIVE-JURISDICTION CLAUSES

Provisions conferring exclusive jurisdiction upon the courts of the lender's country are commonly found in Switzerland. A typical example follows:

> "Any dispute between the bondholders and the debtor arising out of or in connection with the bonds or coupons shall be de-

---

the settlement of disputes by one arbitrator or by a panel or arbitrators. In regard to loans made to enterprises by the High Authority of the ECSC, jurisdiction is conferred upon the Court of Justice of the Communities.

The statement in the text regarding intergovernmental loans must be qualified in the sense that provisions for arbitration are not as frequent as provisions calling for consultation between the parties.

[34] Article 34 of the ICJ Statute. See e.g., Jully, "Arbitration and Judicial Settlement, Recent Trends", 48 Am. J. Int'l L. 380 (1954).

cided exclusively by the ordinary courts of the Canton of Basle-City, subject to appeal to the Federal Tribunal at Lausanne whose judgment shall be final (as translated).[35]

Comparable provisions are also found in loans negotiated in other Continental countries, like the Netherlands or Germany,[36] as well as in the United Kingdom:

"The [Borrower] hereby submits to the jurisdiction of the High Court of Justice in England as regards all matters and questions arising hereunder or under the Bonds."[37]

No such clause is usually found in France.[37a] Apparently French

---

[35] S.A. Pirelli, $4\frac{1}{2}\%$ External Loan of 1955, Prospectus, clause 10. The same provision is found in the following prospectuses: La Rinascente per l'Exercicio di Grandi Magazzini, $4\frac{1}{2}\%$ External Loan of 1955; Montecatini, Società Generale per l'Industria Mineraria e Chimica, Anonima, $4\frac{1}{2}\%$ External Loan of 1955; California Texas Corporation, $4\frac{1}{2}\%$ Loan of 1955. Société Internationale de la Moselle (GmbH) Trèves $4\frac{1}{2}\%$ Loan of 1961, Guaranteed by the Republic of France; Compagnie Française des Pétroles, Paris, $4\frac{1}{2}\%$ Loan of 1963.

[36] See e.g., Article 22 of the trust agreement attached to the prospectus of the Reders Scheepskrediet Vereniging (Shipowners' Ship Credit Association, incorporated in Norway) $5\frac{1}{2}\%$ Bonds of 1961:
"1. This agreement shall be governed by Dutch law.
2. All disputes arising out of the execution or interpretation of this agreement shall be settled by the courts of the Netherlands" (as translated).
Comp. in Germany, the City of Oslo $5\frac{1}{2}\%$ Bearer Bonds of 1959:
"All rights and obligations arising under this loan or in connection therewith shall be governed by the laws of the Federal Republic of Germany.
The courts having jurisdiction and the place of performance for all parties concerned shall be in Frankfurt am Main" (as translated).

[37] Trust Deed between English lenders and an Austrian corporation.

[37a] A recent exception, which may be significant, is found in the French prospectus of bonds (forming part of "parallel" issues in several Continental markets) issued by Ente Nazionale per l'Energia Elettrica with the guarantee of the Italian Government. The relevant provision (as translated) reads as follows:
"Bonds and coupons, both as to form and substance, and all the rights and obligations of the holders, the borrower and the banks acting as paying agents thereunder shall in all respects be governed by French laws.
All disputes arising in connection with such bonds shall be submitted to the French courts and the borrower elects domicile in Paris, with its agents in France, where all notices may be delivered to it.
The bondholders may, however, waive the benefit of the French jurisdiction and bring action in Rome before the Italian courts having jurisdiction, such courts being required to base their decision on French law.
French courts have, however, exclusive jurisdiction in respect of any

lenders believe that they are sufficiently protected by Articles 14 and 15 of the Civil Code, which gives jurisdiction to French courts by reason of the French nationality of the lenders. In addition, French law provides for several other grounds for the jurisdiction of French courts, like the making and performance of the loan contract[38] or the issuance of bonds in France.[39] In this field, like that of the con-

disputes regarding the application of statutes concerning the replacement of bonds lost or destroyed, and statutes applicable to registered bonds."

[38] See e.g., Cass. January 14, 1934, Banque Hypothécaire Franco Argentine v. Bonnaud et Hourtille, Clunet 1934, 1202; S.1934.1.297; Besançon May 15, 1929, Société du Port de Para v. Côte, Clunet 1929, 1253. Comp., Rouen June 26, 1929, Chemin de Fer de Sao Paulo et Rio Grande v. Barbey S. 1930.2.36, Clunet 1931, 630; Paris January 31, 1928, Zelinoff v. Banque de Sibérie, Rev. 1928, 291, aff'd Cass. July 29, 1929, Rev. 1930, 99, S. 1929.1.350; Cass. October 24, 1933, Banque d'Athènes v. Banque Lisboa et Açores, Rev. 1934, 484.

[39] The law of July 11, 1934 provides in its single article:
"Claims concerning the repayment of [the principal of] securities issued [in France] by corporations or collectivities [i.e. municipalities and other political units of a foreign state] or concerning the payment of coupons shall be brought before the courts at the place where the defendant corporation or collectivity has its seat [siège social], if the latter is located in France. If the defendant corporations or collectivities have their seat in a foreign country, such claims shall be brought before the courts of the Seine [Paris], unless, prior to the issuance of bonds, the defendants have elected domicile [agreed to confer jurisdiction upon a certain court] in France, in which case the court at the elected domicile shall have jurisdiction" (as translated).
Article 37 of the decree-law of October 30, 1935 also provides:
"The jurisdictional rules provided for in the law of July 11, 1934, concerning the repayment of securities issued by foreign corporations or collectivities are applicable to any claim involving the rights of holders of bonds or securities of one and the same issue" (as translated).
The view has been advanced that the 1934 and 1935 statutes are "d'ordre public" and that French courts could not be ousted of the jurisdiction specifically conferred upon them by these statutes. See Niboyet, 6 (1) Traité, p. 414. This contention finds support in French decisions concerning other aspects of the same legislation (Cass. March 22, 1944, Chemins de Fer Portugais v. Ash, S. 1945.1.77; Rev. 1940-46, 107). However, since the enactment of a 1955 statute authorizing bondholders' associations to consent to arbitration as a means of settling loan disputes with foreign borrowers, it is possible that a different and less restrictive solution might obtain. See Delaume, "Arbitration of Loan Disputes under French Law", 10 Arb. J. (N.S.) 196 (1955). For an interesting provision waiving the benefit of the law of July 11, 1934, see Section 15.08 of the Indenture dated March 1, 1962, between the Société du Pipe-Line Européen and Morgan Guaranty Trust Company of New York (5½% Sinking Fund Debentures Due 1982) :
"Appointment of Agent for Service. By the execution and delivery of this Indenture, the Company irrevocably designates and appoints the Secretary of Morgan Guaranty Trust Company of New York, in The

flict of laws, French lenders seem satisfied that French law affords them a protection sufficient to make contractual provisions unnecessary[40]

In Canada, where there have been relatively few examples of international loans, no jurisdictional provisions are found in the most recent bond issues, either in foreign governmental bond issues or issues made by foreign private borrowers.[41]

In the United States, lenders are sometimes satisfied with providing specifically for the jurisdiction of American courts,[42] although they frequently insist also upon reserving their right to bring suit also in foreign courts. Stipulations found in American loan instruments, therefore, often fall within the next category of clauses.

City and State of New York, United States of America, as the Company's authorized agent upon which process may be served in any suit or proceeding arising out of or relating to the Debentures or this Indenture and agrees that service of process upon said Secretary, and written notice of said service to the Company (mailed or delivered to its Treasurer at its principal office in Paris, France) shall be deemed in every respect effective service of process upon the Company in any such suit or proceeding. The Company further agrees to take any and all action, including the execution and filing of any and all such documents and instruments, as may be necessary to continue such designation and apointment of said Secretary in full force and effect so long as any of the Debentures shall be outstanding. The Company waives the benefit of the French Decree of July 11, 1934 to the extent necessary to give effect to the provisions of this Section 15.08."

[40] The French practice of relying upon the French statutory or case law in this field may prove dangerous. Thus, foreign countries generally refused to comply with French judgments obtained by French lenders or bondholders (usually on the basis of Article 14 of the Civil Code) to enforce gold clauses.

[41] See e.g., Commonwealth of Australia, Canadian Bonds of 1955.

It should be noted, however, that the $5\frac{1}{2}$-$7\frac{1}{2}\%$ Debentures issued in 1957 by Petrofina, a Belgian company, contain no jurisdictional clause. It is interesting to note, however, that in several loans involving banks and private borrowers resident in different Provinces of Canada, the parties generally agree that the courts of the Province in which the borrower is incorporated shall have jurisdiction. See e.g., the following provision in a Deed of Trust and Mortgage between a British Columbian corporation and a Quebec trustee:

"All questions or controversies as to the liabilities of the Trustee hereunder shall be decided and determined under the laws of, and, if litigation thereon is instituted, by the courts of, the Province of British Columbia."

This exception to the general practice to stipulate the jurisdiction of the lender's court may be more apparent than real because in most cases the lender has an agency or branch, or is acting in participation with bankers, in the Province of the borrower.

[42] See e.g., the Société du Pipe-Line Européen Indenture quoted in note 39 supra. Similar provisions are found in recent indentures relating to debentures issued by private European and Japanese borrowers.

(b) MULTIPLE-JURISDICTION CLAUSES

A typical provision in American indentures is the following:

"The Company hereby subjects itself and its property to the jurisdiction of the Courts of the United States of America and the State of New York and hereby constitutes and appoints The Corporation Trust Company, a New York corporation, or its successor appointed from time to time, having an office in the City of New York, its true and lawful attorney in fact and authorized agent, for it and in its name, place and stead, to make and accept service of all writs, processes and summons in any action, suit or proceeding in any of the Courts of the United States of America or of the State of New York, and upon whom all lawful writs, processes and summons may be served with the same effect as though the Company existed in the State of New York; and said appointment of said The Corporation Trust Company, or its successor, shall be irrevocable so long as any of the Bonds remain outstanding. Any successor to The Corporation Trust Company shall become such attorney-in-fact and authorized agent for the Company without any further act on the part of said The Corporation Trust Company or any such successor. In case The Corporation Trust Company and/or any such successor shall cease to exist, the Company agrees, upon the request of the American Trustee, forthwith to appoint a person or corporation having a residence in the City of New York, selected by the American Trustee, as its true and lawful attorney-in-fact and authorized agent with the powers and for the purposes provided in this Section 15.

The Company also hereby subjects itself and its property to the jurisdiction of the Courts of Hamburg, Germany.

The provisions of this Section 15, however, are not intended in any way to limit the right of the Trustees and of the Bondholders to bring suits, actions or other legal proceedings in any courts which they or any of them may deem proper."[43]

---

[43] Indenture of October 1, 1925, Rudolph Karstad A.G., First Mortgage 7% Sinking Fund Gold Bonds Section 15.

See also the following provision in the Fiscal Agency Agreement dated September 1, 1965 relating to the Aktiebolaget Götaverken (a Swedish Company) 6% Guaranteed (by the Kingdom of Sweden) Dollar Debentures due December 1, 1980:

"Götaverken hereby appoints the Co-Paying Agent as its authorized agent (hereinafter called the "Authorized Agent") upon which process may be served in any action arising out of or relating to the Debentures which may be instituted in any State or Federal court in the State of New York by the holder of a Debenture and expressly accepts the jurisdiction of any

A variation on the same theme, in a condensed form, is the following:

"[The parties] designate the City of Havana, Cuba, or the City of New York, State of New York, or both of said cities, as the Trustee in any case shall elect, as the place where all summonses, citations, writs, legal process and judicial proceedings, which may take place by reason of this Indenture, shall be carried into effect and substantiated . . . "[44]

These clauses offer the maximum security to lenders. They

such court in respect of such action. Such appointment shall be irrevocable so long as any of the Debentures remain outstanding unless and until the appointment of a successor Paying Agent or Co-Paying Agent in the City of New York, New York, as Götaverken's Authorized Agent and such successor's acceptance of such appointment. Götaverken will take any and all action, including the filing of any and all documents and instruments, that may be necessary to continue such appointment or appointments in full force and effect as aforesaid. Service of process upon the Authorized Agent and written notice of such service to Götaverken (mailed or delivered to AB Götaverken, Box 8885, Göteborg 8, Sweden) shall be deemed, in every respect, effective service of process upon Götaverken. Notwithstanding the foregoing, any action based on the Debentures may be instituted by the holder of a Debenture in any competent court of the jurisdiction in which Götaverken has its seat."

Comp. the indenture involved in Ehrlich v. German Sav. Bank & Clearing Ass'n, 132 N.Y.L.J. Aug. 2, 1954, p. 5, col. 3 (American and German courts having jurisdiction).

That even careful wording of this type of jurisdictional clause may not avoid every pitfall, is well illustrated by the case of Weinstein v. Siemens & Halske Aktiengesellschaft, 26 F. Supp. 410 (D.C.N.Y. 1939); aff'd 105 F. 2d 1023. In that case an indenture contained a provision similar to the above-quoted clause, except that the submission to American courts was limited to suits brought against the obligors by the trustee or "any debenture holder". Despite the probable intent of the parties, it was held that this provision could not be invoked by a holder of defaulted coupons. In reaching this conclusion, the court made the rather candid statement that "Whether there was or was not in the minds of the parties a good ground for creating that distinction [between holders of debentures and holders of coupons] cannot concern us, however harsh it may seem for a holder of defaulted coupons to be helpless in respect to personal service on the defendants or any properly designated agent. That is among the hazards involved in dealings with foreign corporations, to say nothing of the inelasticity of a formal agreement such as an indenture". (ibid at p. 412).

[44] Indenture dated July 1, 1935, between Compania Azucarera Vicana (Vicana Sugar Company) and an American Trust Company. This provision was held to refer only to actions maintained by the trustee against the Company, to the exclusion of actions brought against it by any other person, in Wahl v. Vicana Sugar Company, 144 N.Y.S. 2d 613 (1955), affirmed 2 App. Div. 248, 156 N.Y.S. 2d 993. Comp., Grossman v. Sapphire Petroleums Limited, 195 N.Y.S. 2d 851 (1959).

guarantee lenders against pleas to the jurisdiction of American courts, while permitting them to sue the borrower in the courts of its own country or of any other country having jurisdiction.

Because of these advantages, multiple-jurisdiction clauses are also found in markets outside the United States, such as the English or the Swiss markets. A typical example in England is found in a trust deed between English lenders and an Austrian company which, after a recital of express submission to the jurisdiction of the English courts,[45] provides further:

" . . . that nothing in this clause contained shall hinder or prevent the trustees from taking proceedings in the courts of Austria or other countries where the mortgaged premises are situated and from exercising all rights and powers under the laws for the time being in force in Austria or other countries where the mortgaged premises are situated which they would have been entitled to take or exercise if this clause had not been inserted."

The wording of this provision makes it quite clear that by providing for the jurisdiction of the English courts, English lenders do not intend to deprive themselves of any of the remedies to which they would be otherwise entitled.

In Switzerland, a number of recent loan documents contain similar provisions, like the following:

"Any dispute between the bondholders, on the one part, and on the other, the debtor, arising out of or in connection with the bonds or coupons shall be decided *exclusively* by the ordinary courts of the Canton of Basle-City, subject to appeal to the Federal Tribunal at Lausanne whose judgment shall be final. *The bondholders shall have also the right to bring their claims before the Belgian courts*" (as translated) (italics added).[46]

---

[45] See text and note 37 supra. Comp., the following clause in the prospectus of Allmänna Svenska Elektriska Aktiebolaget (ASEA) US$15 million 6% 15 Year External unsecured Loan of 1965:
"13. *PROPER LAW AND ARBITRATION.*—The Trust Deed and the Bonds will be governed by and construed in accordance with the laws of England and the Trust Deed will contain an arbitration clause under which, without prejudice to the right of the Trustee to proceed in the courts of any country in the world, ASEA will be entitled to refer any matters connected with the Loan, the Trust Deed or the Bonds to arbitration in London and any resulting award will be final and binding on ASEA, the Trustee and the Bondholders."
[46] Compagnie Financière Belge des Pétroles, External Loan 4½%, 1963 Prospectus, Clause 10.
See also Compagnie Française des Pétroles, External Loan 4% 1955;

Despite its obvious intent, the wording of this clause is not altogether satisfactory. It seems somewhat contradictory to reserve "exclusive" jurisdiction to Swiss courts, while simultaneously providing that Belgian courts may also have jurisdiction. Jurisdiction in this case is not "exclusive." It is alternative or cumulative as the case may be. This contradiction has been removed from other Swiss prospectuses by the deletion of the word "exclusive." Thus the prospectus of the Union Sidérurgique du Nord de la France, "USINOR," Paris, Loan $4\frac{1}{2}\%$ of 1964, provides that:

> "Any dispute between the bondholders, on the one part, and, on the other, the Company, concerning the bonds and/or the coupons of this loan shall be governed by Swiss law and shall be decided by the ordinary courts of the Canton of Zurich, subject to appeal to the Federal Tribunal at Lausanne whose decision shall be final. To this effect, the Company elects domicile with Union de Banques Suisses à Zurich and designates such bank as its agent . . .
>
> The bondholders shall be free to bring any legal proceedings in the French courts . . . " (as translated) .[47]

An interesting addition to this type of provision appears in a number of recent prospectuses which stipulate that if the bondholders elect to bring action in courts other than the Swiss courts, "Swiss law shall remain the applicable law."[48] This last stipulation is characteristic of the desire of lenders to maintain the unity of the legal status of their loans regardless of the forum before which a dispute

---

Péchiney, External Loan $4\frac{1}{4}\%$ 1954; Instituto Mobiliare Italiano, External Loan $4\frac{1}{2}\%$ 1955; International Standard Electric Corporation, New York, Loans $3\frac{1}{2}\%$ and 4% 1954; Cassa per il Mezzogiorno, Rome, $4\frac{1}{2}\%$ Loan 1960; Istituto Mobiliare Italiano (IMI) $4\frac{1}{2}\%$ Loan 1961; S.A. Acciaierie e Ferriere Lombarde Falck, $4\frac{1}{2}\%$ Loan 1961.

[47] See also the prospectuses regarding the (i) British Aluminum Company, Limited, London $4\frac{1}{2}\%$ Loan of 1960; (ii) Société Norvégienne de l'Azote et de Forces Hydro-Electriques à Notodden (Norvège) $4\frac{1}{2}\%$ Loan of 1959; and (iii) Kjøbenhavns Telefon Aktieselskab, Copenhague $4\frac{1}{2}\%$ Loan of 1959.

[48] See e.g., IBM World Trade Corporation, $4\frac{1}{4}\%$ Loan of 1961, prospectus, clause 10; Istituto Mobiliare Italiano (IMI), $4\frac{1}{2}\%$ Loan of 1961, prospectus, clause 10; Imperial Chemical Industries Limited, London, $4\frac{1}{4}\%$ Loan of 1962, prospectus, clause 11. Comp., Aktiebolaget Volvo Göteborg, $4\frac{1}{2}\%$ Loan of 1961 stating that if action is brought in the Swedish courts, Swiss law shall remain applicable: "pour l'interprétation du texte des obligations et/ou des coupons du présent emprunt." Similar clauses are found in prospectuses regarding bonds issued in Switzerland for foreign governments. See text and note 64 infra.

may be brought. Nevertheless, it cannot be assumed that courts outside Switzerland will necessarily interpret or apply Swiss law as
would Swiss courts, or give up their right to rely on their own characterization or public policy. The practical effect of these clauses,
therefore, appears considerably less clear than their manifest objective.
This is not the same as saying that these clauses are "de trop": As a
clear reminder of the parties' intention, they may prove useful in the
case of an actual dispute.[49]

2. *Loans Made by Domestic Public Agencies*

The practice of domestic public agencies is less consistent than
that of private lenders. Some agencies do not usually stipulate jurisdictional clauses in their agreements, even though the same agencies may
insist upon stipulation of applicable law.[50] Other agencies favor
arbitration.[51] When jurisdictional clauses are found, however, they
bear a marked resemblance to the provisions used by private lenders.
Thus the Export-Import Bank, when it lends to private entities,
frequently insists that the borrower (and the guarantor, if any) consent to be sued either at the place of payment or at the place of
incorporation of the borrower.[52]

B. LOANS CONCLUDED BY INTERNATIONAL PERSONS

1. *Direct Loans*

The frequency of jurisdictional clauses in loan contracts between
private and international persons is proportionate to the expected
effectiveness of such clauses at the proper forum. This explains why
in England, where waivers of immunity are revocable,[53] it is not
customary to provide for the jurisdiction of the English courts in
loans made to foreign governments; whereas such provisions are
commonly found in Switzerland, where waivers of immunity are

---

[49] As to possible complexities arising from multiple-jurisdictional clauses
in the case of guaranteed loans, see text and notes 142 to 144 infra.

[50] This seems to be the practice of the AID in the United States and of
the CDFC in England.

[51] This seems to be the practice of the Export-Import Bank of Japan and
of the Kreditanstalt Für Wiederaufbau.

[52] Townsend, "The Export-Import Bank of Washington: Organization and
Operations", U. of Ill. Law Forum, Legal Problems of Int'l Trade (Spring
1959) 237, at p. 245.

[53] See note 31 supra.

irrevocable,[54] and in the United States where, despite the unsettled status of the law, the binding character of such waivers might be upheld.[55] A typical example is found in the loan agreement of February 8, 1945 between Chase National Bank of the City of New York and the Kingdom of the Netherlands:

> "The Government hereby irrevocably waives all claim or right to sovereign or other immunity in relation to the enforcement in any jurisdiction of any or all of its obligations and of its warranties and representations under this Agreement, including enforcement of the mortgage of the Security hereunder or in relation to any claims for breach of warranty or misrepresentation by the Government based on or arising out of this Agreement, and irrevocably agrees that the rights of the Manager or of the Banks or of any of them with respect to repayment of all advances under the loan, with interest and commitment charges thereon, and in and to the Security and with respect to all of its other obligations hereunder and of its warranties and representations may, to the extent deemed necessary or desirable by them or any of them, be finally adjudged or determined in any court or courts of the State of New York or of the United States of America having jurisdiction in the State of New York, or in any other court having jurisdiction, even though such adjudication finally determines the rights or claims of the Government; and the Government hereby submits generally and unconditionally to the jurisdiction of said courts and of any of them in respect of such advances under the loan, with interest and commitment charge thereon, the enforcement of the mortgage of such Security, the enforcement and execution of any judgment against it, and all of its other obligations hereunder."

This example is particularly interesting in that it reveals the intention of American bankers that the jurisdictional aspects of government and private loans be treated in the same way, as far as possible. From the point of view of lenders, jurisdictional clauses, in either type of loan, are motivated by the same basic considerations. It is not surprising, therefore, that, despite the uncertain effectiveness of waivers of immunity in this country, lenders insist upon inserting in government loans clauses similar to those which are customary in

---

[54] See note 29 supra. The writer is not authorized to quote provisions found in loan contracts between Swiss lenders and foreign governments. However, the relevent language of these provisions is substantially identical to that of jurisdictional clauses found in Swiss prospectus quoted in note 64 infra.

[55] See text and note 30 supra.

private loans. This brings the American practice much closer to the Continental practice than would appear from a comparison of American and Continental cases. Indeed, American jurisdictional clauses, like their Continental counterparts, also appear in loans to foreign political subdivisions, central banks or other entities under foreign governmental control or ownership. The latter loans normally contain stipulations whereby the borrower:

> "to the extent that [it] has or may acquire any right of immunity, hereby irrevocably waives such right of immunity in respect of its obligations under this Agreement [and] irrevocably agrees that any legal action or proceeding with respect to this Agreement may be brought in the Courts of the State of [e.g. New York], or in such other courts in the United States of America or in [the borrower's country] as [the lenders] may elect."[56]

Recently, provisions such as the above have been supplemented by the additional statement that:

> "the borrowings hereunder will be private and commercial acts rather than governmental or public acts."

This characterization of the transaction as an act *jure gestionis* provides additional protection to the lender. Should the waiver of immunity contained in the other part of the provision prove ineffective for any reason, the borrower would nevertheless have difficulty objecting successfully to the jurisdiction of the local courts. In effect, this contractual classification of the loan bargain goes directly to the root of the difficulty, and probably makes the waiver part of the provision somewhat superfluous. It is understandable however that lenders, in their quest for increased protection, are unlikely to relinquish this traditional weapon against pleas of jurisdictional immunity.

In the field of international lending, the distinction between acts *jure gestionis* and acts *jure imperii* has gained importance as a result of the proliferation of international lending organizations. Characteristically, none of these organizations enjoys a general immunity from suit. Such an immunity might have proved harmful to the conduct of their business, and in particular to the success of their borrowing operations in the private capital market. Hence, the general rule that legal proceedings may be brought against these organizations by

---

[56] See also note 70 infra.

their respective creditors, either in any court having jurisdiction,[57] or in certain fora specifically mentioned in the articles of agreement of the particular organization.[58] Under the circumstances it is not surprising to find, in loan contracts between private lenders and lending organizations, jurisdictional clauses of the type commonly used in the country in which the funds are raised.[59]

Jurisdictional clauses in loans made by international lending organizations exhibit considerable variations. Certain organizations, such as the IBRD, the IDA or the IADB, generally provide for the arbitral settlement of disputes arising under agreements between them and their respective borrowers,[60] and it is only in specific instances

---

[57] ECSC, Treaty, Article 40, paragraph 3; EIB, Statute, Article 29, paragraphs 1 and 2. See also Lalive, *L'Immunité de Juridiction des Etats et des Organisations Internationales,* 84 Recueil des Cours 205 (1953), at pp. 376 et seq.; Stein and Hay, "Legal Remedies of Enterprises in the European Economic Community", 9 Am. J. Comp. L. 375 (1960), at pp. 407-412.

Similarly, the BIS, subject to arbitration provisions concerning disputes with central banks, "may proceed or be proceeded against in any court of competent jurisdiction" (Article 57 of the BIS Statutes).

[58] See e.g., IBRD, Articles of Agreement, Article VII, Section 3:

"Actions may be brought against the Bank only in a court of competent jurisdiction in the territories of a member in which the Bank has an office, has appointed an agent for the purpose of accepting service or notice of process, or has issued or guaranteed securities. No actions shall, however, be brought by members or persons acting for or deriving claims from members. The property and assets of the Bank shall, wheresoever located and by whomsoever held, be immune from all forms of seizure, attachment or execution before the delivery of final judgment against the Bank."

The Agreement of June 29, 1951, between the IBRD and Switzerland, which is not a member of the IBRD, contains provisions similar to the above quoted provision (Article II, 216 UNTS 348).

Comp., IFC, Articles of Agreement, Article VI, Section 3; IDA, Articles of Agreement, Article VIII, Section 3; IADB, Articles of Agreement, Article XI, Section 3. See also, Jenks, *International Immunities* (1961), p. 45.

[59] See e.g., the Agreement dated August 1, 1960, between the Deutsche Bundesbank and the IBRD:

"*ARTICLE IX.* This agreement both as to form and content and the rights and duties of the parties arising therefrom, will be exclusively governed by, and construed in accordance with the law of the Federal Republic of Germany. In this respect the Bank submits to the jurisdiction of the German Courts and elects domicile at the office of the Deutsche Bundesbank, Taunusanlage 4-6, Frankfurt am Main, Germany. Both parties choose Frankfurt am Main as the forum . . ." (as translated).

See also the provisions in bonds issued by international lending organizations quoted infra text and notes 65, 71 and 72.

[60] See text and note 79 infra.

and for limited purposes that the determination of controversies between the parties is referred to domestic courts. Such may be the case when a loan is secured by a mortgage or similar security, and recourse to the local courts might prove necessary for the enforcement or foreclosure of the mortgage. Examples of clauses of this kind are found in secured loans made by the IBRD to private borrowers, like the following:

"The provisions for arbitration set worth in this Section shall be in lieu of any other procedure for the determination of controversies between the parties under the Loan Agreement and Guarantee Agreement or any claim by any such party against any other such party arising thereunder provided, however, that nothing herein shall be deemed to preclude any of the said parties from exercising, or instituting any legal or equitable action to enforce, any right or claim arising out of or pursuant to the Trust Deed or the Bonds, and submission to arbitration hereunder shall not be deemed to be a condition precedent or in any way to prejudice such exercise or other enforcement of any such right or claim."[61]

Other organizations, like the EIB or the IFC, ordinarily confer jurisdiction on the courts in the country of the borrower or of the enterprise in which the investment is made. These courts do not always have exclusive jurisdiction, however; and sometimes action may be brought also in other courts specified in the agreement, or courts otherwise having jurisdiction over the subject matter of the dispute.[62] In the case of the ECSC, the organization takes advantage of the exceptional judicial facilities available to it, and stipulates in loan contracts with borrowing enterprises within the Community that disputes thereunder shall be submitted for decision to the European Court of Justice.[63]

---

[61] Loan Agreement dated August 13, 1959, between the IBRD and The Karachi Electric Supply Corporation, Limited, Schedule 3, letter (n), 355 UNTS 129. See also e.g., the IBRD Loan Agreements with: (i) Corporación de Fomento de la Producción and Companía Carbonifera de Lota (July 24, 1957, Schedule 3 (j), 282 UNTS 139); and (ii) Vorarlberger Illwerke Aktiengesellschaft (June 14, 1955, Schedule 3 (g), 221 UNTS 375).

[62] Stein and Hay, op. cit., note 57 supra, at p. 407. See also chapter III, note 28.

[63] Blondeel and Vander Eycken, "Les Emprunts de la Communauté Européenne du Charbon et de l'Acier", La Revue de la Banque (Belgium) 249 (1955), at p. 283; Delaume, "Jurisdiction of Courts and International Loans", 6 Am. J. Comp. L. 189 (1957), p. 211.

174INTERNATIONAL LOANS

2. *Bonds*

Continental lenders usually insist upon stipulating the court or courts having jurisdiction over loan disputes in bonds issued by foreign governments[64] or international organizations.[65]

In contrast with these transactions, most bonds issued by foreign governments in the United States,[66] England,[67] or Canada[68] contain

---

[64] A typical Swiss example is found in Clause 11 of the $4\frac{1}{2}\%$ Loan of 1960 of the Commonwealth of Australia:

"Any disputes between the bondholders, on the one hand, and the Australian Government, on the other, arising out of the bonds or coupons of this issue shall be governed by Swiss law and shall be decided by the ordinary courts of the Canton of Bâle-Ville, subject to appeal to the Federal Tribunal, at Lausanne.

This conventional forum shall have jurisdiction also in respect of the cancellation of lost bonds or coupons. Payment to a holder recognized as creditor by a decision of a Swiss court shall operate as a valid discharge of the Australian Government.

Bondholders shall have also the right to bring their claims and to institute legal proceedings before the Australian courts, renouncing in this case the jurisdiction of the Swiss courts" (as translated).

Comp., in Germany, the City of Oslo $5\frac{1}{2}\%$ Bearer Bonds of 1959:

"The jurisdiction and place of performance for all parties concerned shall be Frankfurt am Main" (as translated).

[65] See e.g., the IBRD 5% Deutsche Mark Bonds of 1959:

". . . The World Bank submits to the jurisdiction of the German courts and elects domicile at the head office of the Deutsche Bank AG. . . . Frankfurt am Main, Germany. All parties concerned choose Frankfurt am Main as the forum" (as translated).

Provisions to the same effect are found in the IBRD $4\frac{1}{2}\%$ Swiss Franc Loan of 1960; $4\frac{1}{2}\%$ Netherlands Guilder Bonds of 1961; 5% Belgian Franc Bonds of 1960; 5% Italian Lire Bonds of 1961.

Comp., the EIB $5\frac{3}{4}\%$ Netherlands Guilder Bonds of 1964:

"This Loan is subject to Dutch law; any dispute between the bondholders and the Bank arising out of the bonds or the coupons of this issue shall be within the exclusive jurisdiction of the competent courts in Amsterdam" (as translated).

and the ECSC, $4\frac{1}{4}\%$ Swiss Franc Bonds of 1956:

"Any disputes between the bondholders, on the one hand, and the High Authority, on the other, which may arise in connection with the loan and the rights thereunder, shall be subject to the jurisdiction of the ordinary courts of the Canton of Zurich, subject to appeal to the Federal Tribunal, at Lausanne, and the High Authority expressly subjects itself to the jurisdiction of these courts" (as translated).

[66] See e.g., the Republic of Panama 4.80% External Secured Bonds of 1958; the Commonwealth of Australia, Fifteen Year $4\frac{3}{4}\%$ Bonds of 1958; the Kingdom of Norway, Fifteen Year $5\frac{1}{4}\%$ External Loan Bonds of 1963; the Republic of Austria, $5\frac{1}{2}\%$ External Sinking Fund Dollar Bonds of 1958; the Belgian Congo, Fifteen Year $5\frac{1}{4}\%$ External Loan Bonds of 1958; the Government of New Zealand, Fifteen Year $5\frac{3}{4}\%$ Bonds of 1961; the Government of Japan, $5\frac{1}{2}\%$ External Sinking Fund Bonds of 1963. But see the Malaysia $5\frac{1}{2}\%$ External Serial Bonds due 1966-1970, prospectus, p. 5:

no jurisdictional provision. The same remark can be made with respect to bonds issued in these countries by the IBRD. However, the absence of a jurisdictional clause in IBRD bonds is not necessarily significant since under the IBRD's Articles of Agreement, action can be brought against that organization in the courts of member countries in which that organization has issued securities.[69]

In the United States, attempts have been made in recent years to include, in bonds issued by public entities other than foreign governments, the clauses found in American loan contracts. A typical example is the following provision in the prospectus of the City of Oslo 5½% Sinking Fund External Loan Bonds of 1958:

> "The City will undertake to effect the irrevocable appointment of the Fiscal Agent as the City's authorized agent upon which process may be served in any action arising out of or relating to the Bonds which may be instituted in any State or Federal court in the State of New York by any holder of a Bond. The City will irrevocably waive any immunity from judicial jurisdiction

---

"The Bonds provide that Malaysia irrevocably waives any immunity from jurisdiction to which it might otherwise be entitled in any action or proceeding arising out of or relating to the Bonds which may be instituted by any holder of a Bond in any state or Federal court in the State of New York. In that connection, the Fiscal Agency Agreement provides that Malaysia irrevocably appoints the Fiscal Agent as the authorized agent of Malaysia upon which process may be served in any such action or proceeding."

A similar clause is found in the City of Helsinki Twelve Year 6¼% External Loan Bonds of 1965, prospectus p. 5.

See also the following provision in the prospectus regarding the European Investment Bank 6% Dollar Bonds of 1965, Due September 15, 1985:

"The Bonds will be governed by, and construed in accordance with, the laws of the State of New York. The Bank will appoint the Fiscal Agent as its authorized agent in New York City upon which process may be served in any action based on the Bonds which may be instituted in any State or Federal court in the State of New York by the holder of a Bond and will expressly accept the jurisdiction of such court in respect of such action. Notwithstanding the foregoing, any action based on the Bonds may be instituted by the holder of a Bond in any competent court of the jurisdiction in which the Bank has its seat. The Bank will irrevocably waive any immunity from jurisdiction to which it might otherwise be entitled in any action based on the Bonds which may be instituted by the holder of a Bond in any State or Federal court in the State of New York or in any competent court of the jurisdiction in which the Bank has its seat." (p. 15)

[67] See e.g., the Kingdom of Norway, 4½% (Shipping) Sterling Registered Stock 1961/66; the Danish Government, 3½% Sterling Loan of 1946; the Republic of Austria US $18 million 6% Bonds 1979/1984 (issued in 1964).

[68] See e.g., Commonwealth of Australia, Canadian Bonds of 1955.

[69] See note 58 supra.

to which it might otherwise be entitled in any action arising out
of or relating to the Bonds which may be instituted by any holder
of a Bond in any State or Federal court in the State of New York."[70]

Another example is supplied by the successive jurisdictional
clauses found in bonds issued in the United States by the ECSC.
Probably because of the difficulty in determining the exact jurisdictional status of the ECSC in the United States, it was originally
provided that bond disputes would be submitted to the Court of
Justice of the Community rather than to American courts.[71] In

---

[70] Comp., the following jurisdictional clause in the prospectus of the City
of Oslo, 4% Loan of 1956 issued in Switzerland:
"Any dispute between the bondholders, on the one hand, and the City of
Oslo, on the other, arising out of the bonds or coupons of this issue
shall be governed by Swiss law and shall be decided by the Tribunal of
the Canton of Zurich, subject to appeal to the Federal Tribunal, at
Lausanne. To that effect, the City of Oslo 'elects domicile' at the Royal
Legation of Norway in Bern.
The bondholders shall also be free to exercise their rights and to insti-
tute legal proceedings before the courts of the Kingdom of Norway" (as
translated).
See also, in the United States the following provision in the Indenture of
April 15, 1963 between the Copenhagen Telephone Company, Incorporated
and First National City Bank, in which the Company, after appointing the
Bank as its authorized agent upon which process may be served, agrees that:
"By the execution and delivery of this Indenture the Company irrevocably
waives any immunity from jurisdiction to which it might otherwise be
entitled in any suit or proceeding arising out of or relating to the Debentures or this Indenture. This waiver is intended to be effective upon
the execution of this Indenture in which it is contained without any further act by the Company before any court, and introduction of a true
copy of this Indenture into evidence shall be conclusive and final evidence of such waiver" (Section 15.11).
A similar provision is found in the Indenture dated March 15, 1959 (Section 17.11 between KLM Royal Dutch Airlines and First National City Trust
Company.
[71] High Authority of the ECSC, $5\frac{1}{2}\%$ Secured Bonds (Seventh Series)
1957-1975, Prospectus, p. 26:
"[The] Eighth Supplemental Indenture will also provide that the jurisdiction of the Court of Justice of the Community shall extend to any
dispute between a holder of Bonds or Serial Notes or a representative . . ., as such holder or representative, on the one hand, and the
High Authority, on the other hand."
This is still the solution obtaining in connection with the $4\frac{3}{4}\%$ Netherlands Guilders Loan of 1962 issued by the ECSC in the Netherlands. See
prospectus, clause 10:
". . . All differences [between bondholders and the ECSC] shall be
submitted to the Court of Justice of the European Communities, which
is expressly declared to be empowered to act in accordance with Article
42 of the Treaty setting up the European Coal and Steel Community"
(as translated).

addition to this stipulation, the bonds most recently issued by the ECSC also provide that:

> "The High Authority hereby waives irrevocably any immunity from jurisdiction to which it might otherwise be entitled in any action arising out of or relating to the Bonds or the Serial Notes or the Bank Loans which may be duly instituted in any State or Federal court in the State of New York by the holder of a Bond or a Serial Note or a Bank Loan. This waiver is intended to be effective upon the execution of this . . . . Supplemental Indenture in which it is contained without any further act by the High Authority before any such court, and introduction of a true copy of this . . . . Supplemental Indenture into evidence shall be conclusive and final evidence of such waiver."[72]

This provision, like those already noted in connection with direct loans to foreign governmental or semi-governmental entities, illustrates the increasing effort by American lenders to circumvent the possible consequences of the doctrine of jurisdictional immunity by way of contractual covenants. Whether this trend will develop into a battle as successful as that which has been waged by Continental lenders, with the support of the judiciary, remains to be seen. It is to be hoped that it will.

This review of market practice would not be complete without

---

[72] See also High Authority of the ECSC, 5⅜% Secured Bonds (Thirteenth Series) 1960-1980, Prospectus, pp. 27-28.

See also the following provision in the Fiscal Agency Agreement dated September 15, 1965 relating to the EIB 6% Dollar Bonds of 1965, Due September 15, 1985:

> "This Agreement shall be governed by, and construed in accordance with, the laws of the State of New York. The Bank hereby appoints the Fiscal Agent as its authorized agent (hereinafter called the Authorized Agent) upon which process may be served in any action based on the Bonds which may be instituted in any State or Federal court in the State of New York by the holder of a Bond and expressly accepts the jurisdiction of any such court in respect of such action.

> . . . .

> Service of process upon the Authorized Agent and written notice of such service to the Bank (mailed or delivered to the President at the seat of the Bank) shall be deemed, in every respect, effective service of process upon the Bank. Notwithstanding the foregoing, any action based on the Bonds may be instituted by the holder of a Bond in any competent court of the jurisdiction in which the Bank has its seat. The Bank hereby waives irrevocably any immunity from jurisdiction to which it might otherwise be entitled in any action based on the Bonds which may be instituted by the holder of a Bond in any State or Federal court in the State of New York or in any competent court of the jurisdiction in which the Bank has its seat."

discussion of a curious clause sometimes found in government loans. This clause provides that disputes between lenders and borrowers shall be decided by the Permanent Court of International Justice (now the International Court of Justice) in the Hague. Examples are found in several pre-World War loans, like the External Loan of the French Republic of 1939 issued both in Switzerland and the Netherlands:

> "The French Government undertakes to subject any disputes which may arise in connection with the bonds or coupons of this loan to the jurisdiction of the Permanent Court of International Justice" (Article 9, as translated).

The effectiveness of this clause, which remains to be tested, is an interesting matter for speculation. Because the Hague Court's jurisdiction was limited to disputes involving states as parties litigant, the Court would have been forced to decline jurisdiction, in a dispute between private lenders and a borrowing government,[73] unless the lenders' government had espoused their claim and brought action in the Court against the borrower.[74] In final analysis, all that this clause could have meant was that, should such an espousal of the lenders' claim take place, the debtor government agreed to submit to the jurisdiction of the Court. That this was the real meaning of the clause is made clear by the following stipulation in a loan of the same period:

> "The Government accepts the jurisdiction of the Permanent Court of International Justice for the determination of possible disputes arising hereunder in any instance in which the Dutch Government or any other Government, *espousing the claims of*

---

[73] Comp., The Anglo-Iranian Oil Case, ICJ Reports 1952, 93.

[74] Cf., e.g., The Serbian and Brazilian Loans Cases, P.C.I.J. 1929, Series A, Nos. 21 and 22; The Case of Certain Norwegian Loans, ICJ Reports 1957, p. 9. It is easier to understand the following provision inserted in loan contracts betwen Czechoslovakia and French bankers in connection with the issuance of bonds of the Czechoslovak Republic *guaranteed* by the French Government:
"Any disputes which may arise as to the interpretation or execution of the present provisions shall be subject to the jurisdiction of the Permanent Court of International Justice at The Hague, acting in execution of Article 14 of the Covenant of the League of Nations. The Czechoslovak State undertakes to lay such disputes before the Permanent Court of International Justice whose jurisdiction it accepts" (Article 22 of 1932 and 1937 contracts, as translated).
The French Government, as guarantor, could effectively bring action before P.C.I.J. in any dispute arising out of the loan contract.

[*holders of*] *bonds of this issue,* should decide to submit such a dispute to the said Court for its decision" (as translated, emphasis added) .[75]

The fact that these provisions did not give private lenders direct access to the Court may be the reason why post-war loan documents, while providing for the jurisdiction of the ICJ, typically confer alternative or subsidiary jurisdiction on domestic courts. This particular type of multiple-jurisdiction clause, involving both international and domestic fora, is found in certain loans floated in Switzerland, like the 1947 loan of the *Régie des Télégraphes et Téléphones,* guaranteed by the Belgian Government:

> "Any dispute between the bondholders and the borrower or the guarantor arising out of, or in connection with the bonds or coupons shall be decided exclusively by the International Court of Justice in The Hague, or in default thereof, by the Swiss Federal Tribunal at Lausanne whose judgment shall be final" (as translated) .[76]

The value of this provision must be cautiously weighed. Its wording, like that of the private-loan provisions,[77] is defective, in that it confers "exclusive" jurisdiction upon the ICJ while providing also for the jurisdiction of the Swiss Federal Tribunal. In addition, the newer clause still falls short of giving the lenders direct access to an international forum. Insofar as the lenders are concerned, all that the clause does is to confer jurisdiction on the Swiss Court. In other words, despite its impressive character, the clause is somewhat misleading. This consideration may explain why reference to the ICJ has disappeared from the most recent government loans issued in Switzerland.[78]

SECTION II. ARBITRATION AGREEMENTS

A. THE ATTITUDE OF LENDERS TOWARDS ARBITRATION

The general trend in recent years to encourage the settlement of international commercial or economic disputes by way of arbitration

---

[75] Loan Agreement dated March 19, 1930, between the Government of the Grand Duché of Luxembourg and Dutch Bankers.

[76] External Loan 4% of 1947, Prospectus, clause 10. See also Société Nationale de Crédit à l'Industrie, External Loan 4% of 1950; Belgian Congo, External Loans 4% of 1950 and 1952—all guaranteed by Belgium.

[77] See text and note 46 supra.

[78] See note 64 supra.

has made some progress in the area of international loans. However, it cannot be said that all lenders have shown equal eagerness to follow the general trend and substitute arbitration in their respective loan contracts for other means of settlement.

Certain institutions, like the IBRD, the IDA or the IADB have made the most consistent use of arbitration. This appears to be due to international legal character of their operations and the fact that possible disputes between them and their respective borrowers might involve financial, economic or technical matters more suitable to determination by experts than to judicial adjudication.[79] Other

---

[79] Section 7.04 of the IBRD Loan Regulations No. 4 which is reproduced below for the convenience of the reader, reads as follows:

"Section 7.04. *Arbitration.*

(a) Any controversy between the parties to the Loan Agreement or the parties to the Guarantee Agreement and any claim by any such party against any other such party arising under the Loan Agreement, the Guarantee Agreement or the Bonds which shall not be determined by agreement of the parties shall be submitted to arbitration by an Arbitral Tribunal as hereinafter provided.

(b) The parties to such arbitration shall be the Bank on the one side and the Borrower and the Guarantor on the other side.

(c) The Arbitral Tribunal shall consist of three arbitrators appointed as follows: one arbitrator shall be appointed by the Bank; a second arbitrator shall be appointed by the Borrower and the Guarantor or, if they shall not agree, by the Guarantor; and the third arbitrator (hereinafter sometimes called the Umpire) shall be appointed by agreement of the parties or, if they shall not agree, by the President of the International Court of Justice or, failing appointment by him, by the Secretary-General of the United Nations. If either side shall fail to appoint an arbitrator, such arbitrator shall be appointed by the Umpire. In case any arbitrator appointed in accordance with this Section shall resign, die or become unable to act, a successor arbitrator shall be appointed in the same manner as herein prescribed for the appointment of the original arbitrator and such successor shall have all the powers and duties of such original arbitrator.

(d) An arbitration proceeding may be instituted under this Section upon notice by the party instituting such proceeding to the other parties. Such notice shall contain a statement setting forth the nature of the controversy or claim to be submitted to arbitration and the nature of the relief sought. Within 30 days after the giving of such notice, each side shall notify the other side of the arbitrator appointed by it.

(e) If within 60 days after the giving of such notice instituting the arbitration proceeding the parties shall not have agreed upon an Umpire, any party may request the appointment of an Umpire as provided in paragraph (c) of this Section.

(f) The Arbitral Tribunal shall convene at such time and place as shall be fixed by the Umpire. Thereafter, the Arbitral Tribunal shall determine where and when it shall sit.

(g) Subject to the provisions of this Section and except as the parties

shall otherwise agree, the Arbitral Tribunal shall decide all questions relating to its competence and shall determine its procedure. All decisions of the Arbitral Tribunal shall be by majority vote.

(h) The Arbitral Tribunal shall afford to all parties a fair hearing and shall render its award in writing. Such award may be rendered by default. An award signed by a majority of the Arbitral Tribunal shall constitute the award of such Tribunal. A signed counterpart of the award shall be transmitted to each party. Any such award rendered in accordance with the provisions of this Section shall be final and binding upon the parties to the Loan Agreement and the Guarantee Agreement. Each party shall abide by and comply with any such award rendered by the Arbitral Tribunal in accordance with the provisions of this Section.

(i) The parties shall fix the amount of the remuneration of the arbitrators and such other persons as shall be required for the conduct of the arbitration proceedings. If the parties shall not agree on such amount before the Arbitral Tribunal shall convene, the Arbitral Tribunal shall fix such amount as shall be reasonable under the circumstances. The Bank, the Borrower and the Guarantor shall each defray its own expenses in the arbitration proceedings. The costs of the Arbitral Tribunal shall be divided between and borne equally by the Bank on the one side and the Borrower and Guarantor on the other. Any question concerning the division of the costs of the Arbitral Tribunal or the procedure for payment of such costs shall be determined by the Arbitral Tribunal.

(j) The provisions for arbitration set forth in this Section shall be in lieu of any other procedure for the determination of controversies between the parties to the Loan Agreement and Guarantee Agreement or any claim by any such party against any other such party arising thereunder or under the Bonds.

(k) If within 30 days after counterparts of the award shall be delivered to the parties the award shall not be complied with, any party may enter judgment upon, or institute a proceeding to enforce, the award in any court of competent jurisdiction against any other party, may enforce such judgment by execution or may pursue any other appropriate remedy against such other party for the enforcement of the award, the provisions of the Loan Agreement or the Bonds. Notwithstanding the foregoing, this Section shall not authorize any entry of judgment or enforcement of the award against the Guarantor except as such procedure may be available against the Guarantor otherwise than by reason of the provisions of this Section."

Substantially the same provision is found in: (i) the IBRD Loan Regulations No. 3, Section 7.03, applicable to loan agreements between a member country and the IBRD; (ii) the IDA Credit Regulations, Section 6.03; and (iii) the IADB loan agreements.

Comp., the following provision commonly stipulated in agreements between the UN Special Fund and recipient countries:

"Any dispute between the Special Fund and [name of country] arising out of or relating to this Agreement which cannot be settled by negotiation or other agreed mode of settlement shall be submitted to arbitration at the request of either Party. Each Party shall appoint one arbitrator, and the two arbitrators so appointed shall appoint the third, who shall be the chairman. If within thirty days of the request for arbitration either Party has not appointed an arbitrator or if within fifteen days of the appointment of two arbitrators the third arbitrator has not been ap▸

lenders, on the other hand, have shown little inclination to deviate from established patterns of doing business, and very rarely provide for arbitration.

Thus, although reference to arbitration is sometimes found in intergovernmental loan agreements or agreements providing for governmental loans to international organizations,[80] most of these agree-

----

pointed, either Party may request the President of the International Court of Justice to appoint an arbitrator. The procedure of the arbitration shall be fixed by the arbitrators, and the expenses of the arbitration shall be borne by the Parties as assessed by the arbitrators. The arbitral award shall contain a statement of the reasons on which it is based and shall be accepted by the Parties as the final adjudication of the dispute."

[80] See e.g., the agreements respectively dated September 17, 1956 (413 UNTS 400) and October 11/20, 1961 (415 UNTS 395) between the Swiss Confederation and the IBRD, which provide that:

"Any dispute between the Confederation and the Bank concerning the application or interpretation of this Agreement or of any supplementary arrangement or agreement which is not settled by negotiation shall be submitted for decision to a board of three arbitrators of whom the first shall be appointed by the Federal Council, the second by the Bank, and a presiding arbitrator by agreement of the contracting parties or, if they shall not agree, by the President of the International Court of Justice, unless in any specific case the parties agree to resort to a different mode of settlement" (as translated).

See also the Loan Agreement dated March 30/April 15, 1957 between the Swiss Confederation and the ILO (40 ILO, Official Bulletin (1957) p. 352, Article 3):

"Any dispute between the International Labour Organisation and the Swiss Confederation on the interpretation or performance of this agreement which cannot be settled by negotiation shall be submitted for settlement to a commission of three arbitrators sitting in Geneva. One arbitrator shall be appointed by the Swiss Federal Council, the second by the International Labour Organisation and the chairman of the arbitral tribunal by the two foregoing or, if they disagree, by the President of the International Court of Justice.

The award of the arbitral tribunal shall be without appeal and shall be immediately executory."

References to arbitration in intergovernmental loan agreements are sometimes formulated in vague terms. See e.g., the Agreement dated May 13, 1959 between Japan and Viet-Nam (373 UNTS 149, Article 5) which provides that:

"Disputes between the two Governments concerning the interpretation and implementation of this Agreement shall be settled, in the first place, through the diplomatic channel. If the two Governments fail to settle the dispute, through the diplomatic channel, the dispute shall be submitted to arbitration in accordance with an arrangement to be concluded by the two Governments" (as translated by the UN Secretariat).

This, of course, is merely an agreement to arbitrate, not an effective arbitration clause. Similar provisions are found in financial agreements (apparently unpublished) between the Soviets and countries receiving Russian aid.

ments contain no provision for the settlement, of disputes arising thereunder, by way of arbitration or otherwise.[81] This practice may be attributable not to a dislike of arbitration *per se*, but rather to considerations of mutual trust and prestige, and to the conviction that any difficulties would be settled at the diplomatic level. In any event current governmental practice affords little ground for expecting a radical change of policy in the near future.

A similar conclusion is probably justified with respect to loans made by private lenders. As yet private lenders do not seem to have made the same extensive use of arbitral compacts as they do of jurisdictional clauses. Provision for the arbitral settlement of disputes has sometimes been made in loan contracts with foreign governments or other public entities,[82] and arbitration agreements are found in a few

---

[81] See e.g., the following agreements between: the State of Brunei and the Government of the Federation of Malaya, March 26-May 1, 1959 (345 UNTS 57); Canada and Belgium, October 25, 1945 (230 UNTS 127); Canada and France, April 9, 1946 (43 UNTS 43); Canada and the United Kingdom, March 6, 1946 (20 UNTS 13); Canada and the Netherlands, February 5, 1946 (43 UNTS 3); India and Burma, March 12, 1957 (312 UNTS 139); New Zealand and France, July 2, 1947 (16 UNTS 219); New Zealand and Czechoslovakia, January 22, 1948 (16 UNTS 229); The United Kingdom and Austria, December 18-23, 1946 (88 UNTS 93); the United Kingdom and Burma, June 28, 1950 (87 UNTS 153); the United Kingdom and Chile, October 21, 1960 (385 UNTS 15); the United Kingdom, France and Turkey, October 19, 1939 (CC LNTS 172); The United States and Ecuador, June 27, 1958 (317 UNTS 52); the United States and Pakistan, September 17, 1952 (227 UNTS 77); and the United States and other governments parties to so-called Agricultural Commodities Agreements, such as those with Ceylon, (March 13, 1959, 342 UNTS 51), India (March 3, 1959, 341 UNTS 235) or Spain (January 13, 1959, 341 UNTS 241).

A number of these agreements provide for consultation between the parties if circumstances so require.

[82] See e.g., the following agreements between American bankers and the Governments of: (i) Nicaragua (September 1, 1911, Article V, Section 2, *Dunn,* p. 344); (ii) El Salvador (June 24, 1922, Article IX, *Dunn,* p. 227; (iii) Haiti (October 6, 1922, Article XXII, *Dunn,* p. 308) and (iv) Argentina (6% Redeemable External Gold Loan, 1925, *L.N. Report,* p. 38). Provision for arbitration was made in the General Bond of the State of Sau Paulo 7% Coffee Realisation Loan (hereinafter the Sau Paulo Loan) floated in England in 1930. A number of loan contracts between bankers and the European Commission for the Danube (E.C.D.) provided expressly for the settlement of disputes by arbitration. See e.g., Loan dated July 21, 1860 between Banque Ottomane and E.C.D.; Loan dated November 28, 1919 between Société Générale and E.C.D.; and Loan dated January 31-March 16, 1928, between Banque des Pays de l'Europe Centrale and E.C.D. (reproduced in *Salmon,* pp. 334, 340 and 342).

Comp., the Free City of Danzig 6½% Loan, 1927 (Tobacco Monopoly), General Bond, Clause 34 and the Kingdom of Bulgaria 7½% Stabilization

contemporary loans to foreign private borrowers.[83] However, these examples are either too old or too isolated to be of real significance.

So far as the motivations of lenders are concerned, there is reason to believe that their guarded attitude towards arbitration is governed by two major considerations. In the first place, most lenders appear to believe that any issues raised in an action against the borrower, particularly if the borrower is a private entity, are likely to be dealt with more effectively in court than by way of arbitration. In the second place, lenders have good reasons not to be overconfident in the practical merits of arbitration agreements, especially in the case of loans to foreign public bodies. Under the laws of many countries, the arbitrability of state or public contracts is still subject to various prohibitions or limitations which may forbid the use of arbitration agreements or cast serious doubts upon their validity. Recent cases in France, concerning arbitration clauses in contracts between the French Government and foreign ship owners, illustrate this remark. To set the problem in proper perspective, it should be recalled that there is no limitation in France upon the authority of public bodies to submit to the jurisdiction of foreign courts; and that under French law, state contracts are not arbitrable.[84] The question at issue was whether agreements in state contracts providing for foreign arbitration should be assimilated to foreign-jurisdictional clauses, in which case the validity of the arbitration clause was assured; or whether the French prohibition was "d'ordre public" and deprived the arbitration clause of any binding effect. Although the first alternative has now prevailed,[85] the fact that extensive litigation was needed to clarify

Loan, 1928, General Bond, Clause 19 (*L.N. Report,* p. 38). See also, Domke, "Arbitration Clauses and International Loans", 3 Arb. J. 161 (1939), and "International Arbitration of Commercial Disputes", in the *Proceedings of the 1960 Institute on Private Investments Abroad* (1960), 131 at pp. 170-171.

[83] See e.g., in *Switzerland*: Anglo-American Corporation of South Africa, Ltd. 4% Loan of 1950; Orange Free State Investment Trust, Ltd. $4\frac{1}{2}$% Loan of 1952; West Rand Investment Trust, Ltd. (WRIT) $4\frac{1}{2}$% Loan of 1954; Anglo-American (O.F.S.) Housing Company, Ltd. $4\frac{1}{2}$% Loan of 1955; *The Netherlands,* Naphtachimie, S.A. Paris $4\frac{1}{4}$% Loan of 1955. (hereinafter Naphtachimie Loan); Recourse to arbitration seems to be viewed with increasing favor in England. See e.g.; Allmänna Svenska Elektriska Aktiebolaget (ASEA) US$15 million 6% 15 Year External Unsecured Loan of 1965 (quoted in note 45 supra); U.S. Rubber Uniroyal Holdings, S.A. £5 million 6% Sterling/DM Guaranteed Loan of 1965; Enso-Gutzeit Osakeyhtiö £4 million $6\frac{1}{2}$% Sterling/DM Guaranteed Loan 1980 (quoted in note 142 infra).

[84] Code of Civil Procedure, Articles 83 and 1004.

[85] Cass. April 14, 1964, Office National Interprofessionnel des Céréales v. Capitaine du "San Carlo", S.1964, 93; Revue de l'Arbitrage 1964, 137.

the issue and place arbitral compacts on the same legal footing as jurisdictional clauses, shows sufficiently the nature of the difficulty. Since the problem is by no means limited to the French system,[86] the caution exhibited by lenders in favoring jurisdictional over arbitral clauses is understandable. Until the existing impediments to a greater use of arbitration are removed, there is no reason to expect that the stipulation of arbitral clauses in loan contracts will become more common.

Although lenders may not be ready to provide for the submission of future loan disputes to arbitration, however, the merits of arbitration may become fully apparent to lenders in the case of an existing dispute. When all other remedies, including those available under jurisdictional clauses, have failed or are likely to prove ineffective, arbitration may be the only procedure available for lenders to seek satisfaction of their claims. The situation existing in France before 1955 and the measures taken to correct it afford a good illustration of this remark. Until 1955, French law sought to protect the interests of lenders, and particularly holders of foreign bonds, by broadening the jurisdiction of the French courts, rather than encouraging the arbitral settlement of loan disputes. In order to provide lenders with a French forum in which to bring their claims, several new grounds for the jurisdiction of the French courts were added to the already long list of cases in which these courts can entertain international jurisdiction.[87] In fact, the French legislature achieved, by statutory enactments, the objective which in the normal case is sought by way of contractual stipulation providing for the jurisdiction of the courts in the lenders' country. This legislation, together with the judicial interpretation of statutes which made it impossible for bondholders' associations to consent to arbitration,[88] was conducive to litigation,

---

[86] See e.g., Domke, "A Report of the 1961 Paris Arbitration Conference", 16 Arb. J. 131 (1961), at p. 139; Vedel, "Le Problème de l'Arbitrage entre Gouvernements ou Personnes de Droit Public et Personnes de Droit Privé", Revue de l'Arbitrage 1961, 116, at pp. 117-120. See also the 1965 Ethiopian Code of Civil Procedure, articles 315 and 3132.

[87] See notes 2, 5, 6 and 39, supra.

[88] The decree-law of October 30, 1935, defining the powers of bond-holders' associations, lists certain matters which can be passed upon by these associations, and other matters which require the consent of each individual bondholder. Since neither list exhausts the possible area of dispute, it rested with the courts to decide whether matters not specifically mentioned could be acted upon by the associations or only by individual bondholders. When first faced with the question, the courts tentatively favored the first alternative, but they finally settled upon the second and more restrictive solution. It is now well

but did not necessarily bring satisfaction to the creditors. If the borrower had no assets in France or its assets were immune from attachment, and the borrower refused to comply with a French judgment, the bondholders had no alternative other than (i) to incur the trouble and expense of seeking enforcement of the French judgment in the borrower's country with variable chances of success; or (ii) gathering whatever support they could from the French decision in their favor, to negotiate a settlement with the borrower. Since, however, there was no assurance that a settlement agreed upon by the majority of bondholders could not be defeated by the minority, the situation of bondholders, despite all the jurisdictional remedies given to them by the French law, became very difficult indeed.[89]

In order to find a solution to this possible impasse, a decree-law of May 20, 1955 was enacted.[90] Article I of the decree now provides:

"In case of a dispute between holders of bonds or other evidences of indebtedness, of the one part, and a foreign 'collectivity', of the other part, the [bondholders] in general meeting may adopt a resolution submitting the dispute to arbitration . . . " (as translated).

---

established that associations enjoy no other prerogatives than those expressly conferred upon them by the decree (Cass. March 10, 1954, Société Tramways et Electricité de Damas v. Caumartin, D. 1954, 489; S.1954.1.153). An illustration is found in the case of Association Nationale des Porteurs Français de Valeurs Mobilières v. Auribault (Cass. June 18, 1958, Revue de l'Arbitrage 1958, 91), which involved a dispute over a gold clause in bonds issued by the Victoria-Minas Railway Company (a Brazilian company) held primarily by French bondholders. In 1952, the Brazilian Government, substituted for the original borrower, had entered into an agreement with the Association Nationale which, disregarding the gold clause in the bonds, provided for the arbitral settlement of the existing dispute with the bondholders. This agreement had been approved by the majority of the bondholders. A dissenting bondholder brought action in the French courts to have the resolution passed by the majority quashed as ultra vires. The action succeeded.

[89] Cass. March 22, 1944, Chemins de Fer Portugais v. Ash, S.1945.1.77; Rev. 1940-46, 107. See also Nadelmann, "Composition—Reorganization and Arrangements—in the Conflict of Laws", 61 Harv. L. Rev. 804 (1948).

[90] Journal Officiel May 22, 1955, p. 5150. The preamble of the decree states that:
"Arbitration is the only procedure at the disposal of bondholders to seek satisfaction of their claim when the debtor is a foreign public collectivity [i.e. municipality or other political unit of a foreign state] which refuses to comply with a French judgment in favor of the bondholders . . . Under the circumstances, and in order to facilitate the satisfactory solution of many disputes, it appears desirable, in cases of disputes between bondholders and a foreign public collectivity, to confer upon the general assembly of bondholders the authority to pass upon a resolution to arbitrate" (as translated).

This provision constitutes an official recognition of the merits of arbitration in the settlement of loan disputes. Its scope, however, may not be as wide as one might have wished. On its face, the decree is limited to disputes between bondholders and a foreign sovereign or other public bodies, such as municipalities and other political units, which are included in the French concept of "collectivity." No mention is made in the decree of possible disputes with foreign private entities. It is true that the two situations are quite different, and bondholders have means to enforce French judgments against foreign private issuers that might be lacking in the case of foreign public borrowers. However, there may still be cases in which submission of private loan disputes to arbitration might be a useful remedy. Whether this remedy is available is not clear. The answer will depend upon the judicial construction of the decree. The courts may hold that in view of the limited terms of the decree, disputes between bondholders and foreign private borrowers are no more arbitrable today than they were before 1955. On the other hand, the courts may conclude that the decree, by repudiating the earlier limitations upon the powers of bondholders' associations, formulates a general principle applicable to cases other than those to which it expressly refers. Such a conclusion would considerably brighten the future of arbitration in the settlement of loan disputes involving the French market.

It is possible of course, that new developments at the national level similar to those which have taken place in France; or the establishment of a new machinery for the settlement of investment disputes between states and nationals of other states,[91] reveal new patterns for settling loan controversies. In the field of international lending, however, it appears doubtful that arbitration will ultimately take precedence over other methods of settlement, and especially conciliation, which has proved particularly successful in recent years as a means to adjust loan disputes of long standing.[92]

---

[91] See the text of the Convention on the Settlement of Investment Disputes between States and Nationals of Other States submitted to Governments by the Executive Directors of the IBRD and Accompanying Report of the Executive Directors, March 18, 1965 (hereinafter the SID Convention). For earlier proposals for the creation of an International Loan Tribunal, see L.N. Report, Section 92 and Annex IV; Rome Institute for the Unificaton of Private Law, Institution d'un Tribunal des Emprunts Internationaux, Etudes, XX, U (nification) D (roit) P (rivé) —1946, Doc. 6; Report on the Activity of the Institute for the Years 1947-1952, in 3 UNIDROIT (1954), p. 65.

[92] Recourse to conciliation considerably facilitated the settlement of controversies of French bondholders with Japan (Imperial Japanese Loan of 1910) and with the City of Tokyo (City of Tokyo Loan of 1912). In both

B. THE ARBITRATION PROCESS

1. *The Parties*

Arbitral clauses in direct loan contracts provide that each party (in the case of contracts between two parties) or each group of parties (in the case of guaranteed loans or loans involving a plurality of parties) shall have the right to request arbitration.[93]

In the case of loans publicly issued, however, steps are normally taken to curb the individual bondholder's right of action and restrict the right to institute proceedings to certain designated persons. Thus it may be provided that the only persons authorized to set the arbitration machinery in motion shall be the debtor, on the one side, and on the other side, some representative of the creditors, such as the trustee,[94] the common representative of bondholders,[95] certain offici-

---

cases, the recommendations of the conciliators (Mr. Von Steyern in the case of the Government loan dispute, and Mr. Black, then President of the IBRD, acting however in his personal capacity, in the case of the City bond controversy) were accepted by the parties.

As to the role of the IBRD in facilitating the settlement of economic (other than loan) disputes, see *The World Bank,* p. 8.

[93] See e.g., IBRD, Loan Regulations No. 3 regarding arbitration between the IBRD and a borrowing member government, Section 7.03 (b) :

"The parties to such arbitration shall be the bank and the Borrower."

Comp., IBRD, Loan Regulations No. 4 regarding arbitration between the IBRD, a borrower other than a member government and a guarantor member country, Section 7.04 (b) :

"The parties to such arbitration shall be the Bank on the one side and the Borrower and the Guarantor on the other side."

This provision, duly amended, has been maintained consistently by the IBRD in loans made by it to several borrowers (see e.g., Loan Agreement dated September 21, 1956, between the IBRD and Osterreichische Elekstri-zitätswirtschafts-Aktiengesellschaft (Verbundgesellschaft) and Osterreichische Donaukraftwerke Aktiengesellschaft, guaranteed by Republic of Austria, Schedule 3 (a), (259 UNTS 43), or to one borrower with the guarantee of several guarantors (see e.g., Loan Agreement dated December 10, 1959, between the IBRD and Société Pétrolière de Gérance, guaranteed by Republic of France and by (i) Société Nationale de Recherche et d'Exploitation des Pétroles en Algérie; (ii) Compagnie Française des Pétroles en Algérie; and (iii) Compagnie Française des Pétroles, Schedule 3 (g) (380 UNTS 319).

[94] See e.g., League of Nations, Draft arbitration clause, *L.N. Report,* paragraph 89 (b), p. 26; Draft International Convention regarding international loans tribunal, Annex IV, (vi) p. 41.

See the prospectus (clause 18) regarding the Naphtachimie Loan (referred to in note 83 *supra*) :

". . . Naphtachimie will appoint one arbitrator; the trustee will appoint the second arbitrator and these two arbitrators will appoint a third arbitrator before the commencement of the arbitration proceedings" (as translated).

ally recognized entities concerned with the protection of holders of foreign bonds,[96] the issuing banking house, or the paying or fiscal agent of the loan.[97] If the bondholders' individual right of action is preserved, measures are taken to keep other parties in interest, such as the trustee or the bankers, informed of the institution of any proceedings in order to give these parties an opportunity to intervene and present evidence.[98]

2. *The Arbitrators*

Arbitration under international loans is normally compulsory: If one party refuses to appoint arbitrators, the other party usually has the right to request that the appointment be made by some independent authority like the President of the International Court of Justice,[99] or that of some other judicial body,[100] the Secretary-

[95] See e.g., *L.N. Report,* Id. loc. See also, the French decree-law of May 20, 1955, referred to supra in note 90.

[96] See e.g., *L.N. Report,* Id. loc. See also the London Agreement of February 27, 1953 regarding the Settlement of German External Debts (TIAS 2792, 333 UNTS 3), Article 29 (relating to public debts) and Annex II, Article VIII (relating to private debts) (hereinafter German External Debts Agreement).

[97] See e.g., *L.N. Report,* Id. loc. See also, Agreement dated September 1, 1911, between Nicaragua and American bankers, September 1, 1911 (Article V, Section 2, *Dunn,* 344); Agreement between Argentina and American bankers relating to the Argentine 6% Redeemable External Gold Loan of 1925, *L.N. Report* p. 38; General Bond of the Free City of Danzig 6½ Loan, 1927, Ibid. See also the 1937 arbitration between the Kingdom of Roumania Monopolies Institute and the Fiscal Agents for the Stabilization and Development Loan of 1929, referred to in Domke, "Arbitration Clauses and International Loans", 3 Arb. J. 161 (1939).

[98] See e.g., the German External Debts Agreement, Article 30, referred to supra in note 96, and the Agreement of November 21, 1956 between the United States and Austria (290 UNTS 181, TIAS 3903) regarding Austrian Dollar Bonds, Articles VI and XIV (2) (hereinafter Austrian Dollar Bonds Agreement).

[99] See e.g., IBRD, Loan Regulations No. 3 (Section 7.03 (c)) and No. 4 (Section 7.04 (c)). Comp., the Sau Paulo Loan, referred to supra in note 82, conferring the power of appointment of the President of the former PCIJ.

[100] An interesting example is that of the IBRD loan to Compagnie Minière de l'Ogooué, a Gabonese mining corporation, which is guaranteed by the Republics of France, Gabon and Congo. It will be recalled that, following the referendum of September 28, 1958, a "Community" was created between France and the former French overseas territories in Africa, including Gabon and Congo, which elected to become autonomous states within the Community. Since one of the organs of the Community was a Court of Arbitration having jurisdiction over controversies between members of the Community, it appeared particularly appropriate to take advantage of the new constitutional set-up, and to stipulate that if the borrower and the three guar-

General of the United Nations,[101] the President of the IBRD,[102] certain technical organization,[103] or a well-known international arbitration association.[104]

Although provisions calling for arbitration by a single arbitrator are not unknown,[105] the great majority of clauses provide for arbitra-

_____

antors could not reach agreement on the arbitrator to be appointed by them in accordance with the IBRD Loan Regulations, such arbitrator would be designated by the President of the Court of Arbitration of the Community. See Loan Agreement dated June 30, 1959 (452 UNTS 67), Schedule 3 (j) reading as follows:

> "The Arbitral Tribunal shall consist of three arbitrators appointed as follows: one arbitrator shall be appointed by the Bank; a second arbitrator shall be appointed by the Borrower and the Guarantors or, if they shall not agree, by the President of the Court of Arbitration of the French Community; and the third arbitrator (hereinafter sometimes called the Umpire) shall be appointed by agreement of the parties or, if they shall not agree, by the President of the International Court of Justice or, failing appointment by him, by the Secretary-General of the United Nations."

[101] Thus, the IBRD Loan Regulations No. 3 (Section 7.03 (c)) and No. 4 (Section 7.04 (c)) provide that, failing appointment of the umpire by the President of the I.C.J., the appointment shall be made by the Secretary-General of the U.N. The Regulations also provide that if either side shall fail to appoint an arbitrator, such arbitrator shall be appointed by the umpire.

Comp., the Sau Paulo Loan which vested in the Council of the League of Nations, as substitute for the President of the P.C.I.J., the power to appoint the arbitrators or the umpire.

[102] SID Convention, Article 30 (Conciliation) and Article 38 (Arbitration), referred to supra in note 91.

[103] See e.g., the Naphtachimie Loan, referred to supra in note 83:

> "If one of the parties shall not, within fourteen days after a request by the other party delivered to it by registered mail, have appointed an arbitrator or in the event of lack of agreement of the third arbitrator, each party may request the chairman of the Chamber of Commerce of Amsterdam to appoint a second and/or third arbitrator" (as translated).

The Sau Paulo Loan, referred to supra in note 82, provided that failing appointment by the President of the PCIJ or by the Council of the League of Nations, the arbitrators would be appointed by "the President for the time being of the Law Society of England".

[104] Thus, the German External Debts Agreement (Article 29 (3) and (4)), referred to supra in note 96, vests the power of appointment in the International Chamber of Commerce.

Comp., the West Rand Investment Trust, Ltd. (WRIT), Johannesburg, $4\frac{1}{2}\%$ Loan of 1954, (hereinafter WRIT Loan) prospectus, clause 13:

> ". . . . Any controversy arising under this agreement shall be submitted to an arbitral tribunal of three members which shall be appointed in accordance with the Rules of Conciliation and Arbitration of the International Chamber of Commerce, in Paris . . ." (as translated).

[105] Sometimes the arbitrator is to be appointed by agreement of the parties at the time of the proceedings. See e.g., the Agreement between Argentina and

tion by a tribunal of three arbitrators. Most loans contracted by private[106] or governmental[107] borrowers, as well as loans made or contracted by international lending organizations like the IBRD,[108] stipulate that each party, or group of parties, is entitled to appoint one arbitrator, the third arbitrator (the chairman or umpire) being appointed by the other two;[109] or by mutual agreement of the parties,[110] or, lacking such agreement, by an independent authority.[111]

In exceptional cases, the number of arbitrators may be increased to account for the particular circumstances of a specific case. For example, it will be recalled that under Loan Regulations No. 1 of the IBRD (applicable to loans made to a borrower other than a member

---

American bankers, supra note 97, (appointment by the Argentine Ambassador to the U.S.A. and by the bankers).

On other occasions, the arbitrator is already designated in the loan documents. See e.g., the Agreement between Nicaragua and American bankers, supra note 97 (Secretary of State of the United States), and the Agreement dated June 24, 1922 (Article IX, *Dunn,* p. 227) between El Salvador and American bankers, (Chief Justice of the Supreme Court of the United States, or another member of the federal judiciary).

[106] See e.g., the Naphtachimie Loan, referred to supra in note 83.

[107] See e.g., the State of Sau Paulo Loan, referred to supra in note 82.

". . . one Arbitrator shall be appointed by each of the parties to the dispute and the Umpire shall be appointed by such two Arbitrators."
See also, the arbitration clause quoted in the Société Commerciale de Belgique Case, PCIJ Series A/B, No. 78, at p. 166; the German External Debts Agreement, Article 29 (2), referred to supra in note 96, regarding the composition of the Court of Arbitration set up to settle disputes arising in connection with the settlement of debts of the Reich and other public authorities; the Agreement of May 31-October 14, 1954, between the United Kingdom and Austria for the validation of Foreign Currency Bonds (204 UNTS 87), Annex, Section 2 (2).

[108] Loan Regulations, No. 3 Section 7.03 (c), and No. 4 Section 7.04 (c). See also, Article 9 of the 1956 Loan Agreement between the Swiss Confederation and the IBRD, referred to supra in note 80.

[109] See the agreements cited supra in note 107.

[110] See e.g., the 1956 Austrian Dollar Bonds Agreement (Article I (2)), referred to supra in note 98; see also note 108 supra; SID Convention, Articles 29 (3) (Conciliation) and 37 (3) (Arbitration), referred to supra in note 91.

[111] See text and notes 99 to 104 supra. Both the Draft Arbitral Clause (*L.N. Report,* para. 86 (e)) and the Draft Convention for an International Loans Tribunal (*L.N. Report,* Annex IV (ii)), prepared by the Loan Committee of the League of Nations contemplated that the arbitrators, or the judges, would be appointed by the Permanent Court of International Justice.

The General Bond of the Free City of Danzig 6½% Loan of 1927 (Tobacco Monopoly), provided for submission of disputes to the Council of the League of Nations or to "any person appointed by the Council to settle the said question". (*L.N. Report* p. 38). See also, Id. loc., the General Bond of the 7½% Stabilization Loan, 1928 of the Kingdom of Bulgaria.

country, with the guarantee of the member in whose territories the project is located) the IBRD, as one party, and the borrower and the guarantor, as the other party, are each entitled to appoint one arbitrator, the umpire being appointed by agreement between the two parties. It will also be recalled that the Loan Regulations provide that if the borrower and the guarantor cannot agree on an arbitrator, that arbitrator shall be appointed by the guarantor.[112] This last solution has been employed in the great majority of IBRD loans made to political subdivisions or agencies of the guarantor. Sometimes, however, especially in the case of loans made to private corporations, this approach has been discarded to give both the borrower and the guarantor the right to appoint separate arbitrators. The case of the 1959 loan to Société Pétrolière de Gérance, a French corporation operating an oil pipeline in Algeria, is in point. The loan is guaranteed by France and also by three oil companies. The loan agreement provides for an arbitral tribunal of five arbitrators, two appointed by the IBRD, the third by the borrower and the guarantor companies (or, if they cannot agree, by the borrower), the fourth by France, and the fifth (the umpire) by agreement of all the parties.[113]

Another example is found in Annex II to the 1953 German External Debts Agreement which, with a view to facilitating the settlement of private debts, provides for the constitution of an Arbitration and Mediation Committee of eight members, appointed in equal proportion by the debtors and the creditors.[114]

---

[112] Loan Regulations No. 4, Section 7.04 (c).

[113] Loan Agreement dated December 10, 1959, Schedule 3 (g) (380 UNTS 319). The relevant provision reads as follows:

"The Arbitral Tribunal shall consist of five arbitrators appointed as follows: two arbitrators shall be appointed by the Bank; the third arbitrator shall be appointed by the Borrower and SN REPAL, CFP (A) and CFP or, if they shall not agree, by the Borrower; the fourth arbitrator shall be appointed by Republic of France; and the fifth arbitrator (hereinafter sometimes called the Umpire) shall be appointed by agreement of the parties or, if they shall not agree, by the President of the International Court of Justice or, failing appointment by him, by the Secretary General of the United Nations."

[114] Annex II, Article IX (2). Paragraph 3 provides that the four creditor members shall be appointed by organizations designated by the respective Creditor Committees of the United States, United Kingdom, Switzerland and The Netherlands. However, at the request of a Creditor Committee of a country whose creditors are especially concerned in a particular case, the same paragraph provides for the replacement of one of the creditor members by a member specifically appointed by the Creditor Committee of the country involved. The appointment of the four debtor members is reserved to the Head of the German Delegation on External Debts.

This last Agreement deserves attention in another respect also. It provides that the chairman of the Committee must be elected among the creditor members.[115] This solution, which was expressly rejected in those provisions of the German External Debts Agreement dealing with the settlement of public debts,[116] is relatively rare in arbitration clauses relating to international loans.[117] Although obviously nationality is a most important element to consider in selecting arbitrators, most arbitration clauses contain no reference to nationality as a factor of qualification or disqualification of the arbitrators. This practice is probably attributable to the feeling of mutual trust which is of the essence of international loan bargains, and to the confidence the parties have in the integrity and good judgment of those authorities entrusted by them with the appointment of arbitrators.[118] It is also noteworthy that arbitration clauses in international loans contain no standards regarding the professional qualification of arbitrators. This is easily understandable, particularly in the case of economic development loans. In most cases it is impossible, at the time of the loan agreement, to know whether possible controversies between the parties will be financial, legal or technical in nature. The selection in the loan documents therefore of members of one rather than another profession might prove inappropriate at the time of an actual dispute.

3. The Proceedings

Provisions in arbitration clauses concerning the conduct of the proceedings are generally intended to insure a high degree of flexibility in the arbitral procedure, and therefore are usually extremely general in character.

As a rule these clauses merely provide that, subject to conducting the hearings with fairness,[119] the tribunal shall be free to decide all matters relating to its competence and shall determine its own rules

---

[115] Article IX (2).

[116] Agreement, Article 29 (2) (c) provides that the chairman of the Court of Arbitration set up by this provision shall be neither a German national nor a national of a creditor country.

[117] See, however, the agreements between American bankers and Latin American countries, note 82 supra. See also, Article I (2) of the 1956 Austrian Dollar Bonds Agreement.

[118] See e.g., Laurent Jully, "Arbitration and Judicial Settlement, Recent Trends", 48 Am. J. Int'l L. 380 (1954), at p. 400.

[119] See e.g., IBRD, Loan Regulations No. 3 (Section 7.03 (h)) and No. 4 (Section 7.04 (h)).

of procedure.[120] In the absence of specific agreement between the parties, therefore, matters such as those relating to the time and place of the hearings,[121] the manner of giving notice of hearings, the presentation of evidence, the representation of the parties by counsel, and the conditions relating to intervention by third parties,[122] are left to the reasonable discretion of the tribunal. One exception to the general rule is that, if several arbitrators are appointed, the arbitration clause ordinarily sets forth the number of votes required for a tribunal decision.[123]

---

[120] See e.g., the 1956 Austrian Dollar Bonds Agreement (Article V), referred to supra in note 98; the German External Debts Agreement (article 29 (6)), referred to supra in note 96, which provides that if the Court of Arbitration fails to determine its rules of procedure, or in matters not covered by such determination, the Arbitration Code of the International Chamber of Commerce applies, and Annex II to that Agreement (Article IX (4)); IBRD, Loan Regulations No. 3 (Section 7.03 (g)) and No. 4 (Section 7.04 (g)).

See also the provision in the Naphtachimie Loan, referred to supra in note 83, that: "the arbitrators shall determine the rules of the arbitral procedure". The Rules of Procedure of the International Loans Tribunal proposed by the Committee of the League of Nations (*L.N. Report,* Annex IV (iv), p. 40) were to be drawn by the PCIJ.

See also, SID Convention referred to in note 91 supra, Article 33 (Conciliation) and Article 44 (Arbitration). For a controversial decision regarding the law governing procedural matters in arbitral proceedings see, Lalive "Un Récent Arbitrage Suisse entre un Organisme d'Etat et une Société Privée Etrangère", 19 Annuaire Suisse de Droit International 273 (1962); Suratgar, "The Sapphire Arbitration Award, The Procedural Aspects: Report and Critique", 3 Col. J. Transnational L. 152 (1965).

[121] See e.g., IBRD Loan Regulations No. 3 (Section 7.03 (f)) and No. 4 (Section 7.04 (f)). Both provisions specify, however, that the tribunal shall first convene at the time and place fixed by the umpire. Thereafter, the tribunal may determine where and when it shall sit.

The 1956 Austrian Dollar Bonds Agreement, referred to supra in note 98, provides (Article IV) that the seat of the tribunal shall be in New York although the tribunal may, in exceptional circumstances, hold sessions elsewhere.

The Naphtachimie Loan, referred to supra in note 83, specifies that the arbitration proceedings shall take place in The Netherlands. The Sau Paulo Loan, referred to supra in note 82, provides for arbitration in London. This is similar to the general practice of conferring jurisdiction on specific courts which are normally those in the lenders' country. See also, SID Convention, Articles 62 and 63, referred to supra in note 91.

[122] See, however, Article VI (3) of the 1956 Austrian Dollar Bonds Agreement, referred to supra in note 98.

[123] Thus, the IBRD Loan Regulations No. 3 (Section 7.03 (g)) and No. 4 (Section 7.04 (g)) provide that decisions of the arbitral tribunal shall be by majority vote.

The 1956 Austrian Dollar Bonds Agreement (Article III), referred to supra

Arbitration clauses are frequently specific in regard to the costs of the proceedings and their apportionment among the parties. There also, however, variations from case to case are noticeable. In some instances, the parties determine the costs of the proceedings, including the remunerattion of the arbitrators and of such persons as may be required for the conduct of the proceedings,[124] on other occasions, the costs are established by the tribunal itself.[125] The costs may then be divided among the parties,[126] or be borne by the debtor,[127] or by the creditor, if it is found that his claim was frivolous or made in bad faith.[128] Generally, each party must defray its own legal and other expenses in the arbitration proceedings,[129] although there are cases

in note 98, and the 1954 UK/Austria Agreement (Section 2 (3)), referred to supra in note 107, respectively provide in substance that all decisions of the tribunal shall be by joint action of its two members if they are in agreement; lacking such agreement, the matter shall be referred to the chairman whose decision shall constitute the decision of the tribunal.

[124] See e.g., IBRD, Loan Regulations No. 3 (Section 7.03 (i)) and No. 4 (Section 7.04 (i)).

[125] See e.g., Annex II (Article IX (5)) to the 1953 German External Debts Agreement, referred to supra in note 96. Comp., the 1956 Austrian Dollar Bonds Agreement (Article XIII) , referred to supra in note 98.

The IBRD Loan Regulations (see preceding note) further provide that if the parties cannot agree on the remuneration of the arbitrators before the tribunal shall convene, the tribunal shall fix an amount "as shall be reasonable under the circumstances".

The draft convention prepared by the Committee of the League of Nations (L.N. Report, Annex IV, (v) , pp. 40-41) contemplated that the PCIJ would fix the remuneration of the judges, the other administrative expenses of the Loan Tribunal being borne equally by the states and members of the League of Nations adhering to the Convention.

[126] See e.g., IBRD Loan Regulations No. 3 (Section 7.03 (i)) and No. 4 (Section 7.04 (i)). The costs are divided equally between the IBRD, on the one hand, and the borrower on the other (if the borrower is a member country) , or both the borrower and the guarantor (if the loan is made to a borrower other than a member with a member's guarantee) . The IBRD has remained faithful to this solution in cases of loans made to several borrowers (see e.g., Loan Agreement dated September 10, 1953, between the IBRD and Corporación de Fomento de la Producción and Compania Manufacturera de Papeles y Cartones, guaranteed by Republic of Chile (188 UNTS 25) , Schedule 3 (f)) , and loans guaranteed by several guarantors (see e.g., the Société Pétrolière de Gérance Loan cited supra in note 113, Schedule 3 (g) .

[127] See e.g., the 1956 Austrian Dollar Bonds Agreement (Article XIII, referred to supra in note 98; the 1954 UK/Austria Agreement (Section 9 (2)), referred to supra in note 107; Annex II to the 1953 German External Debts Agreement (Article IX (5)), referred to supra in note 96. Comp., L.N. Report, Annex IV (v) , pp. 40-41.

[128] See e.g., L.N. Report, Draft Arbitration Clause § 89 (f) , p. 26; Annex II to the 1953 German External Debts Agreement (Article IX (5)).

[129] See e.g., IBRD Loan Regulations, loc. cit. supra, note 126.

in which the debtor is required to bear a reasonable share of the expenses incurred by the creditor when the latter's claim is successful.[130] The financing of arbitration proceedings follows no established pattern, and the prevailing practice does not lend itself to generalization.[131]

4. *The Award*

A common feature of arbitral clauses in international loans is that they prescribe no time limit within which the award must be rendered, a wise solution in view of the complexities frequently involved in international loan disputes. Another feature, consistent with compulsory arbitration, is that the award may be rendered by default.[132]

Subject to these remarks, the prevailing practice conforms generally to that which obtains in other fields of international arbitration. Thus, it is customary to provide that the award, normally reduced to writing,[133] and duly notified to all the parties concerned,[134] shall be "final and without appeal,"[135] "final and conclusive,"[136] or "final and binding upon the parties."[137]

An original situation is that of the decisions rendered by the arbitral bodies set up by the German External Debts Agreement.

---

[130] See e.g., the 1954 UK/Austria Agreement (Section 9(1)), referred to supra in note 107; the 1956 Austrian Dollar Bonds Agreement (Article XIII (2)), referred to supra in note 98. This last agreement contains also an interesting provision compelling the Austrian Government to make available for transfer the dollar exchange required for payments of costs and expenses to be borne by it under the agreement (Article XIII (3)).

[131] See, Hudson, *International Tribunals* (1944), pp. 59 et seq.

[132] See e.g., IBRD, Loan Regulations No. 3 (Section 7.03 (h)) and No. 4 (Section 7.04 (h)). Comp., the WRIT Loan, referred to supra in note 83, referring to the Rules of Arbitration of the I.C.C.

[133] See e.g., IBRD, Loan Regulations. Id. loc.; the WRIT Loan, referred to supra in note 83; the Sau Paulo Loan, referred to supra in note 82, and the Naphtachimie Loan, referred to supra in note 83, by referring to the I.C.C. Rules or to domestic (English and Dutch) law achieve a similar result.

[134] See e.g., IBRD, Loan Regulations, Id. loc. See also, the 1954 UK/Austria Agreement (Section 2(4)), referred to supra in note 107; and compare the agreements cited supra in note 98.

[135] See e.g., the WRIT Loan, referred to supra in note 83, the Agreement between Argentina and American bankers relating to the Argentine 6% Redeemable External Gold Loan of 1925 (*L.N. Report,* Annex III, p. 38).

[136] See e.g., the agreements between American bankers and Nicaragua, and El Salvador, notes 97 and 105 supra.

[137] See e.g., IBRD, Loan Regulations No. 3 (Section 7.03 (h)) and No. 4 (Section 7.04 (h)). Comp., the General Bond of the $7\frac{1}{2}\%$ Stabilization Loan, 1928, of the Kingdom of Bulgaria (*L.N. Report,* Annex III, p. 38).

These decisions are "binding" on the parties as to the terms of settlement set forth in the decision.[138] This means that once a decision has been given, both the debtor and the creditors are obliged to recognize that the terms of the decision are in accordance with the provisions of the Agreement. Although the debtor is compelled to offer the terms set forth in the decision to its creditors, and the creditors' representatives have the duty to recommend acceptance of the offer to the bondholders, the latter remain free to accept or to reject the offer.[139] These decisions, therefore, seem to stand somewhere between a normal arbitral award and the opinions or recommendations of conciliators which, whatever their moral weight, are not legally binding on the parties.

SECTION III. MISCELLANEOUS

A. GUARANTEED LOANS

The lenders' interest in having its relations with the borrower and the guarantor determined within the context of the same legal framework, already noted in connection with stipulations of applicable law,[140] is apparent also from the jurisdictional provisions currently found in guaranteed-loans agreements.

Depending upon the circumstances, jurisdictional clauses in guaranteed loan documents may provide for the exclusive jurisdiction of a designated forum, as in the following example in a Swiss prospectus:

"Any dispute between the bondholders, of the one part, and the debtor or the guarantor, of the other part, concerning the bonds or coupons of this loan, shall be decided exclusively by the Federal Tribunal at Lausanne whose judgment shall be final" (as translated) .[141]

---

[138] Agreement, Article 29 (7) ; Annex II, Article IX (1) (as interpreted by the Sub-Annex to Annex II) .

[139] The Sub-Annex to Annex II makes it clear that even though Article IX (1) states that the creditors shall be "obliged to accept" the terms of the offer, that expression means only that the creditors cannot raise the issue of inconsistency between the terms of the offer and the provisions of the Agreement.

[140] See Chapter III, text and notes 131 to 133.

[141] Prospectus of the Belgian Congo 4% Loan of 1963, guaranteed by Belgium, clause 12.

See also, in Germany, the prospectus of the Prefecture of Osaka and the City of Osaka 6½% DM Loan of 1962, guaranteed by Japan:

"The rights and obligations arising out of this Loan, including the

Or they may authorize the lenders to bring suit in any one of a number of designated jurisdictions, as in the following provision in a German prospectus:

"The place of performance and jurisdiction for the obligations of the debtor and the guarantors shall be Frankfurt am Main. The bondholders shall have also the right to bring their claims before the Austrian courts" (as translated) .[142]

---

guarantee given by Japan, shall be solely determined under the laws of the Federal Republic of Germany.

The place of performance and jurisdiction for all parties concerned shall be Frankfurt am Main" (as translated) .

In most cases the guarantor, like the borrower, is a foreign entity. For a case in which the guarantor was a company incorporated in the lenders' country, see Indian and General Investment Trust, Limited v. Borax Consolidated, Limited, [1920] 1 K.B. 539 (American company, borrower; English company, guarantor) . The relevant indenture clause reads as follows:

"Clause 27: 'These presents shall be construed and the rights of all persons claiming hereunder shall be regulated by the law of England. And the railroad Company [the American borrower] doth hereby agree that in case it shall be necessary for the trustees to take legal proceedings against the railroad company in connection with these presents or for effectuating the security hereby created it shall be lawful for the trustees to sue the company in England in its corporate name and in order to give effect to the intention of the foregoing provision the railroad company hereby agrees to be bound in all things by the jurisdiction of the English Courts and the railroad company shall be deemed to have and at all times during the continuance of this security to retain domicile and residence in England and that service of any writ of summons or other process issued at the suit of the trustees against the railroad company effected by leaving a copy of such writ or other process at the registered office for the time being of the Borax Company [the guarantor] in London shall be deemed to be good and effectual service of such writ or other process upon the railroad company."

[142] Oesterreichische Donaukraftwerke AG 6% DM Loan of 1959, jointly and severally guaranteed by the Republic of Austria and Oesterreichische Elektrizitaetswirtschaft-Aktiengesellschaft-Verbundgesellschaft. See also Suomen Teollisuus-Hipoteekkipankki Oy 6¼% DM Loan of 1963, guaranteed by the Republic of Finland.

Comp., in Switzerland, the prospectus of the California Texas Corporation (Caltex) 4½% Loan of 1955, guaranteed by Bahrain Petroleum Company Limited, Overseas Tankship Corporation and Caltex Oceanic Limited, clause 11:

"Any disputes between the bondholders, of the one part, and the California Texas Corporation or the Guarantors, of the other part, concerning the bonds and/or coupons of this Loan shall be governed by Swiss law and shall be decided by the courts of the Canton of Bâle-Ville, subject to appeal to the Federal Tribunal at Lausanne. To this effect, the California Texas Corporation and the Guarantors elect domicile with the Société de Banque Suisse, at Basel.

The bondholders shall be free to exercise any rights and to bring any

These clauses, which appear with equal frequency in the case of privately guaranteed loans and loans guaranteed by foreign governments, are particularly important in the latter case. The guarantor, by submitting to the jurisdiction of the courts designated in the agreement, may be effectively barred from a successful plea of immunity. Since it is unclear whether a sovereign entity's guarantee of a non-sovereign borrower's loan obligations, by itself, constitutes a tacit waiver of immunity,[143] the lenders' efforts to solve this problem with a jurisdictional clause seems entirely justified.

legal proceedings in the courts of the countries in which the California Texas Corporation and/or the Guarantors are incorporated" (as translated).

See also the Swiss prospectuses concerning: (i) The Tauernkraftwerke Aktiengesellschaft, Salzburg 5% Loan of 1958 guaranteed by the Austrian Government and the Österreichische Elektrizitätswirtschafts-Aktiengesellschaft (Verbundgesellschaft), clause 10; (ii) the Aktieselskabet Dansk Svovlsyreog Superphosphat-Fabrik 4½% Loan of 1961 guaranteed by Norsk Hydro-Elektrisk Kvaelstofaktieselskab Notodden (Norvège) and Dansk Andels Gödningsforretning, Copenhague, clause 11; (iii) the Société Concessionnaire Française pour la Construction et l'Exploitation du Tunnel Routier sous le Mont-Blanc 4½% Loan of 1961, guaranteed by France, clause 11; and (iv) the Association Diocésaine de Besançon 5% Loan of 1963, guaranteed by French real estate companies, clause 9.

See also (i) in England, the prospectus of the Enso-Gutzeit Osakeyhtiö £4 million 6½% Sterling/DM Guaranteed Loan 1980:

"The Trust Deed will contain an arbitration clause under which, without prejudice to the right of the Trustee to proceed in the courts of any country in the world, the Company, the Guarantor or the Trustee will be entitled to refer any matter connected with the Loan to arbitration in London."

and (ii) in Luxembourg, the prospectus of the Oesterreichisch-Alpine Montangesellschaft 5¾% Loan of 1965, Guaranteed by the Republic of Austria:

"The Trustee and, within the framework of the Trust indenture, the bondholders shall be free to enforce their rights in any court in the City of Luxembourg having jurisdiction over the subject matter, in any State or Federal Court in the State of New York, United States of America having jurisdiction over the subject matter and/or in any court in the Republic of Austria having jurisdiction. . . ."

[143] This issue was raised in the case of Société Bauer-Marchal v. Ministre des Finances de Turquie, which involved a dispute between French bondholders and the Turkish Government as guarantor of bonds issued in 1913 by the City of Constantinople. The Court of Appeals of Paris (January 29, 1957, J.C.P. 1957, II, 9779; Clunet 1957, 392) held that although the principal obligor (the City) was subject to the jurisdiction of the French courts, the guarantor government could successfully plead immunity since the act of guaranteeing the loan did not constitute a waiver of jurisdictional immunity. This judgment was quashed by the Supreme Court (Cass. December 19, 1961, J.C.P. 1962, II, 12489) on the ground that the lower court had failed to establish why it had characterized the governmental guarantee as an act *jure*

In guaranteed-loan documents, the object of jurisdictional clauses, like that of stipulations of applicable law, is to settle issues concerning the lenders' rights against the obligors. These clauses make no attempt to solve the various jurisdictional problems which may arise as an aftermath of the adjudication of the primary dispute, between the borrower and the guarantor. These would have to be solved under the relevant conflict-of-laws rules determining the jurisdiction of national courts; or to the extent that the borrower, the guarantor or other parties in interest are subjects of international law, by the principles applicable to international litigation.[144]

Similar problems are inherent in loan documents which provide for the settlement of loan disputes by way of arbitration. Thus, it is clear, that the arbitral provisions found in the IBRD Loan Regulations, or similar clauses in the IADB agreements, refer only to disputes between the lending organization and the contracting parties.[145] They do not purport to resolve jurisdictional issues which might arise between the guarantor and the borrower, for example after full repayment of the loan by the guarantor.[146]

B. THE SPECIAL CASE OF ASSIGNMENT

Although jurisdictional or arbitral clauses in loan contracts and bonds are stipulated primarily for the convenience of lenders, they

imperii rather than an act *jure gestionis*. The case was remanded to another Court of Appeals (Rouen February 10, 1965, Clunet 1965, 655), which adopted the latter characterization.

For earlier French judgments dismissing actions against sovereign guarantors on the ground of jurisdictional immunity, see Trib. Comm. Seine April 11, 1867, Cavour Canal Company Case, D. 1867.2.49; Trib. Civ. Seine November 14, 1934, Huttinger v. Société des Chemins de Fer du Congo, Etat du Congo and Ministère des Colonies de Belgique, Clunet 1935, 623. Comp., Cass. November 21, 1961, Montefiore v. Association Nationale des Porteurs de Valeurs Mobilières, J.C.P. 1962, II, 12521.

[144] See e.g., Sir John Fisher Williams' remarks concerning the Austrian Guaranteed Loans in *La Convention pour l'Assistance Financière aux Etats Victimes d'Agression,* 34 Recueil des Cours 81 (1930), at pp. 137-138.

[145] IBRD Loan Regulations No. 4, Section 7.04 (a) and (b) quoted in note 79 supra.

[146] Certain situations may be particularly complex. See e.g., the Loan Agreement dated June 30, 1959, between the IBRD and Compagnie Minière de l'Ogooué (452 UNTS 67), guaranteed by the Republic of France, the Republic of Congo and the Republic of Gabon; the Loan Agreement dated March 17, 1960, between the IBRD and Société Anonyme des Mines de Fer de Mauritanie (452 UNTS 147), guaranteed by the Republic of France and the Republic of Mauritania; and the Loan Agreement dated December 10, 1959, between the IBRD and Société Pétrolière de Gérance (380 UNTS 319) guaranteed by the Republic of France and three oil companies.

may be of considerable interest to borrowers also. Particularly in the case of widely circulated bonds, a designation in the bonds of a specific judicial or arbitral forum may enable the borrower to resist successfully transferees' efforts to bring action in a forum other than those specified[147]

In the absence of any such designation, the substitution of one creditor for another as a result of a transfer or assignment, may expose the borrower to litigation in completely unexpected fora. For example, foreign bondholders have transferred foreign bonds to French nationals in order to confer jurisdiction upon the French courts on the sole basis of the nationality of the transferee;[148] and contractual rights have been assigned to New York residents by non-residents for the sole purpose of establishing jurisdiction in the courts of that State.[149] Although the French and New York statutes lend themselves particularly well to transactions of this kind, cases in other countries show that the problem is not limited to the eastern and western shores of the Atlantic. A Swiss case is in point. Under a loan agreement between the Greek Government and a Swedish company, the government had issued sterling bonds payable in Athens, New York, London or any other place designated by the lender, subject to notification to the borrower not less than two months before the due date. After the borrower had defaulted on its obligations, one of the bonds was assigned to a Swiss bank, which attached funds deposited in Switzerland by the debtor government. The government pleaded sovereign immunity. The plea was granted, but only on the ground that the

---

[147] See e.g., Cass. July 12, 1950, Montané v. Compagnie des Chemins de Fer Portugais, Rev. 1952, 509; Clunet 1950, 1206; S.1952.1.41. Bonds issued by a Portuguese railway company had been transferred by a foreign bondholder to a French holder who, notwithstanding a clause in the bonds providing for arbitration in Portugal, proceeded to bring suit in the French courts on the basis of article 14 C. Civ. The suit was dismissed on the ground that the French holder was bound by the arbitral clause in the bonds.

[148] See e.g., Trib. Civ. Seine May 4, 1927, Leclerc v. Compagnie des Chemins de Fer Portugais, Clunet 1928, 377. See generally, Niboyet, VI *Traité de Droit International Privé Français* (Part I, 1949), p. 300; Batiffol, *Traité Elémentaire de Droit International Privé* (3d ed. 1959) p. 759; Delaume, *American-French P.I.L.*, pp. 144-145.

[149] See e.g., De Gorter v. Banque de France, 176 Misc. 1062, 29 N.Y.S. 2d 842 (1941), aff'd 262 App. Div. 997, 30 N.Y.S. 2d 815 and Banque de France v. Supreme Court of State of New York, 287 N.Y. 483, 41 N.E. 2d 65 (1942); Wagner v. Braunsberg, 5 A. 2d 564, 173 N.Y.S. 2d 525 (1958). See also, Delaume, *American-French P.I.L.*, pp. 148-149.

Comp., Principality of Monaco v. Mississippi, 292 U.S. 313, 54 S. Ct. 745 (1934).

transaction did not have sufficient contact with the Swiss territory to give jurisdiction to the Swiss courts.[150]

Jurisdictional provisions in international loan instruments are not the only way to anticipate the consequences of future transfers or assignments. Restrictions upon the transferability or assignability of contractual rights may achieve results similar to those obtained by jurisdictional or arbitral clauses. This device is not possible, of course, in the case of bonds or similar evidence of indebtedness, lest their negotiable character be destroyed; but is fairly frequent in loan contracts between bankers and foreign borrowers and in intergovernmental loan agreements.[151] Since these restrictions make it impossible to modify the loan relationship without the borrower's consent, the jurisdictional issue incidental to possible transfers disappears or at least cannot be settled without the borrower's assent.

This description of legal practice would not be complete without referring also to the particular situation which arises as a result of sales of portions of loans made by the IBRD out of its loan portfolio. It has been seen elsewhere[152] that such sales to private investors, which are frequent, may be arranged at, or about, the time of the loan (participations); or after disbursements under the loan have been made (portfolio sales). In either case, it is the IBRD's practice to stipulate that all matters relating to the loan will be administered solely by it, thereby making it clear that the participants or purchasers are not entitled to exercise personally any of the remedies that the IBRD may have against the borrower or the guarantor. All that the IBRD undertakes is to exercise the same care in handling loans as to which it has granted participations or made portfolio sales, as it exercises with respect to loans and portions of loans for its own account. In no instance, therefore, would the participants or purchasers be entitled to institute, or become a party to, an arbitration proceeding under the loan in which they have invested their funds.

A similar situation arises when the IBRD requests the borrower, as it sometimes does, to issue bonds in representation of the loan, and

---

150 T.F. June 6, 1956, Royaume de Grèce v. Banque Julius Bar et Cie, R.O.82.1.75; Int'l L. Reports (1956), p. 195. Regarding the necessary connection of foreign loans with the Swiss territory as a ground for the jurisdiction of the Swiss courts, see note 17 supra. Comp., Amsterdam January 15, 1947, Trust Maatschappij Rokin v. Pester Bank, N.J. 1948, 130, summarized in Clunet 1950, 932 and in 3 Int'l & Comp. L. Q. 102 (1950).

151 See Chapter III, note 114.

152 Ibid, text and notes 122, 123.

sells the bonds to investors. The Loan Regulations expressly provide that in such a case no bondholder is entitled to exercise any rights under the Loan or the Guarantee Agreement; and express mention of this fact is made in the bonds themselves.[153] This does not mean, of course, that the holders of the bonds are deprived of any remedies: They certainly can exercise such remedies as may be available against the borrower or the guarantor under the rules obtaining in any court having jurisdiction. Like other investors participating in IBRD's operations, however, they could not be a party to any arbitration proceedings between the IBRD and the parties to the loan or guarantee agreement.

C. JOINT OPERATIONS

The observations in Chapter III concerning stipulations of applicable law in international loan contracts which are legally or financially interrelated,[154] also apply to jurisdictional clauses in these loans. As a practical matter, lenders in a joint operation, regardless of the degree of association with the other lenders, continue to adhere to their respective methods of doing business, and stipulate in their loan contracts the type of clauses concerning the applicable law and forum which suit their personal preference. To take the same examples as those used in the preceding Chapter, it is characteristic that: (i) in the Air India joint financing, the private lenders insisted upon conferring jurisdiction upon the New York courts; while the IBRD, consistent with its practice, provided for the arbitral settlement of disputes; (ii) in the tripartite financing of the Southern Italy Development Fund, the bonds issued in the United States market contain no jurisdictional provision, while disputes arising under the EIB or the IBRD loans would have to be decided respectively by the Italian courts or by an arbitral tribunal; and (iii) arbitration in one form or another is the exclusive means of settling disputes under the Indus Water Treaty, between India and Pakistan, or the parties to the Indus Development Fund Agreement, or the IBRD and Pakistan under the Loan Agreement with that country; whereas the DLF Agreement with Pakistan contains no jurisdictional clause at all.

---

[153] Id. loc.
[154] See Chapter III, text and notes 57 to 62.

SECTION IV. RECOGNITION AND ENFORCEMENT OF CREDITOR JUDGMENTS AND AWARDS

Despite encouraging developments in recent years, the ideal of prompt and effective enforcement of creditor judgments and awards against international or foreign borrowers frequently remains unrealized. Unless the borrower is able and willing to comply with the terms of the judgment or award (which may well be the case)[155] the creditor may experience considerable difficulty in obtaining satisfaction.

A. SOVEREIGN IMMUNITY

The major obstacle is that which arises from the doctrine of sovereign immunity. In those countries in which the absolute doctrine of immunity still prevails, the recovery of a judgment or award against a sovereign debtor is bound to remain ineffective against a recalcitrant debtor.[156]

Even in those countries which subscribe to the doctrine of restrictive immunity, or view the doctrine with increasing favor, it is far from certain that limitations upon sovereign immunity will be extended to measures of execution. True, it has been held in several countries that when there is no immunity from suit, there should be no immunity from execution.[157] However, the specific circumstances surrounding some of these cases,[158] or the fact that they may be at

---

[155] Voluntary compliance by governments with arbitral awards is a well known phenomenon. See e.g., *L.N. Report* p. 25; Domke "Arbitration Clauses and International Loans", 3 Arb. J. 161 (1939). Non-compliance by a debtor international organization with the terms of a judgment or award against it is almost unconceivable.

[156] See e.g., Duff Development Company, Limited v. Government of Kelantan [1924] A.C. 797.

[157] See e.g., (i) *Argentina,* Supreme Court February 26, 1958, Government of Peru v. S.A. Sociedad Industrial Financiaria Argentina, S.I.F.A.R., 26 Int'l L. Rep. (Year 1958, II), 195; (ii) *Belgium,* Trib. Civ. Brussels April 30, 1951, Socobelge et Etat Belge v. Etat Hellénique, Journal des Tribunaux 1951, p. 298, S.1953.4.1, Clunet 1952, 244, 18 Int'l L. Reports (Year 1951), p. 3; *France,* Cass. February 5, 1946, Procureur Général v. Vestwig, S.1947.1.137, Annual Digest (year 1946), p. 78; *Switzerland,* T.F. February 10, 1960, République Arabe Unie v. Dame X., R.O.86.I.23, Clunet 1961, 458, 55 Am. J. Int'l L. 167 (1961); the *United States,* Harris and Co. v. Cuba, 127 So. 2d 687 (Fla. Dist. Ct. App. 1961).

[158] See e.g., the French supreme court judgment in the Vestwig case (cited in the preceding note), in which the Norwegian Government, whose funds in

variance with other judgments or the decisions of political departments within the same jurisdiction or in other countries,[159] makes it
impossible to reach any general conclusion. Futhermore, as has been
noted elsewhere,[160] there is no consensus of opinion as to whether
foreign borrowing should be characterized as a sovereign or non-
sovereign act. Under the circumstances, therefore, it is entirely possible
that even if two countries subscribe to the restrictive theory, execution against the local assets of a sovereign borrower might be allowed
in one,[161] and barred in the other country.[162]

These difficulties are not necessarily limited to measures of execution taken pursuant to domestic decisions. They may arise also in
connection with the enforcement of international judgments or
awards. As yet, however, there is no definite answer to the question

France were garnished, was acting as agent for private parties to a commercial
transaction. See, Freyria, "Les Limites de l'Immunité de Juridiction et d'Execution des Etats Etrangers", Rev. 1951, 207, at p. 220; Castel, "Immunity of a
Foreign State from Execution: French Practice", 46 Am. J. Int'l L. 520
(1952), at p. 522.

[159] See e.g., in the United States, Weilamann et al v. Chase Manhattan
Bank, 192 N.Y.S. 2d 471 (1959), 28 Int'l L. Rep. 165, 54 Am. J. Int'l L. 640
(1960). See also, Drachsler, "Some Observations on the Current Status of
the Tate Letter", 54 Am. J. Int'l L. 790 (1961); Setser, "The Immunity
Waiver for State-Controlled Business Enterprises in United States Commercial Treaties", Proceedings of the Am. Soc. of Int'l Law 89 (1961); Griffin,
"Execution against the Foreign Sovereign's Property: "The Current Scene",
Ibid., p. 105; Timberg, "Expropriation Measures and State Trading", Ibid.,
p. 113; Delson, "Applicability of Restrictive Theory of Sovereign Immunity
to Actions to Perfect Attachment", Ibid., p. 121; Collins, "The Effectiveness
of the Restrictive Theory of Sovereign Immunity", 4 Col. J. Transnational L.
119 (1965); Note, "Sovereign Immunity of States Engaged in Commercial
Activities", 65 Col. L. Rev. 1086 (1965).

In certain countries, such as Italy (Decree Law of August 30, 1925 and
Law of July 15, 1926, Article I, as translated in Sereni, The Italian Conception
of International Law (1943), p. 239) or Greece (Law 15/1938; see Cass.
Greece, Case No. 460/1962, Revue Hellénique de Droit International 1963, p.
355), no execution can be levied upon the property of foreign sovereigns
without the authorization of the local government. For a concrete case in
Italy, in which this authorization was not given, see British Government and
the Municipality of Venice v. Guerrato, Tribunal of Venice October 30, 1959,
28 Int'l L. Rep. 156.

[160] See text and notes 17 to 19, supra.

[161] Cf. in Switzerland, T.F. June 6, 1956, Royaume de Grèce v. Banque
Julius Bär et Cie., R.O.82.I.75; Int'l L. Reports (Year 1956), p. 195. After
the attachment, by an assignee of the lender, of Greek funds deposited in
Switzerland, a plea of immunity was entered and upheld on the ground that
the loan did not have sufficient connection with the Swiss territory.

[162] Cf. Brussels May 24, 1933, Brasseur and Associates v. The Republic
of Greece, Annual Digest 1931-2, p. 164.

whether the property of a debtor state could be attached or seized for
the purpose of satisfying an international decision.[163]

Special attention must be given also to the situation of creditors
of international organizations. In this last respect, a distinction must
be made between lending and other organizations. Although the
latter organizations may waive immunity from suit, such a waiver
does not ordinarily extend to any measure of execution.[164] It is therefore conceivable, though highly theoretical, that should such an
organization refuse to comply with the terms of a judgment in favor
of a creditor (whether domestic or international in character), a
municipal court might have no effective means of enforcing the
decision against the relevant organization.[165] A contrary solution
obtains in the case of international lending organizations such as the
IBRD, the IDA, the IFC, the IADB or the EIB, whose respective
Articles of Agreement or Statutes provide that if final judgment is
given against the entity involved in a case in which it enjoys no immunity from suit,[166] its property and assets will cease to be immune
from seizure, attachment or other form of execution.[167]

An original solution has been found in the case of the ECSC.
Pursuant to the Protocol on the Privileges and Immunities of the
Community, the assets of the Community cannot be the object of any
measure of execution without the authorization of the European

---

[163] See e.g., Schacter, "The Enforcement of International Judicial and
Arbitral Decisions", 54 Am. J. Int'l L. (1960), at pp. 7 to 14; Jenks, *The
Prospects of International Adjudication* (1964), pp. 706-713.

[164] Jenks, *International Immunities* (1961), pp. 37 to 40.

[165] Id. op., p. 40. Agreements relating to loans made by governments to
international organizations, to the extent that they contain provisions for the
settlement of disputes between the parties, which is not always the case (see
e.g., the loan from the United States Government to the United Nations to
finance the construction of the headquarters building, dated March 3, 1948,
19 UNTS 43), usually provide for the arbitral settlement of such disputes.
See text and notes 80, 81 supra. Arbitration clauses in these agreements,
however, rarely refer to matters concerning the enforcement of arbitral
awards. What appears to be an isolated example is the Agreement dated
March 30-April 15, 1957, between Switzerland and the ILO (40 ILO Off.
Bull. 352 (1957), Article 3), which stipulates that:
> "The award of the arbitral tribunal shall be without appeal and shall
> be immediately executory."

[166] These are suits by persons other than member governments (or persons
deriving their rights from a member government). See e.g., the Articles of
Agreement of the IBRD (Article VII, Section 3), the IFC (Article VI, Section 3), the IDA (Article VIII, Section 3) and the IADB (Article XI, Section 3). Comp., the EIB Statutes, Article 29 and Article 180 (a) of the EEC
Treaty.

[167] Ibid.

Court of Justice.[168] No judgment against the ECSC, therefore, can be enforced against it in the territories of a member of the Community without the consent of the Court of Justice.[169] Outside the Community, the solution of the problem would depend entirely upon the particular degree of immunity that the local courts or authorities recognized in the ECSC.[170]

Additional complexities may arise in the case of guaranteed loans.[171] Suppose, for example, that a loan to a foreign non-sovereign borrower is guaranteed by a foreign sovereign, and that the borrower's property within the jurisdiction is either non-existent or insufficient to satisfy the judgment or award. In a situation such as this, it is entirely possible that if an attempt is made to levy execution upon the local assets of the guarantor, the attempt will be defeated by the guarantor's immunity. This is a situation which is acknowledged in the IBRD Loan Regulations. It will be recalled that these Regulations provide for the arbitral settlement of disputes between the IBRD, on the one part, and the borrower and the guarantor, on the other part.[172] The Loan Regulations make a distinction between the case where the terms of an arbitral award would not be complied with by the IBRD or by the borrower, and the case where non-compliance results from the action or inaction of the member government guaranteeing the loan. In the first instance, the Loan Regulations provide that if the award is not complied with within thirty days after its delivery, judgment may be entered upon the award, or proceedings instituted to enforce the award in any court having jurisdiction, and that such judgment may be enforced against the IBRD or the borrower by execution or any other available remedy. In the second instance, the right of the IBRD to enforce the award against the guarantor government is subject to the important qualifi-

---

[168] Protocol, Article I. See, Stein and Hay, "Legal Remedies of Enterprises in the European Economic Community", 9 Am. J. Comp. L. 375 (1960), at pp. 412-413.

[169] This rule would apply to the enforcement in a member country of a judgment against the ECSC obtained by a bondholder or other lender pursuant to a jurisdictional clause conferring jurisdiction over loan disputes upon the courts of the bondholder's or lender's country. For examples of such clauses, see text and notes 65 to 72, supra.

[170] Conceivable examples would be those of a Swiss or American judgment rendered pursuant to the jurisdictional clauses stipulated in bonds issued by the ECSC in Switzerland or the United States. See text and notes 65 and 72, supra.

[171] See text and note 143, supra.

[172] See text and note 79, supra.

cation that no judgment can be entered nor the award enforced except to the extent that such a procedure may be available against the member concerned at the forum in which enforcement is sought. In other words, the Loan Regulations, while attempting to provide effective means to enforce arbitral awards, acknowledge the fact that by adhering to the arbitral provisions contained in such Regulations, a member government does not necessarily waive its immunity from execution.[173]

Unless and until the restrictive theory of immunity prevails in regard to both immunity from suit and immunity from execution, it is doubtful whether arbitral clauses of a general character, like those adopted by the IBRD, can be more specific. Further restrictions on the doctrine of sovereign immunity, which in the international financial field appears particularly unwelcomed, can only improve the climate of mutual trust and good faith essential to the success of international loan transactions.

B. The Impact of Jurisdictional and Procedural Conflict Rules

Sovereign immunity is only one, albeit a formidable, obstacle to the effectiveness of creditor judgments and awards. Other obstacles are frequent. These include, among many others, the bankruptcy of the borrower, the fact that the borrower has no assets within the jurisdiction and the consequent necessity to seek enforcement of the judgment or award in the borrower's country or a third country, in accordance with the substantive and procedural rules in that country governing the recognition and enforcement of non-domestic decisions. No elaboration is required to bring home the point that the manipulations of these rules—and in particular such doctrines as reciprocity or public policy, or such devices as *révision au fond* (review of the merits of foreign decisions), or security for costs—may enable the losing party to significantly delay or altogether prevent the enforcement of the judgment or award, and force the creditor to bring suit *de novo* in the country in which recognition is sought.[174]

---

[173] See e.g., *Broches,* pp. 372-373. See also, SID Convention, Article 55, referred to supra in note 91.

[174] See e.g., Nadelmann, "Non-Recognition of American Money Judgments Abroad and What to Do About It", 42 Iowa L. Rev. 236 (1957) and "French Courts Recognize Foreign Money Judgments: One Down and More to Go", 13 Am. J. Comp. L. 72 (1964). See also the Bilateral Studies referred to in note 2 supra.

It is true that as a result of judicial, statutory and treaty developments, particularly relating to the recognition and enforcement of foreign arbitral awards,[175] some progress has been made; and the international effectiveness of foreign decisions is assured in an increasing number of cases. However, many of the difficulties connected with the recognition and enforcement of non-domestic judgments and awards still remain.

This last remark applies not only to the decisions of municipal courts or arbitral awards, but also to the decisions of international tribunals. A characteristic example is the judgment of a Belgian court subjecting the judgment of the ICJ in the *Socobelge* Case to the procedure of *exequatur*, the procedure for enforcing foreign judgments and awards in Belgium.[176] A similar solution has also prevailed in France in connection with the enforcement of a judgment of the Mixed Court of Appeals of Tangiers.[177]

Complexities such as these have been eliminated by the provisions of the European treaties regarding the enforcement of the decisions of the Court of Justice of the European Communities within the territories of member governments. The three treaties provide that the decisions of the Court of Justice are binding and enforceable in the territory of each member state, subject only to the requirement of obtaining a local writ of execution. The local authorities can neither review the merits of the Court's decisions nor deny them recognition; they are bound, upon request, to affix their respective writs of execution to the Court's decisions, which thereby acquire the same force and effect as domestic judgments.[178] This procedure would presumably apply to the enforcement of the Court's decisions concerning loan disputes submitted to the Court pursuant to specific jurisdic-

---

[175] See e.g., among an abundant literature, Contini, "International Commercial Arbitration. The United Nations Convention on the Recognition and Enforcement of Foreign Arbitral Awards", 8 Am. J. Comp. L. 283 (1959); Read, *The Recognition and Enforcement of Foreign Judgments in the Common Law Unites of the British Commonwealth* (1938), pp. 304-5; Nadelmann, op. cit. preceding note, 42 Iowa L. Rev. at p. 256; Rivkin, "International Litigation and Arbitration", in *Surrey,* at pp. 985-989.

[176] Trib. Civ. Bruxelles April 30, 1951, Socobelge et Etat Belge v. Etat Hellénique, Journal des Tribunaux 1951, 298; S.1953.4.1; Clunet 1952, 244; 18 Int'l L. Rep. (Year 1951), p. 3.

[177] Trib. Civ. Seine September 29, 1959, Roussel v. Lestrade de Kyvon, Rev. 1960, 591. As to English law, see Seidl-Hohenveldern, "The Foreign Litigant before the Court of Justice of the European Communities", The Journal of Business Law 179 (1964), at pp. 183-185.

[178] ECSC Treaty, Articles 44, 92; EEC Treaty, Articles 187, 192; EURATOM Treaty, Articles 159, 164.

tional clauses in loan agreements between the financial institutions of the Community, e.g. the ECSC, and borrowing enterprises.[179]

This solution, when compared with the ordinary rules regarding the enforcement of non-domestic decisions in the respective territories of the members of the European Communities, constitutes a major improvement. Unfortunately, it is sometimes limited in that it applies only to decisions imposing financial obligations on persons other than states. As to decisions involving states, the rules obtaining in each country may, therefore, remain applicable.[180]

To eliminate this last difficulty, the League Loan Committee, when considering the proposal for the creation of an international loans tribunal, proposed that the decisions of the tribunal should have in each member state "the same force and effect as if [they] had been rendered by a national court of last instance."[181] This would have exempted the tribunal's decisions from the various local practices concerning the enforcement of foreign awards.

Although the loans tribunal was never established, the merits of the Committee's proposals are so apparent that they have inspired the drafters of the Convention on the Settlement of Investment Disputes between States and Nationals of Other States. Article 54 provides that:

"(1) Each Contracting State shall recognize an award rendered pursuant to this Convention as binding and enforce the pecuniary obligations imposed by that award within its territories as if it were a final judgment of a court in that State. A Contracting State with a federal constitution may enforce such an award in or through its federal courts and may provide that such courts shall treat the award as if it were a final judgment of the courts of a constituent state.

(2) A party seeking recognition or enforcement in the territories of a Contracting State shall furnish to a competent court or other authority which such State shall have designated for this purpose a copy of the award certified by the Secretary-General. Each Contracting State shall notify the Secretary General of the desig-

---

179 See text and note 63, supra. See also Seidl-Hohenveldern, op. cit., note 177 supra, at p. 184.

180 As in the EEC Treaty, see note 178 supra. This limitation could, in the case of a loan to a private person guaranteed by a member government, result in a disparity of treatment of the Court's decision, depending upon whether enforcement would be sought against the borrower or the guarantor.

181 *L.N. Report,* Annex IV, paragraph (viii), p. 41.

nation of the competent court or other authority for this purpose
and of any subsequent change in such designation.

(3) Execution of the award shall be governed by the laws concerning the execution of judgments in force in the State in whose
territories such execution is sought".[182]

In other words, each Contracting State, whether or not it is, or
one of its nationals is, a party to the proceedings, must recognize
awards rendered by arbitral tribunals pursuant to the Convention
as binding, and must enforce the pecuniary obligations imposed by
the award as if it were a decision of a domestic court. Because of the
different legal techniques followed in common-law and civil-law countries and the different systems found in unitary and federal or other
non-unitary States, the Convention, however, does not prescribe any
particular method to be followed in connection with its implementation. It requires, nevertheless, that each Contracting State meet the
requirements of the Convention in accordance with the laws in force
in its own system.

---

[182] See e.g., Delaume, "La Convention pour le Règlement des Différends
Relatifs aux Investissements entre Etats et Ressortissants d'Autres Etats",
Clunet 1966, 26, at pp. 38-41; Hynning, "The World Bank's Plan for the
Settlement of International Investment Disputes", 51 Am. Bar Assoc. J. 558
(1965), at p. 563; Sirefman, "The World Bank Plan for Investment Dispute
Arbitration", 20 Arb. J. 168 (1965), at p. 177; "The Convention on the
Settlement of Investment Disputes between States and Nationals of other
States", 20 The Record of the Association of the Bar of the City of New York
1 (1965), at pp. 6-9.

Part Two

SPECIAL RISKS AND AVAILABLE
LEGAL REMEDIES

Chapter V

Secured and Guaranteed Loans

Borrowers may give some sort of security to lenders in order to make loans attractive to lenders, or obtain financing on particularly favorable terms. In the international field of lending, however, the practical significance of security arrangements should never be overestimated. Although a personal guarantee from responsible obligors or a pledge of easily marketable assets within the lenders' reach may prove extremely valuable, excessive reliance on other forms of security, including "assignments" or "pledges" of public revenues or mortgages of foreign assets, would be misplaced.

The many types of security arrangements, though they may basically fulfill the same function and bear similar names, frequently exhibit considerable variations, as a result of different legislative histories[1]. This consideration, together with the relative scarcity of comprehensive comparative studies in a highly technical field, often creates conceptual and drafting problems. Of necessity draftsmen may be compelled to proceed by approximation, in attempting to translate foreign legal concepts in their own language. As long as the draftsmen have a clear perception of the legal characteristics of the security involved, a certain laxity in conveying its technical features to laymen may be tolerable and have, in fact, more significance to investors than lengthy legal explanations.

The danger, of course, is that looseness in drafting reaches such proportions as to create in the minds of lenders a false feeling of se-

---

[1] See e.g., Cohen and Throop, "Investment of Private Capital in Foreign Securities", in *Surrey,* p. 528; Schaeffer, "Le Gage sans Dépossession en Droit Comparé" in *Le Gage Commercial,* edited by Hamel (1953), 626, at p. 648; Bayitch, *Aircraft Mortgage in the Americas* (1960), pp. 13-19. See also text and notes 66 to 73 infra; Slovenko, "Suretyship," 39 Tulane L. Rev. 427 (1965).

curity. Too frequently, investors have relied on doubtful[2] or illusory[3] security covenants which add nothing to the lender-borower relationship and should be banished from loan documents.

SECTION I. GUARANTEED LOANS

A. CATEGORIES OF GUARANTORS

The amount of money involved in most contemporary international loans makes it normally impossible for private individuals to assume the responsibilities of guarantors.[4] Furthermore, among the

---

[2] See e.g., the Indenture dated May 31, 1922 between Bolivia and Equitable Trust Co. of New York (*Dunn,* p. 268). As security for the loan, Bolivia agreed to create first mortgages upon railroad properties, including rolling stock and equipment. Apparently it was not fully established at the time of the loan that movable property could be included in the security since the indenture provided (Article IV, Section 4) that:

> "In case said rolling stock, equipment or any other things belonging to or used in connection with said railroads, or either of them should be held or considered to be personal property not subject to mortgage, there is hereby constituted a special lien and any provisions of law in conflict therewith are hereby waived . . ."

Comp., the following provision in a 1920 American indenture concerning a loan to a European borrower secured by a mortgage upon real property and also upon:

> "all franchises, concessions and rights of the [Borrower] to conduct its business received from the Government of [xxxxx] or any municipality or other subdivision thereof, to the extent that such franchises, concessions and rights may be mortgaged under the laws of [xxxxx]."

[3] For example, a foreign sovereign or one of its political subdivisions may "pledge its full faith and credit" or "charge its general revenues and assets" or "its income from whatever source arising" as security for the loan. Provisions such as these, which are usually foreign to European loan documents, are still in use in England and the United States. See e.g., among recent bond issues in: (i) *England:* the City of Copenhagen (Swiss Frs.) 5% External Loan 1974/1983; the Japanese Government 6% Sterling Loan 1983/1988; the Uganda Government 3½% Stock due 1966/1969; the Kenya Government 4½% Stock due 1971/1978; the Sidney City Council 5½% Registered Stock due 1965/1966; and the New Zealand Government 4% Stock due 1976/1978; and (ii) in the *United States:* the Mexico $40 million External Bonds of 1963; the Republic of Finland $12.5 million Ten Year 6% External Loan Bonds of 1963; and the Belgian Congo $15 million Fifteen Year 5¼% External Loan Bonds of 1958.

[4] See however, as to the practice of the Export-Import Bank, Middleton, "Export-Import Bank", in *Surrey,* 391, at p. 395. Personal guarantees by individuals are not rare in the case of loans made by development banks. See also Boskey, *Problems and Practices of Development Banks* (1959), pp. 82-85.

For historical examples, including loans raised by the royal families of France, England and other European countries with the guarantees of "relatives, courtiers and burghers", see Sack, *La Succession aux Dettes d'Etat,* 23 Recuel des Cours 149 (1928), at pp. 241-242.

various entities which have established sufficient financial standing to undertake such responsibilities, some, including international lending organizations, have so far refrained from using their guarantee power.[5] As a practical matter, therefore, international guarantors consist at present exclusively of private corporations and governmental or other public entities.

As a rule, private guarantees relate only to loans raised by private borrowers, such as clients of a banking or credit institution,[6] or affiliates of the guarantor.[7] Under normal circumstances, private

---

[5] Such is the case of organizations like the IBRD (Articles of Agreement, Article III, Section 4), the EIB (Statutes, Article 18 (4)), and the IADB (Articles of Agreement, Article III, Section 4). There are several reasons why these organizations have not made use of their guarantee power. One reason, which was particularly relevant in the early years of their operations, was the necessity for these organizations to establish their own credit in the market. Loan guarantees, by creating a relationship between the borrower's credit and that of the guaranteeing organization, might have compromised the realization of this objective. Furthermore, guaranteed loans might prove more expensive to borrowers than loans made directly to them by these organizations.

[6] See e.g., the following loans issued by Norwegian companies in Switzerland and the Netherlands with the guarantee of Norwegian banks: Aktieselskapet Union (Union Co.) Oslo 4½% Loan of 1956; A. S. Vaksdal Mølle, Bergen 4½% Loan of 1961; Shipowners' Ship Credit Association, Kristiansand, 5½% (Dutch Guilders) Loan of 1961.
See also the following cases: T.F. September 18, 1934, Nathan Institut A.G. v. Schweizerische Bank für Kapitalanlagen, R.O. 60, II, 294; Clunet 1935, 1096; Cass. October 27, 1943, Société des Grandes Minoteries Bassot et Cie. v. Crédit Foncier de l'Algérie et de Tunisie, S.1946.1.17. Comp., T.F. February 28, 1950, Suleyman v. Tungsram Elektrizitaets A.G., R.O. 76,II,33.

[7] See e.g., the following prospectuses regarding bond issues in: (i) *the Netherlands:* Naphtachimie, S.A. Paris 4¼% Loan of 1955; (ii) *Switzerland:* California Texas Corporation (CALTEX) 4½% Loan of 1955; Société Norvégienne de l'Azote et des Forces Hydro-Electriques à Notodden (Norvège) 4½% Loan of 1959; Mobil Oil Holding, S.A., Luxembourg 4¾% Loan of 1965; (iii) *the United Kingdom:* Wolfson Clore Mayer Corporation Limited (an Israeli corporation) U.S. $5 million 6½% Debenture Stock 1983/88, issued in 1963; and (iv) *Germany:* Du Pont Europa Holdings, S.A., Luxembourg, DM 100 million 6% Bearer Bonds of 1965/1980.
See also, the IBRD loan to: (i) Société Pétrolière de Gérance guaranteed by Société Nationale de Recherche et d'Exploitation des Pétroles en Algérie, Compagnie Française des Pétroles (Algérie) and Compagnie Française des Pétroles, and by the Republic of France (Agreements dated December 10, 1959, 380 UNTS 319); and (ii) Compagnie Algérienne du Méthane Liquide (CAMEL), guaranteed by CONCH International Limited, Bureau de Recherches de Pétrole, Compagnie Française des Pétroles (Algérie) and Société Nationale de Recherche et d'Exploitation des Pétroles en Algérie, and by the Republic of Algeria (Agreements dated May 14, 1964, registered with the Secretariat of the United Nations under No. 7552. See also 3 Int'l Legal Materials 821 (1964)).
Comp., the September 1958 DLF loan to the Liberian-American Agri-

institutions do not guarantee public borrowings; and private borrowers generally do not seek governmental guarantees, since this might result in governmental interference with their internal affairs and the conduct of their business. When such public guarantees are requested, it is usually because they are an indispensable factor in obtaining the loan,[8] or are justified by the particular relationship between the borrower and the guarantor. Thus, when a private corporation operates under a governmental license or concession, or when a portion of its capital stock is governmentally owned, a governmental guarantee, far from being objectionable, may prove a valuable asset: It may give additional assurances to the lenders that the license or concession will be maintained or renewed, or that the guarantor will cause the borrower to comply with the terms of its loan obligations.[9]

cultural and Industrial Corporation (Dep't of State, Press Release, Washington D.C., September 24, 1958).

[8] A typical example is that of convertibility and transfer guarantees. Another example involves IBRD loans: It is the practice of this organization to require that loans made to borrowers other than a member be guaranteed by the government of the member country in whose territories the financed project is located. See e.g., Broches, p. 305; Delaume, "International Machinery for Financing Economic Development", 28 Geo. Wash. L. Rev. (1960) 533, at p. 554; Nurick, "The International Bank for Reconstruction and Development and the International Development Association", in Surrey, 426, at p. 430.

As to the practice of: (i) the IADB, see Arnold, "The Inter-American Development Bank", Id. op., 471, at p. 473; and (ii) the EIB, see Dupont, "Les Institutions Internationales Bancaires de Financement du Développement", in I Les Banques de Développement dans le Monde (1963) 67, at p. 181.

For several years, the High Authority of the ECSC insisted upon receiving a "currency undertaking" from the government of the country in which the borrowing enterprise was located. As to this, and the present practice of the High Authority, see Zimmer, "Legal Experiences of the European Coal and Steel Community in International Loan Operations", in McDaniels, 266, at pp. 275-6.

[9] See e.g., the prospectuses relating to the following bond issues in: (i) Switzerland: Tauernkraftwerke AG, Salzburg, 5% Loan of 1958, guaranteed by Austria; (ii) in Germany: Oesterreichische Donaukraftwerke AG 6% Loan of 1959, guaranteed by Austria and Oesterreichische Elektrizitaetswirtschafts-Aktiengesellschaft-Verbundgesellschaft; (iii) in the Netherlands: Sabena 4¾% Loan of 1961, guaranteed by Belgium; and (iv) in France: Energie Electrique du Maroc Indexed Bonds of 1954, guaranteed by Morocco.

Regarding the practice of such domestic lending agencies as the Export-Import Bank and the AID see e.g., Townsend, "The Export-Import Bank of Washington: Organization and Operation", U. of Ill., Law Forum, Legal Problems of International Trade (1959) Spring Number 237, at p. 244; Middle, "Export-Import Bank", in Surrey, 391 at p. 395; Grant, "Agency for International Development", Id. op., 403, at p. 411.

Governmental or other public guarantees relate primarily to loans raised by public borrowers. Sometimes motivated by purely financial reasons, as in the case of municipal loans,[10] loans raised by public credit institutions[11] or autonomous agencies,[12] these guarantees may also have more or less pronounced political undertones. Examples are guarantees given to external loans raised, within or without the guarantor's territories, by dependent territories[13] or by foreign sov-

[10] See e.g., among recent issues, the Prefecture and City of Osaka 6½% DM Bonds of 1962, guaranteed by Japan.

[11] See e.g., the Vienna Mortgage Institute (Hypotheken-Anstalt) 5% Loan of 1959, issued in Switzerland with the guarantee of the State of Vienna; The Mortgage Bank of the State of Vorarlberg 4½% Loan of 1959, issued in Switzerland with the guarantee of the State of Vorarlberg; The Japan Development Bank Guaranteed External Bonds dated September 15, 1961, issued in the United States with the guarantee of Japan; the Southern Italy Development Loan Fund (Cassa per il Mezzogiorno) Guaranteed External Loan Bonds of 1959, issued in the United States with the guarantee of Italy; the Crédit Foncier de France 5½%, Guaranteed External Loan Bonds of 1959, issued in the United States with the guarantee of France; the Cassa per il Mezzogiorno 4½% Loan of 1961, issued in Switzerland with the guarantee of Italy.

[12] See e.g., the prospectuses relating to the following bond issues in: (i) *Switzerland*: Electricity Supply Commission (ESCOM), Johannesburg 5% Loan of 1959, guaranteed by the Union of South Africa; Régie des Télégraphes et Téléphones (RTT) Bruxelles, 4½% Loan of 1959, guaranteed by Belgium; Société Nationale des Chemins de Fer Belges, Bruxelles, 4% External Loan of 1948, guaranteed (as a co-obligor) by Belgium; (ii) in *the United Kingdom*: Nigerian Ports Authority 6% Sterling Guaranteed Loan Stock 1980/83, issued in 1963 with the guarantee of the Federal Government of Nigeria; (iii) in *the United States*: Nippon Telegraph and Telephone Public Corporation Guaranteed Dollar Bonds 5%, 5⅛%, 5¼% and 6%, issued in 1961 with the guarantee of Japan; and (iv) the "parallel" issues of Ente Nazionale per l'Energia Elettrica, (ENEL) of 6% Bonds 1965/1980, made in *Belgium, France, Germany, Italy, Luxembourg* and *The Netherlands*, with the joint and several guarantee of the Italian government.

See also the Agreement dated July 23, 1955 (Article 5) between Italy and Switzerland (284 UNTS 279), providing for the Italian Government's guarantee of loans made by the Swiss Railway Administration to the Italian Railway Administration.

The Société Internationale de la Moselle (G.m.b.H) Trèves, 4½% Loan of 1961, issued in Switzerland with the guarantee of France, presents an original situation. In 1956, France, Germany and Luxembourg signed a Convention for the improvement of navigation on the Moselle River. This convention provided for the creation of a company, in the form of a German G.m.b.H, wholly owned by the three governments. The project was to be financed by capital stock subscriptions, loans and grants from the shareholder governments; and also by loans raised by the company with the guarantee of a shareholder government. The present loan is guaranteed by France in accordance with the terms of the Convention. See Prospectus, p. 5.

[13] See e.g., the Tunisian Loan of 1884, the Morocco Loans of 1914, 1916, 1920, etc., and the Annam and Tonkin Loan of 1896 all guaranteed by France

ereigns, including allied governments[14] or governments whose stability is deemed to be in the interest of the guarantor.[15]

With the creation of contemporary international organizations, a new type of guarantee has appeared. Until the last World War, and on occasion at the present time,[16] governments have been known to guarantee the financial obligations of international institutions. These guarantees, however, except for the personality of the borrower, do not substantially differ from other types of guarantees given on an *ad hoc* basis. With the creation of such organizations as the IBRD, the EIB and the IADB, however, the situation has changed considerably. Subject to minor variations among these organizations their respective capital stock is divided into two major parts: One part is paid by members to provide the organization with basic lending resources; the other is subject to call to the extent necessary to meet the organization's obligations on funds borrowed (or guaranteed) by it.[17] Each member has the obligation, proportionate to its share of subscribed

---

(Jêze, *La Garantie des Emprunts Publics d'Etat,* 7 Recueil des Cours (1925) 155, 210; I *Moreau-Néret,* p. 173). See also, the loan made by Australia to the Netherlands Indies Government with the guarantee of the Netherlands (Exchange of Notes between the Governments of Australia and the Netherlands, January 24, 1947 (art. 9), 10 UNTS 77).

[14] See e.g., the United States (Dutch) Loan of 1781, guaranteed by France (Jêze, *La Garantie des Emprunts Publics d'Etat* (1924) pp. 97-98; De Martens, *Recueil des Traités* (2nd ed. 1818), III, p. 396); the Czechoslovakia Loans of 1932, guaranteed by France (I *Moreau-Néret,* p. 174), and of 1939, guaranteed by France and England (Cmd. 5933, January 24, 1939); the Agreement of January 17, 1938, between France, the United Kingdom and Czechoslovakia, 196 LNTS 287. See also, the German Imperial Loans of 1795 and 1797, guaranteed by England (Jêze, op. cit., note 13 supra p. 202); the Turkish Loan of 1855, guaranteed by France and England (Ibid., p. 205); the Sardinian Loan of 1855, guaranteed by England (*Borchard,* p. 103).

The Franco-English Loan issued in 1915 in the United States was not guaranteed by the American Government, even though it had the government's moral support (Jèze, op. cit., note 13 supra pp 208-209).

[15] See e.g., the Egyptian Loan of 1885, guaranteed by Austria, England, France, Germany, Italy and Russia (Jèze, op. cit., note 13 supra, p. 192); the Austrian (League Loans) of 1923 and 1933, guaranteed by a number of members of the League of Nations (Ibid., p. 196; I *Moreau-Néret,* p. 175; *Borchard,* p. 103).

[16] Thus, pursuant to a Law of February 7, 1953 (Journal Officiel February 8, 1953, 1255, article 32 at p. 1259), the French Government has agreed to guarantee, within a maximum franc amount, loans issued by UNESCO for the construction of its headquarters building in Paris. See e.g., *Salmon,* pp. 114 et seq.

Regarding governmental guarantees of loans contracted by the European Commission for the Danube, see *Salmon,* pp. 54-59.

[17] See e.g., *The World Bank,* pp. 25-29; Delaume, op. cit. note 8 supra, pp. 538-541; Nurick, op. cit. note 8 supra, pp. 429-430; Arnold, op. cit. note 8 supra, p. 472; Dupont, op. cit. note 8 supra, pp. 78-80, 171-172, 196.

capital, to make payment on any call in either gold or United States dollars (depending upon the organization involved), or in the currencies needed by the organization to meet its obligations. The obligations of each member are independent of each other: A failure by one or more members to answer a call would not excuse any other member from its obligation to make payment. In substance, therefore, the callable portion of capital subscriptions constitutes a joint and several obligation of members to guarantee the organization's obligations, with the extent of each member's guarantee being limited to the uncalled portion of its capital subscription. Another interesting feature of these arrangements is that a member's guarantee does not attach to any particular indebtedness of the organization, but is rather a continuing guarantee covering a series of financial obligations undertaken by the organization. As the uncalled portion of capital subscriptions frequently aggregates sizeable amounts, that portion of the subscribed capital constitutes in fact a huge reserve fund well designed to give confidence to creditors, and help each organization establish and maintain its credit standing in the private capital market. This is particularly important because the private capital market constitutes a significant source from which these organizations draw funds needed for lending operations.[18]

B. Scope of Guarantees

Guarantee arrangements, necessarily tailored to the circumstances of each loan transaction, vary greatly. Depending upon the particular relationship between the borrower and the guarantor or guarantors, the dictates of the lenders, the purpose of the loan and the nature of the risks involved, guarantees may be limited to a simple promise to pay if the borrower defaults, or extend so far as to make the guarantor in effect a co-obligor of the principal debtor.[19]

---

[18] The principal objective of the 1959 capital increase of the IBRD (from $10 to $21 billion) was to raise the guarantee resources of the IBRD so as to increase its borrowing capacity, rather than to add directly to its lending resources. See *The World Bank,* p. 25.

[19] Another type of "guarantee", though not a true guarantee in the legal sense, may nevertheless be extremely valuable for practical purposes. Examples are arrangements between a borrowing corporation and its shareholders (or the most important of them) providing that the shareholders will supply funds to create and maintain the borrower's working capital at a level satisfactory to the lender, or finance any overrun in the cost of the project partly financed out of the proceeds of the loan. Although these arrangements do not make the shareholders guarantors in the legal sense, they may nevertheless give the lenders adequate assurances that the borrower's financial position will not be allowed to deteriorate. Furthermore, once these

Simple promises to pay upon, or after notice of, the borrower's default may prove deceptive when the time comes to enforce the guarantee. Such an arrangement leaves the guarantor free to avail himself of the defenses pertaining to the principal obligor, and may compel the lenders to exhaust all their remedies against the borrower before proceeding against the guarantor. This situation becomes particularly serious if proceedings are required in a number of countries. This type of guarantee is therefore not recommended and is not favored by lenders, except in very specific circumstances where the guarantor's reliability is such as to give the lenders confidence that a call made on the guarantor will be promptly honored.[20]

The problems are substantially the same in the case of stipulations whereby the guarantor agrees to guarantee "unconditionally" the payment of the principal, interest and other charges on the loan.[21] The view is sometimes advanced that an "unconditional" guarantee may permit the lenders to proceed directly against the guarantor. However, the area of doubt which persists as to the exact meaning of this provision [22] makes it advisable to couple it with the stipulation that action can be brought against the guarantor without notice to, or demand upon, the principal obligor; or even better, that the guarantor waives all the defenses of which he could avail himself in the absence of a waiver clause.[23]

arrangements have been concluded to the satisfaction of the lender, they usually cannot be amended without his consent. For concrete examples, see the IBRD loans to (i) Compagnie Minière de l'Ogooué (dated June 30, 1959, Article V, Sections 5.04, 5.06 and 5.07, 452 UNTS 67), and (ii) Société des Mines de Fer de Mauritanie (dated March 17, 1960, Article V, Sections 5.04, 5.05 and 5.08, 452 UNTS 147).

[20] See e.g., the Austrian Government Guaranteed Loan of 1923, guaranteed by Belgium, Czechoslovakia, Denmark, France, Italy, the Netherlands, Sweden and the United Kingdom; the Czechoslovakia 5% External Loan of 1932, guaranteed by France; and the loans to municipalities or public entities referred to in notes 11 to 13 supra.

[21] See e.g., the following public issues in: (i) *Germany*: Prefecture of Osaka and City of Osaka 6½% Partial Debentures of 1962; (ii) *the United Kingdom*: Nigerian Ports Authority 6% Sterling Guaranteed Loan Stock 1980/83; and (iii) *the United States*: The Japan Development Bank Fifteen Year 6% Guaranteed External Loan Bonds due February 1, 1978 (see also note 26 infra).

[22] See e.g., I Dewing, *The Financial Policy of Corporations* (5th ed. 1953), p. 220, note 99.

[23] See e.g., the following provision in the Japan Development Bank Guaranteed External Loan Bonds referred to note 21 supra:

"Japan, pursuant to Article 37-3 of The Japan Development Bank Law, hereby unconditionally guarantees (a) to the bearer of the within Bond (or if said Bond be registered as to principal then to the registered owner

Waivers of this kind are found most frequently, though not always, in agreements providing for joint and several guarantees, regardless of whether the guarantor or guarantors are liable for the entire amount,[24] or a portion only,[25] of the loan. Insistence upon such stipulations is an interesting feature of contemporary lending and legal practice, since in many legal systems the very act of undertaking a

thereof) due and punctual payment of the principal of said Bond and the redemption price, if any, thereof, and the due and punctual payment of the sinking fund payments provided for therein, according to the tenor of said Bond and (b) to the bearer of any of the coupons attached to said Bond and, if interest shall become payable on said Bond after maturity, to the bearer or registered owner thereof, due and punctual payment of the interest on said Bond, according to the tenor of said Bond and coupons; waives any requirement that the holder of the within Bond or the bearer of any of said coupons, in the event of any default in such payment by The Japan Development Bank, first make demand upon or seek to enforce remedies against The Japan Development Bank before demanding payment under, or seeking to enforce, this guarantee; covenants that this guarantee will not be discharged except by complete performance of the obligations contained in said Bond and this guarantee . . ."

Comp., in the United Kingdom, the following provision in the prospectus concerning the Wolfson Clore Mayer Corporation Limited (an Israeli Company) US $5 million 6½% Debenture Stock 1983/88 at par:
"The stock is secured by the unconditional guarantee of the Company's wholly-owned subsidiary, B.I.T.A. Limited ("BITA"), the due performance of which is secured by a first specific mortgage on a leasehold site in Tel-Aviv, and by a first floating charge on the whole of the undertaking and assets of BITA."

See also the following note.

24 See e.g., the following provision in the prospectus regarding the public issue in the *Netherlands* of Naphtachimie 4¼% Bonds of 1955, jointly and severally guaranteed by Pechiney and Seichimé, two French corporations:
"Each of the sureties waives the benefit of the privileges of division and discussion, as well as all the privileges and defenses which the law gives to sureties including the privileges and defenses set forth in Articles 1885 and 1886 of th Dutch Civil Code" (as translated). [The privilege of division is the privilege of one surety to request the creditor to divide his claim among all sureties so that each may bear its own share of the debt. The privilege of discussion is the privilege of a surety to request the creditor to exercise his remedies against the principal debtor before proceeding against the surety.]

Similar provisions are found in the Anglo-American Rhodesia Development Corporation Limited £ 4½% 15 Year Bonds of 1955, guaranteed by the Anglo-American Corporation of South Africa, Limited; the Shipowners' Ship Association, Kristiansand (Norway) 5½% Loan of 1961, guaranteed by the Christiana Bank og Kreditkasse. Comp., in *Switzerland,* the California Texas Corporation (CALTEX) 4½% Loan of 1955, guaranteed by three affiliated corporations (prospectus, clause 7):
"It is understood that the bearers shall have the right at any time to request from any one of the Guarantors payment of all amounts due

joint and several guarantee constitutes by itself a waiver of the defenses normally belonging to an ordinary surety. In this as in other instances, international lenders and their legal advisers seem to believe that contractual stipulations can add something to the protection afforded by relatively well established rules of law. This belief appears justified, since loan guarantees are frequently rooted in different legal systems whose rules may not necessarily coincide or be free of controversy.

---

on account of the payment of the principal of, interest, commissions, taxes and fees on, the loan" (as translated).

In the *United States,* see the Crédit Foncier de France External Loan Bonds of 1959 (See supra note 11 and infra note 34).

See also, the Agreement concerning financial assistance to Czechoslovakia dated January 27, 1939, VIII Hudson, *International Legislation,* 259:

"The Government of the United Kingdom and the Government of the French Republic will. . . . jointly and severally guarantee the principal and interest of a sterling loan to be issued in London by the Government of the Czecho-Slovak Republic. . . ."

25 See e.g., the Société Ferroviaire Internationale de Transports Frigorifiques (INTERFRIGO), Bruxelles 4½% Loan of 1959, guaranteed by eight European Railway Companies, prospectus, clause 5:

"Interest payments and principal repayments of this loan are guaranteed by the founders of INTERFRIGO herinafter specified, each for 1/8, severally and not jointly with the others" (as translated).

See also, the Shareholders Guarantee Agreement dated May 14, 1964 between the IBRD and four shareholders of the Compagnie Algérienne du Méthane Liquide (see note 7 supra), Section 2.01:

"Without limitation or restriction upon any of the other covenants or agreements in this Agreement contained, each of the shareholders, severally and not jointly with the other shareholders, as a primary obligor, and not as a surety merely, absolutely unconditionally and independently of the obligations of any other Guarantor, guarantees the due and punctual payment of the principal of, and interest and other charges on the Loan and the Bonds, all as set forth in the Loan Agreement and the Bonds, provided, however, that the liability of each of the shareholders under this Section shall be respectively limited to the following percentage of any amount due, outstanding and unpaid under the Loan or the Bonds on any date on which such amount shall be due and payable, namely:

CONCH	50%
BRP	10%
CFP (A)	17%
SN REPAL	23%"

Comp., the Companies Guarantee Agreement dated December 10, 1959 between the IBRD and shareholders of Société Pétrolière de Gérance (see note 7 supra), Section 2.01 (a) and (b) providing that the Guarantors' obligations shall, in respect of each category of guarantors

"be limited to an amount equivalent to one-half of any amount due, outstanding and not paid by the Borrower under the Loan or the Bonds on any date on which such amount shall be due and payable."

In a number of instances, guarantors assume obligations to the lenders which go beyond those of a mere surety and transform the guarantor, to a greater or lesser degree, into a primary obligor. The reasons for such undertakings vary. Sometimes the primary purpose of the undertaking is to give additional assurances to lenders that the borrower will at all times be in a position to carry out his obligations. Such is the case when the guarantor agrees to (i) supply the borrower with additional funds needed for the conduct of his operations or the completion of specific projects financed out of the loan proceeds,[26] (ii) provide the borrower with the foreign exchange needed to service the loan,[27] or (iii) refrain from taking any action which would interfere with the borrower's performance of his loan obligations or the conduct of his operations.[28] At other times, the guarantor's undertaking is designed to give the lenders certain rights or advantages which the borrower is in no position to grant, such as a right of inspection within the guarantor's territories,[29] or an exemption from

---

[26] Most frequently, this type of covenant is found in government guarantees. See e.g. French Mail Steamship Lines (Société des Services Contractuels des Messageries Maritimes) 7% External Sinking Fund Gold Bonds of 1924, reading in part as follows:
"Payment of interest and sinking funds on the outstanding bonds are secured:

. . . .

(2) By the payments which the French Government has undertaken to effect . . . if necessary, or to make up any deficiency in the Company's annual income when insufficient to pay charges, including interest on and amortization of loans issued pursuant to the convention."
Comp., the provisions referred to in Irving Trust Co. v. Deutsch-Atlantische Tel., 22 N.Y.S. 2d 581 (1940), at p. 583.
Guarantee agreements under IBRD loans to public entities contain a standard provision to the effect that if there is reasonable cause to believe that the funds available to the borrower will be inadequate to meet the estimated expenditures necessary to carry out the project financed by the IBRD, the guarantor will make arrangements satisfactory to the IBRD, promptly to provide the borrower or cause the borrower to be provided with such funds as are needed to meet such expenditures. See e.g., among many examples, Section 2:02 of each of the following Guarantee Agreements: The Agreement with (i) the Belgian Congo, dated March 30, 1960 (379 UNTS 161); (ii) the Republic of Colombia, dated May 23, 1962 (447 UNTS 39); (iii) the Republic of Ghana, dated February 8, 1962 (449 UNTS 207); and (iv) Japan, dated November 29, 1961 (426 UNTS 3).
[27] See e.g., the Tauernkraftwerke A.G., Salzburg 5% Loan of 1958 (prospectus clauses 5 and 6) jointly and severally guaranteed by the Austrian Government and the Osterreichische Elektrizitätswirtschafts-AG (Verbundgesellschaft). See also Chapter VII, text and notes 36 to 42.
[28] See Chapter II, text and note 34.
[29] See e.g., the standard provision in guarantee agreements relating to IBRD loans:

taxes imposed by the guarantor.[30] On still other occasions, covenants personal to the guarantor are essentially designed to maintain close relations between the guarantor and the lenders. For example, the guarantor may agree to (i) furnish to the lenders periodic information regarding his financial position,[31] (ii) request the lenders' consent before contracting new obligations to other creditors,[32] or (iii) refrain from taking any action which might modify or loosen the relations between the guarantor and the borrower.[33]

"The Guarantor shall afford all reasonable opportunity for accredited representatives of the Bank to visit any part of the territories of the Guarantor for purposes related to the Loan."

[30] See e.g., the prospectus of the Crédit Foncier de France 5½% Guaranteed External Loan Bonds due 1979, issued in 1959 in the United States with the guarantee of the French Government:

". . . . the Republic will agree that the principal of and interest on the Bonds will be free of all present and future taxes and duties of whatsoever nature imposed by the Republic or by any taxing authority thereof or therein, except when the Bonds or coupons, as the case may be, are beneficially owned by any person residing in or ordinarily a resident of the Republic."

[31] See e.g., the standard provision in IBRD Guarantee Agreement stipulating that:

"The Guarantor and the Bank shall cooperate fully to assure that the purposes of the Loan will be accomplished. To that end, each of them shall furnish to the other all such information as it shall reasonably request with regard to the general status of the Loan. On the part of the Guarantor, such information shall include information with respect to financial and economic conditions in the territories of the Guarantor and the international balance of payments position of the Guarantor."

[32] This is achieved by debt-limitation covenants and negative pledge or similar clauses in guarantee agreements.

[33] See e.g., the following provision in the Companies Guarantee Agreement dated December 10, 1959 relating to the IBRD loan to Société Pétrolièr de Gérance (see not 7 supra), Section 3.03:

"Except as the Bank shall otherwise agree:

(a) SN REPAL and CFP (A) shall not, as long as any part of the Loan shall remain outstanding and unpaid, take any action, or sell, transfer or otherwise dispose of any substantial part of their respective holdings of the stock of the Borrower if as a result of any such action, or sale or other disposal, SN REPAL and CFP (A) would part with effective control of the Borrower; and

(b) CFP shall not, as long as any part of the Loan shall remain outstanding and unpaid, take any action, or sell, transfer or otherwise dispose of any substantial part of its holdings of the stock of CFP (A) if as a result of any such action, or sale or other disposal, CFP would part with effective control of CFP (A)."

C. Effects of Guarantees

1. *The Lender-Guarantor Relationship*

It is essential that loan guarantees give lenders prompt and effective remedies against the guarantor or guarantors. To achieve this goal, the guarantee must authorize the lenders to proceed immediately against the guarantor.[34] This can be accomplished by use of one of the waiver clauses above described, or by other arrangements, like a deposit with the lenders or their agents of notes or other evidences of indebtedness issued by the guarantor and immediately enforceable against him in the event of a default.[35] If the loan is guaranteed by a number of guarantors, another method is to provide that one guarantor assumes liability to the lenders for the entire amount of the loan, reserving his right, of course, to reimbursement from the borrower and/or the other guarantors.[36]

---

[34] Provisions giving the guarantor a period of delay after default to make good its guarantee are infrequent. See e.g., the German Imperial Loan of 1795 granting to England, as guarantor, a period of 4 days after default in which to make good its guarantee (see Jèze, op. cit., note 13 supra, p. 203).

Comp., the following provision in the prospectus of the Anglo-American Rhodesian Development Corporation, Ltd., Loan 4½% of 1955, (issued in the Netherlands with the guarantee of the Anglo-American Corporation of South Africa, Limited):

"As mentioned in the Trust Deed . . . the guarantor undertakes, in case the debtor should not fulfill any undertaking in connection with the loan in question to pay interest, redemption payments, additional interest . . ., or costs to be paid by it, to furnish the amount owing by the debtor in connection with this obligation to pay within a fortnight after the guarantor has received a request thereto in writing from the Trustee."

See also, Indian and General Investment Trust, Limited v. Borax Consolidated, Limited [1920] 1 K.B. 539, at p. 541.

A typical example of provisions currently used in leading financial markets, though subject to variations in draftsmanship, is the following stipulation in the Crédit Foncier de France External Loan Bonds of 1959 (see note 11 supra):

"The Republic [of France] will agree that the guarantee may be enforced in the event of default of Crédit Foncier without making prior demand upon or seeking to enforce remedies against Crédit Foncier . . ."

[35] See e.g., article 13 of the General Bond of the Austrian Government Guaranteed Loan of 1923, requiring the guarantors to deposit with the trustee their own bonds payable immediately upon the trustee's request in case of an Austrian default.

[36] Thus, in connection with the Turkish Government Loan of 1855, guaranteed by France and England, the two guarantors agreed that in case of a default by Turkey, the English Government would pay the total sum due, subject to being subsequently indemnified by the French Government for the amounts corresponding to the French share. See Declaration of London July 27, 1855 British and Foreign State Papers, XLV [1855], 20. See also *Borchard*, p. 109, note 32; Jèze, op. cit. note 14 supra, p. 88.

The guarantee should provide that the lenders will receive the amounts, in the currencies and at the places, specified in the loan documents. This consideration is extremely important and may have a decisive influence upon the selection of the guarantor and the determination of the type of guarantee best suited to the circumstances of the particular loan. Thus, if a guaranteed loan is divided into several issues respectively issued in, and payable in the currencies of, a number of countries, it might be advisable to limit each guarantee to a specific issue of the loan rather than rely on guarantees applying, legally as well as financially, to the over-all loan transaction.[37] In the same connection, it is important to make certain that, through proper licensing or by virtue of the guarantor's own exchange-earning capacity, the foreign exchange required to service the loan will be available when needed. Finally, if the guarantee extends to performance of non-financial obligations, like the completion or operation of economic development projects, the lenders should be satisfied that the guarantor is either personally equipped to take over the borrower's duties or is in a position to cause some third party to carry out these duties.

2. *Relations between the Obligors*

It is a general rule that if the guarantor (or one of the guarantors) pays, he succeeds by way of subrogation[38] to the rights of the lenders, including security rights. This consideration may explain why guar-

---

[37] See e.g., the Austrian Government International Guaranteed Loan of 1933, guaranteed by France, England, Italy, Belgium, the Netherlands and Switzerland. Each guarantor was responsible solely for the tranche issued in its own territories. See VI Hudson, *International Legislation,* p. 85; *Borchard,* p. 110, note 34. Comp., the Greek Loan of 1833 issued in three separate tranches in England, France, and Russia, respectively guaranteed by each of the three countries. See Jèze, op. cit., note 13 supra, p. 187.

[38] Subrogation provisions in contemporary loan documents are infrequent. In most cases, the parties merely rely upon the relevant rules of substantive law, and make no attempt to supplement these rules by means of contractual covenants.

When such covenants are included, it appears that their primary objective is not to define the guarantor's rights against the obligor, but rather to restate the general principle that the guarantor's rights acquired by way of subrogation should not impair the lender's rights under the loan, according to the old maxim "Nemo Censetur Subrogasse Contra se". See e.g., the following provision in an American indenture:

"No payment by the Guarantor pursuant to the provisions hereof to all or any of the holders of the Debentures or the coupons appertaining thereto or to the Trustee shall entitle the Guarantor, by subrogation to the rights of the holders of the Debentures or coupons in respect of which

antors do not always insist, though they sometimes do,[39] on obtaining their own lien on the borrower's properties.

If a loan is guaranteed by a number of guarantors and one of them pays more than his share of the debt, he is entitled to reimbursement from his co-guarantor or guarantors for the amount paid in excess of the sum for which he is personally liable. This situation, which is most likely to arise in connection with guarantee obligations which are joint and several and are given for the full amount of the loan,

---

such payment is made or otherwise, to any payment by the Corporation in enforcement of this Indenture or otherwise, except after payment in full of the entire principal and premiums (if any) and interest on all of the Debentures, or provision for such payment satisfactory to the Trustee."

Similarly, the standard form of loan contract between the High Authority of the ECSC and enterprises of the European Community provides in substance that if the guarantor pays the principal debt, the right of subrogation arising thereunder shall not impair the rights of the High Authority to claim the unpaid principal amount, and interest or premium thereon, of the loan.

See also, in connection with the IBRD Loan to CAMEL, the Algeria Guarantee Agreement (Section 3.08) and Shareholders Guarantee Agreement (Section 3.06), referred to in note 7, supra.

[39] See e.g., the Aktieselskapet Union (Union Co.), Oslo 4½% Loan of 1956, issued in Switzerland with the guarantee of the Bergens Privatbank. Clause 8 of the prospectus (as translated) reads in part as follows:

"Bergens Privatbank, Bergen, guarantees the repayment of the principal of this loan and the payment of interest, commissions, taxes and fees up to an aggregate amount of Swiss francs 22 million [the principal amount of the loan was S. Frs. 15 million]. . . .

In the event that A/S Union (Union Co.) cannot or will not pay amounts due and payable under the loan whatever the reason therefor, and if payment is not made immediately upon demand, the Bergens Privatbank, upon being requested to do so, shall pay immediately in Switzerland in free Swiss francs, ...

A/S Union (Union Co.) shall mortgage in favor of Bergens Privatbank, in consideration of its guarantee and until full repayment of this loan, certain real properties owned by A/S Union (Union Co.) and its subsidiaries, as described in a list dated January 16, 1956, namely:

[description of the mortgaged properties]

The real properties so mortgaged shall be free of any other lien; and they shall be freed [i.e., the amount secured by the mortgage shall be reduced] to the extent that principal and interest payments on this loan shall have been made by A/S Union (Union Co.)."

See also, the French Line (Compagnie Générale Transatlantique) External 6½% Sinking Fund Gold Bonds of 1927 (Canadian issue), guaranteed by the French Government and secured in favor of the guarantor by a first mortgage on the vessels to be constructed with the proceeds of the loan.

Comp., the Austrian Government Guaranteed Loan of 1923. Article 15 of the General Bond creating a pledge of revenues in favor of the guarantor governments to rank junior only to that securing the rights of the bondholders.

may also occur when the liability of the guarantors is divided into shares and each guarantor is responsible only for a stated portion of the debt. In this last case, it is conceivable that, should one of the guarantors fail to honor its guarantee obligation, the other guarantor or guarantors will make up for the shortage in order to avoid the drastic consequences of a default.

SECTION II. SECURED LOANS

A. ASSIGNMENT OF REVENUES

Private borrowers frequently assign, as securiy for loans, the monies to be received by them from third parties, particularly if the greatest part of their income is from the sale of goods, or fees for service supplied by them. Examples are assignments of the proceeds of (i) power contracts between a power producer and its consumers,[40] (ii) sales contracts between an industrial enterprise and purchasers of goods manufactured by it,[41] (iii) transport contracts between a company operating an oil pipeline and users of the pipe,[42] and (iv) traf-

[40] See e.g., the Société Electrique de l'Our (SEO), Luxembourg 4½% Loan of 1963 issued in Switzerland, secured by an assignment of monies due by the Rheinisch-Westfälisches Elektrizitäts A.G. (RWE) a German utility company, under arrangements with SEO; and the Tiroler Wasserkraftwerke A.G. (TIWAG), Innsbruck, 5% Loan of 1961 issued in Switzerland; the Rheinisch-Westfälisches Elektrizitätswerk, A.G. 4½% Loan of 1964, issued in Switzerland and secured by an assignment of a power contract between RWE and certain Swiss and German companies.

See also, the following loan agreements between the IBRD and: (i) Österreichische Elektrizitätswirtschafts Aktiengesellschaft (Verbundgesellschaft) and Österreichische Draukraftwerke Aktiengesellschaft, dated July 19, 1954, Article V, Section 5.03 (216 UNTS 305); (ii) Vorarlberger Illwerke A.G., dated June 14, 1955, Article V, Section 5.03 (221 UNTS 375); and (iii) the Tata Hydro-Electric Power Supply Company, Limited, the Andhra Valley Power Supply Company, Limited, and the Tata Power Company, Limited, dated November 9, 1954, Article V, Section 5.04 (309 UNTS 159).

[41] See e.g., Royal Exchange Assurance v. Brownell, 146 F. Supp. 563 (S.D.N.Y. 1956), affirmed 257 F. 2d 582 (1958), concerning the distribution of the proceeds of sales of potash exported to the United States by a German company. The potash has been assigned to English bankers as security for a loan by them to the Company.

See also the IBRD loan to CAMEL (note 7 supra) secured, in addition to various personal guarantees, by an assignment of the proceeds of sales of liquefied gas (Loan Agreement, Article V, Sections 5.10 and 5.11).

[42] Thus, loans were issued in France and the Netherlands in 1961, and in the United States in 1962 by the Société du Pipe-Line Sud-Européen, a French corporation formed by oil companies of different nationalities. These

fic contracts between cable and telegraph companies.[43]

In the great majority of cases, the third party is either notified of the assignment or expressly agrees to it,[44] and becomes obligated to make his payments directly to the lenders either on each payment date,[45] or on the borrower's default,[46] or on the lenders' instructions. If these amounts are sufficient at all times to meet debt service payments,[47] this type of arrangement constitutes one of the most effective

loans are equally and ratably secured by an assignment of amounts payable to the borrower by its shareholders pursuant to a Completion Agreement and a Throughput Agreement. These arrangements are fully described in the various prospectuses, including (in English) the South European Pipeline Company 5½% Sinking Fund Debentures due 1982, prospectus pp. 5 to 7.

[43] See e.g., Irving Trust Co. v. Deutsch-Atlantische Tel. 22 N.Y.S. 2d 581 (1940), concerning the distribution of moneys collected by the trustee under an indenture providing for the assignment of amounts due under traffic contracts between the defendant, a German cable company, and Western Union Telegraph Company. The security provisions of the indenture are reproduced in Kuczynski, *American Loans to Germany* (1927), pp. 293-297.

[44] (i) *Notification.* See e.g., the Société du Pipe-Line Sud Européen loans (referred to in note 42 supra) and in particular Article 5 of the Assignment Agreement dated March 14, 1962 between the Société, Morgan Guaranty Trust Company of New York and Lazard Frères & Cie, which provides that:
"The present document will be notified to the debtor oil companies, in compliance with the provisions of Article 2075 of the Civil Code and Article 91, Paragraph 5 of the French Commercial Code, so that the future debenture holders and American representative body, the beneficiaries of the present Assignment, may be properly secured as regards third parties, and so that the oil companies may be informed of the conditions under which they may or must pay up sums due by them to the Pipeline Company, which sums are the subject matter of the present Assignment."
(ii) *Notice of consent to, or participation in, the assignment arrangements*: See e.g., the IBRD loans referred to in note 40 supra and the IBRD loan to CAMEL referred to note 7 supra.

[45] See e.g., the SEO loan referred to in note 40 supra.

[46] See e.g., the Société du Pipe-Line Sud Européen loans referred to in note 42 supra; the IBRD loan to CAMEL referred to in note 7 supra, the IBRD loans to Yugoslavia and Iraq referred to in notes 49 and 50 infra.

[47] In addition to determining *ab initio* a certain ratio between the assigned revenues and the payments due under the Loan, lenders commonly stipulate that the borrower shall not, without their prior approval, agree to a reduction of these revenues or any other substantial modification of the assigned contract. See e.g., the following provision in an English indenture:
"The [Borrower] hereby covenants with the Trustees. . . . that [it] will not consent to any modification of the terms of the [contract for the sale of electricity] whereby the half yearly revenue to be payable by [the purchasers of electricity sold by the borrower under such contract] to [the borrower] shall be reduced to less than the sums required to cover the whole of the working expenses of [the borrower] and the interest and amortization on the said Loan."

forms of security. In effect, it may constitute an indirect guarantee
of the loan by the third party.[48]

Because of its many advantages, this type of security arrangement
is sometimes used in connection with loans raised by public borrowers. For example, assignments of intergovernmental sales contracts[49]
or oil royalties[50] have secured certain IBRD loans to member governments. These examples are more typical than certain other arrangements, like the assignment of tributes or indemnities payable
to borrowing governments,[51] which are too exceptional to lend them-

_____

[48] This similarity between assignment and guarantee is made particularly
apparent in the SEO loan referred to in note 40 supra: Since the assignment
does not take effect until the power facilities financed out of the proceeds
of the loan begin operation, loan service during construction is secured by a
guarantee from RWE. See prospectus, clause 5. Similar arrangements are found
in other "power" loans issued in Switzerland and England.

[49] See Loan Agreement between the Federal Peoples' Republic of Yugoslavia and the IBRD, dated October 17, 1949 (155 UNTS 3). This loan has
been repaid.

[50] See Loan Agreement between Iraq and the IBRD, dated June 15, 1950
(155 UNTS 267), which has been repaid.

[51] See e.g., the assignment of: (i) *tributes paid by dependent territories,*
like the Egyptian tribute to Turkey, servicing several Turkish loans (see
Brun, "Emprunts Ottomans et Tribut d'Egypte", Clunet 1925, 518; *Wynne,*
pp. 522, 525; Gouvernment Egyptien v. Rothschild and Sons, Mixed Court of
Appeals of Alexandria April 29, 1926, Clunet 1926, 754; and agreement dated
March 17, 1929 between the United Kingdom and Egypt, 90 LNTS 413);
(ii) *war indemnities owed by a defeated belligerent,* like those involved in
the Agreement Regarding the Relief Debts Contracted by the Kingdom of
the Serbs, Croats and Slovenes towards Australia, Denmark, France, Great
Britain, The Netherlands, Norway, Sweden and Switzerland dated August
8/12, 1927 (Article 6, CI LNTS 483), or the Agreement between Poland and
a number of European Governments Concerning the Polish Reconstruction
Debt (Form of Bond, VII Hudson, *International Legislation,* p. 43); or
(iii) *annuities receivable from a foreign government for the use of the borrower's territory,* like the monies due by the United States to Panama. See
the following provision in the Fiscal Agency Contract dated October 1, 1958,
annexed to the prospectus concerning the Republic of Panama 4.80% External Secured Bond of 1958:

"TWELFTH: The Bonds when issued shall be the unconditional
obligations of the Republic; and to the payment of the principal,
premium, if any, and interest thereon, there is pledged the good faith
and credit of the Republic. As a further guaranty and security for the
payment of any and all sums which may at any time become due and
payable on account of the principal, premium, if any, or interest on the
Bonds, the Republic has created and hereby does create a first charge
and lien on $1,000,000 of the $1,500,000 Treaty Payment receivable annually by the Republic from the United States of America, pursuant to
Article I of the Treaty of January 25, 1955, ratifications of which were
exchanged on August 23, 1955, between the United States of America
and the Republic. Said first charge and lien of said $1,000,000 on said

selves to generalization. At a time where there is increasing disaffec-
tion for such disappointing forms of security as the classical "assignment" or "pledge" of public revenues,[52] arrangements such as those

$1,500,000 Treaty Payment is not to exceed $1,000,000 (U.S.) annually. . . .

The Republic is contemporaneously giving irrevocable instructions to
the Secretary of State of the United States of America and is receiving
an acknowledgement thereof. . . . to pay from said $1,500,000 Treaty Pay-
ment the sum of $1,000,000 annually to The First National City Bank of
New York, Fiscal Agent of the Loan, so long as any of the Bonds to be
issued hereunder or the coupons appurtenant thereto remain outstanding and unpaid. . . .

THIRTEENTH: The Republic further covenants that it will not
do, suffer or permit any act or thing whereby the security herein provided for the Bonds might or could be impaired or diminished."

[52] See e.g., *Borchard,* pp. 86-91. This type of security has been rarely used
since the end of the last World War. For a concrete example, see the following provision in the prospectus (p. 4) relating to the 1963 (U.S. issue) City
of Milan 5½% External Loan Bonds:

"Payment Delegations

In order further to secure the payment of interest on and principal of
the Bonds the City will provide for the payment of such interest and
principal out of revenues from the City family income tax by delivering
payment delegations (the "Payment Delegations") on revenues collectible under such tax. Such Payment Delegations will direct the City Collec-
tor of Taxes to pay to Banca Commerciale Italiana, as Collecting Agent
for the bondholders, prior to the respective due dates for interest, sinking fund and principal payments to be made on the Bonds, specified lire
amounts out of such tax revenues. The Collecting Agent will in turn
convert the amounts so received into dollars and transmit these to Dillon,
Read & Co., Paying Agent, for payment to the bondholders. The Payment Delegations will be expressed in lire amounts equivalent (at
the rate of 625 lire to the dollar) to the dollar amounts of interest, sinking fund and principal payments to be made on each semi-annual payment date.

In the Collecting Agency Agreement the City will agree to deliver
additional Payment Delegations on the family income tax revenues or
Payment Delegations on other tax revenues of the City in the event of
declines in value of the lira in terms of the dollar, repeal of the City's
authority to impose the family income tax or insufficiency of revenues
collectible thereunder and the Collecting Agent will agree to waive in
whole or in part payment of the Payment Delegations held by it in respect
of the Bonds in the event of the retirement of Bonds in excess of sinking
fund requirements or satisfaction of the sinking fund obligation by
surrender of Bonds or increases in value of the lira in terms of the
dollar."

Another example, though somewhat less significant, is found in the prospectus (p. 4) of the 1962 (U.S. issue) Government of New Zealand Fifteen
Year 5½% Bonds which provides that:

"Amounts payable in respect of principal and interest on the Bonds will
share a charge upon the public revenues of New Zealand equally and
ratably with such amounts payable on all other New Zealand securities."

under consideration may be the forerunners of new security techniques in international transactions.

B. PLEDGES OF CHATTELS, SECURITIES

To be fully effective, a pledge of chattels or securities must be easily marketable, and must be removed from the borrower's possession. These considerations explain why relatively few items in these categories can qualify as adequate security for international loans.

By far the most important of these are securities held by the borrower in its portfolio, like shares of corporate stock,[53] treasury bonds,[54] or (in the case of loans contracted by banking or other financial institutions), evidences of indebtedness received by the obligor from its own borrowers. The most outstanding contemporary example of this last type of arrangement is the Act of Pledge between the ECSC and the BIS, pursuant to which evidences of indebtedness received by the ECSC from borrowing enterprises in representation of ECSC loans are held in pledge by the BIS, acting as "depositary" "for the equal *pro rata* benefit and security of all lenders to the High Authority."[55]

---

[53] Loans contracted by private corporations are frequently secured by a pledge of shares of other corporations more or less affiliated to the borrower. See e.g., British Controlled Oilfields, Ltd., £800,000, 4½% Secured Loan Stock; The White Pass and Yukon Corporation, Ltd., 4½% First Debenture Stock 1961/76; Loan Agreement dated January 27, 1949, between the IBRD and Brazilian Traction, Light and Power Company, Limited (Article V, Section 1, 152 UNTS 264).

In the case of government loans, lenders frequently insist that the securities pledged with them (or a depositary) be securities issued by corporations organized within their own, or a third, country rather than by corporations organized within the borrower's territories. See e.g., in regard to World-War I loans contracted in the United States and other neutral countries by the French and the British Government, Petit, *Histoire des Finances Extérieures de la France pendant la Guerre* (1914-1919) (1929), pp. 90-91, 340 et seq., 384 et seq., 544 et seq., 564-565, 605 et seq. See also, more recently, the Agreement dated February 25, 1957, between the British Government and the Export-Import Bank, providing for a line of credit secured by a pledge of securities (Article VI, Cmd. 104 (1957)).

[54] See e.g., the 1916 French loans raised in the Netherlands (Petit, op. cit. preceding note, p. 91). See also *Borchard*, p. 85. Comp., the Agreement of December 5, 1921 between Bolivia and American bankers (*Dunn*, pp. 253-254); the Treaty of May 11, 1920, between Germany and the Netherlands (III LNTS 153) concerning a loan to Germany secured by a deposit of Imperial Treasury Bonds of a value equal to the amount of the loan.

[55] See Act of Pledge, fifth "Whereas", p. 2. Some of the legal issues involved in the implementation of these pledges are described by Zimmer (op. cit. note 8 supra, at pp. 272-273) in the following terms:

"The legal principle with regard to pledging in all the Community

Also appropriate, though limited for practical reasons to loans contracted by governments or central banks, is gold or bullion.[56] Much

countries is that, in the event of default, the party on whose behalf an enterprise obligation was pledged first has a priority lien on the proceeds of the sale of the pledge property over all parties on whose behalf the same obligation was pledged at a later date. In addition, by the law of several member States—as for example France—for a pledge to be valid vis-a-vis a third party it is necessary that notice of pledge be served on the debtor by a special Government official in accordance with a prescribed procedure and that the fact of service be officially recorded.

To ensure that all lenders to the High Authority are equally secured, therefore, the following procedure is observed. (a) Holders of Notes of all series must authorize the Depositary on their behalf to waive the priority to which they are entitled on the pledged obligations and security over holders of Notes of later series than their own. (b) Each time en enterprise obligation is lodged with the Depositary, the High Authority and the Depositary sign a separate contract, called the "Acte constitutif de gage," whereby the claim in question is pledged in favor of the holders of all Notes issued up to that date by the High Authority. (c) Each time a new loan is floated, the High Authority and the Depositary also conclude an "Acte constitutif de gage," whereby the property already held in pledge by the Depositary is repledged in favor of the new Noteholders, while the old Noteholders, represented by the Depositary, waive their legal priority rights on the pleged property for the benefit of the new creditors. (d) In some of the Community countries the "Actes constitutifs de gage" have to be officially served on the enterprise borrowers. Even though it can be arranged for several borrowers to appoint a joint representative for the pledging and repledging formalities as they occur, so many loans have nevertheless been floated by the High Authority and so many loans to enterprises have been made of the proceeds that the completion and service of the "Actes constitutifs de gage," and the production of legal opinions certifying that the relevant documents are in order and have been duly served on the parties concerned, all add up to a very complicated and cumbrous procedure. Moreover, the Actes have to be carefully examined to make sure that the pledging operations or the notification of these to the borrowers are not vitiated by errors of form.

Accordingly, the High Authority and the Depositary have agreed that in the case of loans to enterprises in Germany recourse is to be had not to the pledging procedure but to another legal device permitted under German law, a "Sicherungsabtretung." Under a Sicherungsabtretung the legal title passes to the Depositary, which in its relationship to the borrowing enterprise becomes the technical holder of the claim. When the reason for which the Sicherungsabtretung was effected ceases to exist, legal title passes back to the High Authority. Where this arrangement is adopted, difficulties over creditors' priorities do not arise, nor is it necessary to serve notice of every repledging on all borrowers. Unfortunately, it has not been possible for the High Authority to follow this procedure in all the member countries."

[56] See e.g., the 1930 loan made by the BIS to the Central Bank of Spain, secured by a pledge of gold deposited with the Bank of England (see, Hamel, Les Formes Internationales des Crédits Bancaires, 51 Receuil des Cours (1935),

less frequent, though not unknown, is the pledge of commodities such as coffee or art treasures, which would normally lack the vital element of marketability.[57]

Lenders usually insist that the pledged property be deposited with them or with a depositary outside the borrower's country.[58] Exceptions may be made in special cases, like loans between central banks where a justified feeling of trust may require no more than "earmarking" the pledged property for the account of the lender.[59]

Removing the pledged property from the borrower's possession, although essential both legally and practically to the protection of the lenders' interests, should nevertheless be accomplished without impairing the borrower's legitimate rights in the security. A compromise between the respective interests of the lenders and the borrower must be found which gives assurance to the borrower that his rights in the security will not be unduly impaired while the property remains in the possession of the lenders and that such property will not be arbitrarily forfeited in the event of default.

Protection of the borrower's rights in the security until default, or until the security is returned to the borrower, is essentially a matter of contractual agreement between the parties. In the case of a pledge of securities, it is commonly provided that, unless an event of default shall have occurred and be continuing, the pledgor shall exercise all rights arising out of ownership of the pledged securities including

207, at p. 228). See also, the 1945 loan made to the Netherlands Government by a group of American banks (Kriz, "Postwar International Lending", Essays in International Finance, No. 8, Princeton University (1947), p. 4), and the credit extended by Swiss banks to the Government of Roumania secured by a pledge of gold deposited in Switzerland by the National Bank of Roumania (Ibid., p. 12, note 24).

[57] Such was the case in the United States of Brazil 7½% Coffee Security Loan of 1922, secured by "a first hypothecation on about 4,535,000 bags of coffee"; and of the State of Sao Paulo Coffee Realization Loan of 1930, also secured by a pledge of coffee. See *Borchard,* pp. 85-86; *Madden and Nadler* (1929), p. 165. As to pledges of royal jewels and other assets, see Sack, *La Succession aux Dettes Publiques d'Etat,* 23 Recueil des Cours (1928) 149, at p. 241.

[58] See e.g., in regard to securities deposited with the lenders: The 1915-1916 French and British Government loans and the Export-Import Bank 1957 loan to the United Kingdom referred to in note 53 supra. Comp., Tribunal Civil Seine March 3, 1875, Etat Ottoman v. Comptoir d'Escompte, Sirey, 1877.2.25.

See e.g., in regard to securities deposited with the trustee or other depositary: the 1916 French banks' loan in the Netherlands (Petit, op. cit. note 53 supra, p. 91); the IBRD loan of 1949 to Brazilian Traction, etc. referred to in note 53 supra); the Act of Pledge referred to in note 55 supra.

[59] See e.g. Hamel, op. cit. note 56 supra, at p. 225.

the right to vote the securities,[60] receive dividends or interest thereon,[61] exercise preemptive rights to purchase newly issued securities or sell those rights for cash,[62] or substitute for any such securities other se-

[60] See e.g., the Export-Import Bank 1957 Loan to the United Kingdom (referred to in note 53 supra, Article VII, para. 4).

A typical provision is the following:

"Unless an event of default shall have occurred and be subsisting, the Company shall have the right to vote or give consent for all purposes not contrary to the covenants herein contained or otherwise inconsistent with the purpose or purposes of this Indenture, and with the same force and effect as though such shares were not held subject to this Indenture, upon or in respect of all shares of stock held subject to this Indenture; and, from time to time, upon demand of the Company, the Trustee forthwith shall make and deliver, or shall cause to be made and delivered, to the Company or its nominee or nominees, suitable powers of attorney or proxies to vote upon any share of stock which shall have been transferred into the name of the Trustee or its nominee or nominees or to give consent in respect thereof. If an event of default shall have occurred and be subsisting, then in addition to the other remedies herein provided, the Trustee, if it shall deem it advisable, shall revoke all such powers of attorney and proxies and shall vote or cause the nominee or nominees of the Trustee to vote, and shall exercise all the powers of an owner with respect to, any such shares of stock held subject to this Indenture . . ."

Sometimes, however, it is provided that the trustee shall exercise the voting power with respect to the pledged securities for the benefit of the trust estate, as in the following provision:

"The voting power with respect to the Pledged Debentures shall be vested in the Trustee and exercised by it for the benefit of the trust estate in such manner as the Trustee in its discretion shall see fit."

[61] See e.g., the Export-Import Bank loan referred to in the preceding note (Article VII, para. 4); see also the following indenture provision:

"Unless and until any of the events of default enumerated in Section .... hereof shall have happened and be continuing, the Company shall be entitled to receive for its own use all interest paid on the Pledged Debentures and if the Trustee shall receive any such interest it shall forthwith deliver and pay such interest over to the Company; and the Trustee from time to time shall execute and deliver upon the written request of the Company suitable assignments and orders for the payment of such interest in favour of the Company and shall deliver to the Company upon a like request any and all coupons representing such interest, as they mature . . ."

[62] See the following provision:

"In the event that any corporation whose shares of stock are pledged under this Indenture shall issue to the holders of such shares rights to purchase any securities or other property, the Company shall be entitled to receive and exercise such rights or sell such rights for cash as in its discretion it shall determine, provided, however, that if the Company shall sell any of the purchase rights appertaining to the pledged shares, the net proceeds of such sale, after deduction therefrom of all commissions, expenses and taxes, including as income taxes only long term capital gains taxes as estimated as of the time of such sale, payable on or

curities of equal market value.[63]

Protection of the borrower against forfeiture of the security may be the object of specific covenants between the parties. However, this matter is primarily determined by the procedural requirements and the many limitations to contractual freedom set forth in most systems of law. Thus in many countries, it is questionable whether the parties may effectively provide (a) for a foreclosure which dispenses with formalities like notice, judicial authorization to sell, or sale at public auction;[64] or (b) that upon default, title to the pledged property shall become absolute in the pledgee; or (c) that upon default, the pledgor's equity of redemption shall terminate or be forfeited.[65] All

in connection with such sale, shall be applied by the Company toward
    (i) the redemption of Bonds issued under this Indenture, or
    (ii) the payment of the purchase price for such securities or other property as it shall elect to purchase pursuant to such rights, or
    (iii) in part toward the redemption of Bonds issued under this Indenture and in part toward the payment of the purchase price for such securities or other property as it shall elect to purchase . . ."

[63] See e.g., the Export-Import Bank 1957 Loan to the United Kingdom (referred to in note 53 supra, Article VII, para. 3).

[64] See e.g., France, Civil Code, art. 2078, Commercial Code, art. 93; Germany, BGB, arts. 1221, 1235; Chile, Civil Code, arts. 2424, 2397. Comp., Paton's, 3 *Digest of Legal Opinions* (1944), p. 3127; Annotations 76 A.L.R. 705, 109 A.L.R. 1106.

See also, the following provision in a contract dated December 5, 1921 between the Republic of Bolivia and American bankers (*Dunn,* p. 254):
"[The pledgee] may proceed to the sale of the cited pledged bonds at public sale in the city of New York, with previous notification to the Republic of not less than thirty days . . ."

See, however, the following provision in Article IX of the Agreement of February 25, 1957 between the United Kingdom and the Export-Import Bank (referred to in note 53 supra):
"Upon the non-payment of the principal of all such notes declared due as aforesaid, the securities constituting the collateral pledged under Article VI hereof shall at its option be transferred into the name of Eximbank and Eximbank directly or acting through its nominee is empowered to sell, assign, collect and convert into money and deliver the whole or any part of the collateral at public or private sale, without demand, advertisement or notice of the time or place of sale or of any adjournment thereof which are hereby expressly waived. After deducting all expenses of such sale or sales, Eximbank shall apply the residue of the proceeds thereof to the payment of such notes and unpaid interest thereon at the rate specified in such notes, returning the excess, if any, to the United Kingdom . . ."

[65] See e.g., British South Africa Co. v. De Beers Consol. Mines (1910) 2 Ch. 502 (reversed, (1912) A.C. 52, on the ground that the equity of redemption was not really clogged by the transaction involved in this case). See also, Annotation, 24 A.L.R. 822.

Comp., in *Europe:* Belgium, Civil Code, art 2078; France, Civil Code, art.

that is normally possible in most countries, is to release the equity of redemption at some time after the date of the loan.

If the word "pledge" were always used in its classical sense, i.e. to designate a transfer of possession from the pledgor to the pledgee, there would be little to add to the above comments. However in the last few decades, the word "pledge" has acquired a new connotation in many civil-law countries, and is now frequently used in these countries to refer to forms of security which do not entail a transfer of possession. Under such names as "gage sans depossession,"[66] or "prenda sin desplazamiento,"[67] new forms of security have appeared in civil-law countries which provide adequate substitutes for the common-law concept of chattel mortgage, otherwise generally foreign to the civil

---

2078; Germany BGB, art. 1229; Greece, Civil Code, art. 1239; Italy, Civil Code, arts. 1963, 2744; Netherlands, Civil Code, art. 1200; Spain, Civil Code, art. 1859; Switzerland, Civil Code, art. 894; (ii) in *Latin America:* Argentina, Civil Code, art. 3222; Bolivia, Civil Code, art. 1421; Brazil, Civil Code, art. 765; Chile, Civil Code, arts. 2397, 2424; Cuba (pre-Castro), Civil Code, art. 1859; Mexico, Civil Code, art. 2887; Nicaragua, Civil Code, art. 3759; Peru, Civil Code, art. 1024; Uruguay, Civil Code, art. 2308; and (iii) in the *Far East:* Japan, Civil Code, art. 349.

In this connection, two French decisions are interesting. The first is an old judgment of a lower court upholding a forfeiture clause in a loan contract between French bankers and the Turkish Government, which was secured by a pledge of securities deposited with the bankers. The court held that although the forfeiture clause would have been invalid under French law, it was valid under Turkish law, which was found to be the applicable law. See Trib. Civ. Seine March 3, 1875, Etat Ottoman v. Comptoir d'Escompte, S. 1877.2.25. It is hard to say whether this decision was influenced by the consideration that the creditors were French, or was based on the then prevailing opinion that a government must be presumed to contract under its own law. In any event, a forfeiture clause in a contract between a foreign (Dutch) creditor and a French pledgor has since been declared invalid by the French Supreme Court (Cass. May 24, 1933, Société Administratie Kantoor de Mas [or Maas] v. Syndic des Etablissements Ravel [or Bez], S.1935.1.258; Rev. 1934, 142).

[66] See e.g., *Le Gage Commercial,* cited in note 1 supra; Dainow, "Civil Code Revision in the Netherlands: Some New Developments in Obligations and Property," in *XXth Century Comparative and Conflicts Law* (1961), 172, at pp. 181-185; Wagatsuma, "Chattel Mortgages in Japanese Law," The Japan Annal of Law and Politics, No. 3, 99 (1955); von Mehren, *Law in Japan* (1963), pp. 530-537.

[67] See e.g., Folsom, "Chattel Mortgages and Substitutes Therefor in Latin America", 3 Am. J. Comp. L. 477 (1954). In Spain, the corporation law (*Ley de Sociedades Anonimas*) of July 7, 1951 (Art. 114, No. 3) provides expressly that bonds may be secured by a "prenda". See De Arrillaga, *Emision de Obligaciones y Proteccion de los Obligacionistas* (1952), p. 112; Garrigues and Uria, *Comentario a la Ley de Sociedades Anonimas,* vol. 2 (2nd ed. 1953), pp. 469-470.

law.[68] These types of liens, which require publicity in order to be effective against third parties,[69] have been used primarily to secure loans for agricultural or industrial development. They usually involve agricultural or industrial equipment, like livestock, machinery and trucks; or products like crops, crude oil or manufactured goods. No doubt, these new forms of security will play an increasing role in future international lending transactions.[70]

Reference should also be made to the current practice of the European Company for the Financing of Railway Rolling Stock (Eurofima), a corporation owned by European railway companies and operating under a charter granted by the Swiss government pursuant to an international convention.[71] The purpose of Eurofima is to finance the rehabilitation of European railways by purchasing rolling stock and making it available to the member railway companies on a conditional sale basis. Eurofima retains title to such rolling stock until full payment by the railway company involved. This type of agreement may have been influenced also by the American concept of

---

[68] The two major exceptions concern mortgages on aircrafts and ships, which although they are technically classified as chattels, are in many respects treated like realty. See Bayitch, op. cit. note 1 supra, pp. 13-19. For concrete examples, see e.g., the loans dated July 15, 1948 made by the IBRD to several Dutch companies (153 UNTS 211, 259); the loan dated March 20, 1952 made by the IBRD to KLM (the Dutch Airlines) secured by a chattel mortgage on airplanes (159 UNTS 207); and the loan made by the IBRD on March 5, 1957 to Air-India International Corporation, in a joint operation with United States commercial banks, also secured by a chattel mortgage on passenger planes (272 UNTS 201).

[69] In countries like France, where the legislative creation of these new "pledges" has not followed a definite pattern, recordation is made in specific registers relating to each particular category of "pledge". In other countries, where the implementation of such "pledges" has been more systematically organized, special sections have been added to the general property register to permit a centralized registry of liens on chattels and realty. See notes 66 and 67 supra.

[70] See e.g., the following loans made by the IBRD: on September 10, 1953 to Corporación de Fomento de la Producción and Compania Manufacturera de Papeles y Cartones (188 UNTS 25, secured by a "Hipoteca y Prenda Industrial"); on April 19, 1955 to Compania Nacional de Cemento Portland del Norte S.A. (221 UNTS 153, secured by a "Hipoteca" and a "Prenda Mercantil y Minera"); on May 14, 1964 to Compagnie Algérienne du Méthane Liquide (CAMEL), referred to in note 7 supra, secured by a "Hypothèque" and "Nantissement de Fonds de Commerce".

[71] Convention of October 20, 1955. The text of this Convention and the related documents can be found in 3 *European Yearbook* (1957), pp. 411 et seq. See also, Adam, "Société Européenne pour le Financement du Matériel Ferroviaire, Eurofima", Ibid., pp. 70 et seq.

equipment trust.[72] This development is of particular significance because of the important changes that had to be made in the domestic laws of participating countries to give it effect.[73] In this last respect, Eurofima's example constitutes an impressive precedent of great potential interest to the future development of international financing of European investments.

C. MORTGAGES

In taking a mortgage or similar security on the borrower's real property, several formal and substantive factors must be given careful consideration.

As a matter of formal validity, the deed of mortgage is normally drafted in accordance with the legal requirements in effect at the situs of the mortgaged property. This general rule is made imperative in certain countries which require that the deed be "authenticated" by a public officer, like the civil-law "notary," and refuse to give effect to deeds executed in foreign countries.[74]

The local law must also be complied with in regard to all questions concerning recordation.[75] This may raise difficult problems when

---

[72] See Adam, op. cit. preceding note, at pp. 71, 76-79.

[73] Conditional sale agreements are normally subject to many limitations in Continental law. See Adam, op. cit note 71 supra, at pp. 77-78.

[74] This is true under French law (Civil Code, articles 2127 and 2128) and legislations in other countries influenced by the French example, like the Netherlands (Civil Code, article 1218) and the Dominican Republic (Civil Code, articles 2127 and 2128). However other countries, like Belgium, which at one time adopted the Code Napoleon, have since enacted statutes giving effect to mortgages drafted in a foreign form, subject to judicial or other administrative review by the local authorities. See, Belgian Mortgage Law December 16, 1851, article 77. Comp., Nicaragua, Civil Code, article 3823. Some other countries, like Argentina (Civil Code, article 1211) ; Chile (Civil Code, articles 2409 and 2411) ; and El Salvador (Civil Code, articles 677 and 740) limit the recognition of foreign mortgages to mortgages drafted by a public official at the place of drafting. Still other countries seem to give general recognition to foreign mortgages whatever their form, subject only to recordation of the mortgage instrument in the local property register. See e.g., Bolivia (Civil Code, article 1475) ; Colombia (Civil Code, article 2436) ; Ecuador (Civil Code, article 2430) ; Mexico, State of Morelos (Civil Code, article 3005) ; and State of Sonora (Civil Code, article 16) ; Spain, Ruling of February 14, 1947, article 39 (in Medina y Maranon, *Leyes Civiles de Espana*, 1949) ; Uruguay (Civil Code, article 2324).

[75] See e.g., the following provision in an indenture between a German company and two trustees (American and German) :
"The Company will cause the recording consents *(Bestellungsurkunden)* and, to the extent permitted by law, this Indenture to be duly and

the mortgaged property is located in a country which prohibits alien
entities from acquiring title to real estate[76] or does not acknowledge

> promptly filed and registered in such manner and in all recording offices
> (*Grundbuchämter*) to the extent that such filing and registration may be
> necessary in order fully to preserve and protect the security of the holders
> of the Bonds and coupons and the rights of the Trustees, and will promptly,
> after the execution of this Indenture, furnish to the Trustees one or more
> Opinions of Counsel stating that in the opinion of such counsel such
> filing and registration has been duly completed so as to make effective
> the lien of this Indenture and reciting the details of such action or
> stating that in the opinion of such counsel such action is not necessary
> in respect to certain of the said instruments. On or before ————————
> of each year thereafter the Company will furnish to the Trustees one
> or more Opinions of Counsel stating that in the opinion of such counsel
> all action with respect to refiling or re-registration necessary fully to
> preserve, continue and protect the security of the holders of the Bonds
> and coupons and all rights of the Trustees has been taken and reciting
> the details of such action, or stating that in the opinion of such counsel
> no such action is necessary."

For an example of English practice, see e.g., 3 *Palmer's*, p. 322.

In addition to the foreign registration of the mortgage, the English Companies Act, 1948 (11 & 12 Geo. 6, c.38), Section 95, provides that if the
mortgagor is a company registered in England, the mortgage should be filed
with the Registrar of Companies in England.

[76] See e.g., Townsend, op. cit. note 9 supra, at p. 244:

> "There are certain types of security which may not be available to [the
> Export-Import Bank] because of its status as an agency of the United
> States. For example, the laws of some foreign countries prohibit a govern-
> ment, or a government agency, from acquiring, or being a mortgagee of,
> real estate or an assignee of concessions or franchises . . ."

In some countries, there may be difficulty in vesting title to land in an
alien corporation, at least if such corporation has not qualified to do business
within the country. An example is found in the case of the Central Railways of
Buenos Aires, in which the question arose whether an English trustee of a
loan issued in England by an English company and secured by a mortgage
of Argentina property, should qualify to do business in Argentina before
recording the security in the Property Register. The answer, at first found
in the affirmative, turned out to be in the negative, after a change in the
office of the director of the Property Register. See Gaceta del Foro, vol. VIII,
p. 55 (1923), reporting the different opinions of the directors of the Property
Register, as well as an inconclusive decision of Court of Appeals of Buenos
Aires of March 14, 1923. See also, Arguello, "Regimen Internacional de las
Sociedades Anónimas en la Republica Argentina", Revista de la Facultad de
Derecho y Ciencias Sociales 1951, 1159, at 1176-77.

Comp., the Ship Mortgage Act of the United States, which makes it unlawful "to sell, mortgage, lease, charter, deliver, or in any manner transfer"
any American-flag vessel or any interest therein to an alien, without the approval of the Secretary of Commerce. This statute was held applicable in a
case involving a loan by a German corporation secured by a mortgage on an
American vessel, pursuant to an indenture whose Trustee was an American
company. Chemical Bank New York Trust Co. v. Steamship Westhampton,
231 F. Supp. 284 (1964).

such concepts as the common-law trust.[77] Other problems may arise
also. For example, under French law (and similar legal systems), the
appointment of the bondholders' common representatives cannot take
place until the community of bondholders has been organized, i.e.
some time after the issuance of the bonds.[78] To the extent, therefore,
that the bonds are secured by a mortgage or other security requiring
recordation, the recordation in the name of the common representative must be delayed until the bonds have been issued. The danger,
of course, is that during the interim period, the liens of other creditors will be recorded and will acquire precedence over the bondholders' security. To meet this problem, it has become the practice in
France to satisfy all recordation requirements before the date of issue
by recording the security in the name of the "notary" responsible
for its validity, or officers of the issuing house, acting in a fiduciary
capacity for the benefit of the future bondholders.[79]

---

[77] In most civil-law countries, the trustee is treated as an agent for the
lenders (and bondholders in particular). See Chapter II, text and notes 99
to 102. As a consequence of this characterization, before the trustee can record
the security, consent to releases or substitution of the security or foreclose,
he may be compelled to produce specific evidence of authority, in the form,
for example, of an appropriate resolution passed at a bondholders' meeting.
This requirement can result in considerable delays prejudicial to the investors' interests.

One method which has been employed to avoid such difficulties is as
follows. A mortgage deed between the borrower and the trustee is executed
in accordance with the provisions of the *lex situs,* without any reference to
the fact that the trustee is acting in a fiduciary capacity, and recorded in the
trustee's name. Thus the trustee appears as the real party in interest and is
able to consent to releases or substitution of security, or to foreclose in its
own name. At or about the time the mortgage deed is recorded, the benefit
of the security is given to investors under a separate instrument, drawn up
in the common-law form of a trust indenture, which provides that the trustee
holds the mortgage, or the proceeds thereof, in trust for the investors. See e.g.,
*Annual Report of the Special Committee on Private International and Con-
flict of Laws for 1923-1925* to the Association of the Bar of the City of New
York, pp. 426 et seq. As pointed out in the Report, however, this device may
involve:

"a theoretical, if not practical element of risk, as the bank or trust company appears as the only creditor of record in the foreign country where
the mortgage is placed, thereby possibly subjecting the security to claims
of creditors of the banking institution, who might succeed in attaching
the mortgage of record and excluding the bondholders." (p. 427)

[78] Decree-Law of October 30, 1935, article 26. Comp.: in Belgium, Comm.
Code, Title IX, article 91; Brazil, Decree-Law No. 781 of October 12, 1938;
and in Italy, Civil Code, articles 2415, 2417.

[79] See e.g., I *Moreau-Néret,* pp. 330-331. A good example, though relating
to the French law governing the validity of assignments, rather than mortgages, is found in the "Assignment Agreement" securing bonds issued by the

Another delicate issue is whether the documents to be recorded should express the amount of the mortgage in terms of the foreign currency in which the loan is denominated or the local-currency equivalent thereof. Although some countries permit recordation of mortgage documents expressed in terms of foreign currency,[80] other countries require that these documents be expressed in terms of the local currency.[81] From the lenders' point of view, the latter method may present problems. If, after recordation, the foreign-exchange value of the local currency is seriously impaired, the amount recorded in local currency will be substantially less than the foreign-currency amount of the loan and, to the same extent, the loan will become insufficiently secured. If foreclosure becomes necessary, the lenders may not be able to collect more than the local currency amount stated in the mortgage register, and may have to rely on a personal action against the borrower for the balance. There are several possible solutions to this problem. The first is to make the amount recorded in local currency large enough to account for possible minor depreciations of the foreign-exchange value of the local currency.[82] If greater variations of the foreign-exchange value of such currency are anticipated, or if the loan is granted for an extensive period of time, an alternative solution may be more appropriate. This would consist of

Société du Pipe-Line Sud-Européen (filed as an exhibit to the U.S. prospectus of the 5½% Sinking Fund Debentures of the Société due 1982, and dated March 13, 1962). The Agreement provides that certain designated persons are "acting in the name and on behalf of the future debenture holders . . . and of all legal or contractual bodies to represent the holders of said debentures for the protection of their common interest . . ."

[80] Thus, article 2432 of the Civil Code of Chile provides that the deed of mortgage must be recorded, and the recordation must show the amount secured by the mortgage. As the deed itself is recorded, it follows that if it is denominated in a foreign currency, the entry in the register of mortgages will also be denominated in that currency. Similar provisions are in effect in Peru (Civil Code, articles 1014, 1025) and Nicaragua (Civil Code, article 3808).

[81] See e.g., in *Europe,* Austria, GBG, article 14; Belgium, mortgage law of December 16, 1851, article 83; France, Civil Code, articles 2132 and 2148; Germany, BGB, article 1115; Italy, Civil Code, article 2809; Switzerland, Civil Code, article 794;—and in *Latin America,* Argentina, Civil Code, article 3109; Bolivia, Civil Code, article 1477; Colombia, Civil Code, article 2455; Mexico, Civil Code, article 3015; Uruguay, Civil Code, article 2334.

[82] This "maximum mortgage" *(hypothèque maximale)* is now used in European countries. The danger, however, is that if the ceiling is fixed too high, the borrower may seek, and possibly obtain, a judicial decree reducing the amount secured by the mortgage to a lower level. In case of a future depreciation of the local currency, this lower amount may prove insufficient to secure the aggregate foreign-currency amount of the loan.

an agreement by the mortgagor that if the foreign-exchange value of the local currency depreciates to a significant extent, and if the lenders so request, the mortgagor will create additional mortgages so that the aggregate amount in local currency for which the mortgages are recorded will remain equivalent to the aggregate foreign-currency amount of the loan.[83] A third solution, which has the advantage of simplicity but is not always possible under local law, is to record the mortgage amount in the local-currency equivalent of the amount of the loan at the time of recordation, and include a revaluation clause which will automatically result in an increase of the recorded local-currency amount proportionate to the decrease in the foreign-exchange value of that currency.[84]

Considerations of fluctuating exchange rates may influence other provisions of international indentures. Thus, if it is covenanted that the mortgagor shall maintain insurance on the security, it may be necessary to provide also that such insurance shall be taken in a specified currency, and that if the foreign exchange value of that currency depreciates, the amount of the insurance shall be increased accord-

---

[83] See e.g., the following provision in a loan agreement dated June 14, 1955, between the IBRD and Vorarlberger Illwerke AG (221 UNTS 375):

". . . In the event the par value of the currency of the Guarantor [Austria] is reduced or the foreign exchange value of the currency of the Guarantor has, in the opinion of the Bank, depreciated to a significant extent, the Borrower shall from time to time promptly upon the Bank's request execute and deliver to the Bank such additional supplemental first mortgage or mortgages in form and substance satisfactory to the Bank as may be required to make the aggregate amount in the currency of the Guarantor for which all mortgages created hereunder may be recordable or may have been recorded equivalent to the aggregate amount in the currencies other than the currency of the Guarantor required for the payment of principal of, and interest on, the Loan and the Bonds, calculated on the basis of such reduced par value or depreciated foreign exchange value respectively, and for the purpose of such calculation the par value or the foreign exchange value of the currency of the Guarantor in terms of any such other currency shall be as reasonably determined by the Bank.

All such mortgages shall equally and ratably secure payment of the principal of, interest, premium, if any, on prepayment or redemption, and other charges on, the Loan and the Bonds." (Article V, Section 5.04).

[84] An amendment of the French Civil Code (Article 2148 and Decree of October 14, 1955, article 57) has made it possible to record mortgages in France by stating the original aggregate amount of the debt value in French currency, together with a revaluation clause. The mortgage thereafter secures, with the same priority, all the successively revalued French franc amount of the original debt, and no additional recordation is necessary.

ingly.[85] Similarly, covenants relating to the release and substitution of the security are usually supplemented by provisions regarding the determination of the fair value of the mortgaged property to be released or substituted, both in terms of the local currency and the currency in which the loan is denominated.[86] These provisions are intended to give lenders the assurance that the fair value of the property will be properly assessed, and that the ratio between the aggregate value of the security and the amount of the loan will at all times be maintained.

Another problem is presented by the fact that the concept of mortgage, as incorporated in the law of the situs, may automatically include assets which, in the lender's country, would have to be specifically designated as security. Thus in many civil law countries, the law subjects to the lien of the mortgage not only the real property involved and fixtures permanently attached to it, but also various movables which, though not physically attached to such property, are nevertheless so indispensable to its normal use and exploitation as to be deemed, for the purpose of hypothecation, part of the immovable property which they serve. Examples are cattle, machines, trucks and other agricultural or industrial equipment. This concept, which has the advantage of broadening the scope of the security, may nevertheless prove inconvenient. If the borrower wishes to dispose of or replace movables like trucks or machines which have become worn out or obsolete, he must request a specific release from his lender. This may be a cumbersome and costly procedure in view of the cost of

---

[85] See e.g., the following provision in an English trust deed with a Continental borrower:

". . . Every insurance effected by the [Borrower] under this clause shall be effected for such amount as the Trustees shall approve and if the proportion which such amount bears to the value of the property insured shall be diminished either through the depreciation of the currency in which such insurance is effected or through the appreciation in value of the property or from any other cause the amount of such insurance shall be increased accordingly . . ."

[86] Thus, an indenture between a German company and an American trustee and German co-trustee provides that, in addition to the usual officer's and appraiser's certificate and opinion of counsel regarding the property to be released and the conditions of the release, the German co-trustee shall be supplied with a special certificate whenever the value of such property is equal to or exceeds 10 per cent of the Deutsche mark equivalent, at the current rate of exchange, of the aggregate principal amount of all outstanding bonds. The additional certificate, to be executed by an independent appraiser, is required to state the fair value in Deutsche marks of the property involved. The indenture also provides that this information shall be forwarded by the co-trustee to the American trustee for final determination.

registration fees and the formalities, including notations in the register of mortgages, required to perfect the release and the substitution, if any, of the security.

One way to remedy this difficulty is to provide that, up to a specific amount for a given period of time, such as a year, the mortgagor shall be entitled to sell or dispose of worn out or otherwise unusable movables subject to the lien of the mortgage.[87] However this solution, in spite of its apparent simplicity, may be subject to a practical impediment, namely the difficulty of proving that the amount of permissible release has not been exceeded at the time of a proposed sale. In the absence of some sort of statement by the mortgagee, the mortgagor may have difficulty convincing third parties that the property offered for sale will be freed from the mortgage lien, or satisfying the registrar of mortgages that he may proceed with the necessary modification of the mortgage registration.

For these reasons, another solution is sometimes preferred: The exclusion *ab initio* from the lien of the mortgage of all or specific classes of movables.[88] This method, of course, enables the mortgagor

---

[87] See e.g., the following provision in an American-German indenture:
"The Company shall have full power, from time to time in its discretion, to

(a) sell, exchange or otherwise dispose of, free from the lien of the Indenture, in any calendar year, machinery and equipment, or other tangible property constituting part of the Trust Estate and having an aggregate fair value in Deutsche Marks equivalent, at the current rate of exchange in effect at the time of such sales, exchanges or other disposals, to $25,000;

(b) sell, exchange or otherwise dispose of, free from the lien of the Indenture, machinery and equipment, or other tangible property constituting part of the Trust Estate which may have become worn out, unserviceable, obsolete, disused, undesirable or unnecessary for use ir the conduct of its business; *provided,* that the Company shall, at any time prior thereto, contemporaneously therewith, or within six months thereafter, replace the same with, or substitute therefor, other machinery and equipment, or other tangible property, which need not be of the same character but shall be of equal value to the Company, shall be useful and desirable or necessary in the conduct of its business, shall cost not less than the amount realized or realizable on a sale, of the property so replaced or substituted, and shall be subject to the lien of the Indenture or, if not so subject, shall forthwith be subjected to the lien of the Indenture, by creation of equally ranking joint and several security mortgages *(gleichrangige Gesamtgrundschulden)* with respect thereto . . ."

[88] See e.g., the following provision in an American-Canadian indenture:
". . . there is expressly excepted and excluded from the lien of the mortgage hereby constituted the following described property of the Company, whether now owned or hereafter acquired:

(a) All cash on hand or in bank, contracts, shares of stock,

to dispose of these assets freely in the course of its operations. Although this solution limits the scope of the security, it has the great advantage of avoiding unnecessary friction between the mortgagor and the mortgagee, and preventing possible delays in the normal conduct of the borrower's business.

These are essentially contractual limitations to the ordinary scope of the security. Other limitations may result from the statutory requirements of the *lex situs*. Thus in most countries, it is impossible to create a valid mortgage on real property within the public domain. Even if the creation of such a mortgage were legally possible, it would be unrealistic to expect that the mortgage could be effectively enforced in the event of a default. Again, in the many countries which still forbid or strictly regulate the mortgaging of after-acquired property the mortgage must be confined to property owned at the time of its creation, unless the general prohibition admits of certain exceptions.[89]

---

bonds, notes, evidences of indebtedness and other securities, bills, notes and accounts receivable, patents, patent rights, patent applications, trade names, trademarks, claims, credits, choses in action and other intangible property;

(b) All . . . materials, supplies and other personal property which are consumable in their use in the conduct of the business of the Company;

(c) All other property produced or manufactured, or in process of production or manufacture, in the conduct of the business of the Company or otherwise acquired or held for the purpose of sale in the ordinary course of the business of the Company;

(d) All automobiles, buses, trucks, tractors, trailers and similar vehicles, railway rolling stock other than such as is used exclusively within the bounds of the trust estate, boats, barges, repair docks and other marine equipment, aircraft, and office furniture and fixtures, and the accessories and supplies used in connection with any of the foregoing;

(e) All hand tools, movable machinery and equipment and other similar property not permanently placed or located on or about the real property now or hereafter subject to the lien hereof . . ."

[89] See e.g., French Civil Code, article 2130, paragraph 1, subject however to the important exception in paragraph 2 of this article: If at the time of the mortgage, the mortgagor does not own sufficient property to fully secure the loan, he may undertake to mortgage future-acquired property as and when such property is acquired; such additional mortgages to take effect, however, only as of their own respective dates. Similar rules obtain in other civil countries like Belgium (see VI *Répertoire Pratique du Droit Belge, Hypothèques* (1950), para. 1318); Argentina (Civil Code, article 3126); Chile (Civil Code, article 2419); Colombia (Civil Code, article 2444); Uruguay (Civil Code, article 2332).

For a concrete example, see the Loan Agreement dated September 10, 1953, between the IBRD and Corporación de Fomento de la Producción and

These technicalities, together with the complexities of enforcing
a mortgage (including the representation of investors and the right
of action of the trustee or the bondholder's common representative)[90]
make the effectiveness of mortgage securities largely dependent upon
the circumstances of each case. In this, as in the case of other forms
of security, the trade-name of the institution covers many different
situations and should not be relied on without extensive investigation
into the particular set of laws and facts involved.

D. FLOATING CHARGES

In the United Kingdom, and other countries which have followed
the English example, it is not uncommon to stipulate that in addition
to the lien of the indenture or trust deed, the loan will be secured by
a floating charge upon all of the borrower's assets, present and future,
real and personal, tangible and intangible.[91]

Compania Manufacturera de Papeles y Cartones (188 UNTS 25, Article V,
Section 5.01), which provides for the creation of: (i) a mortgage on property owned by the borrower at the time of the loan; and (ii) supplemental
mortgages on properties included in the project financed by the loan.

[90] See Chapter II, text and notes 91 to 96, 98 and 99.

[91] See e.g., 3 *Palmer's*, p. 48; Gower, "Some Contrasts between British and
American Corporation Law," 69 Harv. L. Rev. 1369 (1956), at p. 1397; Pen-
nington, "The Genesis of a Floating Charge," 23 Mod. L. Rev. 630 (1960);
Coogan and Bok, "The Impact of Article 9 of the Uniform Commercial Code
on the Corporate Indenture," 69 Yale L. J. 203 (1959), at pp. 251-259.

A good example of a floating charge covenant is the following:
"The Company doth hereby charge, as and by way of a first floating
charge, in favour of the Trustee, with the payment of all principal,
premium (if any) and interest on all Bonds at any time outstanding
under this Indenture and all other moneys for the time being and from
time to time owing on the security of this Indenture and of the Bonds,
all its undertaking, property and assets (other than those parts of the
Specifically Mortgaged Property which have been effectively subjected
to the Specific Lien of this Indenture) for the time being, present and
future, of whatsoever kind and wheresoever situate, including but without limiting the generality of the foregoing, its . . . goodwill, trade marks,
inventions, processes, patents and patent rights, materials, supplies, in-
ventories, furniture, implements, rents, revenues, incomes and sources of
money, moneys, rights, powers, privileges, franchises, benefits immunities,
contracts, agreements, leases, licenses, book debts, accounts receivable,
negotiable and non-negotiable instruments, judgments, securities, choses
in action, and all other property and things of value of every kind and
nature, tangible and intangible, legal or equitable, which the Company
may be possessed of or entitled to or which may be hereafter acquired by
the Company; provided, that, until the security hereby constituted shall
have become enforceable and the Trustees or either of them shall have
determined or become bound to enforce the same, the floating charge
created by this Section shall in no way hinder or prevent the Company

The effect of such a charge is to create an equitable lien on the assets of the borrower which operates as an immediate and continuing charge on its property, subject however to the borrower's power to deal freely with such property in the ordinary course of its business.[92] The lien remains effective until the lenders intervene to enforce their claims and a receiver is appointed, or winding-up proceedings are commenced. In such an event, the charge ceases to be "floating" and becomes fixed or "crystallized," and the borrower can no longer dispose of, nor can its other creditors effectively claim, the charged property.

Whether this form of security will be recognized and enforced as to property located outside England or other common-law countries following the English example, depends on the provisions of the *lex situs*. At least one American decision has given effect to an English floating charge,[93] even though this form of security is not generally

at any time and from time to time from selling, alienating, leasing, paying dividends out of profits or out of any distributable surplus available for the payment of dividends or otherwise disposing of or dealing with its property and assets (other than Specifically Mortgaged Property) in the ordinary course of business and for the purpose of carrying on the same . . ."

See also the following agreements between the IBRD and: (i) Sui Gas Transmission Company, Limited, dated June 2, 1954, Article V, Section 5.05 (324 UNTS 59); (ii) Karnaphuli Paper Mills, Limited, dated August 4, 1955, Article V, Section 5.09 (236 UNTS 195); (iii) The Karachi Electric Supply Corporation, Limited, dated June 20, 1955, Article V, Section 5.04 (230 UNTS 41); (iv) The Indian Iron and Steel Company, Limited, dated December 18, 1952, Article V, Section 5.04 (201 UNTS 241); (v) The Tata Hydro-Electric Power Supply Company, Limited, The Andhra Valley Power Supply Company, Limited, and the Tata Power Company, Limited, dated November 9, 1954, Article V, Section 5.04 (309 UNTS 159); and (vi) The Dead Sea Works, Limited, dated July 11, 1961, Article V, Section 5.04 (429 UNTS 3).

[92] Unless otherwise provided in the indenture or trust deed, the borrower remains free to sell or mortgage the charged property, as if the property were free of any lien. See the covenant quoted in the preceding note.

[93] See, Pennsylvania Co. for Insurance on Lives and Granting Annuities v. United Railways of Havana & Regla Warehouse, Ltd., 26 F. Supp: 379 (D.C. Me. 1939). The plaintiff, a Pennsylvania corporation, had attached shares of a Maine corporation owned by the defendant, an English corporation conducting business in Cuba, with its principal place of business in London. At the time of the attachment, the shares were subject to a floating charge valid under English law. Subsequently, an English receiver was appointed and the charge, by proceedings for crystallization, became a specific lien which, under English law, took precedence over all other claims, including those attempted to be enforced by attachment. It was held that because the crystallization of the floating charge destroyed the attachment, the latter must be quashed.

used in American practice. In civil-law countries, however, it is doubtful whether a similar solution would be reached in the absence of a statute specifically providing for such a result.[94]

SECTION III. NEGATIVE-PLEDGE CLAUSES

It is customary for loan documents to provide that the borrower shall not create liens or charges on its assets or revenues in favor of creditors other than the lenders without causing the lenders to share equally and ratably in the security.[95] This type of stipulation, com-

---

[94] The concept of floating charge has infiltrated certain civil-law countries, especially in Latin America, where important English investments have been made and local lawyers have had the opportunity to appreciate the merits of this institution. See e.g., as to Argentina and Paraguay, De Arrillaga, *Emision de Obligaciones y Proteccion de los Obligacionistas* (1952), p. 110; Zavalo Rodriguez, I *Código de Comercio y Leyes Complementarias* (1961), pp. 850-851; Rivarola, II *Sociedades Anonimas* (1957), p. 266; Malagarriga, I *Derecho Comercial* (2d ed. 1958), pp. 511-512; Cappa, "The Corporate Debenture System of South American Countries", 43 Yale L. J. 570 (1934), at p. 577.

[95] Another type of provision which is sometimes used flatly prohibits the borrower from creating liens on his assets without the prior consent of the lender or the trustee. See e.g., the following provision in the French prospectus (p. 4) of the SACOR Loan of 1962:
"This loan is not secured by any personal guarantee or lien on [the borrower's] property. However, in the event that SACOR would wish to create such securities for other loans, existing or future, it would have to obtain the prior consent of the Trustee." (as translated).
See also: (i) the Government of Czechoslovakia External 5% Loan of 1932, issued in France with the guarantee of the French Government, which provided, among other things, that:
"The Government of Czechoslovakia has undertaken that as long as the bonds shall be outstanding, it will not create any priority, security or charge upon the net revenues of the Tobacco Monopolies which would rank in priority to or *pari passu* with the present Loan" (as translated).
(ii) Article XII of the General Bond of the German Government International 5½% Loan of 1930 (the Young Loan):
"Pursuant to the Hague Agreement and in particular subject to the charge securing the German External Loan 1924 the German Government shall not while any part of the unconditional or the said postponable annuities remains outstanding create without the consent of the Bank for International Settlements acting in accordance with the Hague Agreement any mortgage or charge upon the Customs, the Tobacco Taxes, the Beer Tax or the Tax on Spirits (Administration of the Monpoly) to secure any other loan or credit of the German Government in priority to or pari passu with the said annuities."
and (iii) Article 6 of the Loan Agreement dated March 23, 1948, between the United States and the United Nations (19 UNTS 43):

monly referred to as a "negative-pledge" or "pari passu" clause, is found in all kinds of loan instruments, including those involving borrowings in the private-capital market by foreign corporations,[96] mu-

"The United Nations agrees that . . . it will not, without the consent of the United States, while any of the indebtedness incurred hereunder is outstanding and unpaid, create any mortgage, lien or other encumbrance on or against any of its real property in the headquarters district as defined in [the Headquarters] Agreement. The United Nations also agrees that the United States, as a condition to giving its consent to any such disposition or encumbrance, may require the simultaneous repayment of the balance of all installments remaining unpaid hereunder."

Comp., Article VI, Section 6.06 of the Act of Pledge:

"The High Authority, considering that it is essential that all creditors, direct and indirect, of the High Authority shall have assurance that no one of them will receive any preference over any of the others as to the aforesaid levies which the Treaty authorizes the High Authority to maintain and collect and which underlie the credit of the High Authority, and considering that the levies and the guaranty fund resulting from them should be at all times available to protect, without discrimination, all engagements of the High Authority, whatever their form, hereby states that it does not propose to create, and agrees that it will not create, any mortgage, pledge or other priority on its revenues coming from the levies or on the accumulated levies from time to time resulting therefrom or, except as provided herein, on any other assets of the High Authority."

[96] See e.g., the following provision in the prospectus concerning The Compagnie Française des Pétroles, Paris 4½% Loan of 1963, issued in Switzerland:

"Compagnie Française des Pétroles undertakes that, as long as the loan shall be outstanding and unpaid, it shall not create in favor of other holders of bonds any security without causing the holders of bonds of this issue to share equally and ratably in such security" (as translated).

Similar provisions are found in other capital markets. See e.g., in the Netherlands, the prospectus regarding the Compagnie Internationale des Wagons-Lits et des Grands Express Européens, S.A., Bruxelles 4¾% Bonds of 1961; and in Canada, the prospectus regarding Petrofina, a Belgian company) 5½-7½% Debentures issued in 1957; and in the United States, the following provision (Section 5.06) in an Indenture dated April 15, 1963 between the Copenhagen Telephone Company, Incorporated and the First National City Bank:

"After the date of the execution and delivery of this Indenture and so long as any of the Debentures shall be outstanding, the Company agrees that if the Company secures any loan, debt, guarantee or other obligation, now or hereafter existing, by any lien, pledge or other charge upon any of its present or future assets or revenues, the Debentures shall be secured by such lien, pledge or other charge equally and ratably with such other loan, debt, guarantee or other obligation, and the instrument creating such lien, pledge or other charge shall expressly provide that the Debentures shall be so secured; provided, however, that the Debentures shall not be secured by (and no instrument shall be required to provide that the Debentures shall be secured by) any lien, pledge or other charge on any real estate property, if the aggregate principal amount of the

nicipalities or other public bodies or agencies,[97] governments,[98] and

> obligations of the Company secured by all liens, pledges or charges on real estate property does not exceed the value of all the land and buildings subject to such liens (excluding the value of the telephone equipment installed on or in such land or buildings irrespective of whether or not regarded as fixtures under Danish law) as assessed by Danish authorities for tax purposes. The term "real estate" as used herein shall mean land and buildings owned by the Company, but shall not include the telephone plant and equipment of the Company except to the extent installed on such land or in such buildings and considered as fixtures under Danish law."

[97] See e.g., in the United States, the prospectus regarding the City of Copenhagen 5⅜% Sinking Fund External Loan Bonds due May 15, 1978, reading in part as follows:

> "The City will agree that if it shall in the future secure any loan, debt, guarantee or other obligation, now or hereafter existing, by any lien, pledge or other charge upon any of its present or future revenues or upon the assets of its revenue-producing utilities (as defined), the Bonds will be equally and ratably secured by such lien, pledge or other charge, provided, however, that the Bonds will not be required to be so secured if the lien, pledge or other charge on the assets of the City's revenue-producing utilities is created or granted to secure the purchase price or cost of construction of such utilities or any improvement or addition to such utilities or to secure any loan or portion of a loan (but only to the extent of such portion) used to pay such purchase price or cost. Revenue-producing utilities are defined to include electric generating, transmission and distribution facilities, district heating plants and related distribution facilities, gas production, transmission and distribution facilities, public transit facilites (including streetcar and bus lines) and water supply facilities, including all equipment used in or in connection with such facilities or plants."

A similar clause is found in the prospectus regarding the Swiss Francs 60 million 5 per cent External Loan 1974/1983 issued by the same borrower in the United Kingdom.

Similar provisions are found in Continental countries such as Germany (prospectus regarding the City of Oslo 5½% Bearer Bonds of 1959), the Netherlands (prospectus regarding the City of Oslo 5% Loan of 1961) or Switzerland (prospectus regarding the City of Quebec 4½% Loan of 1960).

[98] See e.g., in Switzerland, the prospectus concerning the Argentine Republic 6½% External Loan 1961/1973 of U.S. \$25 million, General Bond, Clause XII, reading as follows:

> "In case the Government should create or issue or guarantee in accordance with the Argentine Constitution any loan or bonds secured by means of a charge on any of its revenues or assets, or if it should assign any part of its revenues or assets in any guarantee of any obligation whatsoever, the Bonds of this Loan shall be secured equally and rateably with such loans or bonds or guarantees."

and in the United States, the prospectus concerning the Kingdom of Denmark 5¼% Fifteen Year External Loan Bonds of 1963:

> "The Kingdom will agree [in the bonds] that if it shall, in the future, secure any loan, debt, guarantee or other obligation, now or hereafter existing, by any lien, pledge or other charge upon any of its present or future assets or revenues, the Bonds shall *ipso facto* share in and be

international lending organizations,[99] as well as in loan agreements
between these organizations and their respective borrowers.[100]

> secured by such lien, pledge or other charge equally and ratably with such
> other loan, debt, guarantee or other obligation."

and in the United Kingdom, the prospectus regarding the Japanese Government 6% Sterling Loan 1983/88:

> "The Japanese Government agrees that if it shall, in the future, secure
> any loan, debt, guarantee or other obligation constituting external debt,
> now or hereafter existing, by any lien, pledge or other charge upon any
> of its present or future assets or revenues, the Bonds will *ipso facto* share
> in and be secured by such lien, pledge or other charge equally and
> rateably with such other loan, debt, guarantee or other obligation."

[99] See e.g., the following provision in the prospectus concerning the IBRD
Twenty Year Bonds of 1962, issued in the United States:

> "So long as any of the Bonds shall be outstanding and unpaid, the Bank
> will not cause or permit to be created on any of its property or assets
> any mortgage, pledge or other lien or charge as security for any bonds
> or other evidences of indebtedness heretofore or hereafter issued, assumed
> or guaranteed by the Bank for money borrowed (other than purchase
> money mortgages, pledges or liens on property purchased by the Bank
> as security for all or part of the purchase price thereof) unless the Bonds
> shall be secured by such mortgage, pledge or other lien or charge equally
> and ratably with such other bonds or evidence of indebtedness."

Similar provisions are found in IBRD bonds issued in Austria, Belgium,
Germany, Italy, the Netherlands, Switzerland and the United Kingdom; and
in bonds issued by the EIB in the Netherlands.

Comp., the following provision in the ECSC 5½% Sinking Fund Bonds,
due April 15, 1982, issued in the United States:

> "The Community will also agree not to issue any obligations for money
> borrowed which are secured by any mortgage, pledge or other priority
> on any revenues or assets of the Community or which shall be entitled
> to the benefit of any commitment of the Community which might require
> it at any time to secure such obligations (either alone or with other
> indebtedness) by any such mortgage, pledge or other priority, but such
> provisions shall not prevent the issue of additional secured bonds and
> notes pursuant to the terms of the Act of Pledge or the pledge of or
> other priority on the assets held or to be held by the Depositary [i.e. the
> BIS] thereunder as security for the secured bonds and notes heretofore or
> hereafter issued pursuant thereto."

[100] The standard negative-pledge clause in IBRD agreements with member countries reads as follows:

> "It is the mutual intention of the Borrower and the Bank that no other
> external debt shall enjoy any priority over the loan by way of a lien
> on governmental assets. To that end, the Borrower undertakes that,
> except as the Bank shall otherwise agree, if any lien shall be created
> on any assets of the Borrower as security for any external debt, such lien
> will *ipso facto* equally and ratably secure the payment of the principal of,
> and interest and other charges on, the Loan and the Bonds, and that in
> the creation of any such lien express provision will be made to that
> effect, provided, however, that the foregoing provisions of this Section
> shall not apply to: (i) any lien created on property, at the time of
> purchase thereof, solely as security for the payment of the purchase price

The scope of these provisions vary. Those found in bonds issued by foreign governments are usually formulated in the most general terms, while other clauses contain various exceptions designed to achieve flexibility in their implementation. Examples are provisions excepting from the operation of the clause transactions like purchase-money mortgages or liens arising in the ordinary course of business and securing short-term debts.[101]

The successful administration of negative-pledge clauses depends on a close working relationship between borrowers and lenders. Unless the lenders are kept informed of the borrower's intentions, they may be unable to prevent the borrower from diverting to other purposes assets on which they relied for the protection of their investment. In this respect, the shortcomings of the existing machinery for the representation of bondholders and the protection of their interests are particularly apparent, and have sometimes led to the conclusion that: "Perhaps negative pledge clauses in securities should be outlawed."[102] When, however, the lenders maintain a continuing relationship with the borrower (as in the case of direct-loan contracts),

----

of such property; or (ii) any lien arising in the ordinary course of banking transactions and securing a debt maturing not more than one year after its date.

    The term "assets of the Borrower" as used in this Section includes assets of the Borrower or of any of its political subdivisions or of any agency of the Borrower or of any such political subdivision, including the [name of central bank] or any institution performing the functions of a central bank."

The standard negative-pledge clause in IBRD agreements with borrowers other than a member government reads as follows:

    "The Borrower undertakes that, except as the Bank shall otherwise agree, if any lien shall be created on any assets of the Borrower as security for any debt, such lien will *ipso facto* equally and ratably secure the payment of the principal of, and interest and other charges on, the Loan and the Bonds, and that in the creation of any such lien express provision will be made to that effect; provided, however, that the foregoing provisions of this Section shall not apply to: (i) any lien created on property, at the time of purchase thereof, solely as security for the payment of the purchase price of such property; (ii) any lien on commercial goods to secure a debt maturing not more than one year after the date on which it is originally incurred and to be paid out of the proceeds of sale of such commercial goods; or (iii) any lien arising in the ordinary course of banking transactions and securing a debt maturing not more than one year after its date."

Similar clauses, adapted to the particular taste of each organization or the circumstances of specific cases, are found in agreements between the IADB, the ECSC or the EIB and their respective loan partners.

[101] See the provisions quoted in notes 96, 98, 99 and 100 supra.

[102] *SEC Report,* p. 15.

negative-pledge clauses provide the lenders with a substantial assurance of equality of treatment. Furthermore, these clauses may operate as a check against excessive borrowing by enabling the lenders to insist on sharing in a particular security transaction thereby making potential creditors wary of lending. In this respect, a negative-pledge clause may help achieve one of the most important objectives pursued by secured lenders, namely establishing a limit on the borrowing capacity of the debtor.[103]

---

[103] Note, however, that negative-pledge clauses do not prevent the borrower from selling or otherwise disposing of its assets, a fact which may adversely affect its financial position and the rights of its creditors. This idea is clearly expressed in the following provision in an indenture between an American trustee and a foreign corporation:

"The Company will not, so long as any of the Debentures shall be outstanding, voluntarily create or permit to be created any lien on any real estate now owned by the Company (*so long as such real estate shall be owned by it*) unless it shall secure all of the Debentures equally and ratably with the other obligations secured by such lien so long as such other obligations are so secured." (emphasis added)

Chapter VI

Maintenance-Of-Value Clauses

After a period of temporary disuse, maintenance-of-value clauses have progressively regained the favor of a large segment of the international financial community.

When World War II ended, maintenance-of-value clauses, and in particular gold and multiple-currency clauses, were rarely used in the private sector of international lending. In that sector, these clauses were usually omitted. Even if included, they could not be implemented properly, for example because of currency restrictions and existing exchange-control regulations.

In the years immediately following the War, the situation remained substantially the same. It is true that because of the considerable increase in the volume of intergovernmental transactions, and the creation of international lending organizations whose capital and other resources had to be protected against currency depreciation, maintenance-of-value clauses acquired an unprecedented importance. However, these clauses were essentially confined to the public sector of international lending.

With the gradual removal of exchange and other restrictions, and the improvement of market conditions, maintenance-of-value clauses soon reappeared in securities issued in the private capital market. They reappeared first in the form of multiple-currency clauses and later in the form of covenants expressed in "units of account," whose declared purpose is to increase the financial stability of international loans while avoiding the legal or economic objections to which gold clauses may still be subject.

So far, however, this renewed use of maintenance-of-value clauses in international loans is essentially a European phenomenon. With one remarkable exception in the form of a multiple-currency clause in dollar bonds issued by the Republic of Austria in 1958, maintenance of value clauses have failed to reappear in the United States market. Whether financial or legal factors are responsible for this situation is an interesting matter of speculation.

SECTION I. MAINTENANCE-OF-VALUE CLAUSES IN THE PUBLIC SECTOR OF INTERNATIONAL LENDING

A. INTERGOVERNMENTAL TRANSACTIONS

The overwhelming majority of intergovernmental loans and loans made by governments to international organizations are denominated in the currency of the lender government and contain no maintenance-of-value clause.[1]

Some of these agreements do give the borrower the right to repay the loan either in the currency in which the loan is denominated or in gold, at his option.[2] In these cases, however, it is clear that gold as such is not *in obligatione* but merely *in facultate solutionis*, and that repayment in gold is considered only as a convenient means for

---

[1] This is the general practice of Canada, the United States, and the countries in Western Europe. Occasionally, intergovernmental loans are denominated in the currency of a third country. See e.g., the reference to: (i) the English pound sterling in the Agreement dated July 2, 1947, between New Zealand and France (16 UNTS 219); and (ii) the United States Dollar in the Agreement dated June 6, 1959, between Yugoslavia and Ethiopia (386 UNTS 243).

[2] See e.g., the Agreement dated October 25, 1945, between Canada and Belgium (230 UNTS 127), providing for a Canadian dollar loan to Belgium and stipulating that Belgium shall have the option to repay the loan in Canadian dollars or in gold and that, in the latter alternative:

> "the value of fine gold shall be calculated on the basis of the buying price of gold of the Canadian Foreign Exchange Control Board (or successor agency) on the date of its delivery" (Article 9).

A similar provision is found in the Agreement dated February 5, 1946, between Canada and the Netherlands (43 UNTS 3) Article 9. See also, the Agreement dated October 15, 1945, between the United States and the USSR, regarding the disposition of lend-lease supplies (278 UNTS 151). Article II provides that the USSR may elect to make payment in dollars or in gold:

> "which will be valued at the buying price for gold provided in the provisional regulations issued under the Gold Reserve Act of 1934 as the same may be in effect at the time of each delivery [of gold]."

The Agreement dated July 25, 1947, between the USSR and Yugoslavia (130 UNTS 315), Article 10, regarding the repayment of a U.S. dollar 135 million credit, provides that:

> "Gold shall be accepted by the State Bank at Moscow at the official rate of gold at New York on the date of payment after deduction of expenses in connection with the transfer of gold to New York."

the borrower to discharge a financial obligation whose quantum may vary with the fluctuation of the designated currency.

A different situation is presented by most of the financial agreements between Russia and other socialist countries or neutral nations. In contrast to Western countries, the USSR makes an extensive use of gold clauses in its agreements with borrowing nations. A typical example is the 1950 agreement between the USSR and Communist China, which provides for a loan of "US $300 million, at the rate of US $35 per ounce of fine gold," repayable in dollars.[3]

Another example is the 1959 agreement with Iraq[4], which is substantially more complex than the simple arrangement with China. The Iraq agreement provides for a "500 million roubles (1 rouble is equivalent to 0.222168 gramme of fine gold)" and specifies that if during a seven year period of disbursement the gold value of the rouble is altered:

> "The portions of the loan expressed in roubles shall [in order to] preserve the gold equivalent of the amount of the loan, be recalculated in accordance with such change" (Article 5).

The agreement further provides that service payments will be made as follows:

> "The repayment of the loan and the payment of accrued interest thereon shall be made by the Government of the Republic of Iraq by the deposit of the sums due in Iraqi dinars (1 dinar = 2.48828 grammes of fine gold) in a separate account to be opened in the Central Bank of Iraq in the name of the State Bank of the USSR.
>
> The conversion of roubles into Iraqi dinars shall be effected on the basis of the gold value of the rouble and the Iraqi dinar on the day of payment.
>
> The sums deposited in this account may be used by the Soviet Union for the purchase of Iraqi goods in accordance with the terms of the Trade Agreement in force between the USSR and the Republic of Iraq and/or may be converted into a convertible currency to be determined by agreement between the State Bank of the USSR and the Central Bank of the Republic of Iraq.
>
> The conversion of Iraqi dinars into the convertible currency

---

[3] Agreement dated February 14, 1950 (226 UNTS 25), Article 1. Although reference to gold in connection with the repayment of dollars by Communist China is omitted from the relevant provision of the Agreement (Article 3) there can be little doubt that the latter provision is governed also by the gold definition contained in Article 1.

[4] Agreement dated March 16, 1959 (346 UNTS 107).

shall be effected on the basis of the gold value of the two currencies on the day of conversion.

If the exchange rate of the Iraqi dinar is changed, the balance existing in the account of the State Bank of the USSR in the Central Bank of the Republic of Iraq on the day of such change shall be adjusted proportionally to the change which has taken place in the gold value of the Iraqi dinar."[5]

Another type of arrangement is found in the 1960 agreement providing for a "US $100 million (1 dollar = 0.888671 gramme of fine gold)" credit to Cuba.[6] Under the agreement, the credit is to be repaid in equal instalments over a twelve-year period in the form of deliveries of sugar or other Cuban goods and/or freely convertible currencies. In the latter case:

"Conversion of the freely convertible currencies into US dollars shall be made at the official dollar exchange rate on the day of payment.

In the event of any change in the gold content of the US dollar referred to in Article 1 of this Agreement, the balance of the accounts referred to in this Article shall be adjusted to offset such change."[7]

---

[5] Article 7. See also, the Agreement dated November 9, 1957, between India and the USSR for co-operation in establishing industrial enterprises in India (Government of India, New Delhi, 1957), Article V:

"(1) The Government of the USSR will extend credit to the Government of India for 500,000,000 (five hundred million) roubles (one rouble equals to 0.222168 gramme of fine gold) . . .

(6) Payments to cover the credit and interest accrued thereof shall be effected in Indian rupees (one rupee equals to 0.186621 gramme of fine gold . . . Roubles shall be recalculated into rupees basing on the aforesaid gold parity of the rouble and the rupee . . .

(7) In case of change in the gold parity of the Indian rupee, with the exception of cases when a change in the gold parity of the rupee is brought about by a change of the official price of gold in US dollars (the price of one troy ounce of gold equals 35 US dollars), the balance of the account with the Reserve Bank of India on the date of such change will be revalued proportionately to the change of the gold parity of the rupee."

Comp., the Agreement dated December 1, 1962, between the USSR and Laos, 472 UNTS 3 (Articles 4 and 6).

[6] Agreement dated February 13, 1960 (369 UNTS 3).

[7] Article 5. The reference to conversion at the rate of exchange on the day of payment appears also in an Agreement dated June 2, 1961, between the USSR and the Somali Republic (457 UNTS 263). However, this Agreement makes no reference to possible variations in the gold content of the rouble in which the loan is expressed. This omission is rather surprising since the rouble used as currency of reference is defined in terms of its gold content.

All these agreements, regardless of the variations between them, present the common feature that they clearly define at the outset the terms of disbursement and repayment. In certain cases, however, these terms are left flexible. A good illustration is found in the 1954 agreement providing for a loan to Finland:[8]

".... in gold, United States dollars or other currencies as agreed upon between the State Bank of the USSR and the Bank of Finland, to a total amount equivalent to 8,886,720 grammes of fine gold, or 40 million roubles on the basis of a rouble fine-gold content of 0.222168 gramme."

The agreement provides further that:

"Repayment of the loan shall be made in gold—the quantity of which shall not be less than received—in United States dollars or in some other currency agreed upon between the Banks, such dollars and currency to be calculated in roubles on the basis of their gold parity rate on the date of repayment and of a rouble fine-gold content of 0.222168 gramme" (Article 4).[9]

An Agreement dated February 28, 1960, between the USSR and Indonesia (392 UNTS 173) does not raise the same problem since the currency of reference, i.e. the U.S. dollar, is not defined as a "gold" dollar. Reliance, for conversion purposes, upon the rate of exchange at the time of payment between the US dollar and the other currencies in which the loan may be repaid is, therefore, understandable.

[8] Agreement dated February 6, 1954 (221 UNTS 143) A simpler solution was that of the Agreement dated February 2, 1956, between the USSR and Yugoslavia (259 UNTS 111), providing for a loan to be disbursed by agreement between the parties "in United States dollars, in other convertible currencies or in gold" (Article 1) and to be repaid "in United States dollars, in other convertible currencies or in gold, according to the form in which the loan was drawn. (Article 4).

[9] There is an interesting resemblance between the above-quoted provision and the stipulation commonly found in agreements for the repayment of credits granted within the framework of the former European Union. These agreements usually gave the debtor the option to repay the credit:

"(i) in gold or (ii) in United States dollars calculated at the official price for gold of the United States Treasury at the date of payment or (iii) in any other currency acceptable to [the creditor country]. If the payment is made otherwise than in gold or United States dollars the amount of the payment shall be calculated at a rate of exchange, between the unit of account and the currency of payment, agreed between the two Contracting Governments."

Since the "unit of account" referred to in this stipulation was defined in terms of gold (i.e., 0.88867088 gramme of fine gold, see EPU Agreement dated September 19, 1950, article 26, Clunet 1950, 996), the second sentence of the stipulation did not materially vary the terms of the gold clause contained in the first sentence. See e.g., Delaume, "Gold and Currency Clauses in Contemporary International Loans", 9 Am. J. Comp. L. 199 (1960), at p. 202

In view of the use of gold clauses in contemporary intergovernmental

B. THE TRANSACTIONS OF INTERNATIONAL
   LENDING ORGANIZATIONS

With the creation of international lending organizations since
World War II, and the need to maintain the value of their respective
capital resources, (lest their respective credit and operations be at
the mercy of currency fluctuations), maintenance-of-value clauses have
received considerable attention.

Though the capital resources of most international lending organizations are expressed in terms of gold,[10] a substantial part of these
resources consist not of gold but of currency holdings derived from
subscription payments made by members in their own currency or in
freely convertible currencies.[11] To protect the value of these currency holdings, the respective charters of most lending organizations
provide in effect that if the par value of a member's currency is reduced, or if, in the opinion of the organization involved, its foreign
exchange value has depreciated to a significant extent, the member
must pay to the organization, within a reasonable time, an additional
amount of its own currency sufficient to maintain the gold value of
the organization's holdings of that currency.[12]

---

agreements, the view expressed by Mann (*Money in Public International Law*,
96 Recueil des Cours 7 (1959), at p. 118) that:

> "There is hardly any treaty in the books, which contains an elaborate
> gold clause making it clear whether the clause is merely a descriptive
> "clause de style", whether it is a gold coin, gold value or gold bullion
> clause, how the weight and fineness of the gold is to be ascertained or as
> at what date such determination has to be made."

appears outdated. This does not mean, of course, that all international agreements are equally well drafted and that some of them do not show a remarkable lack of precision as to the determination of the exact quantum of the
obligation. See e.g., the Agreement dated February 2, 1956, between the USSR
and Yugoslavia referred to in the preceding note.

[10] Expressing capital resources in terms of gold is not without precedent.
For example, the authorized capital of the Bank for International Settlements (BIS) in Basle, Switzerland, created in 1930, is expressed in terms of
"500 million Swiss Gold francs equivalent to 145,161,290.32 grammes of fine
gold" (Article 5 of the Statutes of the BIS).

An exception to the general rule is that of the International Finance Corporation (IFC) whose authorized capital is expressed in United States dollars
without any definition of the dollar's weight and fineness (IFC, Articles of
Agreement, Article II, Section 2(a)).

[11] See the Statutes of the EIB (Articles 4 and 5); and the Articles of
Agreement of the IBRD (Article II, Sections 2 and 7); the IDA (Article II,
Section 2); and the IADB (Article II, Sections 2 and 4).

[12] See the Statutes of the EIB (Article 7, paragraph 1); and the Articles
of Agreement of the IBRD (Article II, Section 9(a)); the IDA (Article IV,
Section 3(a) and (d)); and the IADB (Article V, Section 3(a)).

The scope of this maintenance-of-value obligation varies greatly, however, depending upon whether the concept of "currency holdings" is limited to amounts initially paid in by members and not yet used by the relevant organization in its operations; or whether the concept is broadened to include also amounts outstanding on loans made or disbursed in the currency of a member paid on account of its capital subscription. In the first instance, the organization involved, if it does not wish to assume the risk of monetary depreciation following the use of a member's currency for lending purposes, must find appropriate means to pass the risk on to the borrower. In the second instance, the organization may rely on the member's maintenance-of-value obligation to make up for any loss arising from the depreciation of the member's currency between the date of disbursement and the date of repayment. The respective practices of the IDA and the IBRD nicely illustrate the problem.

The Articles of Agreement of the IDA provide that the maintenance-of-value obligations of a member shall apply only to the extent that the currency of that member paid on account of its capital subscription has not been disbursed or exchanged by the IDA for the currency of another member.[13] This provision makes it clear that the IDA bears the risk of currency depreciation once it has used a member's currency for lending purposes. In order to offset this risk, the IDA currently insists upon stipulating in its credit agreements with borrowers that the principal amount of the credit repayable to the IDA:

> "shall be the equivalent (determined as of the date, or respective dates of repayment) of the value of the currency or currencies withdrawn from the Credit Account expressed in terms of United States dollars of the weight and fineness in effect on January 1,

---

This maintenance-of-value obligation continues to obtain even in the event of a uniform proportionate change in the par values of the currencies of all members of the relevant organization. In that case, however, a waiver is possible. See the Statutes of the EIB (Article 7, paragraph 4); and the Articles of Agreement of the IBRD (Article II, Section 9 (c)); the IDA (Article IV, Section 2 (c)); and the IADB (Article V, Section 3 (c)). The relevant decision can be taken by a majority vote.

The respective charters of these organizations also provide that if the par value of a member's currency is increased, the organization involved shall return to the member, within a reasonable time, an amount of that member's currency equal to the increase in the value such currency held by the organization. See the Statutes of the EIB (Article 7, paragraph 2); and the Articles of Agreement of the IBRD (Article II, Section 9 (b)); the IDA (Article IV, Section 2 (b)); and the IADB (Article V, Section 3 (b)).

[13] IDA, Articles of Agreement, Article IV, Section 2 (a).

1960 [i.e. the gold dollar in which the IDA's capital is expressed],
determined as of the respective dates of withdrawal."[14]

In other words, and subject to two important exceptions which
may import a desirable flexibility into the IDA's practice,[15] the general rule is that the outstanding amount of each IDA credit is originally (i.e. at the time of each disbursement) computed in terms of
gold and is repaid on the same basis.

The IBRD, when it began its first lending operations, was faced
with a situation somewhat comparable to that of the IDA. Though
the IBRD's Articles of Agreement provide for the value maintenance
of certain "currency holdings,"[16] it is not clear whether this expression applies only to the cash balances of the members' currencies
paid in and "held" by the IBRD, or whether it also covers amounts
in these currencies outstanding on loans. Under the first interpretation, the IBRD would have been exposed to losses resulting from
currency depreciation. Its initial response to this problem was to shift
the risk of depreciation to borrowers, and request them to repay in
the currency or currencies disbursed an amount equivalent to the
currency in which the loan was denominated, i.e. the United States
dollar.[17]

---

[14] Development Credit Regulations, Section 3.03.

[15] The first exception (Section 3.03 (i)) applies in the case of a uniform
proportionate reduction in the par values of the currencies of all the members of the IMF. In that case, amounts outstanding on credits are automatically
reduced by the same proportion as that by which the par value of currencies
are reduced.

The second exception (Section 3.03 (ii)) concerns the case of a substantial
reduction in the par value or the foreign-exchange value of one or more
major currencies of IDA members in terms of the gold-dollar reference used
by the IDA. In that case, the IDA, if it deems it appropriate, may decide that
the reduction in the value of the currency or currencies involved justifies a
general reduction in the principal amount repayable on development credits
then outstanding.

[16] Articles of Agreement, Article II, Section 9.

[17] See e.g., the Loan Agreement between the IBRD and Crédit National
pour faciliter la Réparation des Dommages Causés par la Guerre, dated
March 9, 1947 (152 UNTS 111, Article II, Section 9). Even at the time of
this loan, the first made by the IBRD, it was careful enough to provide that:
"If and when it shall be finally decided in accordance with Article IX
of the Articles of Agreement of the Bank that the provisions of Section 9
of Article II of such Articles are applicable to currencies of members
paid on account of their subscriptions to the capital stock of the Bank
during any period which such currencies have been loaned by the Bank,
this Section shall cease to apply."
After the interpretation of the Articles of Agreement by the Executive
Directors on May 23, 1950, which gave affirmative answer to this question, the
above-quoted provision ceased to be applicable.

This solution, however, had several inconveniences. In the first place, the dollar-equivalent clause in loan agreements failed to reflect the multi-currency element in the IBRD's lending resources and operations. Further, the clause did not protect the organization against a possible depreciation of the dollar. For these and other reasons, the matter was referred to the Executive Directors of the IBRD who, under the power of interpretation vested in them,[18] decided on May 23, 1950, that the maintenance-of-value obligation should be broadly construed and applied to currencies outstanding on loans.

As an immediate consequence of this interpretation, the dollar-equivalent clause disappeared from the IBRD loan agreements. All that these agreements now provide is that the borrower shall repay to the IBRD the amount of the currency disbursed.[19] The IBRD relies on the members whose currency is involved to make good any loss resulting from the depreciation of their currency between the date of disbursement and that of repayment,[20] a solution which is

---

[18] Articles of Agreement, Article IX. Regarding the interpretation by international organizations of their Articles of Agreement, see e.g., *Broches*, pp. 364, 369-370; Fawcet, "The Place of Law in an International Organization", 36 B.Y.B.I.L. 321 (1960), at pp. 329-336; Gold, "The Interpretation by the International Monetary Fund of its Articles of Agreement", 3 Int'l & Comp. L. Q. 256 (1954); Hexner, "Interpretation by International Organizations of their Basic Instruments", 53 Am. J. Int'l L. 341 (1959).

[19] This rule is subject to one exception. If the currency disbursed (e.g. dollar, sterling or Swiss franc) has been purchased with another currency (e.g. DM), the loan is to that extent repayable in the latter currency (DM in this example). See Loan Regulations No. 3 and No. 4, Section 3.03 (a) reading as follows:

> "The principal of the Loan shall be repayable in the several currencies withdrawn from the Loan Account and the amount repayable in each currency shall be the amount withdrawn in that currency. The foregoing provision is subject to one exception, namely: if withdrawal shall be made in any currency which the Bank shall have purchased with another currency for the purpose of such withdrawal, the portion of the Loan so withdrawn shall be repayable in such other currency and the amount so repayable shall be the amount paid by the Bank on such purchase."

[20] There remains one difference, however, between the IBRD's members' maintenance-of-value obligations regarding cash balances of their currency, and amounts of such currency outstanding on loans, respectively. In the first case, the obligation accrues immediately upon a reduction of the par value of the currency concerned or a notification by the IBRD that a depreciation of such currency has occurred. In the second instance, the member's obligation is postponed until its currency has been effectively repaid to the IBRD.

It should be noted, however, that the maintenance-of-value provision does not protect the IBRD against the loss corresponding to interest payments in a depreciating currency between the time such currency begins to depreciate and the time the loan is repaid.

Furthermore, the 1950 interpretation of the IBRD Articles of Agreement does not apply to the IBRD's holdings of non-member currencies, such at

now expressly embodied in the charter of sister organizations like the EIB.[21]

The foregoing remarks apply only to the maintenance-of-value of currency holdings derived from capital subscription payments. Amounts borrowed in the private-capital market or from other sources, are not covered by the maintenance-of-value obligation. However, since the borrowings made by international lending organizations rarely carry a gold or other maintenance-of-value clause,[21a] the risk

the Swiss franc, frequently used in IBRD's lending operations. However, a devaluation or depreciation of the latter currency would raise no serious problem for the IBRD. To the extent that the Swiss francs held by the IBRD come out of its own borrowings in Switzerland, the IBRD would suffer no loss from a devaluation of that currency, since the IBRD's loans raised in Switzerland contain no valorisation clause. A loss on loans made out of Swiss francs would, therefore, be offset by a corresponding gain on borrowings in the same currency.

If the Swiss francs lent by the IBRD have been purchased by it with another currency, e.g. marks, the borrower is obliged to repay marks to the IBRD and, to the extent that the mark would depreciate, the IBRD would be protected by the maintenance-of-value provision described in the text above, with the result that Germany would have to pay to the IBRD an additional amount of marks to maintain the gold value of the IBRD's holdings of German currency.

[21] EIB, Statutes, Article 7, paragraph 1:
"Where the par value of the currency of a Member State in relation to the unit of account as defined in Article 4 (i.e. in terms of gold) is reduced, the amount of that State's share of the capital paid up by it in its national currency shall be adjusted, proportionately to the change occurring in the par value, by a complementary payment made to the credit of the Bank by the State concerned. The amount subject to adjustment may not, however, exceed the *total amount of loans granted by the Bank in the currency concerned and the Bank's holdings in that currency. The complementary payment shall be made within a period of two months or, to the extent that it corresponds to such loans, on the dates on which such loans shall fall due*" (Underlining supplied).

This provision, like the corresponding one in the case of the IBRD, does not protect the EIB for the loss incurred in connection with interest payments between the time when the currency involved depreciates and the time when additional payments are made to maintain the value of such currency.

Regarding the lending practice of the EIB, see e.g., Dupont, "Les Institutions Internationales Bancaires pour le Financement du Développement", in I *Les Banques de Développement dans le Monde* (1963) 67, at p. 182; Barre, "La Banque Européenne d'Investissement", Droit Social 1961, 197, at p. 202; Sertoli, "The Structure and Financial Activities of the European Regional Communities", 26 Law & Contemporary Problems (Summer 1961) 515, at p. 535.

[21a] An exception is found in the General Arrangements to Borrow between the IMF and certain of its members. Under the Arrangements the IMF is obligated to repay to the member involved, in the member's currency, an

of monetary depreciation affecting the repayment of loans made out of borrowed currencies is non-existent. Any loss on a loan made out of borrowed funds would be offset by a corresponding profit on the amount repayable by the organization to its own creditors.

SECTION II. MAINTENANCE-OF-VALUE CLAUSES IN THE PRIVATE SECTOR OF INTERNATIONAL LENDING

A. GOLD CLAUSES AND CURRENCY OPTIONS

During the pre-World War II era, the two major devices used to protect lenders against monetary fluctuations were gold clauses and currency options. Of these two devices, only one (i.e. currency options) has now regained its pre-War status, while the gold clause has fallen into disuse.[22]

The first reappearance of currency options in post-World War II loans by private lenders to foreign borrowers originated in Switzerland in connection with a 1950 loan issued by the Anglo-American Corporation of South Africa Ltd., a South African corporation. The bonds of that issue give the holder the option to claim payment in Switzerland, in Swiss francs; or in South Africa, in South African pounds which can be used in that country or converted into United States dollars or such other currency as the South African Reserve Bank may authorize from time to time.[23] In this and other cases, the

---

amount equivalent to the gold value of that currency at the time of the loan. The IMF, however, incurs no risk since, after a sale to another member for its currency of the currency borrowed by the IMF, the gold value of the repurchase obligation of the purchasing member will, under the relevant provisions of the IMF Articles of Agreement, be maintained. As stated by Gold: ". . . The Fund, having borrowed currency for the benefit of a purchaser, will always receive from the purchaser the equivalent in gold value of what the Fund will be bound to repay to the lender" (*Maintenance of the Gold Value of the Fund's Assets* (IMF, 1965), pp. 28-29).

[22] This remark assumes that the "unit of account" formula discussed below in the text is not itself a gold clause.

The unpopularity of gold clauses is not necessarily attributable to legal factors. In a number of countries, particularly in Europe, gold clauses in international loans would still be valid notwithstanding the statutory enactments of the nineteen thirties. In those countries at least, the disappearance of gold clauses is probably due to a clear perception of the fact, noted by the Financial Committee of the League of Nations, that:

". . . a gold clause may well be so rigid in the only circumstances in which it would be called into application as to be likely in fact to be ineffective . . ." (*L. N. Report*, Annex 1, para. 8).

[23] 4% Loan of 1950, prospectus, clauses 1 and 4.

alternative promises are completely independent: payment in each
currency can be requested only in the designated country, and variations in the value of one currency do not affect the amounts payable
in the other currency.[24]

A second type of currency option is found in the 1953 loan issued
in Switzerland by the Belgian Congo with the guarantee of the Belgian Government. These bonds give the holder the option to claim
payment in Switzerland in Swiss francs, or in the Belgian Congo in
Congolese francs at the fixed rate of exchange of 11.40 Congolese
francs per one Swiss franc.[25]

With the improvement of the economy of other European countries and the relaxation of exchange controls, currency options soon
reappeared in bonds issued in Germany,[26] Luxembourg,[27] the United
Kingdom[28] and other countries.[29]

Outside Europe, currency options have been stipulated in foreign

-----

[24] See e.g., Orange Free State Investment Trust, Ltd., 4½% Loan of
1952; Government of Australia 4% Loan of 1953; Electricity Supply Commission (ESCOM) Johannesburgh 5% Loan of 1959.

[25] 4% Loan of 1953, Prospectus clauses 4 and 6. Similar provisions are
found also in other "Congolese" loans issued in Switzerland in 1950, 1952 and
1956, except that the rate of exchange between the "Congolese" and Swiss
currency was the object of various definitions.

[26] Anglo-American Corporation of South Africa, Ltd., 5½% Loan of
1958:
"All payments of principal and interest are to be made in Deutsche Mark.
The bondholders are [however] entitled to request such payment to be
made in South African currency at a fixed conversion rate of South African £1 = 11.70 DM" (as translated).
See also, the City of Oslo 5½% Loan of 1959 and the Sabena 5¾% Loan
of 1959, both providing for an option between the DM and the US dollar.

[27] ECSC 4¾% Bonds of 1962, providing for an option between Luxembourg francs, DM (at the fixed rate of exchange of F. Lux. 12.50 = DM 1.00)
or US dollar (at the fixed rate of F. Lux. 50 = $1.00).

[28] City of Turin £5 million 6½ per cent. Sterling/Deutsche Mark Bonds
1984 (issued in 1964), providing that:
"Payments will be made in sterling or at the option of the bearer in
Deutsche Marks of the Federal Republic of Germany at the fixed rate of
DM 11.06 to £1. . . ."
This is the first loan since World War II expressed in sterling with a cur-
rency option.

[29] Thus the Argentine Republic 6½% External Loan 1961/1973 of US
$25 million was placed by a syndicate of 17 leading European banks, includ-
ing banks in Switzerland, Germany, Belgium, England, France, Italy and the
Netherlands. Under the bonds, the holder has an option to demand pay-
ment in US dollars, Swiss francs, DM, Belgian francs, sterling, French francs,
Italian lire or Dutch Guilders. The relevant provisions read as follows:
"Article I
The Government creates a Loan of a nominal amount of US $25,000,000
. . . or its equivalent in Swiss francs, Deutsche mark, Belgian francs,

bonds issued in Canada[30] and the United States. Thus, the 1958
bonds of the Republic of Austria provide for payment:

> Pounds sterling, New French francs, Italian lire and Dutch guilders, that
> is to say in the nominal amount of Sw. Fcs. 108,250,000. . . . or DM
> 100,000,000. . . . or B. Fcs. 1,250,000,000. . . . or £ 8,928,571.8.7 . . . or
> NF 123,426,500. . . . or Lit. 15,625,000,000. . . . or Fl. 90,500,000. . . . in
> Bearer Bonds of the Argentine Public Debt which will carry interest at
> the rate of 6½% . . . per annum and which will be redeemed in the
> amounts and on the conditions indicated below.
>
> *Article II*
> The Loan shall be represented by 20,000 Bearer Bonds of US $500.-
> nominal value each or its equivalent of Sw. Fcs. 2,165. . . . or DM 2,000.
> . . . or B. Fcs. 25,000. . . . or £178.11.5 . . . or NF 2,468.53 . . . or
> Lit. 312,500. . . . or Fl. 1,810. . . . Nos. 1 to 20,000 and by 15,000 Bearer
> Bonds of US $1,000.-nominal value each or its equivalent of Sw. Fcs.
> 4,330. . . . or DM 4,000. . . . or B. Fcs. 50,000. . . . or £357.2.10 . . . or
> NF 4,937.06 . . . or Lit. 625,000. . . . or Fl. 3,620. . . . Nos. 20,001 to
> 35,000.
>
> *Article VII*
> The coupons to be attached to each Bond of US $500.— (five hundred
> dollars) will each be in the amount of US $16.25 . . . or Sw. Fcs. 70.36 . . .
> or DM 65. . . . or B. Fcs. 812.50 . . . or £5.16.1 . . . or NF 80.227
> . . . or Lit. 10,156.25 . . . or Fl. 58.82 . . . The coupons to be attached
> to each Bond of US $1,000. . . . will each be in the amount of US $32.50
> . . . or Sw. Fcs. 140.72 . . . or DM 130. . . . or B. Fcs. 1,625. . . . or
> £11.12.2 . . . or NF 160.454 . . . or Lit. 20,312.50 . . . or FL. 117.65 . . .
>
> The rates of exchange used for the calculation of these equivalents as
> well as of those indicated in Articles I and II are the following: 4.33
> Swiss francs per US $1.—; 4.— Deutsche mark per US $1.—; 50.— Belgian
> francs per US $1.—; 2.80 US dollars per £1.—.—; 4.93706 New French
> francs per US $1.—; 625 Italian lire per US $1.— and 3.62 Dutch guilders
> per US $1.—.
>
> *Article VIII*
> The payment of the coupons and of the Bonds due for repayment will,
> at the option of the bondholder, take place either in US dollars or at the
> equivalent in the legal currency of Switzerland, Germany, Belgium, Eng-
> land, France, Italy or the Netherlands in the amounts indicated in Arti-
> cles II and VII respectively, regardless of the domicile of the Paying
> Agent.
>
> In order to obtain payment in a currency other than US dollars, the
> bondholders will have to present their coupons and/or Bonds to any
> of the banks named in Article IX hereunder thirty days before maturity,
> i.e. before June 1st or December 1st, as may be appropriate, with the
> irrevocable order to cash such coupons and/or Bonds at their due dates
> in the currency indicated by the respective holders.
>
> Any coupons and/or Bonds not presented before the dates indicated
> above will be paid on presentation in US dollars.
>
> Payment of interest and capital will be effected by cheque or by trans-
> fer. Payment in cash is only obtainable by the bondholders in the cur-
> rency of the country where the payment is made."

[30] Pertofina, S.A. (a Belgian corporation) 5½%-7½% Debentures of
1957:
"Principal and interest will be payable in lawful money of the United

"in New York . . . in such coin or currency of the United States
as at the time of payment is legal tender for public and private
debts, or at the option of the holder, (i) in Vienna, Austria . . .
in Austrian schillings at the fixed rate of 26 schillings per U.S.A.
dollar, or (ii) in London . . . in British pounds at the fixed rate
of one pound per 2.80 U.S.A. dollar, or (iii) in Frankfurt a/M,
Germany . . . in German marks of the Federal Republic of Germany at the fixed rate of 4.20 marks per U.S.A. dollar . . ."[31]

In view of the controversial character of American judicial decisions invalidating currency options, at least when one of the currencies
in obligatione is the United States dollar,[32] the exact legal status of the

---

States of America or, at the holder's option, in its equivalent in lawful
money of Belgium, Switzerland or the Netherlands at the fixed rates of
exchange of 50.35 Belgian francs, 4.285 Swiss francs and 3.83 Dutch florins
to $1 US respectively . . ."
This provision reads further:
". . . or, at the holder's option, in its equivalent in lawful money of
Canada either (i) at the prevailing buying rate of exchange at the
time and place of payment on the due date, or (ii) if payment is made
subsequent to said due date, at the closing buying rate of exchange at
the place of payment on said due date . . ."
thereby adding to the currency option (*option de change*) contained in the
first quoted sentence, an option of collection (*option de place*) making it
possible for the holder, after selecting one of the currencies *in obligatione*,
to obtain the equivalent thereof, at the current rate of exchange, in Canadian
currency, the currency *in solutione*.

[31] Republic of Austria 5½% External Sinking Fund Dollar Bonds of 1958.
Prospectus p. 3. According to the prospectus,
"The bonds will also provide that the above-mentioned provisions relating to payment in any currency other than USA dollars shall be governed by the laws of the country in which such payment is to be made."
The exact meaning of this provision is obscure. The provision cannot be
construed as a stipulation of applicable law governing the substance of the
debt. Its scope must be limited to matters relating not to the quantum of
the debt but merely to the manner and medium of payment, in which case
the provision would seem to constitute a tautology.

[32] See, Guaranty Trust Co. of New York v. Henwood, 307 U.S. 247 (1939);
Bethlehem Steel Co. v. Zurich General Accident and Liability Ins. Co., 307
U.S. 265 (1939). But see, Anglo-Continentale Treuhand, A.G. v. St. Louis
Southwestern Ry. 81 F 2d 11 (2d cir. 1936), cert. den. 298 U.S. 655; Eng-
lish Transcontinental Ltd. v. Puebla Tramway Light and Power Co., 61 N.Y.S.
2d 356, 186 Misc. 481 (1946).
See e.g., *Nussbaum,* pp. 435-436; *Mann,* p. 156, note 5. See also, Steven-
son, "Legal Aspects of the Public Offering of Foreign Securities in the United
States Market", 28 Geo. Wash. L. Rev. 194 (1959), at pp. 198-200; Note, "The
Unit of Account: Enforceability under American Law of Maintenance-of-Value
Provisions in International Loans", 71 Yale L. J. 1294 (1962), at pp. 1301-
1312.

above stipulation is not free of doubt. It may be significant that this attempt to reintroduce currency options in American lending practice has not been repeated.[33]

B. LOANS EXPRESSED IN EUROPEAN UNITS OF ACCOUNT

The great advantage of currency options is that they give creditors the assurance that, should any of the currencies involved depreciate or be devalued, the creditor will be able to request payment in the strongest currency. From the borrower's viewpoint, however, currency options may constitute a heavy burden. This is particularly true if one of the currencies is revalued rather than devalued, since in that case the borrower may be forced to pay more than he had bargained for.[34]

In order to achieve an equitable distribution of the monetary risk between lenders and borrowers, and to promote the development of a European capital market by facilitating the simultaneous placement of loans in several markets,[35] a new stabilization formula has been devised.

Under this formula, loans, rather than being denominated in a national currency, are expressed in terms of an agreed measure of value, called the "unit of account," with a specific gold content de-

---

[33] Clarification of the status of maintenance-of-value clauses in the United States by means of congressional action has been suggested as the most effective method to dispel persisting doubts regarding the validity of these clauses. See Note, "The Unit of Account, etc." referred to in the preceding note, at p. 1315.

[34] This situation, though infrequent, is far from theoretical. An example is the 5% revaluation of the Deutsche Mark in 1961. To the extent that bondholders of the Republic of Austria loan of 1958 (see text and note 31 above), elected to be repaid in DM, the revaluation increased the Republic's debt.

[35] See e.g., Collin, *The Formation of a European Market* (1964) pp. 11-16. Blondeel, "A New Form of International Financing: Loans in European Units of Account", 64 Col. L. Rev. 995 (1964), at p. 995; Segré, "Foreign Bond Issues in European Markets", 68 Banca Nazionale del Lavoro 43 (1964), at p. 66; Elman, "Move Toward Development of a European Capital Market", Export Trade December 16, 1963, p. 10; Jonckheere, "L'Unité de Compte: une Formule Peu Connue", 22 Annales de Sciences Economiques Appliquées 185 (1964), at pp. 206-207; van der Mensbrugghe, "Bond Issues in European Units of Account", 11 IMF Staff Papers 446 (1964) ; Ingram, "Unit-of-Account Bonds; Their Meaning and Function", Moorgate and Wall Street (London) Autumn 1964, pp. 65-80; Abs. "The European Security and New Issues Market with a view to International Financing" Report of the Deutsche Bank, A.G., presented to the Institut International d'Études Bancaires, November 6, 1964, p. 51.

fined at the time of issue.[36] The purpose of the formula is to maintain the value of the lenders' claim as constant as possible throughout the life of the loan. However, variations in the gold content of the unit of account are made possible by tying its fate to that of seventeen European currencies[37] (the currencies of reference) whose value at the time of issue (the base value) is determined by comparing their respective gold values with that of the unit of account.

These variations, which make it impossible to consider the formula a gold clause in disguise,[38] are subject to strict conditions. No change in the value of the unit of account is possible unless the gold values of each currency of reference has been altered. In other words, as long as at least one of the currencies of reference has not been devalued or revalued, the lender is assured that the value of his claim remains unaffected by individual variations in the base value of one or several currencies of reference.[39]

If the base value of all the currencies of reference have changed, the value of the unit of account may change also, but only if at least two-thirds of the currencies of reference have moved in the same direction. In other words, variations of the currencies of reference in different directions would leave the definition of the unit of account intact if a two-third majority cannot be ascertained.

If both conditions are fulfilled, the gold value of the unit of account is adjusted in the same direction as the currencies of reference

---

[36] The content at present is 0.88867088 gramme of gold (equal to the unit of account of the former European Payments Union).

[37] These are the currencies of Austria, Belgium, Denmark, France, Federal Republic of Germany, Greece, Iceland, Ireland, Italy, Luxembourg, the Netherlands, Norway, Portugal, Sweden, Switzerland, Turkey and the United Kingdom.

In all cases, except that of Switzerland, which is not a member of the IMF, the gold value of each national currency has been determined on the basis of the par value designated by agreement between the country involved and the IMF. In the case of Switzerland, the gold content of the Swiss franc is based on the definition contained in the Swiss Federal Coinage Law of December 17, 1952.

[38] See the authors referred to in note 35 supra.

[39] As pointed out by Blondeel, op. cit. note 35 supra, at p. 1000, the fact that no change in the value of the unit of account is possible unless all the gold values of the currencies of reference have been altered is a factor of primary importance to each country whose currency is included in the currencies of reference: These authorities:

"can prevent a change in the value of the unit of account and control the magnitude of such change; [and] . . . control the degree of the burden on their citizens who have borrowed money through the issuance of unit of account obligations."

forming the two-third group. However, as an additional assurance of stability, the formula provides that the gold content of the unit of account, when so adjusted, will vary only to the same extent as the currency of reference which has changed the least from its previous base value.[40] In effect, therefore, the value of the loan obligation is linked with that of the strongest currency in the group.

This solution, it should be noted, would also be reached under an ordinary multiple-currency clause when several of the currencies listed in the clause are devalued: The lender would naturally request payment in the currency which is devalued the least. In both cases, therefore, the value of the loan obligation is tied to that of the most stable currency included in the group.

In the event of revaluation, however, the two types of provisions lead to very different results. Under a multiple-currency clause, a change in the value of only one of the currencies listed is sufficient to alter the content of the obligation; whereas such an alteration, in the case of a unit-of-account loan, is possible only if all the currencies of reference vary from their base value. Furthermore, in the case of a currency option the value of the obligation follows the fate of the currency which varies the most; whereas under a unit-of-account loan the value of the obligation varies only in the same proportion as the currency which varies the least.[41]

Under the circumstances, it is clear that the unit of account constitutes a useful stabilization device not only for the lenders but also for the borrower. It assures the borrower that: (i) the burden of the loan obligation will remain unchanged as long as his national currency (which is always one of the currencies of reference) remains unchanged or is not devalued by a greater percentage than other currencies of

---

[40] It should be noted that the "previous" base value is not necessarily the "initial" base value, since monetary variations during the life of a loan may cause the gold value of the unit of account to be changed several times. In order to reduce the frequency of such changes, the latest unit-of-account loan documents provide for a two-year period during which a change in the gold value of the unit of account does not have to be followed by a change in the base value of the currencies of reference. At the end of the period, the necessary re-adjustment is made and the base value is confirmed or redefined depending upon the circumstances.

[41] The difference between the two situations was clearly illustrated by the 5% revaluation of the German mark in 1961. To the extent that holders of the Republic of Austria bonds referred to above (see notes 31 and 34) requested payment in Germany, the revaluation of the DM increased the debt of Austria. On the other hand, the revaluation had no effect on the obligations of SACOR, a Portuguese company, under a loan expressed in units of account. See Blondeel, op. cit. note 35 supra, p. 1003.

reference; and (ii) if the unit of account is subject to an upward read-justment, the corresponding increase in the value of the loan obliga-tion will be kept to the lowest possible level.[42]

The unit-of-account formula, though its advantages are apparent, is nevertheless particularly complex. However adequate it may be to measure the value of loan obligations, the unit of account is only a monetary yardstick which, at the time of payment, must be con-verted into the national currency or currencies in which payment is to be made. A simple solution to this conversion problem would have been to provide that conversion should be made on each occasion on the basis of the base value of each currency involved. However this solution has not prevailed: It would have ignored the important fact that national currencies can be obtained on the market at rates which do not necessarily correspond to their respective par or base value. Under the circumstances, reliance on the base value of each national currency, though attractively simple, would have encouraged specu-lation and arbitrage among the various currencies of reference. In order to prevent short-term speculation in foreign exchange, which might have enabled lenders to acquire cheaply unit-of-account bonds by purchasing them with a currency of reference obtainable on the market below par, borrowers have always limited the number of cur-rencies in which subscription payments could be effected. In all cases so far, the currency or currencies in which such payments could be effected have always been among the strongest currencies of reference. As a counterpart to this limitation, which is intended to provide the borrower with the greatest possible amount in his national currency, most unit-of-account bonds have given bondholders the option to request payment, on each payment date, in the currency of reference of their choice. In one case, however, this option was removed from the bondholders and the selection of the currency of reference used for the purpose of conversion was left to the discretion of the bor-rower and the fiscal agent.[43]

These complexities, which have been brought in sharper focus with the passage of time, may be unavoidable. On the other hand, it is possible that, with further experience, some of them can be eliminated or substantially reduced. In any event, it is clear that the

---

[42] See the authors referred to in note 35 supra, particularly Collin, p. 28; Segré, p. 64.

[43] The Cassa per il Mezzogiorno 1963 Loan. See also, Blondeel, op. cit. note 35 supra, pp. 1004-1005; Jonckheere, op. cit. id. loc. pp. 202-204; van der Memsbrugghe, op, cit. id. loc., pp. 451-452.

sponsors of the unit-of-account formula hope that it will succeed in promoting the formation of a truly European capital market.[44]

C. Loans Denominated in a Stable Currency

The lenders' desire to avoid currency depreciation can sometimes be satisfied simply by denominating the loan in a particularly strong currency whose value can reasonably be expected to remain stable. The interest shown by European investors in purchasing U.S. dollar bonds issued in the United States by foreign borrowers is a good illustration of this remark.[45]

Another illustration is the spectacular success of recent issues of bonds denominated in U.S. dollars and Swiss francs which, though they were technically issued in London, were sold primarily to Continental investors by international banking concerns organized by English and Belgian banks.[46]

It is nevertheless clear that, however justified the lenders' confidence in the currency involved, reliance on the stability of that currency throughout the life of the loan may prove excessive. The monetary risk, though it may be considerably reduced, cannot be entirely ruled out. In this respect, loans denominated in a single strong currency do not afford lenders the same protection as currency options or other stabilization devices.

---

[44] See e.g., Blondeel, op. cit. note 35 supra, at pp. 1010-1111; Collin, op. cit. id. loc., at p. 16; Segré, op. cit. id. loc. at pp. 67-69.

[45] See e.g., Stevenson, "Legal Aspects of the Public Offering of Foreign Securities in the United States Market", 28 Geo. Wash. L. Rev. 194 (1959), at p. 202; Samuels, "The Investment Banking Background of Issuing and Marketing Foreign Securities in the United States", address delivered at a conference on Legal Problems of International Financing at the Yale Law School March 1-3, 1962, pp. 2-5.

[46] See e.g., the City of Copenhagen Swiss Frs. 60 million 5% External Loan 1974/1983; the Autostrade Concessioni e Costruzioni Autostrade S.A. US $15 million 5½% Guaranteed Bonds 1972/78; the Republic of Austria US $18 million 6% Bonds 1979/1984; the Republic of Portugal US $20 million 5¾% Bonds 1979/1984; the Kingdom of Norway US $30 million 5½% 20 year External Loan of 1965.

See also, Pulay, "London's Come-back as a Capital Market", 182 Statist (November 8, 1963) 417; Segré, op. cit. note 35 supra, pp. 59-63. As noted by Segré:

". . . the concept of 'market of issue' becomes in this case an extremely vague one, since the various elements of such a concept, which are generally grouped together, are here scattered to such a degree that it has been possible to speak in these cases of 'issues in London' only because the issuing concerns were generally managed by English banks." (at p. 60).

SECTION III. AN OUTSTANDING PROBLEM OF INTERPRETATION: ASCERTAINING THE EXISTENCE OF A MAINTENANCE-OF-VALUE CLAUSE

The draftsmanship of contemporary maintenance-of-value clauses, when compared with the frequently deficient terminology of stabilization devices used in earlier decades, constitutes a marked improvement. Though some of the clauses presently in use are far from simple, they are generally expressed in language which clearly reflects the intention of the parties. Since, however, the most careful draftsmanship does not necessarily rule out possible controversies in times of economic stress, and since the construction of earlier contractual covenants is still an occasional object of dispute, a brief summary of the canons of interpretation used by courts in ascertaining the parties' intention may usefully supplement the preceding remarks concerning contemporary contractual lending practice.

A. THE TERMS OF THE LOAN DOCUMENTS AS A FACTOR OF DETERMINATION

Among other factors relevant to ascertaining the parties' intention, the terms of the loan documents are of paramount importance. Normally, and subject to invalidating statutes or public policy, there is no difficulty in giving effect to the parties' intention if that intention is expressed in clear language. Thus in the several instances in which foreign governments, corporations or other entities issued bonds in the United States which were payable "in gold coin of the United States of America of the standard of weight and fineness existing [at the time of issue]," the courts generally construed the provision as a gold clause.[47] This construction was also placed on similar clauses

---

[47] See e.g., Supreme Court of Austria, November 26, 1935 and July 10, 1936, Austrian Government Guaranteed Loans Cases, Rev. 1936, 717; Clunet, 1936, 334; Nouvelle Revue de Droit International Privé 1936, 597; Supreme Court of Denmark, January 30, 1939, Vereeniging voor den Effectenhandel te Amsterdam v. Ministère des Finances, 40 B.I.J.I. 284 (1939), Clunet 1954, 490; Helsingfors City Court, December 23, 1937, Amsterdam Stock Exchange Committee v. Government of Finland, 38 B.I.J.I. 280 (1938); Supreme Court of Norway, December 8, 1937, Minerva Ins. Co. v. Norwegian Government, 38 B.I.J.I. 71 (1938); Supreme Court of Sweden, January 30, 1937, Skandia v. National Debt Office, 36 B.I.J.I. 327 (1937).

Comp., Conseil d'Etat November 28, 1958, Langlois et Rolland de Chambaudoin d'Erceville, Clunet 1960, 444; Rev. 1959, 117; J.C.P. 1959, II, 10896; D.1959, 361.

in bonds denominated in French francs,[48] pounds sterling,[49] or Norwegian crowns.[50]

In this connection, it is important to note that courts have rejected efforts sometimes made by borrowers to negate the effectiveness of gold or multiple-currency clauses clearly stated in the loan by contending that the clause in question was a purely "routine expression" (clause de style) devoid of substantial significance. For example, in the Brazilian Loans Case, the Permanent Court of International Justice rejected the contention of the Brazilian Government that a gold clause in the bonds had no particular meaning under the circumstances. This contention, said the Court:

> "would eliminate the word 'gold' from the bonds. . . . A reference to a well known standard of value [the gold franc] cannot be considered as inserted merely for literary effect, or as a routine expression without significance. The Court is called upon to construe the promise, not to ignore it."[51]

However, reference to gold, or to various currencies, may not be sufficient to constitute a gold or a multiple-currency clause if there is a lack of precision in the "language of equation,"[52] (i.e. the specifi-

---

[48] PCIJ, Judgments No. 14 (Serbian Loans Case) and No. 15 (Brazilian Loans Case), Series A No. 21 (1929), at pp. 32-33 and 35, and pp. 116-117, respectively.

[49] Feist v. Société Intercommunale Belge d'Electricité [1934] A.C. 161.

[50] Supreme Court of Norway, May 2, 1962, Association Nationale des Porteurs Français de Valeurs Mobilières v. the Norwegian Government, the Mortgage Bank of Norway and the Small Holding and Workers' Housing Bank, as summarized by Bahr, "The Norwegian Gold Clause Case", 12 Am. J. Comp. L. 1 (1963). See also, Hambro, "L'Affaire des Emprunts Norvégiens devant les Juridictions de Norvège", Clunet 1965, 613.

[51] PCIJ Judgment No. 15 (Brazilian Loans case) Series A, No. 21, at p. 116. Comp., Bahr, op. cit. preceding note, at p. 8 in the case of the Norwegian loans.

In connection with the construction of a clause in bonds issued by the City of Vienna providing for payment in Austrian crowns or foreign currencies at fixed rates of exchange to the crown, the Tripartite Claims Commission (US, Austria and Hungary), constituted under the Agreement of November 26, 1924 (VI Reports of Int'l Arbitral Awards (1955), p. 244), held that the clause could not be construed to give bondholders a mere option of collection rather than a currency option, since such a construction would have rendered meaningless the stipulation of fixed rates of exchange. Said the Commission:
> "The maker of the bond agreed at the election of the bearer to pay at New York at the fixed rate of exchange of one hundred crowns equal twenty dollars United States gold coin. This provision is equally bind-

cation of the standard of weight and fineness of the currency involved
or the determination of fixed rates of exchange between the currencies
in which the loan is payable). An American case is in point. Prior
to the First World War, an American corporation had issued in England "First Mortgage Gold Bonds." The word "Gold" was super-
imposed over the text of each bond in letters over an inch wide;
and the resolutions adopted by the stockholders and the directors of
the borrower to authorize the loan and the creation of a mortgage as
security therefor also mentioned that payment was to be made "in
gold coin" of the United Kingdom. Despite these various references
to gold, it was held that since the parties had failed to determine the
standard of weight and fineness of the English "gold coin" referred
to in the bonds, their intention must have been merely to describe
the currency of payment, which at the time happened to be on a gold
standard, rather than to stipulate a genuine gold clause in the bonds.[53]

<hr/>

ing with all other provisions of the bond. To hold that the bearer for his
convenience could demand payment in New York, but that the amount
which he could demand must be stated in crowns translated into dollars at
the current rate of exchange at the time of payment, would be to hold the
quoted provision meaningless" (Ibid. at p. 246).

[52] Lemaire v. Kentucky and Indiana Terminal Railroad Co., 140 F. Supp.
82, 86 (1956); affirmed 242 F. 2d 884 (1957).

[53] Ibid. Said the Court:

"The plaintiff seeks a construction which would require us not only to
imply the standard of weight and fineness of the gold but also the language of equation. The language of equation, we feel, is the essence of
a gold value clause unless there exist extrinsic circumstances such as
supply the defect. (Gold coin no longer being in circulation or reference to an artificial gold unit, etc.) . . . It is our opinion, therefore,
that . . . this bond does not contain a gold value clause . . ." (140 F.
Supp. at pp. 86-87).

Comp., Derwa v. Rio de Janeiro Tramway Light and Power Co. [1928]
4 D.L.R. 542.

When parties have stipulated payment in "francs", "dollars" or "pounds",
domestic and international courts alike have refused to read into private or
governmental loan contracts an implicit reference to the gold standard of
value of the currency in which the loan was denominated, even though such
currency was pegged with gold at the time of the loan. See e.g., (i) in the
United States: State of Maryland v. Baltimore and Ohio Railroad Co., 89
U.S. 105 (1874); (ii) in the United Kingdom: New Brunswick Railway Co. v.
British and French Trust Corporation [1939] A.C. 1; and (iii) in France:
Cass. January 23, 1924, Riegert v. Banque Hypothécaire de Bâle, Clunet 1925,
169; Cass. January 11, 1926, Dreyfus v. Banque Hypothécaire de Bâle, Clunet
1926, 441; Cass. January 14, 1931, Bonnaud v. Ville de Tokio, D.P. 1931.1.5,
Rev. 1934, 537; Cass. December 21, 1932, Vuatrin v. Cie. du Chemin de Fer de
Rosario, and Cie. du Chemin de Fer de Rosario v. Bonnaud, Clunet 1933,
1201; Cass. December 6, 1933, Bedin v. Cie Internationale des Wagons-Lits,

Similarly it had been held that when a loan was issued simultaneously in France and in England; and the bonds issued in France in French francs mentioned the existence of a simultaneous bond issue in England in pounds sterling, such a provision could not be construed as giving holders of the French bonds the right to be paid in pounds sterling or to claim the equivalent thereof in French currency, especially when, in the court's opinion, the two bond issues, though serving a common financial purpose, were technically independent of each other.[54]

Another troublesome situation is that in which the bonds provide for payment in one of several currencies at the holder's option, and refer to gold only in respect of one of these currencies. In such a case, it has sometimes been held that the gold clause in question should be

Clunet 1934, 946; Cass. January 24, 1934, Maljean v. Chemin de Fer de Sao-Paulo, D.P. 1934.1.73. Comp., Mixed Tribunal of Tangiers (Appellate Division) May 18, 1935, Tilley v. Bengelloun Maspero, Rev. 1936, 131.

Similarly, the courts have dismissed the claims of "franc" bondholders that they are entitled to receive in French currency the equivalent of a so-called "international gold standard of value" corresponding to the gold content of the franc (as defined at the time when the Latin Monetary Union was in existence which coincided with the time of issue), rather than the nominal amount of the bonds in depreciated French francs. See e.g., Cass. December 21, 1932 (cited in the preceding paragraph). This case is particularly interesting since it deals both with gold and multiple currency clauses. Before World War I, the debtor company had issued bonds in France, Argentina and Switzerland. The bonds were denominated in "francs" and were payable in each of the named countries. After the French franc had been depreciated, a French bondholder argued that the standard of value referred to in the bonds was the "international" gold standard of value created by the Latin Union, and that if the bonds were paid in French currency he should receive an amount equal to the gold value stipulated in the bonds. His claim was denied. He also contended that, even if there was no gold clause in the bonds, they contained at least a multiple currency clause since at the time of issue the French and Swiss francs were interchangeable and bondholders could, therefore, claim payment at their option in the French or the Swiss currency. This argument was also rejected. Said the court:

"The Monetary Convention of December 23, 1865 between France, Belgium, Italy and Switzerland concerns exclusively the minting . . . of gold and silver coins of the weight, fineness and diameter that the [convention] determines, but [the Convention] does not create an international franc qualified "franc of the Latin Union" which could be substituted for the monetary unit whose value is fixed by statutes in each of the contracting Parties . . ." (as translated).

[54] Supreme Court of Japan December 27, 1934, Case of the City of Tokyo Bonds, 13 Daishin-in Minji Hanzei-Shū (Reports of the Supreme Court decisions), p. 2386 (1934). Contra: the French Supreme Court decisions in two cases involving the same bonds: Cass. January 14, 1931, Bonnaud v. Ville de Tokio and Ville de Tokio v. Roussey, D.P. 1931.1.5. Rev. 1934, 537.

extended also to the other currency or currencies.[55] On other occasions, however, the courts have held that the gold clause was limited to the currency to which it specifically referred.[56]

Contradictory results have also been reached in the case in which the existence of a gold clause was not in question, but the clause referred only to the payment of principal and not to that of interest; or, conversely, referred to the payment of interest without mentioning that of principal. The latter situation was submitted to the P.C.I.J. in the *Brazilian Loans Case*. The Court held that since "it would be an anomaly to have the interest of bonds payable in gold while the principal was not so payable,"[57] the clause must apply to both payments. However, where a gold clause was limited to the payment of the principal, the House of Lords refused to extend the scope of the clause to interest payments.[58]

B. ANCILLARY INFORMATION

Instruments ancillary to the loan contract or the bonds are sometimes used to construe ambiguous language in the loan documents.

For instance, when a loan was secured by a "gold" mortgage or pledge, reference in the bonds to the existence of the "gold" security has been considered sufficient evidence that the parties intended to contract on a gold basis.[59] In one case, the recordation in France, in terms of French francs, of a mortgage securing a loan raised in Switzerland by a French corporation and payable in "francs" has been held evidence of an implicit intention of the parties to contract on the basis of the French, rather than the Swiss, franc. This solution appears questionable, however, since the validity of a recordation in France of a mortgage securing a debt expressed in a foreign currency

---

[55] See e.g., T.F. February 11, 1931, Société d'Heraclée v. Badan Rev. 1931, 726; Clunet 1931, 510; R.O. 57.II.69. See also, in regard to Norwegian bonds, the decision of the minority in the judgment of the Supreme Court of Norway referred to in note 50 supra, at p. 10.

[56] See the decision of the majority in the judgment of the Supreme Court of Norway referred to in the preceding note, id. loc. and also at p. 15. Comp., Cass. July 7, 1931, Bret v. Société d'Héraclée, Rev. 1931, 703, reversing the decision of the Court of Appeals of Paris in the same case.

[57] Judgment No. 15, Series A, No. 21 (1929) at p. 114. Comp., the French Government "Réplique" in the Case of Certain Norwegian Loans, I.C.J., Pleadings (1957) at p. 390.

[58] New Brunswick Railway Co. v. British and French Trust Corporation [1939] A.C.1

[59] Cass. February 14, 1934, Reynaud v. Banque Hypothécaire Franco-Argentine, and Banque Hypothécaire Franco-Argentine v. Bonnaud, Clunet 1934, 1202, S. 1934.1.297.

was a matter of controversy at the time the judgment was rendered.[60] More satisfactory results have been achieved in other cases in which the courts refused to permit references in the security instruments to the existence of "gold" pledges or guarantees to vary the clear terms of bonds providing for payment in legal tender of the monetary system involved.[61]

Resolutions adopted at stockholders' meeting or by directors of the borrower have also been taken into account to construe language in loan documents. In one case, bonds issued in France by a Brazilian corporation provided for payment in "francs," but the stockholders' resolution authorizing the loan, which had been published in a Brazilian official gazette and was expressly referred to in the bonds, provided for a "franc loan producing interest in gold at the rate of 5% per annum." It was held that the borrower was bound to pay an amount in French francs sufficient to give to the bondholders the gold value of the coupons.[62] In this and other cases,[63] reliance on action

---

[60] Cass. July 19, 1937, Société des Hôtels Splendides v. Biscardy, Clunet 1938, 76, Rev. 1938, 276. A similar solution was reached in the case of Papeteries Berges (Cass. July 21, 1936, Clunet 1937, 299), although in this case the loan had been issued both in France and Switzerland. The assumption, therefore, that payments in French currency only had been promised would appear more justified than in the Sociétés des Hôtels Splendides case. See also, in the case of a direct loan, as opposed to a bond issue, Chambery, November 25, 1929, Orsat v. Caisse Hypothécaire de Genève, Clunet 1930, 1226. As to the existing status of the French law, see Chapter V, text and notes 81 and 84.

[61] Appellate Division of the Mixed Tribunal of Tangiers, Tilley v. Bengelloun Maspero, Rev. 1936, 131. Comp., Cass. January 24, 1934, Maljean v. Chemin de Fer de Sao Paulo, D.P. 1934.1.73. In the latter case, a Brazilian railway company had issued bonds in France and the prospectus mentioned that the Brazilian government had granted to the borrower a "gold guarantee" which was security for the loan. This reference in the prospectus was held insufficient to import a gold clause in the bonds. Comp., the Lighthouses Concession Case (Affaire Relative à la Concession des Phares de l'Empire Ottoman) 12 Reports of International Awards, at p. 226.

[62] Cass. January 24, 1934, Chemin de Fer de Sao Paulo v. Portalier, D.P. 1934.1.73. In another case concerning the same corporation, the plaintiff had not invoked the shareholders' resolution before the lower courts and, for procedural reasons, the Supreme Court refused to take judicial notice of the resolution. The plaintiff lost his suit. Cass., January 24, 1934, Maljean v. Chemin de Fer de Sao Paulo, D.P. 1934.1.73.

[63] Lemaire v. Kentucky and Indiana Terminal Railroad Co., 140 F. Supp. 82, 87 (1956), affirmed 242 F. 2d 884 (1957):
"We think, after examining the bond, the interest coupons attached, the mortgage to which the bond refers, the shareholders' resolution contained in the mortgage, the directors' resolution also contained therein, the prospectus . . . that no gold value clause was expressed or intended."

taken internally by the borrower prior to the raising of the loan may be entirely justified insofar as it helps ascertain the original intention of the borrower and prevents him from modifying unilaterally the terms of the loan to the disadvantage of the lenders. Yet the possibility cannot be ignored that, between the time of the original action and the actual raising of the loan, market conditions may have improved and the borrower may have felt it unnecessary to obtain new authority to contract the loan on terms more favorable than those previously approved. If this fact were established, it would give the lenders an unfair advantage to hold the borrower bound by the terms of the original resolution rather than the express terms of the bonds.

Whatever the merits of the above decisions, it is clear that arrangements between the borrower and its bankers or underwriters, even though they may be incidental to the loan transaction, should have no bearing upon the construction of the loan documents, unless the terms of these arrangements have been incorporated into such documents.[64] A dramatic illustration of this remark is found in the following French case. In 1914, a French corporation issued bonds in France and Switzerland. The bonds were denominated in "francs" and were payable either in France or in Switzerland. In an action by a Swiss bondholder to recover payment in Swiss francs, the debtor corporation demurred on the ground that the Swiss banks through which the bonds had been issued in Switzerland had stated in their correspondence with the debtor that the subscription had been received in French francs, the amount of which had been credited to the debtor corporation. The French Supreme Court held this defense valid.[65]

C. CIRCUMSTANTIAL EVIDENCE

If the language of the loan documents is imprecise, consideration may have to be given to the circumstances surrounding the making

[64] As a rule, courts have refused to give consideration to underwriting agreements in the construction of bonds (see e.g., Supreme Court of Sweden, January 30, 1937, note 47 supra; Supreme Court of Austria, November 26, 1935 and July 10, 1936, note 47 supra; comp., Supreme Court of Norway, May 2, 1962, note 50 supra, at pp. 8-9), unless there was a clear indication in the bonds that they incorporated the terms, or some of the terms, of the underwriting agreement (see e.g., Helsingfors City Court, December 23, 1937, note 47 supra).

[65] Cass. June 5, 1934, Société l'Est Lumière v. d'Acher de Montgascon, Clunet 1935, 90.

of the loan, especially the financial usages or customs of the lender
or the market of issue. For example, it has been held on several occasions that when bonds issued by Middle Eastern borrowers provided
for payment in "Turkish pounds" or "francs," without further specifi-
cation, such a provision should be construed as importing a gold value
clause into the bonds, in accordance with the financial usages prevailing at the time of issue. Thus, in *Batache v. Compagnie du Port,
des Quais et Entrepôts de Beyrouth*,[66] the borrower had issued bonds
denominated in "francs 500 = Turkish pounds 22." There was no
reference to gold in the bonds. In an action by bondholders seeking
payment in gold or at gold value, the borrower demurred on the
ground that the bonds provided merely for an option of currency
and contained no gold clause. The lower court so held. However, the
judgment was reversed by the Supreme Court of Lebanon on the
ground that at the time of issue the Turkish pound referred to in the
bonds was pegged with gold and that a reference to gold was implicit
in any instrument referring to Turkish pounds executed in the Turkish empire. A similar solution also prevailed in Egypt where the
French franc had been incorporated into the Egyptian monetary system in 1834. A reference to "francs" in bonds issued by the Suez
Canal Company (and also in rates of passage due to the Company)
was on several occasions construed as referring either to an "international" gold standard of value,[67] or the gold franc "nationalized and
adopted" by Egypt, i.e. an Egyptian gold standard of value.[68]

Solutions contrary to those which prevailed in the Middle East,
although based also on local usages, have been reached in Latin
American countries, where the term "gold" preceding the name of
the local currency does not necessarily imply the existence of a gold

---

[66] Cour de Cassation du Grand Liban March 24, 1933, Clunet 1933, 696.
See also, Cour de Cassation Libanaise June 20, 1928, Compagnie des Eaux
de Beyrouth v. J.E., S. 1929.4.1. For other cases involving Middle Eastern
countries, see *Mann*, pp. 109 et seq.

[67] Mixed Court of Appeals of Alexandria, June 4, 1925, Compagnie Uni-
verselle du Canal Maritime de Suez v. Dabbah et al., Clunet 1925, 1080;
June 18, 1931, Shallam & Sons etc. v. Compagnie Universelle du Canal de Suez,
Clunet 1932, 202, 207; and May 17, 1947, Hoirs Setton v. Compagnie Uni-
verselle du Canal de Suez, Journal des Tribunaux Mixtes No. 3372, May 26-27,
1947.

[68] Mixed Court of Appeals of Alexandria, February 18, 1936, Crédit
Foncier Egyptien v. Attalah, Crédit Foncier Egyptien v. Sursock, and Land
Bank of Egypt v. Levy, Clunet 1936, 1004.

clause and may refer merely to the legal tender of the country involved.[69]

When it is not clear whether the use of the word "gold" means that the parties intended to contract on a gold basis or only in local currency, it has been held that the second alternative should prevail, as this construction was more favorable to the borrower.[70] This solution is consistent with the principle generally accepted in most countries that in case of doubt as to the extent of the debtor's obligations, the interpretation most favorable to the debtor should prevail.[71] However, this rule of interpretation can hardly receive application in the majority of publicly issued loans, where the borrower itself is directly or exclusively responsible for the drafting of the prospectus or the bonds. In these cases, in accordance with the maxim "contra proferentem," any ambiguity in the terms of the loan documents should be construed against the borrower and in favor of the lenders.[72]

Sometimes events subsequent to the making of the loan have been taken into account to solve the difficulty. For example, when payment of interest is made on a gold basis over a protracted period of time, it may be possible to conclude that a gold clause was originally intended by the parties.[73] Conversely, when the lenders have accepted payment in a depreciated currency for many years, their subsequent claim to payment on a gold basis,[74] or in a different currency

---

69 See *Nussbaum,* pp. 243-247. This was also the argument advanced by the Norwegian Government in the Case of Certain Norwegian Loans (I.C.J. Pleadings (1957), at p. 263), objected to by the French Government (Ibid., at pp. 390 et seq.) and rejected by the Supreme Court of Norway on May 2, 1962 (see Bahr, op. cit. note 50 supra, pp. 8-9).

70 See *Nussbaum,* pp. 245-247. Comp., in regard to the determination whether French or Swiss "franc" had been promised, Levy v. Cleveland, C.C. & St. L. Ry. Co., 206 N.Y.S. 261, 210 App. Div. 422 (1926); Court of Appeals of Brussels, March 11, 1921, 6 B.I.J.I. No. 1260 (1922).

71 *Nussbaum,* loc. cit., insists upon the rather chauvinistic character of these cases since in each one of them the debtor was also a national of the country of the forum.

72 PCIJ Judgment No. 15 (Brazilian Loans Case) Series A No. 21, at p. 113 (1929). See also International Institute for the Unification of Private Law, *Preliminary Draft Uniform Rules Applicable to International Loans* (Revised Edition), U.D.P. 1947, Papers: XX, International Loans—Doc. 5a (1), Rule 3 (4): "In doubtful cases, the bond shall be interpreted in favor of the holders."

73 Paris May 16, 1951, Trésor Public et Société Royal Bank of Canada v. Schumann, J.C.P. 1952, II, 6887, affirmed on other grounds Cass. January 24, 1956, Clunet 1956, 1012; J.C.P. 1956, II, 9400; D. 1956, 317. See also Apostolic Throne of St. Jacob v. Said [1940] 1 All E.R. 54.

74 Lemaire v. Kentucky and Indiana Terminal Railroad Co., 140 F. Supp.

having the same denomination as that in which payment was received,[75] is unlikely to succeed. In cases such as these, however, it must be quite clear that payment was made or accepted without protest. Otherwise neither the lender nor the borrower could be considered as having waived any of their respective rights.[76]

D. PRESUMPTIONS

Recourse to presumptions to determine the scope of the parties' rights and obligations is an ultimate means of interpretation which presupposes that all other available evidence is insufficient to make the proper determination. In the monetary field, the situation in which courts have had recourse to this means of interpretation concerns the case where a loan is denominated in terms of a unit of account which is in common use in various countries, although it may designate separate currencies, such as "dollars," "pounds" or "francs"; and it is not clear in which particular currency the loan was intended to be paid. In such a case, courts have frequently assumed that in the absence of any positive evidence to the contrary, the money of the place of payment designated in the loan documents is also the money of account. In other words, the presumption is that when a loan or bond is payable in a certain place, the money *in solutione* is also the money *in obligatione*.[77] This presumption, however, is rebuttable and should be weighed with the greatest care.[78] When a bond or prospectus refers to several places of payment, the above presumption may lead a court to read into the bonds or the prospectus a multiple-currency clause where merely an option of place of payment was intended. That the latter danger is not theoretical is sufficiently illus-

---

82 (1956), affirmed 242 F. 2d 884 (1957), at 888. See, however, Supreme Court of Norway, May 2, 1962, referred to in note 50 supra, at pp. 15-17.

[75] Cass. July 17, 1935, Biscardy et Vacher v. S.A. Brasseries Sochaux, Clunet 1936, 880.

[76] PCIJ Judgment No. 14 (Serbian Loans Case) Series A, No. 20, p. 38 and Judgment No. 15 (Brazilian Loans Case) Series A, No. 21, p. 119 (1929). See also, Paris June 2, 1959, Trésor Public v. Veuve Hermann, Gaz. Pal. 1959.II.170.

[77] See e.g., Cass. June 3, 1930, Crédit Foncier Franco-Canadien v. Bordier, Rev. 1930, 480, Clunet 1931, 103; T.F. May 23, 1928, Huttinger v. Crédit Foncier Franco-Canadien, Clunet 1929, 498. See also *Mann,* pp. 190-193.

[78] See e.g., Cass. November 28, 1932, Sallé v. La Baloise, Clunet 1934, 133; December 21, 1932, Compagnie du Chemin de Fer de Rosario, Clunet 1933, 1201, at 1204, 1207; December 6, 1933, Bedin v. Cie Internationale des Wagons-Lits, Clunet 1934, 946; Gand March 6, 1930, Cie d'Assurances la Génevoise v. Grondel, Clunet 1931, 729. See also R. Piret, *Les Variations Monétaires et leurs Répercussions en Droit Privé Belge* (1935) No. 27.

trated by *Auckland Corporation v. Alliance Assurance Co.*[79] In that case, the City of Auckland had issued bonds in terms of "pounds" payable at the holder's option in England or in New Zealand. Certain bondholders exercised the option to be paid in England, and the question arose whether they were entitled to payment in English, or in New Zealand, currency. The first alternative prevailed and it was held that the nominal amount of the bonds should be paid in London in English currency, a decision highly favorable to the bondholders but which probably had very little basis in the contract.[80] A better result was achieved in the case of *Bonython v. Commonwealth of Australia.*[81] In 1895, the Government of Queensland had issued bonds in terms of "pounds sterling" payable, in Australia or in England at the holders option. In 1932, the Commonwealth of Australia took over the public debt of Queensland and issued consolidated bonds of the Commonwealth against the surrender of the original Queensland bonds. The rights of the holders were to be the same under the new, as under the old, bonds. The question at issue as in the Auckland case, was whether by exercising his option to be paid in England a bondholder was entitled to receive payment at the face value of the bonds in English currency, or could claim in that currency only the equivalent of the face value of the bond in Australian currency. The latter alternative prevailed on the ground, among others, that since, at the time of issue, nobody contemplated a possible divergence in the value of the Queensland and the English pound, it was safe to assume that it could not have been intended that the borrowing government would be placed under a different liability, according to the place of payment. The option given to bondholders to be paid in England or Australia was purely a matter of convenience having no impact on the determination of the substantial obligation of the borrowing government.

In the same connection, an American case should be noted.[82] An American company had issued bonds in France payable at the bearer's option in Paris, Belgium or Switzerland. The bonds were written in the French language and were denominated in francs. The language of the bonds as well as the currency were common to the three

---

[79] [1937] A.C. 587. See also, Adelaide Electric Supply Co. v. Prudential Assurance Co. [1934] A.C. 122.

[80] See *Mann*, pp. 202-203.

[81] [1951] A.C. 201.

[82] Levy v. Cleveland C.C. & St. L. Ry. Co., 210 App. Div. 422, 206 N.Y.S. 261 (1926). But see contra, *Nussbaum*, pp. 395-6.

countries involved. However, the bonds provided for the payment of principal and interest in France without deduction for French taxes. No such provision existed as to payments in Belgium or in Switzerland. The exclusive reference to French taxes was construed as proof of the intention of the parties that the principal place of payment was France, and the money *in obligatione* was the French currency. The clause providing for payment in Belgium or in Switzerland was, therefore, a mere option of collection and did not import a multiple-currency clause. Cases in other countries are in accord with this judgment.[83]

In the *Serbian and Brazilian Loans Cases,* the bonds issued by the debtor governments in terms of gold francs provided for payment in Paris and also in foreign places "at the rate of exchange on Paris." The debtors argued that the latter clause showed that no payment in gold or at gold value had been promised, but merely a payment in French currency, together with an option of collection. The court rejected this argument, holding that an option as to the place of collection had no bearing upon the amount of the debt.[84] This case and those referred to above show that, although there are some instances in which courts have very likely misconstrued an option of collection clause by reading into it a multiple currency clause, the general trend of decisions has been to distinguish carefully the two types of clauses.

Another presumption which has sometimes been used concerns the determination of the money of account of government bonds providing for payment in a unit of account which may refer to various currencies, including the currency of the borrowing government. In such a case, it has been held that the government of a self-governing country, using the terms appropriate to its own monetary system (e.g. "pounds" as referring to the Australian currency), must be presumed to refer to that system whether or not those terms could also apply to another system (e.g. "pounds" as referring to the English currency), and that in the absence of anything to rebut that presumption, it must prevail.[85]

The presumption can be overcome however, if the loan documents or the circumstances surrounding the making of the loan warrant a different interpretation. The case of *National Mutual Life*

---

[83] See note 78, supra.
[84] Series A, No. 20, p. 35 and No. 21, p. 110 (1929).
[85] Bonython v. Commonwealth of Australia [1951] A.C. 201.

Association of Australasia Ltd. v. Attorney General for New Zealand,[86] is in point. In the years 1925-1926, the Government of New Zealand had issued bonds denominated in pounds sterling and payable as to interest and principal at Melbourne, Australia, "free of exchange." At the time of issue, the New Zealand currency was at par with that of Australia, but in 1948, the latter currency had depreciated in comparison with the New Zealand currency. The appellant, a bondholder, claimed that the debtor government could discharge its obligations only by paying the nominal value of the bonds in New Zealand currency (the money *in obligatione*) or its equivalent in Australian currency (the money *in solutione),* at the current rate of exchange. The whole issue revolved around the exact meaning of the words "free of exchange." The appellant contended that these words did not affect the substance of the obligations, which had to be measured in terms of New Zealand currency, but related to matters of performance and meant merely that the debtor government had undertaken to bear any bankers' charges incurred in connection with the effective payment of the bonds. The respondent's views were that its obligation was to pay the nominal amount of the bonds in Australian currency only, and that the words "free of exchange" had been inserted in the bonds to show that no question of exchange, due for example to the transmission of funds from New Zealand to Australia or to a variation of the rate of exchange between the two currencies, was to be brought into the matter. The latter construction prevailed on the ground that the stipulation "must have meant from the beginning that the rate of exchange between the two currencies at the time when payment became due was to be disregarded in determining the amount of Australian currency payable.[87] The words "free of exchange"

> "indicate [d] that, if the New Zealand Government [had] to perform an exchange operation in order to make payment at Melbourne, that operation [should] not be taken into account in determining the Australian currency which [had] to be paid."[88]

---

[86] [1956] 2 W.L.R. 532, [1956] I All E.R. 721. See also, Mann, "Free of Exchange", 19 Modern Law Review 424 (1956); Note, 72 Law Quarterly Review 161 (1956); Haughey, "The Meaning of Pound", 32 New Zealand L.J. 246 (1956), at p. 267. Cowen, "The Meaning of the Words 'Pound' and 'Pound Sterling' in Statutes", 78 L.Q.R. 533 (1962).
[87] [1956] 2 W.L.R., at p. 543.
[88] Ibid. at p. 544. The Court also pointed out, at p. 543, that
"During the period when the two currencies remained equivalent in value

the rate of exchange could not depart from parity, and the effect of the
stipulation that payments must be made free of exchange must have been
small. But the meaning of the stipulation could not change when the
values of the currencies diverged, and it applied to repayment of principal as well as payment of interest. Their lordships must therefore hold
that the obligation of the New Zealand Government is to repay in Melbourne in Australian currency a number of pounds equal to the face value
of the stock."

Chapter VII

Exchange Controls

The return of many countries to convertibility, and the relaxation of exchange restrictions by other countries have considerably improved the international investment climate in recent years.

Yet no responsible lender can ignore the risk of exchange restrictions. This is particularly true since, with the establishment of the IMF, the private international law of exchange controls has undergone considerable changes and lenders are now deprived in most cases of the legal weapons, including public policy, formerly available to them to limit the damaging consequences of exchange restrictions.

From a financial viewpoint, this change in the legal climate regarding the recognition of foreign-exchange controls, though characteristic of the spirit of collaboration between members of the IMF, might have had regrettable consequences. By compelling potential lenders to acknowledge the existence of foreign exchange controls, the new legal order might have discouraged them from embarking on new foreign ventures.

In light of the new law of foreign exchange controls, some arrangements had to be made which, while respecting the powers of exchange authorities in the administration of foreign-exchange resources, would also protect lenders against the detrimental consequences of that administration. This is the object of the contractual arrangements described below. In order, however, to appreciate the significance of stipulations found in contemporary loan documents, the description of lending practice must be preceded by a brief summary of the new law of exchange controls in its relation to international lending operations.

SECTION I. INTERNATIONAL LOANS AND THE RECOGNITION OF FOREIGN EXCHANGE CONTROLS

Before the IMF Agreement took effect, the exchange-control regulations of one country were likely to be viewed with little sympathy in the courts of other countries. Although some courts agreed to give effect to foreign-exchange controls when they were found to be part of the applicable law, as determined by the rules of conflict of laws obtaining at the forum,[1] in most cases recognition was denied either on the ground that the applicable law was that of a country other than that whose exchange regulations were involved,[2] or on the ground of public policy.[3]

The creation of the IMF has changed this situation, at least in the relations between its members. Today, members of the IMF cannot rely on public policy to refuse recognition to the exchange-control regulations of other members which are maintained or imposed consistently with the IMF Agreement. Pursuant to Article VIII, Section 2 (b), of this Agreement:

"Exchange contracts which involve the currency of any member and which are contrary to the exchange control regulations of that member maintained or imposed consistently with this Agreement shall be unenforceable in the territories of any member."

In an interpretation of this remarkable provision by the Board of Executive Directors of the IMF (IMF Circular No. 8 of March 15, 1950), it is stated:

"An obvious result of the foregoing undertaking is that if a party to an exchange contract of the kind referred to in Article VIII, Section 2 (b) seeks to enforce such a contract, the tribunal of the member country before which the proceedings are brought will not, on the ground that they are contrary to the public policy (ordre public) of the forum, refuse recognition of the exchange control regulations of the other members which are maintained or imposed consistently with the Fund Agreement. It also follows that such contracts will be treated as unenforceable notwithstanding that under the private international law of the forum, the law under which the foreign exchange control regulations are maintained or imposed is not the law which governs the exchange contract or its performance."

---

[1] See *Nussbaum,* pp. 465 et seq.; *Mann,* pp. 360, 363 et seq. See, more recently, Re Helbert Wagg [1956] 1 All E.R. 129.

[2] See *Nussbaum,* pp. 471 et seq.; *Mann,* pp. 361, 367 et seq.

[3] See *Nussbaum,* pp. 461 et seq.; *Mann,* pp. 355 et seq. See also the cases cited in note 24 infra.

Article VIII, Section 2 (b), has radically modified the pre-existing law regarding the recognition of the exchange control regulations of other countries.[4] In the first place, that provision eliminates public policy as a ground for refusing to enforce foreign-exchange controls. Furthermore, it modifies the ordinary rules of conflict of laws insofar as the determination of the enforceability of exchange contracts is concerned. Exchange contracts within the scope of this provision must be treated as unenforceable even though, under the conflict of laws rule of the forum, the law under which the exchange-control regulations are maintained or imposed is not the law which governs the contract or its performance.

The case of *Lann v. United Steel Works Corporation*,[5] decided in 1938, illustrates the significance of these new principles. The defendant, a German corporation, had issued bonds providing for payment, at the holder's option, in Germany, Holland or Sweden. After the bonds had been called for redemption in advance of maturity, an American holder elected to receive payment in Holland. Payment was refused on the ground that it was forbidden by German exchange control regulations. In an action brought in New York, the court found that the plaintiff, by demanding payment in Holland, had fixed that country as the place of performance and that, under the conflict of laws rule of New York, Dutch law governed. Since under Dutch law, German exchange control restrictions were no excuse for non-performance, it was held that reliance on such restrictions constituted no valid defense.

Now, given the same set of circumstances, a different solution would be reached. The United States, the Netherlands and Germany are all members of the IMF and, assuming that the German exchange restrictions were imposed or maintained consistently with the IMF Agreement, the courts in New York or Amsterdam would be bound to treat the optional currency clause in the bonds as unenforceable, regardless of the fact that under the conflict rule of the forum, Dutch law is the applicable law.[6]

---

[4] See e.g., *Nussbaum*, pp. 525 et seq.; *Mann*, pp. 378 et seq.; Meyer, "Recognition of Exchange Controls after the International Monetary Fund Agreement", 62 Yale L.J. 867 (1953) ; Gold, *The Fund Agreement in the Courts* (1962), pp. 9-10.

[5] 166 Misc. 465, 1 N.Y.S. 2d 951 (1938).

[6] No example dealing with corporate or governmental loans has been found. However, the reasoning of the court in Re Sik's Estate (205 Misc.

The removal of conflict-of-laws considerations from the determination of the enforceability of exchange contracts produces another
unique result. Under Article VIII, Section 2 (b), it is now conceivable that one exchange contract may involve the currencies of several
members of the IMF, and that the issue of enforceability will have
to be determined under the exchange-control regulations of each of
these members. The perfect example is an optional currency clause of
the type involved in the *Lann* case. In that situation enforceability
of the clause would have to be determined under each of the exchange control regulations maintained or imposed (consistently with
the IMF Agreement) by Germany and each of the other specified
countries.

In certain respects, the language of Article VIII, Section 2 (b) of
the IMF Agreement is somewhat ambiguous and lends itself to various
interpretations which may vary its scope considerably.

The first area of difficulty is caused by the lack of a definition of
the words "exchange contract" in Article VIII, Section 2 (b). This
expression has been variously construed as meaning only contracts
for the sale or payment of currency,[7] or as referring to all types of
transactions which affect a country's exchange resources, whether

---

715, 129 N.Y.S. 2d 134 (1954)), a case involving a loan between two individuals, is of interest. During the German occupation of Yugoslavia, a resident
of that country lent another resident an amount of Yugoslav currency repayable, as soon as possible after the war, in New York at a fixed rate of
exchange between the dinar and the dollar. At the time of the loan, both
parties were subject to persecution and immediate arrest by the occupying
authorities. It was contended that since the transaction had not been authorized and was therefore invalid under the exchange control regulations of
Yugoslavia, it could not be enforced in New York. The court found that
the validity of the contract should be determined under the law of New York,
the law intended by the parties. However, the court acknowledged that the
contract might nevertheless be unenforceable there if it were contrary to the
exchange control regulations of Yugoslavia. The court thus clearly recognized
that for purposes of Article VIII, Section 2 (b) of the IMF Agreement, the
lex causae and the regulations involved are not necessarily the same. The
court found, however, that in view of the circumstances at the time of the
contract, the parties could not conceivably have requested a foreign exchange
license. To have asked the occupying authorities for such an authorization
would have been to court disaster. The court held that under these circumstances the failure to obtain a license did not render the contract unenforceable.

[7] *Nussbaum,* p. 452. See also Banco do Brasil, S.A. v. A.C. Israel Commodity Co., Ins., 12 N.Y.S. 2d 271, 190 N.E. 2d 235, 239 N.Y.S. 2d 872 (1963),
cert. denied 84 S. Ct. 657 (1964). But see Gold, "The Fund Agreement in
the Courts VIII", 11 IMF Staff Papers 457 (1964), at pp. 459-460, 471-473.

involving currency or other tangible or intangible property.[8] Whatever the respective merits of these views, it seems clear that transactions involving bonds, debentures, notes or similar forms of securities, and international loans in general which call for the payment of currency, fall within the scope of Article VIII, Section 2 (b). Such a loan or bond, if contrary to the "exchange control regulations" of a member of the IMF would be "unenforceable" in the territories of other members, two expressions which also need clarification.

"Exchange control regulations" have been defined as "laws passed with the genuine intention of protecting [the state's] economy in times of national stress and for that purpose regulating *(inter alia)* the rights of foreign creditors."[9] Clearly, they do not include trade or tariff restrictions or trading-with-the-enemy and similar regulations, although the distinction is not always easy to make. An illustration is found in the 1953 case of *De Sayve v. De La Valdene*.[10] Under a contract entered into in France by two French residents, the debtor had agreed to pay in several installments certain sums in pounds sterling and United States dollars. In an action brought in New York by the creditor, the debtor argued that the contract had become unenforceable under French statutes introducing *"cours forcé"* in France. It was held that the French statutes involved were merely in the nature of monetary laws defining the French currency at the time France went off the gold standard and made paper money inconvertible, and did not constitute exchange control regulations. Under the circumstances, Article VIII, Section 2 (b) was not applicable, and the court could rely on public policy to deny recognition to the French statutes.

Another example can be easily imagined. Most statutes invalidating gold clauses make no distinction between gold-commodity and gold-coin clauses, on the one hand, and gold-value clauses, on the other. Under these statutes none of these clauses can be enforced. However, exchange control regulations are generally limited to gold-commodity and gold-coin clauses. Assuming, therefore, that an exchange contract provides, as many international loans did, for the payment of gold coins and this provision is contrary to the exchange regulations of a member of the IMF, under the conditions specified in Article VIII, Section 2 (b), other members of the IMF must treat this contract

---

[8] *Mann*, pp. 381-2; Gold, op. cit., note 4 supra, pp. 54, 83-84, 92-94, 96, 106, 116-117, 146, 152.

[9] Re Helbert Wagg [1956] 1 All E.R. 129, at 142.

[10] 124 N.Y.S. 2d 143 (1953).

as unenforceable. Suppose, however, that a loan contract containing a gold-value clause is not contrary to the exchange regulations of a member of the IMF, but is invalid under its domestic law on gold clauses. Other members of the IMF are not bound to recognize the invalidating statute and may still refuse to do so on the ground of public policy. In this connection, the distinction between ordinary statutory law on gold clauses and exchange control regulations is of permanent interest.

The exchange control regulations referred to in Article VIII, Section 2 (b), must be maintained or imposed "consistently" with the IMF Agreement. This reference to the supervisory powers vested in the IMF raises a practical problem of proof. One solution, consistent with that frequently resorted to in the conflict of laws regarding proof of foreign law, is to place the burden of proof on the parties.[11] This solution is objectionable in that it leaves the application of Article VIII, Section 2 (b), entirely to the discretion of the parties. A better solution would be for the judicial or administrative authorities involved to take notice of foreign exchange control regulations and to make the proper determination.[12] In view of the IMF's readiness:

> "to lend its assistance in connection with any problems which may arise in relation to the foregoing interpretation or any other aspect of Article VIII, Section 2 (b) . . . [and] to advise whether particular exchange control regulations are maintained or imposed consistently with the Fund Agreement,"[13]

the proposed solution should not, despite the complexity and the rapid evolution of this field of the law, prove too burdensome for the authorities concerned.

Assuming that it is established that an exchange contract falls within the scope of the exchange control regulations of a member of the IMF, maintained or imposed consistently with the IMF Agreement, there remains the problem of determining whether the contract is "contrary" to such regulations, since it is only in that case that the contract will be treated as "unenforceable." Ordinarily this determination, will be easy enough to make. However, if the regulations

---

[11] See the unreported judgment of a Belgian court summarized by Delaume, "De l'Elimination des Conflits de Lois en Matière Monétaire Réalisée par les Statuts du Fonds Monétaire International et de ses Limites", Clunet 1954, 332, 358, and by Gold, op. cit., note 4 supra, pp. 79-82.

[12] See the unreported judgment of a German court summarized by Gold, op. cit., note 4 supra, pp. 82-86.

[13] IMF Circular No. 8 of March 15, 1950.

have changed, or have been imposed, after the date the contract was made and before performance is to take place, the question arises which of these two dates should be relevant to make the proper determination.

Although the view has sometimes been advanced that the relevant date should be the date of the making of the contract rather than the date of performance,[14] this solution appears unsatisfactory on several grounds. It would mean that an exchange contract, valid when made although contrary to the exchange control regulations of a member at the time of performance, could still be enforced at that time in the territories of other members. Thus a loan validly issued by a borrower located in country A would be enforceable in the territories of country B after the imposition of exchange restrictions, by country A. This result would achieve exactly the same objective as that which was reached in the many pre-war decisions on the ground of public policy, even though public policy, as among members of the IMF, is excluded by Article VIII, Section 2 (b). Also, this solution would, in the converse case of a contract originally contrary to the regulations of a member, perpetuate its unenforceability after the removal of such regulations or after the member concerned would have ceased to belong to the IMF. These results are difficult to reconcile either with economic realities or with the freedom that members of the IMF retain vis-à-vis restrictions imposed by non-member countries. The better view, therefore, seems to be that according to which the necessary determination would be made on the date of performance.[15]

If, on that date, an exchange contract is found to be contrary to the exchange control regulations of a member under the conditions set forth in Article VIII, Section 2 (b), that contract must be considered "unenforceable" in the territories of other members of the IMF. What is meant by this expression is simply that the judicial or administrative authorities of other member countries will not enforce a party's claim designed to get performance of the exchange contract in question. The provision does not require the judicial or administrative authorities of one country to treat an exchange contract which comes within the scope of the provision as invalid, nor does it require a member country to prevent persons within its jurisdiction from

---

[14] Mann, "The Private International Law of Exchange Control under the International Monetary Fund Agreement", 2 Int'l & Comp. L.Q. 97, 106 (1953).

[15] See e.g., Delaume, op. cit., note 11 supra, at pp. 352-356. Gold, op. cit., note 4 supra, at pp. 62-66, 77-78, and op. cit. note 7 supra, p. 464.

entering into contracts contrary to the exchange control regulations of other members. All that is required from members and authorities within their territories is that they refuse to enforce certain contracts. In other words, the obligation of members under Article VIII, Section 2 (b), is purely negative in character, and entails no positive undertaking to give further effect in their territories to the exchange control regulations of other members.[16] This absence of positive obligation is illustrated by the following example. Suppose that a foreign borrower has an account with a New York bank and that his government, a member of the IMF, invokes its own exchange control regulations and brings action in a New York court to take possession of the New York assets. The court has no obligation under Article VIII, Section 2 (b), to order the transfer, it is free to adjudicate the issue on the basis of the law of New York.[17] Nor have the courts any obligation to penalize the borrower if he attempts to dispose of his assets in a manner contrary to the exchange control regulations of his government. Their obligation is confined to a refusal to enforce any contract contrary to such regulations which is brought before them.

The case of *Frantzmann v. Ponijen*[18] is in point. A loan contract between two Indonesian residents, disbursed in Indonesian rupiahs, provided for repayment in the Netherlands in Dutch guilders. No license had been granted. In an action in the Netherlands, the court held that the loan, which was "in essence an exchange of currencies and, consequently, constitute[d] an exchange contract" within the meaning of Article VIII, Section 2 (b), could not be enforced in Holland. Although it appeared that the contract was governed by Indonesian law applicable under the Dutch rules of conflict of laws, the court made it clear that its decision was based exclusively on the binding character of the IMF Agreement in the Netherlands.

---

[16] The obligation is a negative one only, in the absence of specific agreement between the members concerned. The possibility of such an agreement is recognized by the second sentence of Article VIII, Section 2 (b) , which reads as follows:

> ". . . In addition, members may, by mutual accord, cooperate in measures for the purpose of making the exchange control regulations of either member more effective, provided that such measures and regulations are consistent with this Agreement."

[17] Cf., Solicitor for the Affairs of His Majesty's Treasury v. Bankers Trust Co., 304 N.Y. 282, 107 N.E. 2d 448 (1952) . Comp. Banco do Brasil S.A. v. A.C. Israel Commodity Co., Inc., cited in note 7 supra.

[18] District Court of Maastricht, June 25, 1959, N.J. 1960, No. 290; 8 Nederlands Tijdschrift voor International Recht 190 (1961) .

The case of *Lessinger v. Mirau*,[19] is also interesting. In 1949, a loan contract was entered into in Vienna by Austrian citizens. The loan, made to finance a gambling enterprise, was for an amount of 30,000 Austrian schillings. The lender, the plaintiff in this case, had advanced to the defendant a sum of $1,000, the countervalue of the Austrian currency specified in the contract. In an action brought in Germany, where the defendant had removed himself, it was held that the loan contract was governed by the law of Austria, including Austrian exchange regulations, under which the contract was invalid. Referring to Article VIII, Section 2 (b), of the IMF Articles of Agreement, the court held that, since the contract was unenforceable under Austrian exchange regulations, an action in Germany based on the contract must also fail. Furthermore, the court held that the plaintiff could not recover the money lent on the basis of unjust enrichment, since the enrichment had taken place in Austria and under Austrian law no such restitution was possible.

This case is important also in another respect, namely the determination of the consequences of the unenforceability of an exchange contract. In the *Lessinger* case, these consequences were governed by the law of Austria, which happened also to be the country whose exchange regulations were involved. This situation is purely fortuitous, however. It has been seen that under Article VIII, Section 2 (b), the determination of the enforceability of an exchange contract is made exclusively on the basis of the exchange control regulations of the member whose currency is involved, even when the proper law of the contract is that of another country. In this respect, a careful distinction must be made between the *lex monetae* involved, which is applicable for the purposes of Article VIII, Section 2 (b), and the *lex causae* which governs the contractual relations of the parties and should be consulted to assess the consequences of the enforceability or unenforceability of the exchange contract in question.

For instance, in an action to enforce an exchange contract, e.g. one containing a gold-value clause, once it is determined that the contract is not contrary to the exchange control regulations of the relevant member or members of the IMF, it is still necessary to determine whether it satisfies all the conditions of validity required by the law applicable under the conflict-of-laws rule of the forum. In

[19] Schleswig-Holstein Oberlandesgericht in Schleswig, April 1, 1954, Lessinger v. Mirau (unreported) summarized by Gold, op. cit., note 4 supra, pp. 90-94.

this example, the court would have to determine whether gold-value clauses are valid under the *lex causae*. Furthermore, it is conceivable that the clause, although enforceable under Article VIII, Section 2 (b), and valid under the proper law, may be denied effect if the public policy of the country of the forum prohibits the enforcement of gold clauses. The facts in the case of *Compania de Inversiones Internacionales v. Industrial Mortgage Bank of Finland*,[20] illustrate the foregoing. In that case, the question at issue was whether the Joint Resolution of Congress of 1933 was applicable to bonds held by a person domiciled in Colombia and issued by a Finnish corporation in New York and payable in New York in gold coins of the United States. It was held that the gold clause was unenforceable because the bonds were governed by the law of New York. However, by way of a dictum, the Court stated also that gold clauses were contrary to American public policy and were unenforceable in the United States even when the clauses were governed by a foreign law and were valid under that law. This decision, although reached before the creation of the IMF, could be reached in a similar case today.[21] By hypothesis the gold clause, if not contrary to the exchange control regulations of Colombia and if valid under the applicable law, for instance the law of Finland, could still be denied effect in New York if contrary to American public policy.

If the contract is unenforceable under the exchange control regulations of the relevent member or members of the IMF, the law applicable under the conflict-of-laws rule of the forum must be consulted to determine the consequences of this unenforceability. This law determines whether the fact that the contract cannot be enforced amounts to an impossibility of performance or a case of *force majeure;* whether restitution should be made of money already paid by one

---

[20] 198 N.E. 617, 269 N.Y. 24 (1935). For a review of the present status of maintenance-of-value clauses in the United States, see Stevenson, "Legal Aspects of the Public Offering of Foreign Securities in the United States Market", 28 Geo. Wash. L. Rev. 194 (1959), at pp. 198-200.

[21] This solution is not altogether certain. In the case of Perutz v. Bohemian Discount Bank in Liquidation, 110 N.Y.S. 2d 446 (1952); 304 N.Y. 533, 110 N.E. 2d 6 (1953), the Court of Appeals of New York, while refusing to enforce an exchange contract contrary to the exchange control regulations of Czechoslovakia, did not base its decision on the specific provisions of Article VIII, Section 2 (b), but rather on the more general effect of membership in the IMF (See Gold, op. cit., note 4 supra, pp. 52-53). It therefore appears that courts might be willing to recognize exchange controls among members of the IMF even in cases outside the scope of Article VIII, Section 2 (b) merely on the basis of membership in the IMF and the general impact of the IMF Agreement on the relations between its members.

party, or whether such restitution should not take place in accordance with the maxim *"In pari delicto. . ."* The latter solution was reached in the *Lessinger* case and at least one reported case involving foreign exchange brokers.[22]

Conflict-of-laws issues, of course, remain paramount in the relations between members of the IMF and non-members, since these relations fall outside the scope of Article VIII, Section 2 (b), of the IMF Agreement.[23] As to these relations, the law as it existed before the creation of the IMF remains unchanged, at least in the absence of specific bilateral agreements between members of the IMF and non-members which provide for the mutual recognition of exchange restrictions imposed by the signatories; and the recognition of foreign exchange control regulations depends exclusively upon the rules of conflict of laws or the public policy of the forum.[24]

In this case, therefore, the classical remedies against the consequences of foreign exchange controls, are still available to lenders. Such remedies include recourse against guarantors outside the country imposing exchange restrictions, and attachment of the borrower's assets at the forum. It is well known, however, that these remedies, important as they may be in the case of relatively small transactions between individuals, are of little practical value in the case of loans raised by institutional borrowers.

Both in the case of loans falling outside the scope of the IMF Agreement (because of the inadequacy of the available remedies) and in the case of loans covered by that Agreement (because of the binding character of its provisions) it is clear that, before embarking on foreign ventures, lenders must be satisfied that their capital will be protected from the detrimental effects of foreign exchange restric-

---

[22] White v. Roberts, 33 Hong Kong Law Reports 231 (1949); Annual Digest, Year 1949, p. 27. See Gold, op. cit., note 4 supra, pp. 82-86, 87-90; Gold, op. cit., note 7 supra, pp. 468-473.

[23] See IMF Articles of Agreement, Article XI.

[24] See e.g., (i) in the United States: Sulyok v. Penzintezeti Kospont Budapest, 279 App. Div. 528, 111 N.Y.S. 2d 75 (1952), affirmed 304 N.Y. 704, 107 N.E. 2d 604 (1952) (Hungarian exchange restrictions); Stern v. Pesti Magyar Kereskedelmi Bank, 303 N.Y. 881, 105 N.E. 2d 106 (1952) (Hungarian exchange restrictions); Kaufman v. Miedzynarodowy Bank Handlowy S.A., 126 N.Y.L.J. 55 Col. 4 (1951) (Polish exchange restrictions *after* Poland had ceased to be a member of the IMF); Stephen v. Zivnostenska Banka National Corporation, 140 N.Y.S. 2d 323 (1955) Czechoslovak exchange restrictions *after* Czechoslovakia had ceased to belong to the IMF); and (ii) in Germany: Wöllert, BGHZ 31-367; NJW 1960, 1101; also summarized in Rev. 1961, 312; Federal Constitutional Court, January 24, 1961 (2 BvR 168/60), summarized in 55 Am. J. Int'l L. 996 (1961).

tions. The modern history of international lending practice bears ample testimony to this remark.

SECTION II. INTERNATIONAL LENDING PRACTICE

As a result of the contemporary law of exchange control no responsible lender or borrower would now consider entering into a loan bargain without being fully satisfied that the proposed operation has been approved by the relevant exchange control authorities. Indeed, contemporary loan documents expressly state or even advertise (especially in the case of bond issues) that all consents and authorizations essential to the validity of the loan under the exchange control regulations involved have been duly and validly given or obtained.[25] This elementary rule of sound modern international lending practice explains why legal problems concerning the effects of unlicensed transactions, which may arise in connection with other international contracts, including loans between individuals,[26] are foreign to loans involving institutional lenders and borrowers like private corporations or public entities, including international organizatons, governmental bodies, municipalities and administrative agencies.

---

[25] See text and notes 36 to 45 infra. The proper authorizations, usually limited to the currency or currencies in which the loan is payable, are sometimes qualified in other respects. Thus, on occasion, it is provided that the entire loan must be issued in specific markets and cannot be offered for subscription in the borrower's, or some other specified, country. See e.g., the propectus of the Sabena (the Belgian airline) 5¾% Loan of 1959 issued in Germany reading as follows:

"The bonds shall not be sold, directly or indirectly, in the United States or Belgium. The sale in Germany is reserved, until December 18, 1958, inclusive, to [two German financial establishments] which undertake not to sell in markets other than the German market" (as translated) .

On other occasions, the authorization may prescribe that the entire loan be subscribed or purchased by non-residents. See e.g., the prospectus relating to the Union of South Africa 4% Loan of 1952, issued in Switzerland, which reads:

"Neither the bonds nor the coupons can be negotiated in South Africa. They may be held in South Africa by authorized dealers only as defined in the Exchange Control Regulations in force in the Union of South Africa. Such authorized dealers can hold such bonds and collect payment on the coupons only on behalf of non-residents" (as translated) .

As to governmental controls of foreign loans and restrictions concerning foreign lending operations, see Chapter I, text and notes 53 to 58.

[26] See *Mann,* pp. 344 et seq.; *Nussbaum,* pp. 446 et seq. See also Roblot, "Les Répercussions de la Réglementation Française des Changes sur la Formation et l'Exécution des Obligations", Droit Social 1954, 129; Pédamon, "Le Régime Contemporain des Clauses Monétaires", D. 1958, Chronique XVIII, p. 101.

Compliance with exchange control regulations gives the exchange control authorities an opportunity to pass judgment on the specific characteristics of the loan and the merits of the proposed operation. From the lenders' viewpoint, however, such compliance constitutes merely an additional assurance that among all the legal requirements essential to the validity of the loan, those imposed by the regulations have been satisfied. This legal assurance, of course, is no guarantee that foreign exchange will be made available to the borrower at maturity or that, if available, such foreign exchange will be freely transferable by the borrower to make the payments required under the loan. Thus, despite covenants requiring the borrower to apply from time to time for such licenses as may be necessary to obtain the foreign exchange required to service the loan,[27] the necessary licenses may nevertheless not be issued, or if issued may be revoked, thereby putting the loan in jeopardy.

A similar remark can be made in connection with stipulations, not infrequently found in international loans, providing that in case of default judgment can be recovered against the borrower in the currency or currencies payable under the loan or, if this is not permissible under the local law, that the judgment be expressed in an amount of local currency sufficient to purchase such currency or currencies on the actual date of payment at the rate or rates of exchange on that date.[28] Such a stipulation, which may prove extremely valuable under normal circumstances,[29] may afford lenders no protection at all in times of exchange restrictions when courts may refuse either

---

[27] See e.g., the following provision in an indenture concerning the settlement of pre-war dollar bonds issued in the United States by a German corporation:

"So long as payments [by the borrower] of currency of the United States of America under this Plan can be made only upon the issue of licenses or the enactment of regulations by the competent German foreign exchange authorities providing for the payment and transfer of such currency, [the borrower] shall take all appropriate action to obtain all necessary licenses for such payments and transfers."

[28] See e.g., Indenture dated May 15, 1928 (Article VI, Section 1) relating to the Tokyo Electric Light Co., Ltd., First Mortgage Gold Bonds 6% dollar series due 1953, reprinted in *Japanese Foreign Currency Bonds,* published by the Ministry of Finance of Japan (August 1951) No. 29-25, Appendix III–1, pp. 53-54. Similar provisions are found in English trust deeds.

[29] This type of stipulation is likely to be most effective in the courts of most European countries which do not favor the rule of compulsory conversion obtaining in common law countries like England and the United States, and which permit judgments to be rendered in foreign currency. See *Nussbaum,* pp. 364 et seq.; *Mann,* pp. 307 et seq.

to render a judgment in foreign currency or to compel the borrower to make provision in local currency preparatory to conversion and payment in foreign exchange, until a proper license is issued.[30]

For these reasons, the above types of stipulations are usually supplemented by additional provisions to the effect that, unless the lenders elect on the due date to receive payment in local currency,[31] such a payment (or any other payment in any currency other than that stipulated in the loan or the bonds) shall not discharge the borrower, whose obligations shall continue until payment is made in accordance with the terms of the loan or the bonds.[32] To the extent at least that the loan or the bonds are governed by a law other than that under which exchange restrictions are imposed,[33] these provisions

---

[30] See e.g., Supreme Court of Colombia, March 5, 1941, Marine Midland Trust Co. of New York v. Departamento del Tolima (51 Gaceta Judicial 415, Clunet 1940-45, 593).

[31] Thus, the indenture referred to in note 28 supra, provides that if, despite the borrower's efforts, an appropriate license for the purchase and transfer of dollars payable under the bonds should be refused or revoked, the borrower shall, upon request by the bondholders, pay in accordance with their demand, a sum in German currency which equals, at the official German rate of exchange on the day preceding such payment, such portion of the principal of, and interest on, the bonds as the holders shall specify; and that such payment shall discharge the borrower of its obligations *pro tanto*.

[32] The following provisions are typical:

". . . The primary obligation [of the borrower to pay principal, interest or premium] shall not be deemed to have been discharged or satisfied by any tender of or recovery of judgment expressed in any currency other than [e.g. dollar, sterling] except to the extent to which such tender or judgment shall result in the effective payment of the said aggregate amount in [dollars, sterling] and accordingly the primary obligation shall continue enforceable for the purpose of recovering in [dollars, sterling] the amount (if any) by which any such effective payment shall fall short of the said aggregate amount."

"[The borrower] further agrees that, if because of the requirement of any applicable law, [the borrower] shall be unable lawfully to pay [dollars, sterling] or shall be permitted to discharge its obligation in a currency other than [dollars, sterling] or the holder of this [bond] shall be required to demand, or accept, payment in any currency other than [dollars, sterling], then [the borrower's] obligation shall not be discharged except to the extent that any such payment in such other currency shall result in the effective payment (whether at maturity, after judgment or otherwise) of the said aggregate amount in [dollars, sterling]."

[33] See e.g., Re Helbert Wagg [1956] I All E.R. 129. In that case, a sterling loan made by an English company to a German company was governed by German law (or so the court construed the loan agreement), with the result that payment in reichsmarks into a blocked account was held to discharge the borrower.

The statement in the text above regarding the merits of such provisions remains true even in cases in which Article VIII, Section 2 (b) of the IMF

have the substantial advantage of maintaining the lenders' rights against the borrower. The resumption of service payments (albeit subject to adjustment) on industrial loans contracted in the 'twenties and the early 'thirties by German corporations, forced to default on their obligations after the imposition of Nazi exchange restrictions, is a clear illustration of the merits of such provisions. Yet this example is also a good reminder of the fact that, between the time of actual default and the settlement of pre-war loans, some two decades have lapsed during which protracted litigation and bitter frustration were the lenders' only alternatives.

To obviate these results, lenders may insist that the loan be guaranteed by reliable guarantors outside the country of the borrower, in the hope that if restrictions are imposed in the borrower's country, the guarantors will remain able to meet their personal obligations.[34] Here again, however, unless it is made quite clear that the obligations of the guarantors are governed by a law other than that of the borrower's country, lenders may experience difficulty in seeking to enforce the guarantee against a reluctant guarantor which may argue that its obligations are governed, and that performance may be excused, by the law applicable to the borrower's indebtedness. Moreover, since the creation of the IMF, stipulations of applicable law may be

---

Agreement would apply. Assuming that the loan contract would have to be held unenforceable in the lenders' country because it is contrary to the exchange restrictions of the borrower's country, or some other member of the IMF, the contract could nevertheless be enforced if and when the restrictions are removed. This remark clearly illustrates what has been said earlier in regard to (i) the date on which the determination necessary for the application of Article VIII, Section 2 (b) should be made (see text and notes 14 and 15 supra) ; and (ii) the difference between invalidity on the one hand, and unenforceability under the IMF agreement on the other (see text and notes 16 to 19 supra) .

[34] See e.g., the California Texas Corporation 4½% Loan of 1955, issued in Switzerland and jointly and severally guaranteed by three subsidiaries of Standard Oil Company of California and Texas Company, incorporated in Canada, Panama and the Bahamas, respectively. The prospectus provides:

"In the event that, because of exchange restrictions or for any other reason, the California Texas Corporation shall fail to pay, or shall be prevented from paying on the due date the amounts due under the Loan and if such payment is not made immediately upon notification or after the due date, the Bahrain Petroleum Company Limited, the Overseas Tankship Corporation and Caltex Oceanic Limited shall pay, upon request, in free Swiss francs the amount due and payable, any bilateral or multilateral payment, or clearing, agreement to the contrary notwithstanding. It is agreed that the holders shall have the right to demand payment from any one of the guarantors of the aggregate outstanding amount of principal, interest, fees, taxes and charges" (as translated) .

insufficient to protect the lenders' interests. To the extent that performance, either by the borrower or by the guarantor, would be contrary to the exchange control regulations of a member or members of the IMF, under the conditions set forth in Article VIII, Section 2 (b) of the IMF Agreement, performance could not be obtained in other member countries, regardless of express provisions of applicable law in the loan or the guarantee agreement.[35]

The best solution, therefore, is to obtain specific undertakings from the appropriate exchange control authorities before a loan is made, that (i) they will make foreign exchange available to the borrower as and when needed for the servicing of the loan, and that (ii) they will not restrict transfer of such foreign exchange for purposes of the loan. This is the object of the so-called "transfer clauses," commonly found in contemporary international loans.

A typical example is found in the prospectus relating to bonds issued in the United States by the City of Oslo, which reads as follows:

> "The Bank of Norway has advised the City that, under all circumstances and notwithstanding any existing or future exchange control restrictions, the Bank of Norway will authorize the City to buy, against payment of Norwegian national currency at the then current rate of exchange and to transmit to the Fiscal Agent, the United States dollars required for the payment of the interest on and principal of the Bonds (including payments required for the sinking fund on the Sinking Fund Bonds) and that such authorization is irrevocable and is given to the City for the benefit of the holders of the Bonds. The Ministry of Commerce and Shipping of the Kingdom has recognized on behalf of the Kingdom that this currency authorization has been granted to the City by the Bank of Norway on behalf of the Kingdom and has pledged the full faith and credit of the Kingdom that the authorization will not be revoked."[36]

---

[35] Apparently no case involving the impact of Article VIII, Section 2 (b) upon guarantee obligations has been reported. However, the statement in the text above is clearly in line with the IMF interpretation of that provision and with the decisions in which the application of Section 2 (b) has been considered.

[36] City of Oslo 5½% Sinking Fund External Loan Bonds of 1958, prospectus, pp. 5-6. See also, Montecatini (an Italian corporation) 5½% Sinking Fund Dollar Debentures, issued in 1959, prospectus p. 30; K.L.M. Royal Dutch Airlines 4¾% Convertible Subordinated Debentures, issued in 1959, prospectus p. 40, reading as follows:
"The Company has been granted a license by De Nederlandsche Bank N.V. authorizing it to sell the Debentures as dollar obligations of the Company, to make payments in United States dollars of principal,

This type of clause, subject to relatively minor drafting variations depending on the circumstances of each case and the practices of each financial market, is commonly used in connection with loans contracted by private or public entities in countries other than the United States, like Canada,[37] Switzerland,[38] and Germany.[39] Covenants to

premium (if any) and interest thereon, and to issue and deliver Common shares upon conversion of the Debentures, all in accordance with the provisions of the Indenture."

[37] See e.g., the Prospectus relating to the Petrofina (a Belgian corporation) $5\frac{1}{2}\%$-$7\frac{1}{2}\%$ Debentures, issued in 1957, (containing a multiple currency clause) :

"The Company has obtained the necessary authorization from l'Institut Belgo-Luxembourgeois du Change to obtain and pay the amounts of principal and interest on the due dates thereof in the currencies elected by the holders of the Debentures."

[38] See e.g., the prospectus concerning the Union Sidérurgique du Nord de la France "USINOR", Paris $4\frac{1}{2}\%$ Loan of 1964:

"The Company has received a letter from the Minister of Finance and Economic Affairs, dated July 29, 1963, in which the Minister authorizes the Company to contract the present loan in Switzerland. In the same letter, the Minister of Finance and Economic Affairs also authorizes the Company to undertake to pay in freely convertible Swiss francs the interest and to repay the principal of this loan on each payment date, under all circumstances, without any restrictions, without regard to any limitations of any kind which might be in force in France at the time, without discrimination on the ground of nationality, domicile or residence of the bondholders and without requesting presentation of an affidavit or the fulfilment of any other formalities. Furthermore, the Minister authorizes the Company to acquire in France the freely convertible Swiss francs necessary to service the loan, and to transfer them to Switzerland notwithstanding any bilateral or multilateral payment or clearing agreement that may be in existence on each payment date. The Company undertakes to comply with the conditions set forth in the letter of the Minister of Finance and Economic Affairs, a photostatic copy of which has been furnished to the Banks" (as translated) .

Similar clauses are found in the following prospectuses: Joseph Lucas (Industries) Limited, Birmingham, $4\frac{1}{2}\%$ Loan of 1963; Société Electrique de l'Our, Société Anonyme (SEO) , Luxembourg, $4\frac{1}{2}\%$ Loan of 1963; Compania Sevillana de Electricidad, Sevilla, 5% Loan of 1963.

But see the following provision in the prospectus concerning the Société Ferroviaire Internationale de Transports Frigorifiques (INTERFRIGO) , Bruxelles $4\frac{1}{2}\%$ Loan of 1959:

"The Institut Belgo-Luxembourgeois du Change has undertaken the irrevocable commitment, for the duration of the loan, to authorize the purchase of free Swiss francs required for payments, and to permit amounts so purchased to be placed at the disposal of the banks involved, without restriction and under any circumstances, *except in case of force majeure*" (as translated, underlining added) .

[39] See e.g., the prospectus concerning the City of Oslo 6% Bearer Bonds of 1964:

"The Bank of Norway (Norges Bank) has granted to the City of Oslo

the same effect are also stipulated by international organizations like the IBRD,[40] or the High Authority of the ECSC,[41] and lending agencies like the Export-Import Bank of Washington,[42] in connection with loans made by them to non-governmental borrowers.

In the case of loans to foreign governments, when the "availability" of foreign exchange is not ordinarily in question, provision is made in the loan documents only for the free "transfer" of sums due under the loan or the bonds. This is the general practice of leading financial markets[43] and international lending organizations.[44] In unusual cases,

---

unrestricted and irrevocable authority to acquire the necessary amounts in Deutsche Marks for the payment of interest and repayment of principal of this Loan and to transfer them for the purpose of servicing the Loan" (as translated).

Similar clauses are found in the following prospectuses: Prefecture of Osaka-City of Osaka 6½% Bonds of 1962 (Guaranteed by Japan); City of Oslo 5½% Bearer Bonds of 1959; Industrie-Hypothekenbank in Finland AG, Suomen Teollisuus-Hypoteekkipanki Oy (Industrial Mortgage Bank of Finland) Helsinki 6¼% Bonds of 1964.

[40] It is the IBRD's practice, in accordance with a provision of its charter (Article III, Section 4(i)), to require a guarantee of each of its loans by the government of the country in which the particular project is located. A standard clause in such guarantee agreements provides that:

"The principal of, and interest and other charges on, the Loan and the Bonds shall be paid free from all restrictions imposed under the laws of the Guarantor or laws in effect in its territories."

[41] See infra text and notes 47 and 48.

[42] See Townsend, "The Export-Import Bank of Washington: Organization and Operation", U. of Ill., Law Forum, Legal Problems of International Trade, vol. 1959, Spring Number 237, 244.

[43] See e.g., the prospectus relating to the Kingdom of Denmark 4½% Loan of 1959, issued in Switzerland:

"The Government of the Kingdom of Denmark undertakes: (a) that the free transfer of amounts in Swiss francs required for the payment of the interest on and the principal of the loan shall be made in due time and that said Swiss francs shall be freely usable at the time of payment, under all circumstances and notwithstanding any bilateral or unilateral payment, or clearing agreement that may be in existence at the time of payment;

(b) that the payment of the interest on and the principal of this loan shall be made to the holders under all circumstances and without any limitation, any restrictions then in force in the Kingdom of Denmark to the contrary notwithstanding, regardless of the nationality, residence or domicile of the holders and without requesting presentation of an affidavit or the fulfilment of any other formality." (as translated).

Similar clauses are found in the prospectuses concerning Swiss issues by: (i) the Republic of Finland 5% Loan of 1961; (ii) the Republic of Austria 5% Loan of 1961; (iii) the Kingdom of Norway 4% Loan of 1960; (iv) the Kingdom of Denmark 4½% Loan of 1962.

See also, in Germany, the following provision in the prospectus relating to the 6% Bonds of 1964, issued by Japan:

however, a different solution may prevail. Thus, when the administration of foreign exchange is entrusted to a central bank or some similar agency, the lenders may require in addition to the borrowing government's undertaking regarding freedom of transfer, a separate undertaking by the central bank or agency concerned to furnish the borrower, against local currency, the sums in foreign currency or currencies necessary to enable the borrower to meet its obligations under the loan or the bonds.[45]

"Japan will transfer all amounts necessary for the fulfilment of the payment obligations arising out of this Loan to the Deutsche Bank AG, Frankfurt am Main, in the legal currency of the Federal Republic of Germany. This obligation includes the punctual transfer in all circumstances and irrespective of any bilateral or multilateral payment or clearing agreement that may be in force at the time of payment and without regard to the nationality, residence or dimicile of the person entitled to payment and without requiring the execution of any affidavit or the fulfilment of any other farmilities." (as translated).

Similar clauses are found in the prospectuses concerning German issues by: (i) the Republic of Finland 6% Loan of 1964; (ii) the Kingdom of Norway 5¼% Bonds of 1963; (iii) the Kingdom of Denmark 5¼% Bonds of 1963.

See also, in the Netherlands, the prospectus concerning the Commonwealth of Australia 5% bonds of 1961:

"The Commonwealth of Australia undertakes:

(a) to remit in good time to the Amsterdamsche Bank N.V. of Amsterdam, in Dutch guilders, all monies necessary for the payment of coupons and redeemable bonds of this Loan and to make these Dutch guilders available on the due date, without deductions, whatever the circumstances, without regard to any future restrictions on transfer and irrespective of any bilateral or multilateral payment or clearance agreements which may exist at the time of payment;

(b) to cause the payment of the coupons and redemable bonds of this Loan to be made to all bondholders, irrespective of the circumstances and of any restrictions of any kind which may be in force in the Commonwealth of Australia at that time, without regard to nationality, residence or domicile of the bondholders and without requiring any affidavit or the fulfilment of any other formalities." (as translated).

[44] Loan agreements between the IBRD and a member government contain a covenant similar to that stipulated in guarantee agreements related to loans to borrowers other than members, quoted in note 40 supra.

[45] See e.g., the prospectus relating to the 6% Loan of 1959, issued in Germany by the Austrian Danube Power Company, jointly and severally guaranteed by the Republic of Austria and an Austrian power company:

"The Austrian National Bank, the competent Austrian foreign exchange authority, has assumed the unconditional obligation to put at the disposal of the debtor or the guarantor the necessary amounts of DM against payment of the corresponding schilling equivalent for the purpose of paying principal and interest in accordance with the terms of the loan" (as translated).

See also the prospectus relating to the Aktiebolaget Götaverken 6%

Borrowings by international lending organizations, which increase steadily in size and frequency, also deserve close attention. Because the respective resources of these organizations, however substantial, are not unlimited; and because it is their purpose to mobilize private capital and utilize it in their operations, those organizations have made, or are in a position to make, extensive borrowings in the private capital market. To facilitate these borrowings and to give potential lenders adequate security of repayment, various devices have been used which are best illustrated by examples of the practices respectively followed by the High Authority of the ECSC and the IBRD. The experiences of these two veterans of modern international lending have, to a greater or lesser extent, inspired the drafters of the charters of other international lending organizations.

The practice adopted by the High Authority of the ECSC follows closely the general trend of the international money market regarding the stipulation of transfer clauses. Some of the original features of its practice, however, can be understood only in light of the machinery set up in the "Act of Pledge" between the High Authority and the Bank for International Settlements (the BIS).[46] That instrument provides that the BIS, acting as "Depositary," receives all the proceeds of the High Authority's borrowings and disburses them to borrowing enterprises within the European Community at the High Authority's request. Each debt of the High Authority and each loan made by it to a borrowing enterprise are represented, respectively, by "Notes" of the High Authority delivered to, and by "enterprise obligations" pledged with, the BIS. Payments due on enterprise obligations are collected by the BIS and applied by it to the satisfaction of the Notes issued by the High Authority. Both the Notes and the enterprise obligations are denominated in one and the same currency, namely that borrowed by the High Authority.

To complete this machinery, the Act of Pledge, as originally

Guaranteed Dollar Debentures due December 1, 1980, issued in New York City in 1965 with the guarantee of the Kingdom of Sweden:

"Sveriges Riksbank has given its written approval for the issuance of the Debentures. Such bank has also given an authorization, irrevocable by its terms, pursuant to which Götaverken (and Sweden under the guarantee) may purchase in exchange for Swedish Kroner sufficient freely transferable United States dollars to pay principal, premium, if any, and interest on the Debentures in accordance with their terms."

[46] Act of Pledge dated November 28, 1954, 238 UNTS 340; TIAS 3126.

See e.g., Zimmer, "Legal Experiences of the European Coal and Steel Community in International Loan Operations", in *McDaniels,* 266.

drafted, provided that before making a loan to an enterprise, the
High Authority should deliver, or cause to be delivered to the BIS
a "currency undertaking" from the government in whose territory the
enterprise was situated.[47] The scope of such a currency undertaking
varied according to whether the enterprise obligations and the High
Authority Notes were payable in the currency of the government
giving the undertaking or in some other currency. In the first instance, the undertaking provided merely that payments due on the
obligations or the Notes would be made free from restrictions imposed
by the government concerned. In the second instance, i.e. when payment was to be made in a foreign currency, the government in whose
territories the enterprise was located undertook to make foreign exchange available, against national currency, to the enterprise and/or
to the High Authority, or to the BIS for the account of the High
Authority, at the time or times and in the amounts necessary to permit
prompt and full payment in such foreign currency of principal and
interest due on the enterprise obligations or on the related Notes of
the High Authority.[48]

Following the improvement of economic conditions in Europe
and the progressive return of European countries to convertibility,
the Act of Pledge was amended and a new system adopted in 1960.
Under this system, each member of the ECSC, instead of furnishing specific currency undertakings on the occasion of each loan operation, simply supplies the ECSC with a statement that its currency is
freely convertible and that it accepts the obligations set forth in Article

[47] Article IV, Section 4.01. A similar requirement was provided in the
1954 loan made by the United States Government to the High Authority, the
first loan contracted by that institution (Agreement of April 23, 1954 as
amended, TIAS 2945 and 3126; 229 UNTS 229 and 228 UNTS 340). Article
II of the Loan Agreement provided that the dollars lent to the High Authority
would be disbursed:

". . . only when and to the extent that Eximbank has received a statement or statements signed by a duly authorized official of the High
Authority setting out that the High Authority has received from one
or more governments Currency Undertakings as required by the Indenture [the so-called Act of Pledge between the High Authority and
the BIS] in respect of such disbursement. A copy of each such undertaking shall forthwith be transmitted to Eximbank."

[48] The Act of Pledge (Article I, Definitions, definition of "currency
undertaking") further provides that:

"Each Currency Undertaking shall contain an acknowledgement of the
government entering into the same that it is given for the benefit of the
holders of the Notes referred to therein and for the purposes of inducing
such holders to make advances to the High Authority."

VIII, Sections 2, 3, and 4 of the IMF Articles of Agreement. In other words, the member undertakes not to restrict the convertible character of its currency without the prior approval of the IMF[49] The advantage of this solution, in addition to its simplicity, is that transfer assurances, instead of being given on an *ad hoc* basis as in the case of the original currency undertakings, now constitute a permanent feature of the lending and borrowing operations of the ECSC. This places the ECSC in a position somewhat similar to that of the IBRD and those organizations more or less inspired by the IBRD example.

Transfer assurances regarding borrowings made by the IBRD are not derived from isolated undertakings by its members at the time of each borrowing, but rather from specific provisions in its Articles of Agreement. It has been seen elsewhere[50] that only part of the IBRD's capital has been paid in, and that the major part of this capital is subject to call as and when needed by the organization to meet its contractual obligations on loans raised or guaranteed by it. The un-called portion of the IBRD's capital constitutes, therefore, a huge reserve fund on which the organization can draw by making calls on its members. Conversely each member has the obligation, propor-tionate to its share of the subscribed capital and the extent of the un-called balance of its capital subscription, to supply the IBRD with gold, United States dollars or the currency required to discharge the IBRD'S obligations.[51] In addition, the Articles of Agreement provide that all property and assets of the IBRD are free from restrictions, regulations, controls and moratoria of any nature.[52] The combination of these provisions assures the IBRD and its creditors that the cur-rency required to satisfy its obligation, or a medium to obtain it, will be available when needed; and that such currency shall be freely usable by the organization to make payment on its obligations. In other words, the Articles of Agreement of the IBRD contain the two characteristic elements of transfer clauses, namely the availability of exchange and the freedom of such exchange from restrictions. Since a large portion of the capital of the IBRD has been subscribed by countries whose external debt record is outstanding, creditors of the

---

[49] See e.g., pamphlet explaining the proposed Amendments to the Act of Pledge issued on June 14, 1960 by the High Authority, pp. 4 to 6; Zimmer, op. cit., note 46 supra, at pp. 275-276.

[50] See Chapter V, text and notes 17 and 18.

[51] IBRD Articles of Agreement, Article II, Sections 5 (ii) , 7 (ii) and (iii) , Article IV, Section 7 (c) .

[52] IBRD Articles of Agreement, Article VII, Section 6.

IBRD for all practical purposes, have the assurance that the IBRD, if and when necessary, would have the exchange required to satisfy their respective claims. A similar remark can be made in regard to newer organizations whose charters are more or less patterned after the IBRD Articles of Agreement.[53]

---

[53] See e.g., EIB Statutes, Articles 5, paragraph 2, and 25; IADB Articles of Agreement, Articles II, Section 4 (ii) , III, Section 4 (ii) and XI, Section 6. See also the publications cited in Chapter V, note 17.

Chapter VIII

The Political Risk

Since international loans are usually made for protracted periods of time, the danger is great that political changes may adversely affect the interests of lenders before the loan is fully repaid. Although lenders are sometimes able to identify expected changes at the outset,[1] they are normally in no position to forecast with any serious degree of accuracy the possible occurrence of political upheavals or other events, more or less politically flavored, which may adversely affect their interests.

Lenders have learned to anticipate problems concerning governmental interference with the borrower's affairs or its juridical existence, including nationalization,[2] and have devised means to protect them-

---

[1] This is the case if a country is on the eve of independence or on the verge of a revolution; or if the relations between the parties are likely to be affected by the imminent outbreak of a war or existing war-time conditions.

[2] It has been seen elsewhere (see Chapter II, text and notes 34 and 35) that when the chances of governmental interference with the borrower's affairs are great, because of the nature of its business or its relations with the authorities in question, lenders generally insist on direct commitments from the relevant authorities that they will not arbitrarily prevent the borrower from performing its loan obligations. Because public authorities generally refuse to renounce unconditionally their sovereign prerogatives, such commitments usually preserve their right to take action against the borrower if there is just cause for such action. However, these undertakings afford lenders a substantial degree of protection. Like any other contractual agreements between lenders and governmental or other public authorities, they establish a direct relationship between the parties and provide additional remedies to safeguard the lenders' interests. Furthermore, these commitments are frequently complementary to other arrangements between the lenders and the public authorities involved, including financial guarantees. Under the circumstances, the relevant authorities would become directly liable to the lenders if they ignored their non-interference obligations.

Such contractual arrangements do not always exist, however. Sometimes the parties do not believe them necessary at the time of the loan, or are anxious to preserve the purely private character of the transaction. At other

selves against arbitrary governmental action or discrimination.[3] However, the effectiveness of contractual remedies in time of crisis is often negligible. This becomes particularly true when the existence of the state as a recognizable juridical entity is in issue, or the self-preservation of a belligerent state is at stake. In cases like these, the protection of lenders' interests depends in the final analysis less upon specific covenants in loan documents than (i) on the legal principles applicable to the particular situation involved, or (ii) the conclusion of *ex post facto* settlements whose terms generally reflect the respective bargaining position of the parties, rather than strictly legal considerations.

SECTION I. POLITICAL CHANGES

A. CHANGES IN THE FORM OF GOVERNMENT

It is generally agreed that changes in the leadership or the form of government of a state do not affect the continuity of its existence

times, as lawyers are well aware, the solution of the issue may simply be too delicate to settle during the loan negotiations. Whatever the reason for the omission, it is clear that in the absence of any such covenants, the situation of lenders may be far from enviable. Thus in the overwhelming majority of cases following the nationalization of enterprises in Eastern Europe and other countries, lenders, to the extent that their claims have been included in debt settlement plans, have not fared better than other creditors. See e.g., Moreau-Néret, *Valeurs Etrangères* (1956), pp. 146-204; Foighel, *Nationalization* (1957), p. 103; Bindschedler, *The Protection of Private Property in Public International Law*, 90 Recueil des Cours 173 (1956), pp. 218-219.

[3] This is the purpose of negative-pledge clauses (See Chapter V, text and notes 95-103), transfer assurances (see Chapter VII, text and note 43) and similar covenants. Preferential treatment of certain creditors would, in cases like these, constitute a flagrant violation of the borrower's contractual undertakings. (See e.g., *Borchard*, p. 262 and *Wynne*, pp. 232, 234-235; *SEC Report*, Part V, pp. 380-381; T.F. May 26, 1936, Aktiebolaget Obligationinteressenter v. The Bank for International Settlements, R.O.62, II, 140, League of Nations Doc. I.L. 18, Geneva February 11, 1937; United States Secretary of State's Note dated November 33, 1934 to Germany, *SEC Report*, Part V, p. 433; Hackworth 5 *Digest of International Law*, pp. 627-628).

Not all situations are, however, as clear as the foregoing. Sometimes, under the veil of general legislation or regulation, a debtor government in fact adopts measures directed exclusively against foreign creditors or certain classes of creditors. This was the case when in 1936, the German Reich enacted a statute specifically intended to take advantage of foreign laws abrogating gold clauses (see T.F. February 1, 1938, Allgemeine Elektrizitätsgesellschaft and Siemens & Halske AG. v. Journaliag, Annual Digest 1938-1940, p. 115; Dutch Supreme Court May 26, 1939, Osram Gold Dollar Loan, Annual Digest 1919-1942, p. 29). A Belgian regulation issued on May 1, 1933 falls probably within the same category. The regulation provided that only those holders of gold dollar bonds of Belgium who would turn in their bonds for stamping in Belgium would thereafter be entitled to receive payment at the gold value of the dollar. The other holders would be paid at the depreciated value of the paper dollar. Because of the short period during which the stamping was to take place (four days) many foreign holders could not be expected to fulfill the necessary formality in time. Apparently, however, the regulation gave rise to no official protest (see Piret, *Les Variations Monétaires*, (1935), pp. 271-272; *Nussbaum*, p. 427; *Van Hecke*, p. 240).

Discrimination, of course, does not lose its obnoxious character merely because it is dressed up in terms of measures of general application (see e.g., The Treatment of Polish Nationals in Danzig, PCIJ Series A/B, No. 44, at p. 28), and "piercing the veil" is often required to give the facts of the case their genuine significance. That the necessary characterization is not always an easy process is sufficiently illustrated by the respective arguments put forward by France and Norway in the Case of Certain Norwegian Loans (ICJ Reports 1957, p. 9). During the years 1885-1909, several loans were issued in foreign markets by the Government of Norway and Norwegian credit institutions. The bonds were payable in gold kroner and various other currencies. After the abrogation of gold clauses in Norway, the bonds were serviced on the basis of their nominal value only. An exception was made in respect to Danish and Swedish bondholders: They received payment in Danish and Swedish kroner, respectively, which, once at a par with the Norwegian kroner, were at a premium over the latter currency. France, which had espoused the claims of French bondholders, argued that Norway, by according the Danish and Swedish bondholders a treatment more favorable than that granted to French bondholders, had discriminated against these bondholders in violation of international law (*Pleadings*, vol. I, pp. 166, 175, 178-179, 401). Norway answered that the preferential treatment of Danish and Swedish bondholders was an act *ex gratia* based on considerations other than the terms of the loan contract, and that no rule of international law prevented a borrower from granting certain advantages to some of its creditors not extended to other creditors. In other words, discrimination would not be contrary to international law if it were made *in favor of,* rather than *against* a particular class of creditors (*Pleadings*, pp. 254-258, 293, 443-444). The Court had no opportunity to settle the issue, since the French claim was dismissed on jurisdictional grounds. However, some of the Judges expressed some doubts as to the merits of the Norwegian argument (see in particular the separate opinions of Judge Read (ICJ Reports, pp. 88-89) and Judge Lauterpacht (Ibid. p. 38). The issue was raised again in the Norwegian courts in the case of Association Nationale des Porteurs Frànçais de Valeurs Mobilières v. The Norwegian Government, the Mortgage Bank of Norway and the Small Holding and Workers' Housing Bank (Supreme Court of Norway May 2, 1962, summarized by Bahr, "The Norwegian Gold Clause Case", 12 Am. J. Comp. L. 1 (1963)). Though the majority of the Court upheld the Norwegian Government's contention, one Justice registered his dissent (see Bahr, op. cit., p. 16).

It should be pointed out that, though debtors frequently make an independent decision to discriminate among their debtors, on occasion creditors must bear their share of the blame. Instances in which creditors have put sufficient pressure on borrowers to obtain preferential treatment are not rare. A typical example is that of the chaotic situation brought about by pre-World War II diplomacy concerning Germany's public debt (see e.g., *SEC Report*, Part V, pp. 427 et seq.). It is with a view to preventing the recurrence of the pre-war negotiations between Germany and her creditors that the London Agreement on German External Debts of February 27, 1953 (333 UNTS 3)

and its international obligations,[4] so long as the identity of the state is preserved. This general rule is acknowledge by state practice,[5] and by judicial precedents, both domestic and international.[6] The fact that the rule has not been complied with on occasion,[7] does not put its existence into question.

---

prohibits both Germany and her creditors from making or seeking any discrimination or preferential treatment in respect of the various debts subject to the settlement plan. To that end, Article 8 of the Agreement provides that:

> "The Federal Republic of Germany will not permit, nor will any creditor countries seek from the Federal Republic of Germany, either in the fulfilment of terms of settlement in accordance with the present Agreement and the Annexes thereto or otherwise, any discrimination or preferential treatment among the different categories of debts or as regard the currencies in which debts are to be paid or in any other respect . . ."

However, the London Agreement does recognize that particular categories of debts subject to the over-all settlement may receive a differential treatment, even though such treatment is not to be considered discriminatory under the Agreement. A concrete example involves the American issues of the Dawes and Young loans. Under the Agreement, gold clauses in dollar bonds were disregarded, and a dollar clause was substituted for the original gold clause in bonds denominated in other non-German currencies (see text and note 76, infra). To account for the substantial revaluation of the latter bonds as a result of this substitution as well as for the elimination of gold clauses from dollar bonds, it was agreed that the dollar issue of the Young loan would receive better treatment than the European issues in respect to interest (5% instead of 4½%), and that preferential treatment would be granted to the dollar issue of the Dawes loan in regard to both interest (5½% instead of 5%) and amortization (sinking fund of 3% as compared with 2% for the European issue). See Annex I, Sections 1 and 2. The compromise arrived at in London in regard to the settlement of the Dawes and Young loans illustrates the spirit of cooperation characteristic of the London negotiations. It would be improper to see in this compromise more than an *ad hoc*, and a limited, exception to the general principle of non-discrimination most emphatically expressed in the Agreement. To refer, therefore, to the preferential treatment of American creditors without mentioning also the substantial advantages given to European creditors is somewhat misleading (see *van Hecke,* p. 258, note 28).

[4] See e.g., Hackworth, I *Digest of International Law,* 387; Moore, I *Digest of International Law,* 248; Feilchenfeld, *Public Debts and State Succession* (1931), 609-611; Politis, *Les Emprunts d'Etat en Droit International* (1894), 106; Marek, *Identity and Continuity of States in Public International Law* (1954), 26.

[5] See e.g., Marek, op. cit., preceding note, pp. 31-34.

[6] See e.g., the Ottoman Debt Arbitration of April 18, 1925, I *Reports of International Arbitral Awards* (1948), 529; The Tinoco Arbitration of October 18, 1923, 18 Am. J. Int'l L. 147 (1924); The Ship Sapphire, 11 Wall. 164 (1871); Lepeschkin v. Gosweiler, T.F. February 2, 1923, J. T. 1923, 582; Lazard Brothers and Co. v. Midland Bank Ltd., [1933] A.C. 289; Annual Digest 1931-1932, p. 140; Lowinsky v. Receiver in Bankruptcy of the Egyptisch-Türksche Handwerksigarettenfabriek "Jaka" Ltd., District Court of Amsterdam June 7, 1932, Annual Digest 1931-1932, p. 40.

[7] The repudiation of Russia's public debt by the Soviets in 1918 is one of the most frequently cited examples of non-compliance with the rule. It was

The principle of state continuity, as applied to international loan obligations, has been best illustrated by the many decisions rendered, on both the domestic and international levels, in the *Guano Loan Cases,* involving a series of disputes between Peru and her creditors. In 1869, Peru sold to Dreyfus Brothers, a French company, a quantity of guano, with the understanding that the company would have a monopoly for the resale of guano to various European countries. In return Dreyfus Brothers agreed to make a loan to Peru. Numerous disputes over the contract were brought before the Peruvian courts and in 1880 the company entrusted the final decision of the dispute to the President of Peru, Nicolas de Pierola, who had assumed extraordinary executive, legislative and judicial powers. The President ruled that some £3 million were due to Dreyfus Brothers. Subsequently a new government was elected which enacted a law annulling all internal acts of the Pierola Government. In several suits brought against Peru in England and Belgium, the courts rejected the Peruvian contention that because the Pierola government was unconstitutional, Peru was not bound by the acts of that government.[8] The same solution was reached in the 1901 award of a Franco-Chilean Arbitral Tribunal,[9] and in the 1921 award of an arbitral tribunal set up by France and Peru in accordance with the provisions of the Hague Convention of 1907 for the Pacific Settlement of International Disputes.[10]

---

on this occasion that Great Britain and France issued the joint declaration of March 28, 1918, which stated that:

> "no principle is better established than that according to which a nation is responsible for the acts of its government without a change in its authority affecting the obligations incurred."

For an interesting discussion of the history of the repudiation and the subsequent negotiations, see Marek, op. cit, note 4 supra, pp. 34-38.

[8] Republic of Peru v. Peruvian Guano Co. (1887) L.R. 36 Ch. D. 489 and Republic of Peru v. Dreyfus Brothers and Co. (1888) L.R. 38 Ch. D. 348; Brussels July 10, 1888, La Belgique Judiciaire, XLVI, 1218.

[9] Descamps et Renault, *Recueil International des Traités du XXe Siècle* (1901), p. 294. The award of July 5, 1901 reads in part as follows:

> "According to a principle of the law of nations . . . applied . . . in a series of cases today universally accepted, the capacity of a government to represent the state in its international relations depends in no degree whatever upon the legitimacy of its origin; so that . . . the usurper who exercises power in fact, with an express or tacit consent of the nation, acts and concludes validly in the name of the state treaties which the legitimate government, upon its restoration, is bound to respect."

[10] Scott, *Hague Court Reports,* 2d Series (1932), p. 31. The award reads in part as follows:

> "Whereas, Nicolas de Pierola was proclaimed supreme chief of the Republic by popular assemblies and maintained by numerous plebiscitary

Under the circumstances, provisions like that found in the December 1, 1925 Declaration of Trust regarding the Province of Lower Austria Secured Sinking Fund 7½% Gold Bonds, which read as follows:

> "When reference is herein made to the Republic of Austria, it shall be deemed to apply to any successor government which may at any time during the life of this agreement govern the territory now embraced within the territorial boundaries of this Province" (Article XV, Section 6),

can be considered as merely declaratory of existing law. This may explain why provisions of this kind are rarely stipulated in contemporary loan documents.

B. CHANGES OF SOVEREIGNTY

The legal principles governing the effect on the public debt of a change of sovereignty are much less firmly settled than those respecting changes in the form of a debtor's government. In light of the abundant literature in this confused field, which reflects all shades of legal, political and philosophical thinking;[11] and the instances of

---

adhesions; whereas he exercised the legislative power, the executive power and, in part, the judicial power; whereas, on June 28, 1881, he voluntarily resigned these functions but was immediately invested with the presidency of the Republic by the National Assembly; whereas, his government was recognized especially by France, England, Germany and Belgium; whereas, finally, the High Court of Justice of England (decree of February 23, 1888), the Court of Appeals of Brussels (decree of July 10, 1888), the Franco-Chilean Arbitral Court (award called Award of Lausanne of July 5, 1901), being decrees and an award of which the arbitral court adopts the reasons, have deemed that this government represented and bound the nation;

Whereas, it is of slight importance that a Peruvian law of October 25, 1886, declared 'all the internal acts of the government performed by Nicolas de Pierola null,' *since this law can not be applied to foreigners who treated in good faith"* (p. 33, emphasis added).

[11] See e.g., Sack, *Les Transformations des Etats sur leurs Dettes Publiques et Autres Obligations Financières* (1927, hereinafter *Les Transformations,* etc.); *La Succession aux Dettes Publiques d'Etat,* 23 Recueil des Cours 149 (1928); Paenson, *Les Conséquences Financières de la Succession des Etats, 1932-1953* (1954); O'Connell, *The Law of State Succession* (1956); Castrén, *Aspects Récents de la Succession d'Etat,* 78 Recueil des Cours, 385 (1951); Jèze, *Le Partage des Dettes Publiques au cas de Démembrement du Territoire* (1921); Feilchenfeld, op. cit. note 4 supra; Hyde, I *International Law* (2d ed. 1947), 400 et seq.; Hudson, I *Digest of International Law* 593 et seq.; Vallat, "Some Aspects of the Law of State Succession", 41 Transactions of the Grotius Society 1955 (1956) 122.

state practice, which exhibit remarkable historical and geographical variations, it is impossible to formulate any universal rule.

There are clear indications that the international community is conscious of the need to protect the legitimate interests of creditors. However, the conscience of nations is not necessarily aroused with the same intensity in the various situations which may arise on the occasion of a change of sovereignty. All that can be stated generally, yet with caution, is that states appear more inclined to respect the rights of creditors when the personality of the debtor is completely extinguished (i.e. total succession by absorption into another state or dismembership) or in which the debtor acquires a new juridical personality (i.e. secession or independence), and less inclined to respect such rights in situations in which the transfer of sovereignty over part of the debtor's territory leaves its existence as a juridical entity intact (i.e transfer of part of the debtor's territory to another state).

It is commonly stated that in case of total successions the successor state or states succeed to the public debt of the former debtor. Whether the successor state's obligation is based on the principle of acquired rights or unjust enrichment,[12] or on "international financial law,"[13] is an interesting matter of speculation. In any event, state practice generally acknowledges the existence of the obligation, although several exceptions have occurred in recent decades.[14] The practical question, therefore, is not whether the successor state is bound to respect the public debt of its predecessor, but rather the extent of its liability therefor. This, in turn, may depend on whether the debtor's personality is extinguished by absorption into another state or by dismemberment.

---

[12] See O'Connell, op. cit., preceding note, pp. 145-149.

[13] See Sack, *Les Transformations*, etc., pp. 84-90.

[14] One significant exception was the annexation of Austria by the Reich (see e.g., O'Connell, op. cit., note 11 supra, pp. 152-154; Paenson, op. cit., note 11 supra, pp. 146-148). Another was the incorporation of the Baltic States into the Soviet Union (see e.g., Castrén, op. cit., note 11 supra, pp. 419, 465 and 474).

It should be noted, however, that although the Reich took the position that it was not legally bound to assume the debts of Austria, it concluded agreements with creditor countries like the United Kingdom, France, Belgium, the Netherlands and Sweden, pursuant to which it had accepted a certain liability for the Austrian debts. The bargaining position of European countries was apparently greater than that of the United States, which did not succeed in reaching agreement with the Reich (see I *Hyde,* op. cit., note 11 supra, pp. 418-420).

The principle of Germany's liability for Austrian debts between 1938 and 1945 is acknowledged in the London Agreement of February 27, 1953 (Article 19 (1) (b), 333 UNTS 3).

In the case of absorption, it has been suggested that if the former state retains a recognizable entity as a fiscal unit, the successor state's liability is commensurate with the revenues administered by such unit; whereas if the successor state merges its revenues with those of the acquired territory, it incurs an unlimited liability. Whatever may be the merits of this suggestion, the fact is that state practice reveals few examples in which a successor state has been willing to assume an unlimited liability for the debts of an acquired territory under such circumstances.[15] In the overwhelming majority of cases involving changes of sovereignty by way of annexation or federation, the successor states have been careful to preserve the separate fiscal identity of the acquired territory, and prevent any confusion between the respective revenues of the successor state and the acquired territory. In most cases, successor states have insisted that the public debt of the acquired territory be serviced out of the latter's revenues.[16] When suc-

---

[15] One of the few cases in which unlimited liability was assumed involved the annexation of Tahiti by France in 1880, and of Korea by Japan in 1910. See Feilchenfeld, op. cit., note 4 supra, pp. 369 and 378. Comp., the position taken by the United Kingdom regarding the Fiji debts, Feilchenfeld, id. op., pp 290-293.

[16] See e.g., Feilchenfeld, op. cit., note 4 supra, pp. 287, 369-373; O'Connell, op. cit., note 11 supra, pp. 149-150, 151-152, 154-156, I Hyde, op. cit., id, loc., pp. 415-417.

The situation following the cession of the Independent State of the Congo to Belgium is less clear. The Treaty of Cession of November 28, 1907 (Article 3) provided that the cession included all the debt and financial undertakings including foreign loans) of the Congo. However, on the same day that the Treaty was approved, the Belgian Parliament voted a law of October 18, 1908, which provided *inter alia* for the separation of the assets and liabilities of Belgium and the new Colony of the Congo (the *Charte Coloniale*, Article I). This apparent contradiction between the provisions of the Treaty and those of the statute has been the object of much controversy among writers. See e.g., Durieux, *Le Problème Juridique des Dettes du Congo Belge et l'Etat du Congo,* Académie Royale des Sciences d'Outre-Mer, (1961); Waelbroeck, "A Propos des Emprunts Congolais", 15 Chronique de Politique Etrangère 57 (1962). Certain writers have taken the extreme position that Belgium was fully responsible for the Congo debt; others have contended that that debt remained the exclusive responsibility of the ceded territory; and still other writers have sought to make a distinction between debts incurred before the cession (which would have been assumed by Belgium pursuant to the Treaty), and Congolese debts incurred thereafter (which would be the exclusive responsibility of the Congo). When the issue was brought up before Belgian courts, they upheld the binding character of the *Charte Coloniale* and ruled that creditors should look to the Congo rather than Belgium for payment of their claims (Cass. Belgium, April 27, 1933, Sarot du Beilay v. Colonie du Congo Belge et Etat Belge, Clunet 1933, 379). The French Supreme Court took a similar position in the case of Montefiore v. Association Nationale des Porteurs de Valeurs Mobilières (Cass. November 21, 1961,

cessor states have assumed direct liability in respect to the debt of an acquired territory, it has generally taken the form of *ex post facto* guarantees. Examples are guarantees of the debt of a protectorate by a protector state,[17] or of a province by a newly formed federation.[18]

J.C.P. 1962, II, 12521; Rev. 1962, 329; Clunet 1962, 686). A recent Belgian decision (Trib. Civ. Bruxelles September 23, 1964, Demol v. Etat Belge, Ministre des Finances, Journal des Tribunaux 1964, 600) maintains the distinction between Congolese debt and Belgian debt with respect to a 1956 Congo loan, and dismisses a claim for payment directed against Belgium. See also Trib. Civ. Gand December 19, 1963, De Kerr Maurice v. Etat Belge Journal des Tribunaux. 1964, 61, and note 22 infra.

[17] See e.g., as to the French Guarantee of Tunisia's debt in 1884 (in exchange for which other creditors agreed to waive their rights to pledged revenues securing the Tunisian debt), Silvera, "L'Evolution des Rapports Financiers et Economiques Franco-Tunisiens", Revue Juridique et Politique d'Outre-Mer 1960, 89 at pp. 91-92.

[18] See e.g., the Guarantee Agreement dated October 2, 1954 between the Federation of Rhodesia and Nyasaland, and (i) the IBRD, (ii) the United Kingdom, (iii) the Colony of Southern Rhodesia and (iv) the Territory of Northern Rhodesia (201 UNTS 179). In March 1953, the IBRD had agreed to make a loan to the Territory of Northern Rhodesia to assist in financing the Development Program of the Rhodesia Railways. As part of the project was to be carried out in the Colony of Southern Rhodesia and its financing depended on the joint efforts of the two Rhodesias, the Loan Agreement between the Territory and the IBRD was supplemented by a Subsidiary Agreement between the Colony, the Territory and the IBRD. The subsidiary Agreement contained specific undertakings of the Colony and the Territory concerning the project and related matters. The over-all transaction was guaranteed by the United Kingdom pursuant to a Guarantee Agreement with the IBRD (see Loan, Subsidiary and Guarantee Agreements dated March 11, 1953, 172 UNTS 115).

Following the creation of the Federation in October 1953, the Federation, with the concurrence of the two Rhodesias and the United Kingdom, entered into a Guarantee Agreement with the IBRD. Pursuant to that Agreement, the Federation undertook to guarantee the financial obligations of the Territory under the Loan Agreement and, "within the limits of its constitutional powers", to carry out or cause to be carried out all the obligations to be performed by the Territory and/or the Colony under the Loan and/or the Subsidiary Agreement.

Comp., the Guarantee Agreement dated October 2, 1954 (201 UNTS 171) between the Federation of Rhodesia and Nyasaland, and (i) the IBRD, (ii) the United Kingdom and (iii) the Colony of Southern Rhodesia, providing for a solution similar to that described above in respect to the railway loan, in connection with an earlier IBRD power loan to the Colony of Southern Rhodesia, guaranteed by the United Kingdom (see Loan and Guarantee Agreements dated February 27, 1952, 159 UNTS 181).

Another example is the Agreement dated March 25, 1953 between the United Kingdom and Libya (172 UNTS 281), pursuant to which the new federal government agreed to guarantee the repayment to the United Kingdom of a 1949 loan to Cyrenaica, one of the new Provinces of the Federation of Lybia.

In the case of dismemberment or secession, the successor states have generally accepted a share of the public debt of the extinguished state. This has sometimes been done by apportioning existing debts among the successor states.[19] However on at least one occasion (the

[19] See e.g., in the case of the partition of Belgium and Holland in 1830 and in regard to the dissolution of the federal state of Colombia in 1829, Feilchenfeld, op. cit., note 4 supra, pp. 191-209 and 296-297.

A more recent example is afforded by the arrangements between the IBRD and the Rhodesias concluded at the time of the dissolution of the Federation of Rhodesia and Nyasaland in December 1963. Pursuant to these arrangements Northern and Southern Rhodesia resumed direct responsibility for loans originally made to them, and subsequently guaranteed by the Federation after its establishment (see the 1953 railway loan to Northern Rhodesia and the 1952 power loan to Southern Rhodesia referred to in the preceding note). In the case of the loan made to the Federal Power Board (see Loan Agreement dated June 21, 1956, between the IBRD and the Federal Power Board and the Guarantee Agreements of even date therewith between the United Kingdom, on the one hand, and on the other the Federation of Rhodesia and Nyasaland, and the IBRD, 285 UNTS 317) and in the case of the railway loan made to the Federation (see Loan Agreement dated June 16, 1958, between the Federation of Rhodesia and Nyasaland and the IBRD and Guarantee Agreement of even date therewith between the United Kingdom and the IBRD, 309 UNTS 35), agreed to guarantee (in the case of the power loan) or to assume (in the case of the railway loan), each for one-half the obligations of the original borrower (see Loan Assumption Agreements dated December 30, 1963 between the IBRD, Central African Power Corporation (successor to the Federal Power Board) and the United Kingdom, and Guarantee Agreements between (i) the Colony of Southern Rhodesia and (ii) the Territory of Northern Rhodesia, and the IBRD and the United Kingdom; Loan Assumption Agreements dated December 30, 1963, between (i) the Colony of Southern Rhodesia and (ii) the Territory of Northern Rhodesia, and the IBRD, the Rhodesia Railways and the United Kingdom).

In the case of the 1960 IBRD loan to the Federation for the development of agriculture in Southern Rhodesia, (see Loan Agreement dated April 1, 1960, between the Federation and the IBRD; the Project Agreement of even date therewith between the Colony of Southern Rhodesia and the IBRD, and the Guarantee Agreement of even date therewith between the United Kingdom and the IBRD, 379 UNTS 397), Southern Rhodesia alone assumed the original obligations of the Federation. See Loan Assumption Agreement dated December 30, 1963 between the Colony of Southern Rhodesia, the IBRD and the United Kingdom. In all these cases, the guarantee of the United Kingdom continued in effect. To indicate its concurrence with these arrangements, the United Kingdom joined in signing the Loan Assumption and Guarantee Agreements.

As to the distribution of other items in the public debt of the Federation, see The Federation of Rhodesia and Nyasaland (Dissolution) Order in Council 1963 (No. 2085) Section 16 and Schedule I.

Following the unilateral declaration of independence by Rhodesia on November 11, 1965 and the subsequent freezing of Rhodesia's reserves in England, the Smith regime declared that it considered itself absolved from responsibility for servicing and repaying (a) bonds issued in the London

partition of British India in 1947) one of the successor states (India) agreed to remain liable for the debt of the former Central Government (subject to her claim against Pakistan for financial contribution).[20] This solution, which has the advantage of maintaining the unity of the debt and dispensing with the need for creditors to divide their claims among the new debtors, is somewhat exceptional. In most cases, it is doubtful that any one of the successor states would be willing to underwrite in effect the other's obligations, regardless of its own capacity to pay.

Secession from the mother state does not necessarily imply that the mother state loses its own personality. It may mean merely that some territorial entity acquires a new international personality, distinct from that of the mother state. This is the case when a former dependent territory or colony becomes independent. In such a situation, the problem of whether the new state is liable for debts of the mother state generally turns on the distinction between the national debt of the mother state on the one hand, and, on the other hand, the local debts contracted by the territory achieving independence or by the former mother state on its behalf. As a general rule, and subject to financial arrangements between the mother state and its formerly dependent territories, liability for the national debt has remained the exclusive responsibility of the mother country,[21] whereas local debts have continued to be serviced by the newly independent state.[22]

---

market; (b) debt due to the British Government and its agencies; and (c) debt which was guaranteed by the United Kingdom. This last category included existing IBRD loans. Since November 11, 1965, the UK has made payment as Guarantor under IBRD Loans of amounts due from Rhodesia and the Central African Power Corporation.

[20] See O'Connell, op. cit., note 11 supra, p. 166.

[21] This was the case when the United States became independent from Great Britain, and when Latin American countries became independent from Spain. See e.g., Feilchenfeld, op. cit., note 4 supra, pp. 53 and 251; O'Connell, op. cit., note 11 supra, p. 160.

[22] This principle was followed by: (i) the Latin American countries after achieving independence from Spain, (see e.g., Feilchenfeld, op. cit., note 4 supra, pp. 251 et seq.; (ii) the Philippines Republic in 1946 (see Treaty of July 4, 1946, between the United States and the Philippines, Article 4, 7 UNTS 4); (iii) each of the territories of the British Commonwealth on achieving independence or attaining Dominion status (see O'Connell, op. cit., note 11 supra, pp. 178-180). See also, in regard to loans raised by the former Government General of Algeria, the information given by the French Minister of Finance on February 22, 1963, *Annuaire Français du Droit International* 1963, p. 1016.

In several cases, including those which have occurred with increasing

Although these precedents are encouraging, they have not always been followed. For example, in connection with the settlement of the debt of the former Palestine administration, the United Kingdom contended that upon the termination of the British Mandate, the new state of Israel should succeed to the debt of the mandatory government. This view proved unacceptable to Israel. Negotiations between the two countries led to a compromise agreement pursuant to which Israel agreed to be liable for bearer bonds held and registered in that country, and the United Kingdom assumed responsibility for bonds held outside Israel.[23] In the case of a loan, the proceeds of which had been applied to railway projects in Palestine, the United Kingdom, although it remained solely liable to the bondholders, received a finan-

---

frequency since the last World War, the assumption of local debts has been arranged before, or concomitantly with, the change of status of the former dependent territory. This solution, favorable to creditors, also serves to establish the international credit of the debtor state.

The practice of the Latin American Republics was less consistent. While some countries recognized and assumed local debts before the signing of treaties of recognition with Spain (see e.g., in regard to Mexico and Bolivia, Feilchenfeld, op. cit., note 4 supra, p. 251, notes 253 and 255), other countries agreed to service debts only after ratification of such treaties (see e.g., with respect to Bolivia, Costa Rica, Argentina, Venezuela and Nicaragua, Feilchenfeld, ibid., p. 254).

On February 6, 1965, the Democratic Republic of the Congo and Belgium concluded an agreement for the settlement of operations concerning the public debt and the portfolio of the former Belgian Congo. Insofar as the public debt is concerned, the agreement makes a distinction between three categories of debts: (a) the Congo Republic assumes responsibility for the debt expressed in Congolese francs or held by Congolese public institutions; (b) Belgium assumes responsibility for the debt expressed in currencies other than Congolese francs and guaranteed by the Belgian Government; and (c) Belgium and the Congo Republic agree to create a Belgo-Congolese Fund (*Fonds belgo-congolais d'Amortissement et de Gestion*) for the purpose of refunding the debt expressed in currencies other than Congolese francs and not guaranteed by the Belgium Government (with the exception of the debt held by Congolese public institutions). The Fund's resources for interest and redemption payments and other charges are supplied both by Belgium and the Congo Republic. To that end, the two Governments have given to the National Bank of Belgium a permanent order to draw the necessary amounts from the account of the Belgian Treasury and from the account of the National Bank of the Congo with the National Bank of Belgium (see Krediet-bank, Weekly Bulletin April 3, 1965).

In the case of the 1958 Dollar bonds of the Congo, the above arrangements resulted in a substitution of Belgian franc bonds for original dollar bonds. For a criticism of this "cross-currency settlement", see Wall Street Journal, February 3, 1966, p. 17.

For the special case of Rhodesia, see note 19 supra.

[23] Agreement of March 30, 1950 (Article 4), 86 UNTS 231.

cial contribution from Israel equivalent to the amounts spent on railways taken over by Israel.[24]

The case of the Indonesian debt is also significant. In 1949, the new Republic of Indonesia agreed to assume responsibility for loans of the former Netherlands Indies.[25] In 1956, however, the Indonesian Government announced that it would no longer recognize, or make payment on, the Indonesian debt to the Netherlands. As this announcement was limited to a particular class of creditors, however, it does not constitute a complete repudiation by Indonesia of the general practice respecting succession to local debts.

Such a repudiation was advocated by the United States during the Cuban debt controversy with Spain in 1898. The United States took the position that the loans in question, some of which were secured by Cuban revenues, had been incurred by Spain for purposes hostile to the interests of Cuba, and that therefore Cuba was not liable for the loans. In any event, it was questionable whether the loans involved were actually "local debts." If the loans were to be considered part of the national debt of Spain rather than local debts, the weight of precedents would have supported the United States' contention that Spain alone remained liable, regardless of the "hostile" or "odious" nature of the loans.[26]

Despite these examples, the principle of succession to local debts appears to remain generally valid. Although it may be too early to state that this principle has acquired the force of a positive rule of international law, state practice, past and present, shows a general willingness by governments to abide by the principle.

No such consensus of opinion can be said to exist in regard to limited changes of sovereignty involving partial transfers of territory from the debtor to another state without a corresponding change in the juridical personality of either state. It is true that state practice in Continental Europe during the nineteenth century and on the occasion of the various post-World War I peace treaties adhered to a certain extent to the principle of state succession in this kind of sit-

---

[24] Article 2 (b). See Paenson, op. cit., note 11 supra, pp. 75-76.

[25] Round Table Conference Agreement of November 2, 1949 (69 UNTS 3), Draft Financial and Economic Agreement, Section D (69 UNTS 252). Regarding the negotiation of the Financial Agreement, see McTurnan Kahin, *Nationalism and Revolution in Indonesia* (1952) pp. 438-445. Regarding the debt record of Indonesia, see Moody's, *Municipal and Government Manual,* 1964, p. 2803.

[26] See e.g., I Hyde, op. cit., note 11 supra, pp. 410-411; O'Connell, op. cit., id. loc., pp. 188-189; Feilchenfeld, op. cit., note 4 supra, pp. 329 et seq.

uation. However, the European attitude has been inspired by such particular political and economic considerations as to make it impossible to characterize the European practice as a clear illustration of a positive rule of international law.[27] Furthermore, countries outside Europe have consistently denied that a limited transfer of sovereignty imposed any liability upon the successor state,[28] at least when the debt involved was not a local debt proper to the transferred territory or otherwise specifically secured by assets located within that territory.

Although the view has been frequently advanced that secured debts pass to the successor state with the transferred territory in accordance with the maxim *res transit cum suo onere,* state practice gives only limited support to that view. Although successor states have recognized the rights of creditors in tangible assets within the ceded territory,[29] which constitute security for a debt, it is much less certain that debts secured by an assignment or a pledge of revenues will be equally protected.[30]

The many shortcomings of the law regarding succession to public debt raise the question of how interests of creditors can be more effectively protected. Direct improvement of the law by means of a code of substantive rules or international agreements, although desirable, appears a rather remote possibility at present. Indirectly, additional protection might result from the improvement of the international machinery for the settlement of loan disputes, either by creation of permanent international loan tribunals or similar bodies, or by

---

[27] See e.g., Feilchenfeld, op. cit., note 4 supra, pp. 263 et seq.; Paenson, op. cit., note 11 supra, pp. 29-31; O'Connell, op. cit., id loc., pp. 161, 163-165; Castrén, op. cit., id. loc., pp. 407-411.

[28] See e.g., as to the practice of the United States, Feilchenfeld, op. cit., note 4 supra, pp. 257-258, 346-353. In general, see Ibid., pp. 675-676; O'Connell, op. cit., note 11 supra, pp. 159-167; Paenson, op. cit., id. loc., p. 196; Castrén, op. cit., id. loc., pp. 421-422, 476-478.

[29] See in particular the provisions of the Treaties of Saint Germain and Trianon concerning debts secured by "railways, salt mines, or other property" in Austria-Hungary; Feilchenfeld, op. cit., note 4 supra, pp. 479 et seq.

[30] See generally, Feilchenfeld, op. cit., note 4 supra, pp. 817-819, Castrén, op. cit., note 11 supra, pp. 482-484; O'Connell, op. cit., id. loc. pp. 167-173. Paenson, op. cit., id. loc., p. 215, considers that secured creditors remain protected in "all cases"; Sack (*Les Transformations,* etc., pp. 201 et seq.) takes a negative attitude. See, in connection with the perception by Greece (as an occupying power) of lighthouse dues payable under concessionary arrangements between the Ottoman Empire and a French company, which had been pledged as security for Turkish loans: the Lighthouses Concessions Case (Affaire Relative à la Concession des Phares de l'Empire Ottoman) 12 Reports of International Arbitral Awards, at pp. 201-203.

increased use of arbitration.[31] Without minimizing in the least the attractiveness of this last alternative, over-confidence in its effectiveness might be unwise. It is not at all certain that a successor state would feel bound by an agreement entered into by its predecessor, to arbitrate or submit to the jurisdiction of an international court or body. If a successor state repudiated such an agreement, the expected remedy would fail creditors at the time it would be needed most.

Unfortunately, this remark is also applicable to most of the other covenants which may be included in loan documents to anticipate possible changes of sovereignty. In many cases, the detrimental consequences of a change of sovereignty stem from the refusal of the successor state to respect contractual arrangements between its predecessor and that state's creditors.

Although this consideration may appear discouraging, it should not deter creditors from including provisions in loan documents which may improve their position by making it morally difficult for the successor state to disown its predecessor's obligations. For example, a provision obligating the contracting state to maintain the priority of the loan over other debts, or to assign or pledge its revenues as security for the loan, even though it may not necessarily always achieve its objective, may considerably strengthen the bargaining position of the creditors in debt settlement negotiations.

Furthermore, there do exist a number of covenants which should afford effective legal protection to creditors in specific cases. Consider, for example, a clause in a loan agreement providing for consultation in the event that a change of sovereignty might adversely affect the rights of creditors, or requiring the debtor state to cause its successor or successors to maintain the rights of creditors. Although such a clause might not protect creditors against the consequences of a brutal annexation of a revolutionary dismemberment, it might prove extremely valuable in case of a voluntary cession of territory or the peaceful transition by a former territory to an independent state.[32] The practical difficulty, of course, is that such provisions are usually unacceptable to the contracting state. Although states may be perfectly prepared to take all steps necessary to preserve the interests of creditors in the event of organized transfers of sovereignty,

---

[31] See e.g., Feilchenfeld's proposal regarding the creation of a Permanent Financial Commission for the handling of debt settlements, op. cit., note 4 supra, pp. 892-894. See also Chapter IV, text and notes 91 and 181-182.

[32] See e.g., Feilchenfeld, op. cit., note 4 supra, pp. 900 and 903. Comp., The Lighthouses Concessions Case, referred to supra in note 30, at p. 199.

they are usually extremely reluctant, for obvious political reasons, to agree in loan documents to such limitations upon their sovereign prerogatives. This consideration apparently explains why no concrete illustration has been found.

In practice, two major devices have been used to solve the difficulty. The first device consists in characterizing the situation against which protection is sought as an objective event of default authorizing the creditors to exercise the remedies available under the circumstances.[33] The second device, which can be used exclusively or in addition to the first one, is to obtain the guarantee of reliable guarantors capable of meeting the liabilities of the borrower. The well-known example of the fulfillment by Belgium, France and the United Kingdom of their obligations as guarantors of Austrian loans, after Austria had been annexed by the Reich, proves sufficiently the effectiveness of this remedy.[34]

---

[33] See e.g., the following provision identifying an event of default, which is found in several IBRD Loan Agreements:

"An extraordinary situation shall have arisen which shall make it improbable that the Borrower or the Guarantor will be able to perform its obligations under the Loan Agreement or the Guarantee Agreement, or there shall occur any such change in the nature and constitution of the Borrower as shall make it improbable that the Borrower will be able to carry out its obligations under the Loan Agreement."

It should be pointed out in this connection that: (i) the IBRD has taken the position that as a matter of international law the liabilities of a dependent territory arising out of a loan or guarantee agreement with the IBRD continue as liabilities of the independent state; and (ii), no territory, on becoming an independent state, has ever refused to make any repayment for which it was responsible under a loan or guarantee agreement with the IBRD, or carry out any other obligation arising thereunder and incurred while it was a territory. For these reasons, the IBRD has not generally thought it necessary to obtain specific acknowledgment from the newly independent country that it is bound by the obligations to the IBRD incurred by the territory. The Supplemental Agreement dated April 2, 1964, between Kenya, the IBRD and the United Kingdom (503 UNTS 340) is an exception to the practice generally followed by the IBRD. This Supplemental Agreement refers to an earlier loan made to the Colony and Protectorate of Kenya, with the Guarantee of the United Kingdom (see Loan and Guarantee Agreements dated November 29, 1961, 426 UNTS 49). In this case, it was necessary to make rather extensive changes in the existing Loan Agreement after Kenya had gained its independence, and the amending agreement was, therefore, an opportunity to recognize the succession of the new entity to the rights and obligations of the Colony and Protectorate.

For the special case of Rhodesia, see note 19 supra.

[34] See also Sch. v. Germany, German Supreme Court April 14, 1932, Annual Digest, 1931-1932, 62. Prior to World War I, the German Debt Administration had issued bonds on behalf of the former German colonies. The bonds, which were secured by colonial revenues, constituted a joint and several obli-

SECTION II. WAR

A. GENERAL EFFECTS OF WAR

1. *Effect of War on Loans between Enemies*

Since war-time loans between enemy countries are inconceivable and loans between the citizens of such countries are prohibited upon the outbreak of war,[35] the only loans which have to be considered here are loans between states which subsequently become belligerents or individuals subject to the laws of such states.

Pre-war interstates loans raise no particular difficulty. Since it is clear that a belligerent state cannot be expected to contribute to the financial resources of its enemy by discharging its loan obligations during the war, normalization of the relationship must be postponed until the end of the war and the conclusion of a peace treaty between the parties.[36]

The practical problem, therefore, is limited to loans, governmental or private, subscribed to or made by private enemy investors. It is sometimes stated that such loans are not abrogated by, but are merely suspended upon, the outbreak of war.[37] However, this statement is not altogether correct. A distinction must be made between matters relating to the existence of the loan relationship and matters

---

gation of the colonies, and were guaranteed by Germany. After the War, the colonies were placed under mandates and the Mandatory Powers refused, both in their names and on behalf of the Territories to assume any liability for the pre-War loans. They based this position on the provisions of the Treaty of Versailles (Article 257; see Feilchenfeld, op. cit., note 4 supra, pp. 552 et seq.). This solution made *tabula rasa* of the colonies' indebtedness (see e.g., Verein Für Schutzgebietsanleihen E.V. v. Conradie, N.O., Supreme Court of South Africa October 28, 1936, Annual Digest 1935-1937, p. 128). Germany's guarantee obligation, however, was upheld by the German Supreme Court.

In this connection also, it should be recalled that the Articles of Agreement of the IBRD provide that a loan to a borrower other than a member, including a loan to a dependent territory, shall be guaranteed by the particular member state involved (Article III, Section 4 (i)). The guarantee remains in effect after the independence of the territory. See e.g., O'Connell, "Independence and Succession to Treaties", 38 B.Y.B.I.L. 84 (1962), at p. 138. As to payments made to the IBRD by the United Kingdom, as Guarantor of Rhodesian loans, see note 19 supra.

[35] See generally, McNair, *Legal Effects of War* (1944), especially at pp. 101-107, 233-238.

[36] See e.g., Fisher-Williams, *Chapters on Current International Law and the League of Nations* (1929), pp. 359-361.

[37] See e.g., Schering, Ltd. v. Stockholms Enskilda Bank Aktiebolag, [1946] 1 All E. R. 36.

regarding performance of the loan obligations in time of war. There is a general consensus of opinion that the intervention of a state of war does not impair the debtor-creditor relationship created by the original contract.[38] At the same time, however, to the extent that performance of the loan obligations would entail an actual transfer of funds across enemy lines, any dealings between enemy borrowers and lenders must be discontinued for the duration of the war. In the great majority of cases, the lender has performed his part of the bargain at the outset, and the sole obligations affected by the outbreak of war are those of the borrower. To say, therefore, that the loan "contract" is suspended during the war is to overstate the legal implications of war: What is suspended is not the contract but the obligation of the borrower to transmit funds to the lender, and the lenders' corresponding right of action.[39] So much the more, since notwithstanding transfer prohibitions, the borrower may choose to make service payments in its own country for the account of enemy creditors, for example by paying loan monies to the Custodian of Enemy Property.[40] Whether such payments would be recognized as a valid discharge in other countries, including the lender's country after the war,[41] or whether the borrower would be exposed to double liability,[42] is, of course, another question.

---

[38] State practice, especially as evidenced by peace treaties, gives general recognition to this principle. See text and notes 67 to 94 infra.

[39] See McNair, op. cit., note 35 supra, p. 238. Whether interest ceases to run during the war is of relatively minor practical importance, since it would be most unlikely that debt settlements in, or following, peace treaties would fail to solve the issue of unpaid arrears of interest. See text and notes 77, 89 to 91, 93 and 94 infra. Furthermore, the applicable trading-with-the-enemy legislation may provide for payment of interest to the Custodian of Enemy Property. See *McNair*, op. cit., note 35 supra, pp. 105-107. On this problem, generally, see Chadwick, "Foreign Investments in Time of War", 20 L.Q.R. 167 (1904) ; Gregory, "Interest on Debts when Intercourse between Debtor and Creditor is Forbidden by a State of War", 25 L.Q.R. 297 (1909) .

The case of Re Fried Krupp Aktiengesellschaft [1917] 2 Ch. 188, involved a German World War I regulation which exonerated German subjects from the payment of interest on contractual debts to enemies of Germany. This cancellation of interest, which went beyond a mere prohibition of payment during the war, was held contrary to the "usage of nations" and was denied effect in England. Query whether this solution would have obtained in the United States in view of the existing case law regarding suspension of interest on loans between enemies. See e.g., Hoare v. Allen, 2 Dall. 102, 1 L. Ed. 307 (1789) ; Brown v. Hiatts, 15 Wall. 177, 21 L. Ed. 128 (1873) .

[40] See e.g., McNair, op. cit., note 35 supra, p. 105; Domke, *Trading with the Enemy in World War II* (1943) , pp. 165-166.

[41] In the case of Re Helbert Wagg & Co., Ltd. [1956] 1 All E.R. 129, it is clearly indicated that a German regulation directing that loan monies due

What is the effect of war upon loans not yet disbursed or fully withdrawn on the outbreak of war, such as loans providing for progressive disbursements upon justification of expenditures made or to be made by the borrower, or some similar financial arrangement? In this case, unlike the case of an ordinary loan, the obligations of *both* parties remain executory at the outbreak of war, and it might be argued that the unwithdrawn portion of the loan is abrogated. This question does not appear to have raised much difficulty in practice,[43] probably because this type of loan usually contains provisions authorizing the lender to suspend or terminate the contract should an "extraordinary situation" occur, a concept sufficiently general to include war.

Attempts have sometimes been made to provide for the continuation of service payments in time of war, regardless of the nationality of the bondholders. This kind of provision, which became fashionable between the two World Wars, both in governmental[44] and pri-

---

English bondholders be paid to a German Custodian would not have offended: "any principle of public policy of this country or of international law" (at p. 144).

[42] See Cities Service Co. v. McGrath, 342 US 330, 72 S. Ct. 334, 96 L. Ed. 650 (1952). The Attorney General, as successor to the Alien Property Custodian, had issued a vesting order respecting obligations issued by an American corporation in the form of bearer bonds which, although owned by a German national, were last reported to be in Russian hands. The corporation and the trustee objected to the order on the ground that if the bonds were transferred to a *bona fide* holder and the holder brought action in a foreign court, they would be exposed to double liability. It was found, however, that if a foreign judgment should be rendered against the borrower and the trustee, they would have a cause of action against the United States Government to the extent of their double liability. The objection was consequently dismissed.

[43] Comp., the decision of the Mixed Arbitral Tribunal (French-German) of October 27, 1923, Société Française de Reports et de Dépôts v. National Bank fur Deutschland, III Recueil des Décisions, 694. But see, Seligman v. Eagle Insurance Co. [1917] 1 Ch. 519, and McNair, op. cit., note 35 supra, pp. 120-121.

[44] See e.g., the following provision in the General Bond for the Austrian Government Guaranteed Loan of 1923:

"The principal and interest of the bonds will be paid in time of war as well as of peace and no matter whether the holders of the bonds are subjects of a state friendly or hostile to the Austrian State" (Article 12, para. 2).

Similar provisions are found in loans between American bankers and Latin American Republics. See e.g., the Loan Contract dated June 24, 1922 between the Republic of El Salvador and Minor C. Keith, Article XI, para. 1 in fine, reprinted in *Dunn*, p. 222 at p. 228. See also *Borchard*, p. 150, note 1.

vate[45] loans, was bound to prove ineffective after the widespread adoption of trading-with-the-enemy legislation. A good example is found in the unsuccessful attempt of the Deutsches Kalisyndikat (the Syndicate), a German corporation, to maintain service on sterling bonds held in England after the outbreak of World War II.

The Syndicate loan provided *inter alia* that the proceeds of all export sales of potash, made by the Syndicate on a world-wide basis, would be used for the payment of interest and sinking-fund requirements; and that service would be made "in time of Peace or War and whether the holders be subjects of a friendly or hostile country." During the early months of World War II, the Syndicate arranged several meetings in neutral territory with the English underwriters to seek a practical solution to the problem of future loan service. The Syndicate suggested that, if it were authorized by the English Government to export potash through the blockade to countries outside Europe, it would be able to raise sufficient funds to maintain loan service in England. This suggestion was rejected, however, and the Syndicate ceased payments on the English bonds.[46] Only after the conclusion of the 1953 London Agreement on German Debts was a settlement plan made possible.[47] In view of the obvious desire of the

---

[45] See e.g., the following provision, typical of private American-German loan agreements of the 'twenties:
"The Company covenants that notwithstanding the existence at any time of a state of war between Germany and the United States of America or any other international or national disturbance in German affairs, it will, *unless expressly prohibited by law,* continue to make all deposits and payments required by this Indenture and the Bonds, and in all other respects will continue to comply with and perform the several provisions of this Indenture and of the Bonds" (underlining added)
The same indenture also specifies that if a war occurs and payments cannot be made at the places agreed upon by the parties, payments shall be made in The Netherlands; or, if that country and Germany are also at war, then in Switzerland.
Similar stipulations are found in American-Japanese indentures of the same period. See e.g., the indenture dated May 15, 1928 between the Tokyo Electric Light Company, Limited and the Mitsui Bank, Limited, Article VI, Section 1, reprinted in *Japanese Foreign Currency Bonds,* published by the Ministry of Finance of Japan (1951), Memorandum No. 29-27, Appendix III-1.

[46] For a detailed exposé of the 1939-1940 negotiations, see Royal Exchange Assurance v. Brownell, 146 F. Supp. 563 (1956), aff'd, 257 F. 2d 582 (1958).
During the war, the borrower was able to make payments to bondholders in The Netherlands, Switzerland and Sweden. See *Stock Exchange Official Y.B.* vol. II, 1948, p. 1674. For the Settlement Agreement of 1956, see Id. op. 1959, vol. II, p. 2955.

[47] The history of post-War negotiations and the settlement can be traced

Syndicate to continue loan service during the hostilities, this is an excellent example of the principle that relations between enemy debtors and creditors cannot be insulated effectively against the consequences of modern warfare. This may explain why provisions of the kind involved in the Syndicate loan have apparently disappeared from contemporary loan instruments.[48]

In the case of loans, as with other contracts, the enactment of trading-with-the-enemy acts makes it imperative to define the term "enemy" with precision. As long as that definition is based on the nationality of the parties, there is little difficulty in determining the enemy character of the creditor (except of course the problem of "piercing the veil" of corporations). Difficult problems may arise, however, when a national concludes a transaction in another country. Thus, In *Boissevain v. Weil*,[49] a Dutchman had made several loans in 1944 to a British lady, who like him was involuntarily residing in Monaco due to war conditions. The purpose of the loans was to help the woman's son avoid internment in a German concentration camp. The funds, advanced in francs, were repayable in sterling in London after the war. In an action brought in England by the lender, the lower court held that the contract was governed by the law of Monaco; that the Defense (Finance) Regulations, which prohibited British subjects from buying or borrowing foreign exchange without a license from the Treasury, was unapplicable; and that the contract was enforceable. On appeal, however, the decision was reversed and it was held that the loan contract was unenforceable in England, primarily on the ground that Defense (Finance) Regulations applied to British subjects, wherever located.

The case of *Schering, Ltd. v. Stockholms Enskilda Aktiebolag*,[50] is also interesting. It is a characteristic feature of trading-with-the-enemy acts that their scope is not limited to direct dealings between enemies, but also extends to a ban on any payments which might in-

---

in the *Stock Exchange Official Y.B.* 1953, vol. II, p. 2816; 1954, vol. II, pp. 2836 and 3526; 1957, vol. II, p. 3056, and 1960, vol. II, p. 2947.

[48] Some provisions relating to exchange transfers are so general in character that they could be construed as being applicable "under all circumstances", including war-time situations. See Chapter VII, notes 36 to 42. Their basic purpose, however, remains limited to the imposition or implementation of exchange restrictions.

[49] [1948] 1 All E.R. 893; [1949] 1 All E.R. 146; [1950] 1 All E.R. 728.

[50] See note 37, supra. Comp., Arab Bank Ltd. v. Barclays Bank [1954] 2 All E.R. 226 and Re Helbert Wagg & Co., Ltd. [1956] 1 All E.R. 129, at 144.

directly benefit the enemy. In the *Schering* case, a Swedish bank had advanced funds to a German company pursuant to a 1936 "contract of debt." The debt was guaranteed by an English and an Indian Company, both of whom were controlled by the German obligor. In an action against the English Guarantor, it was held that performance of the guarantee obligation would contravene the provisions of the Trading-with-the-Enemy Act, and that consequently the obligations of the Guarantor, even though concluded with a neutral, were suspended upon the outbreak of war.

2. *Effect of War on Loans between Non-Enemies*

The relations between non-enemy lenders and borrowers have been the object of relatively scant attention. Either the issue is summarily dismissed,[51] or it is dealt with in connection with loans from neutrals to belligerents.[52] It is of course true that usually the legal relations between non-enemies are not impaired by the existence of a state of war. Yet it is only too apparent that, as in the *Schering* case, wartime legislation may adversely affect the rights of neutrals or, at the least, have a nuisance value making it more difficult to comply with the terms of the original promise. Trading-with-the-enemy restrictions require that creditors, before receiving payment, establish the *bona fide* quality of their claims. This requirement assumes that certain formalities are satisfied. In the case of foreign loans, particularly when the loan is evidenced by bearer bonds held in many countries, compliance with these formalities may prove a difficult and time-consuming process. Non-enemy holders outside the country imposing the restrictions may be prevented from proving the validity of their claim because of a disruption of communications or some other cause attributable to the existence of a state of war. If a distribution of service monies is to be made, delicate problems may arise. The situation involved in *Irving Trust Co. v. Deutsch Atlantische Tele-graphengesellschaft*,[53] illustrates the practical issues which may confront trustees and bondholders. Bonds issued in the United States by a German cable company were secured by an assignment of traffic contracts between the obligor and American cable companies. Pursuant to this arrangement, the trustee had received funds aggregating about one hundred thousand dollars, which it was ready to dis-

---

[51] Fisher-Williams, op. cit, note 36 supra, p. 359.
[52] *Borchard,* pp. 151-152.
[53] 22 N.Y.S. 2d 581 (1940).

tribute to the bondholders, some of whom resided in Europe. It was anticipated that it would take some time to notify the European bond-holders of the situation, and that more time would be needed for them to prove the validity of their claims. To ignore their rights altogether and allocate the funds to local creditors only would have been in-equitable. At the same time, postponing the distribution indefinitely would have been unfair to those bondholders whose title was already established. The court solved the difficulty by authorizing a limited, although immediate distribution to local bondholders, and instruct-ing the trustee to hold the balance for a period of time sufficient to enable European creditors to present affidavits showing the non-Ger-man character of their bonds and share in the final distribution.[54]

Another illustration is found in *Hoirs Setton v. Compagnie Uni-verselle du Canal de Suez*.[55] In that case, the question at issue was the determination of the rate of conversion into Egyptian currency of "gold francs" promised in bonds issued by the Suez Canal Com-pany. World War II had interrupted the relations between France and Egypt, thereby making it impossible to ascertain the value of the franc in terms of gold. However, the court found that it was still possible to translate the gold content of the French franc into United States dollars and to convert the dollar equivalent into Egyptian pounds at the rate of exchange on the payment date.[56]

Aside from these technical difficulties, the mere existence of a state of war may have a direct impact upon loans between non-enemies. For example, the borrower may be deprived of an impor-tant part of its assets or unable to apply its resources to the satisfac-tion of its loan obligations. Thus during World War II, only certain allied governments in exile could dispose of sufficient "free" funds to be in a position to pay interest,[57] and sometimes meet amortization

---

[54] Regarding the terms of the post-War settlement offer, see Moody, *Public Utility Manual*, 1960, pp. 1383-4.

[55] Mixed Court of Appeals of Alexandria, May 17, 1947, Journal des Tri-bunaux Mixtes No. 3372, May 26-27, 1947.

[56] For the possible use of par values determined by the IMF in situations such as that involved in the Setton Case, see Gold, *The Fund Agreement in the Courts* (1962), p. 6.

[57] The Norwegian Government in London continued to service its bonds in allied countries and pay interest on sterling bonds of Norwegian institu-tions guaranteed by Norway, provided the "non-enemy" character of the holder was established. See, Kingdom of Norway $15 million External Bonds of 1955, prospectus, p. 35. The Government also provided the funds neces-sary to pay interest on the dollar bonds of Oslo and Akershus, although not

payments,[58] on bonds owned by non-enemy holders in other allied or neutral countries. Most governments in occupied Europe, although they promptly settled their foreign loan commitments after the war, were forced to suspend payment on foreign bonds, either from the beginning of the occupation until the end of the war,[59] or for varying periods during the war,[60] depending upon the whim of the occupation authorities.

The impact of a war on loans between non-enemies is not limited to loan relationships existing at the outbreak of war: It may also prevent new loans from taking place, such as loans between neutral governments and belligerents. A neutral government cannot give financial assistance to a belligerent without violating its obligation of neutrality.[61] In recent years, however, the implementation of this prohibition has become somewhat more difficult than in the past.

---

obliged to do so under any guarantee. See Moody's *Municipal and Government Manual,* 1964, p. 2842.

The Belgian Government in London continued to pay interest on dollar bonds until 1946, when sinking fund payments, suspended from 1943 to 1945, were resumed and all arrears paid up. See *Moody's,* id. op., 1964, p. 2699, and prospectus concerning Kingdom of Belgium $30 million External Loan Fifteen Year Sinking Fund 5½% Bonds due 1972, p. 22.

[58] Amortization payments of the Kingdom of Norway 3% Loan of 1938, payable in Swiss francs, were fulfilled by the Norwegian Government in London through the purchase of bonds. See prospectus concerning Kingdom of Norway $15 million External Bonds of 1955, p. 35.

[59] Thus payments on French francs bonds held by residents of the United Kingdom were suspended following the German invasion in June 1940. Service was resumed and arreages paid in 1945. See *Stock Exchange Official Y.B.,* 1690, vol. I, 151. In January 1942, payments to holders of certain Danish bonds residing outside of Denmark were suspended; they were resumed in 1950. See prospectus concerning Kingdom of Denmark $20 million 5½% Fifteen Year External Loan Bonds of 1959, p. 42. In September 1940, Yugoslavia arranged to make partial payment of coupons in sterling in London. Service was suspended in October 1940. See *Stock Exchange Official Y.B.,* 1964, vol. I, 237.

[60] Payments of Belgian-French francs loans by Belgium were suspended during the first year of World War II by decision of the occupying authorities, although they were resumed to some extent in 1943. See prospectus cited note 57 supra, p. 22, and *Association Nationale des Porteurs de Valeurs Mobilières, Report* 1943, p. 6. Payments on Swiss francs-Dutch guilders bonds of the French Government were suspended after June 1940, partially resumed in 1941-42, and suspended again until the end of the war. See *Manuel des Valeurs Cotées à la Bourse de Genève* 1959, p. 39. Payments on Danish Government bonds payable in Swedish kronor, Dutch guilders, pounds sterling and Swiss francs were temporarily suspended for varying periods. See prospectus cited in the preceding note, id. loc.

[61] *Borchard,* p. 151; Lalive, *Le Droit de la Neutralité et le Problème des Crédits Consentis par les Neutres aux Belligérants* (1941) ; Oppenheim, 2 *International Law* (7th ed. 1952) p. 743.

New types of financial arrangements have emerged like clearing agreements, which, although of substantial benefit to a belligerent, may be absolutely vital to the preservation of the economy of the neutral government in question. Under the circumstances, it would be improper to hold such a government responsible for the advantages which may accrue indirectly to the other contracting party. Thus it is significant that, even though the German-Swiss clearing agreement proved beneficial to the Reich, it was never contended by the Allied Powers that Switzerland violated its obligation of neutrality by extending credits to the Reich under this agreement.[62]

This obligation, in any event, is limited to intergovernmental financial assistance. A neutral government is under no obligation to prevent its nationals from extending loans and credits to a foreign state which is at war,[63] although it is free of course to treat such loans as contrary to the spirit of neutrality and discourage or forbid them altogether.[64] These loans must be distinguished from loans made to finance a revolution or insurrection. Courts in neutral countries have generally considered such loans illegal, and have refused to entertain actions for recovery of the proceeds.[65] Furthermore it may be assumed that, should the revolutionary attempt fail, the victorious government would refuse to recognize the existence of the debt; and it is not altogether certain that, should the revolution succeed, the new government would necessarily assume the burden of the loan.[66]

B. POST-WAR SETTLEMENTS

The Peace Treaties following World War II provide for the maintenance of loan obligations suspended by the war, and reaffirm the liability of borrowers, governmental or private, for pre-war ex-

---

[62] As to the 1946 arrangement between the Allied Powers and Switzerland, see Calm, "The Responsibility of the Successor State for War Debts", 44 Am. J. Int'l L. 477 (1950). As to the final settlement of the clearing debt between Switzerland and the Federal Republic of Germany, see Guggenheim 2 *Traité de Droit International Public* (1954), p. 538, note 3.

[63] See e.g., Oppenheim, op. cit., note 61 supra, p. 744; Guggenheim, op. cit., preceding note, pp. 536 et seq.; *Borchard*, p. 151.

[64] As to the United States' attitude during World War I, and the United States Neutrality Acts of 1937 and 1939, see 3 Hyde, *International Law* (2nd ed 1945) pp. 2302-5, Hackworth, VII—*Digest of International Law*, pp. 657-661; *Borchard*, p. 151. See also, Guggenheim, op. cit., note 62 supra, p. 537.

[65] See e.g., De Wutz v. Hendricks (1824) in Scott, *Cases and Opinions on International Law* (1893) p. 438; Kennett v. Chambers, 14 How. 38, 14 L. Ed. 316 (1852), Scott, Id. op., p. 441; Trib. Civ. Seine July 2, 1932, Flörsheim v. Delgado, Rev. 1934, 770.

[66] See e.g., Feilchenfeld, op. cit., note 4 supra, p. 697; *Borchard*, p. 152; O'Connell, op. cit., note 11 supra, pp. 187 et seq.

ternal debts.[67] The Treaties take certain steps to permit creditors to preserve their rights, for example by extending the periods of prescription or limitation of right of action.[68] However, they leave the final settlement of pre-war loans to future negotiations between the parties.

Satisfactory settlement of pre-war loans has not been possible in all cases.[69] The settlements which have been successful generally give recognition not only to the restoration of creditors' rights, but also to the financial capacity of the respective debtors. The following examples clearly illustrate this remark.

1. *Settlement of the German Debts*

(a) *Negotiation of the London Agreement.* In an exchange of notes dated March 6, 1951, between the Allied High Commissioners (representing, respectively, the Government of France, the United Kingdom and the United States) and the Federal Republic of Germany, the latter Government: (i) confirmed that it was liable for the pre-war external debt of the Reich; (ii) acknowledged in principle

---

[67] Peace Treaty with Italy dated February 10, 1947 (Art. 81) 49 UNTS 3. Comp., the treaties of the same date with Roumania (Art. 29), Bulgaria (Art. 27) and Hungary (Art. 31). See Wolff, *The Problem of Pre-War Contracts in Peace Treaties* (1946) and "Treatment of Pre-War Contracts in the Peace Treaties of Paris", 1947, Transactions of the Grotius Society 1947, 213 (1948) Drost, *Contracts and Peace Treaties* (1948), pp. 146 et seq.

Ses also the Exchange of Notes dated March 6, 1951 between the Allied Commissioners and the Federal Republic of Germany, 106 UNTS 141; the Peace Treaty with Japan, dated September 8, 1951 (Art. 18) 136 UNTS 45.

Regarding the clearing machinery provided by Article 296 of the Treaty of Versailles after World War I, see, Sir John Fisher Williams, *Chapters on Current International Law and the League of Nations* (1929) p. 360; Borchard, p. 150; Drost, op. cit., pp. 147 et seq.

[68] Peace Treaty with Italy, Annex 16 Section B(1); Peace Treaty with Japan, Protocol Annexed Section B(1); London Agreement of February 27, 1953 regarding the Settlement of German External Debts (333 UNTS 3), Article 18. See also, Fitzmaurice, *The Juridical Clauses of the Peace Treaties,* 73 Recueil des Cours, 259 (1948), at p. 344 et seq. A number of domestic statutes to the same effect were enacted after the war in most of the liberated Western European countries, anxious to honor their commitments to foreign creditors.

[69] The pre-War loans of Eastern European countries either remain in complete default, or have been seriously impaired to the extent that they have been dealt with in global settlements providing for compensation for nationalization. See e.g., in regard to the pre-War external debt of: (i) Bulgaria, Moody's, *Municipal and Government Manual* 1964, p. 2721; (ii) Hungary, *Moody's,* Id. op., 1964, p. 2797; (iii) Poland, *Moody's,* Id. op., 1964, p. 2859; and (iv) Roumania, *Moody's,* Id. op., 1964, p. 2866.

the debt arising from the economic assistance furnished to Germany by the Allies since the end of World War II, and declared itself ready to accord priority to such debt over all other foreign claims against Germany or German nationals; and (iii) expressed its desire to resume payments on the German external debt and participate with the three Powers in the formulation of a plan for the settlement of public and private claims against Germany and German citizens.[70]

This agreement constituted the first and most important step toward the termination of German default, the restoration of German credit, and the re-establishment of normal economic relations between Germany and other countries. Yet the situation which confronted the German Government and the Tripartite (Allied) Commission, set up to work out a reasonable settlement plan, was somewhat appalling. German pre-war debts amounted to more than the equivalent of $2.5 billion, and the debt representing post-war economic aid was equivalent to more than $3.5 billion. These amounts exceeded by far the Federal Republic's capacity to pay. Furthermore, to the extent that repayment of post-war debt was granted priority over the pre-war claims, as contemplated in the 1951 agreement, it was clear that the chances of achieving a satisfactory settlement of German pre-war debts were rather remote.

To overcome this last obstacle, the three Powers agreed to modify the priority accorded to their claims, provided an equitable settlement of pre-war debts could be reached. France and the United Kingdom declared themselves ready to reduce the amount of their respective claims by 25% (i.e., from the equivalent of $15.7 million to $11.8 million in the case of France; and from the equivalent of $562.8 million to $420 million in the case of the United Kingdom),

---

[70] 106 UNTS 141. As a result of the operation of the European Payments Union, Germany acquired substantial balances against France (484,800,000 units of account) and the United Kingdom (378,900,000 units of account). At the close of the Union in December 1958, Germany decided to take advantage of this situation by making prepayments on its indebtedness to these two countries. There was a provision in the Agreement of February 27, 1953 between Germany and the United States (TIAS 2795) to the effect that if Germany prepaid its corresponding debts to France and the United Kingdom, Germany would make a proportionate repayment to the United States. Accordingly, an agreement was concluded on March 20, 1959 between the United States and Germany (TIAS 4200) setting forth the terms of a prepayment of $150 million. See 53 Am. J. Int'l L. 921 (1959). See also, the Exchange of Notes dated April 25, 1961 (410 UNTS 340; TIAS 4737) concerning the purchase by the Deutsche Bundesbank of a partial amount ($587 million) of the United States outstanding claim against Germany.

and to fund the balance, payable without interest, over a twenty-year period. The United States was willing to reduce its claim by 62.5% (i.e. from $3.8 billion to $1.5 billion), the balance, with 2½% interest repayable after a five-year period of grace, in thirty annual instalments.

On the basis of these offers, the Federal German Government and the three Powers agreed to call an international conference to work out a settlement for pre-war debts.

The conference opened in London on February 28, 1952. It was attended by representatives of 28 creditor nations and private creditor representatives, and by representatives of the German Government and German debtors. Despite the difficulty of working out recommendations for a satisfactory settlement plan,[71] the conference was able to issue on August 8, 1952, a report containing detailed proposals for each category of debt and a few guiding principles applicable to all debts in general. These recommendations were incorporated into the Agreement signed on February 27, 1953 by the Federal Republic of Germany and the Governments of eighteen creditor countries.[72]

(b) *General Terms of the Agreement.* The Agreement and its

---

[71] The following excerpt from the message of the President of the United States dated April 10, 1953 to the Senate regarding the debt settlement agreements with Germany (83d Congress, 1st session, Senate, Executives D, E, F and G, at p. 14) gives a dramatic summary of the problems raised at the London Conference:

"The process of arriving at a satisfactory agreement on settlement terms and procedures for the various categories of debts within the framework of an overall arrangement proved to be complex and difficult because conflicts existed not only between the debtors and creditors, but also among the several creditor groups over a considerable number of technical problems. Among these problems was the extent of liability of German debtors for payments on debts which had been made, pursuant to legislation adopted during the Nazi regime, to the Konversionskasse (Conversion Office), the extent to which the gold clause should be given effect, the extent to which debts could be paid in deutschemarks and the uses to which such deutschemarks could be put, the extent to which adjustment should be made in the debts of the German Reich because of the territorial limitation of the Federal Republic, and conflicting views as to the relative treatment to be given to various categories of debts."

[72] See note 68, supra. Regarding the history of the settlement see e.g., in addition to the President's message to Congress referred to in the preceding note, Dernburg, "Some Basic Aspects of the German Debt Settlement", 8 The Journal of Finance 298 (1953); Simpson, "The Agreement on German External Debts", 6 Int'l & Comp. L. Q. 472 (1957); Sinay, "L'Accord de Londres du 27 Février 1953 sur les Dettes Extérieures Allemandes", J.C.P. 1954, II 1158.

many Annexes[73] are governed by a few principles intended to facilitate an orderly over-all settlement of pre-war debts, and reconcile as far as feasible the respective interests of Germany and its creditors.

An orderly settlement was possible only if haphazard negotiations, which had characterized pre-war arrangements between Germany and its creditors, were absolutely forbidden. To that end, and also to ensure that the favorable economic or political position of certain creditor countries would not result in advantages denied to other creditor countries or their nationals, the Agreement emphatically prohibits any discrimination among the debts subject to the proposed settlement plan, or as regards the currencies in which such debts are to be paid. Under this prohibition, Germany as well as her creditors are respectively forbidden to permit or seek any discriminatory or preferential treatment.[74]

Upon the settlement of this fundamental issue, it was possible to formulate the general terms of a settlement plan which would preserve the rights of Germany's creditors insofar as this goal was possible in light of Germany's capacity to pay and her existing and prospective foreign exchange resources.

To preserve the rights of creditors, the Agreement and Annexes I and II thereto, relating respectively to public and private loans, provide that in all respects other than those indicated in these documents, the terms of the original loan contracts are to be maintained.[75] The limitations authorized include the elimination of gold clauses from dollar and Swiss franc loans and the substitution of dollar clauses for gold clauses in loans denominated in other currencies.[76] The Agreement also provides for the reduction of the amount of interest

---

[73] In addition to loans, the Agreement also covers non-contractual pecuniary obligations and pecuniary obligations arising out of contracts other than loans fixed or due before May 8, 1945 (Article 4).

Article 5, which defines the debts excluded from the Agreement, refers, inter alia, to debts arising from the first and second World Wars, and credits acquired by Germany on clearing accounts with occupied countries.

[74] See note 3 supra.

[75] See e.g., Annex I, paras. 1 (e), 2 (f), and 3 (f); Annex II, Article V, para. 1. See also Annex II, Article V, para. 12. This paragraph provides generally that security arrangements in the original loan contract shall remain unchanged, unless the security no longer corresponds to the new principal amount of the settled debt or circumstances have otherwise changed since the loan agreement was entered into (e.g. because of the loss of assets during the War or after the partition of Germany).

[76] See the publications referred to in note 72 supra. See also Delaume, "Gold and Currency Clauses in Contemporary International Loans", 9 Am. J. Comp. L. 199 (1960), at pp. 211-212.

arrears,[77] the reduction of interest rates,[78] the extension of maturity dates,[79] and the postponement of amortization payments.[80] It should be noted that these limitations were motivated essentially by the necessity to account for Germany's capacity of transfer, and were not included in the interest of individual debtors.[81] Indeed, except in very specific cases,[82] the Agreement does not relate the extent of creditors' concessions to the individual debtor's capacity of payment.

[77] Arrears of interest on German public loans were recalculated at lower rates, e.g. at 5% instead of 7% in the case of the Dawes Loan; 4½% instead of 5½% in the case of the Young Loan; and 4% instead of 6% in the case of the External (match) Loan of 1930. Annex I, paras. 1 (d), 2 (d) and 3 (c), respectively. On practically all private loans one-third of the unpaid interest was waived (Annex II, Article V, para. 4) while a similar waiver extended to two-thirds of the arrears of interest in the case of the Konversionskasse bonds (Annex I, para. 4 (d)).

[78] Interest was reduced: (i) in the case of the Dawes Loan, from 7% to 5½% on the American issue and 5% on the other issues; (ii) in the case of the Young Loan, from 5½% to 5% on the American issue and 4½% on the other issues; (iii) in the case of the External (match) Loan of 1930, from 6% to 4% (Annex I, paras. 1 (a), 2 (a), and 3 (a) respectively). On practically all other public and private loans the interest rate was reduced to 75% of the original rate (Annex I, para. 7 (1) (a); Annex II, Article V, para. 5).

[79] The maturity of the Dawes Loan was extended from 1949 to 1969; that of the Young Loan from 1965 to 1980; that of the External (match) Loan of 1930 from 1980 to 1994 (see Annex I, paras. 1 (c), 2 (c), 3 (d)). The maturity dates of public bonds other than those of the State of Prussia were extended by 20 years from the contractual maturity dates (Annex I, para. 7 (1) (d). The maturity of private loans was extended by 10 to 25 years from January 1, 1953 (Annex II, Article V, para. 9).

[80] Amortization payments were postponed until 1958. Annex I, paras. 1 (b), 2 (b), 3 (b), 4 (b), 7 (c); Annex II, Article V, para. 8.

[81] This consideration is clearly reflected in various provisions of the Agreement. Thus, if a debtor fails to discharge his obligations and the creditor recovers judgment against him in Germany, the creditor is not "entitled to the transfer in non-German currency of the principal sum which becomes due as a result of such failure sooner than would have been the case if the debtor had not failed to discharge such obligations" (Agreement, Article 17 (1) (b)). Another illustration is found in Article 34 of the Agreement, which provides for consultation between Germany and creditor countries if circumstances so warrant.

[82] See paragraph 11 of Article V of Annex II providing in substance that if the debtor cannot make a settlement offer in accordance with the terms specified in the Agreement because of a loss of assets or other reasons due to extraordinary circumstances, the debtor and the creditor may make such (less favorable) adjustments as may be necessary under the circumstances. See also, Annex I, paragraph 7 (e) regarding the settlement of external bonds issued or guaranteed by German states (other than the State of Prussia), municipalities and other public bodies.

Another example relates to the extension of the maturity date of private

Another important feature of the Agreement is that it does not purport to compel creditors to accept the terms of the settlement plan or any offers of settlement made thereunder. Essentially, the settlement plan and specific proposals for settlement are merely offers which, to become binding, require the creditors' consent.[83] Only when such consent has been given and the parties have agreed on the terms of a mutually satisfactory arrangement is the debt deemed to have been duly "settled."[84]

These remarks would not be complete without reference to the procedure for the "validation" of German foreign-currency bonds, which constitutes an essential part of the settlement machinery. Before the War, a large number of bonds had been repurchased and repatriated in Germany. Many of those bonds, which had never been presented to the trustees or paying agents for cancellation, had been looted or had otherwise disappeared during the war or soon thereafter. It was feared that unlawful holders of bonds might attempt to negotiate them or file claims against the debtors, trustees or paying agents, a fear which was not unjustified.[85] This situation would not only have been unfair to the German debtors, but would also have proved detrimental to *bona fide* creditors by reducing the amount of foreign exchange available to satisfy their claims. The same type of problem was faced by many European countries invaded or occupied during the hostilities. Germany, like these other countries,[86] solved the problem by establishing a procedure specifically intended

---

loans. Unlike other concessions recommended to creditors, which were general in character, (such as those relating to a reduction of the interest rate or a postponement of amortization payments), extension of maturity in each case was left to negotiation between the parties, subject only to being fixed on a date within 10 to 25 years after the original maturity. Annex II, Article V, para. 9.

[83] According to Annex I, para. 8 (b) and Annex II, Article VIII, offers of settlement were to be forwarded to individual lenders either directly or, in the case of bondholders, through their representatives or bondholders' committees. See also Article 30 of the Agreement regarding the supply of information to, and the powers of, trustees.

[84] Agreement, Articles 15 and 16. The Agreement also provides for arbitration and mediation as means of settlement in case of disagreement between debtors and creditors (Annex II, Article IX, Section 1). Little use seems to have been made of these modes of settlement. See Domke, "Dispute Settlement of International Loans", in *McDaniels* 525, at pp. 536-539.

[85] See e.g., State of The Netherlands v. Federal Reserve Bank of New York, 201 F. 2d 455 (1953). Comp., Cities Service Co. v. McGrath, 342 U.S. 330, 72 S. Ct. 334, 96 L. Ed. 650 (1952).

[86] Moreau-Néret, *Valeurs Étrangères* (1956), pp. 136 et seq.

to determine the validity of foreign bonds so that only those bond-holders who satisfied certain standards would be entitled to payment. This was accomplished by a German law of August 25, 1952, which contains elaborate provisions regarding the submission of bonds for registration, registration periods, the evidence to be submitted, etc., and by several agreements between Germany and the governments of creditor countries providing for mixed validation boards intended to accelerate the final determination of the large volume of claims involved.[87]

2. *Other Post-War Settlements*

The realistic approach which characterizes the German debt settlement was followed also in the settlements regarding the foreign debts of Italy, Japan and Austria. In each case attempts were made, with various success, to preserve as much as possible of the terms of the original loan contracts while accounting also for the borrower's capacity of payment and foreign exchange resources. These two major considerations explain why the concessions made by the creditors exhibit substantial variations from case to case. There was no reduction of the principal amount due in any case. The only other significant feature common to all three settlements is the postponement of the original maturity dates, although the length of postponement, like the other terms of the respective settlements, exhibits considerable variations.[88]

The settlement of dollar, sterling and Swiss franc bonds of Italy provided that bondholders would be offered new 30-year bonds, the face amount of which would include the original principal amount plus accrued interest from June 10, 1940 to January 1, 1947, calcu-

---

[87] See e.g., the Agreement between the United States and Germany dated February 27, 1953 regarding the Validation of Dollar Bonds of German Issue (223 UNTS 167), which contains the text of the German law of 1952, as supplemented by the Agreements of April 1, 1953 (224 UNTS 3) and August 16, 1960 (418 UNTS 235).

[88] In the case of Italy, the maturity date was extended to 1977 (See Moody's *Municipal and Government Manual*, 1960, p. 2519; *Stock Exchange Official Y.B.*, 1960, I, p. 174; *Manuel des Valeurs Cotées à la Bourse de Genève*, 1959, p. 42). In the case of Austria, the new maturity date was 1980 (*Moody's*, Id. op., p. 2387; *Stock Exchange Official Y.B.*, 1960, vol. I, 112; *Manuel des Valeurs Cotées à la Bourse de Genève*, 1959, p. 32; *Annuaire Desfossés* 1959, vol. I, p. 127).

The original maturity date of Japanese loans containing an option of currency was extended by fifteen years; that of loans which contained no currency option was intended by ten years. See, Agreement dated November 21, 1952 (the U.K.-Japan Agreement), Article 3 (172 UNTS 303); *Foreign Bondholders Protective Council, Report* 1951-1952, p. 169.

lated at the original interest rate. The new and lower interest rate was to be 1% from 1947 to 1950, increasing to 2% in 1950 and 1951, and 3% thereafter. Sinking fund operations were suspended until 1952.[89]

Agreement regarding the settlement of dollar and sterling Japanese bonds was reached on September 26, 1952 at a conference in New York. The settlement, which covered both government loans and non-governmental bonds incorporated into the Japanese public debt by a 1943 statute, provided that all interest, accrued or future, would be paid at the contractual rate. Interest due before the war and between the date of the settlement and December 22, 1952 was to be paid on the latter date; interest payable subsequently would be paid on the due date. Coupons, representing interest arrears for the period from the outbreak of the war through September 25, 1952 were to be given to bondholders and were to be payable in each case ten years after the original payment date. Sinking fund payments would be resumed as of 1953 in accordance with the terms of the original contracts, subject to certain adjustments.[90]

No agreement was reached at the time regarding French franc bonds of the Imperial Japanese Government and the City of Tokyo. It was only in 1955 and 1960, respectively, that these two loans were settled, on the basis of recommendations by *ad hoc* conciliators appointed to propose concrete and workable settlement plans.[91]

The settlement of pre-war Austrian loans was a complicated affair. In the first place, the Reich, after annexing Austria had refused to acknowledge any liability for the Austrian debt. Furthermore, certain loans, like the Austrian Government International Loan of 1930 and the Austrian Government Guaranteed Conversion Loan of 1934, were guaranteed by several foreign countries, most of whom had honored their guarantee obligations.[92]

In 1952, a conference was held in Rome, which grouped the

---

[89] For references, see the preceding note. See also Southern Italy Development Fund (Cassa per il Mezzogiorno) Guaranteed External Loan Bonds of 1959 (US issue), prospectus, p. 41.

[90] See note 88, supra.

[91] See *Annuaire Desfossés* 1959, vol. I, 172 summarizing the settlement plan of the 1910 Imperial Government Loan. Regarding the City of Tokyo Loan of 1912, see the recommendations of Mr. Eugene R. Black, then President of the IBRD, contained in a "Plan for the Resumption of Payment of Principal of and Interest on the French Tranche of the [city of Tokyo 5%] Loan". See also, Broches, Am. Soc. of Int'l L. Proceedings 1961, p. 72; Domke, op. cit., note 84 supra, pp. 542-543.

[92] No payments were made by Czechoslovakia after March 1939; Italy suspended payment in 1939 but resumed payment in 1948.

representatives of Austria, the guarantor governments and the various creditors. On December 6, 1952, the Conference issued a report containing its recommendations, which was accepted by Austria and the guarantor governments represented at the Conference. It provided for a reduction of interest rates[93] and a postponement of amortization payments until 1959. Arrears of interest after May 8, 1945 were to be recalculated at a lower interest rate and paid eight-and-a-half years after the original coupon payment dates. The Guarantors (with the exception of Czechoslovakia) agreed to pay the difference between the sums provided by Austria and the amounts payable under the original terms of the bonds, while Austria agreed to reimburse the guarantors for payments already made and payments to be made by them under their guarantee obligations. Such reimbursement was to be made in annual instalments from 1954 to and including 1980, without interest.

There remained the problem of the payment of arrears of interest accumulated between March 1938 and May 1945. The issue was settled a year after the Rome Conference, at the London Agreement on German debts, when the Federal Republic of Germany acknowledged liability for such arrears of interest.[94]

[93] Interest was reduced from 7% to 4½% on the Austrian Government International Loan of 1930, and from 5% to 4½% on the Austrian Guaranteed Conversion Loan of 1934. See Moody's, *Municipal and Government Manual,* 1960, p. 2387; *Stock Exchange Official Y.B.,* 1960, vol. I, 112; *Annuaire Desfossés* 1959, vol. I, 127; *Manuel des Valeurs Cotées à la Bourse de Genève,* 1959, p. 32.

[94] Article 19 and Subsidiary Agreements, 333 UNTS 3, 379.

Table of Cases

Table of Cases

Estarella Vincensini v. Aubaniac
Cass. March 28, 1960,
Clunet 1961, 776; Rev.
1960, 202 ....141, n. 217

Etat de Céara v. Dorr
Cass. Oct. 24, 1932,
Clunet 1933, 644; D.1933.
1.196 ....158, n. 22

Etat Français v. Comité de la
Bourse d'Amsterdam
Cass. Jan. 1, 1950,
S.1951.1.1; Rev. 1950, 609;
D.1951, 749; J.C.P. 1950,
II, 5812 ....114, n. 137

Etat Français v. Veuve Hermann
Cass. Oct. 29, 1964,
Clunet 1965, 637 ...115, n. 140,
116, n. 143

Etat Ottoman v. Comptoir d'Escompte
Trib. Civ. Seine March 3,
1875,
S.1877.2.25 ....200, n. 95, 103, n.
104, 236, n. 58, 239, n. 65

Etat Yougoslave v. S.A. Sogerfin
T.F. Oct. 7, 1938,
61 La Semaine Judiciare
327 (1939) ....159, n. 29

Etchegoyen v. Leray
Cass. July 5, 1827,
D.P. 1827.1.295; S.1828.
1.105 ....136, n. 201

Feist v. Société Intercommunale
Belge d'Electricité
[1934] A.C. 161 ......277, n. 49

Feldman v. Etat de Bahia
Brussels November 22, 1907,
Pasicrisie 1908.II.55; Clunet 1908, 210 .....157, n. 20,
158, n. 22

Fields v. Predionica I Tkanica
A.D.
265 App. Div. 132, 37
N.Y.S. 2d 874 (1942) ...160,
n. 30

Flörscheim v. Delgado
Trib. Civ. Seine July 2,
1932,
Rev. 1934, 770 ......337, n. 65

Frantzmann v. Ponijen
D. Ct. Maastricht June 25,
1959,
N.J. 1960, No. 290; 8 Ned.
T. voor Int'l R. 190
(1961) ....297, n. 18

Frazier v. Foreign Bondholders
Protective Council
125 N.Y.S. 2d 900, 283 App.
Div. 44 (1953) ....155, n. 16,
157, n. 20

Frazier v. Foreign Bondholders
Protective Council
133 N.Y.S. 2d 606 (1954) ..155,
n. 16, 157, n. 20

Frazier v. Hanover aBnk
119 N.Y.S. 2d 319, aff'd 119
N.Y.S. 2d 918, 281 App.
Div. 861 (1953), reargu-
ment and appeal denied
127 N.Y.S. 2d 815, 283
App. Div. 655 ....155, n. 16,
157, n. 20

Fried Krupp Aktiengesellschaft
(In Re)
[1917] 2 Ch. 188 ...123, n. 164,
330, n. 39

Gentini Case (1903)
Ralston's Report, 724 ...144,
n. 225

German Interests in Polish Upper Silesia Case
P.C.I.J. Series A, No. 7, p.
42 (1926) ....122, n. 163

Gledhill v. Schiff
224 N.Y. 593, 120 N.E. 863
(1918) ....157, n. 20

Goodman v. Deutsch-Atlantische
Telegraphen Gesellschaft
2 N.Y.S. 2d 80, 166 Misc.
509 (1938) ......117, n. 145,
131, n. 183

Gouvernement du Maroc v.
Laurans

Index

Index

Index